Dawn Rose on a Dead Body

CALIFORNIA SERIES IN PUBLIC ANTHROPOLOGY

The California Series in Public Anthropology emphasizes the anthropologist's role as an engaged intellectual. It continues anthropology's commitment to being an ethnographic witness, to describing, in human terms, how life is lived beyond the borders of many readers' experiences. But it also adds a commitment, through ethnography, to reframing the terms of public debate—transforming received, accepted understandings of social issues with new insights, new framings.

Series Editor: Ieva Jusionyte (Brown University)

Founding Editor: Robert Borofsky (Hawaii Pacific University)

Advisory Board: Catherine Besteman (Colby College), Philippe Bourgois (UCLA), Jason De León (UCLA), Laurence Ralph (Princeton University), and Nancy Scheper-Hughes (UC Berkeley)

Dawn Rose on a Dead Body

ARMED VIOLENCE AND POPPY
FARMING IN MEXICO

Adèle Blazquez

Translated by H. W. Randolph

UNIVERSITY OF CALIFORNIA PRESS

University of California Press
Oakland, California

Library of Congress Cataloging-in-Publication Data

Names: Blazquez, Adèle, 1988- author. | Randolph, Henry W., translator.
Title: Dawn rose on a dead body : armed violence and poppy farming in
    Mexico / Adèle Blazquez ; translated by H. W. Randolph.
Other titles: Aube s'est levée sur un mort. English | California series
    in public anthropology ; 59.
Description: Oakland, California : University of California Press, [2025] |
    Includes bibliographical references and index.
Identifiers: LCCN 2024044634 (print) | LCCN 2024044635 (ebook) |
    ISBN 9780520405257 (hardback) | ISBN 9780520405264 (paperback) |
    ISBN 9780520405271 (ebook)
Subjects: LCSH: Opium poppy growers—Social aspects—Mexico—
    Badiraguato. | Drug traffic—Social aspects—Mexico—Badiraguato. |
    Organized crime—Social aspects—Mexico—Badiraguato. | Violence—
    Mexico—Badiraguato. | Opium poppy—Mexico—Badiraguato.
Classification: LCC HV5840.M42 B33313 2025 (print) | LCC HV5840.M42
    (ebook) | DDC 305.9/63375097232—dc23/eng/20241126
LC record available at https://lccn.loc.gov/2024044634
LC ebook record available at https://lccn.loc.gov/2024044635

Manufactured in the United States of America

34 33 32 31 30 29 28 27 26 25
10 9 8 7 6 5 4 3 2 1

CONTENTS

LIST OF ILLUSTRATIONS

FIGURES

MAPS

ACKNOWLEDGEMENTS

This book is the result of an investigation for which I owe a debt of gratitude to many people. First, I want to thank the residents of Badiraguato for their hospitality and generosity. They housed me, fed me, helped me, protected and defended me; they shared their life stories, made me laugh, and left me inspired and outraged by their situation. I would especially like to thank the women and men who are named here as Tamara, Lamberto, Enrique, and Gonzalo; Teofilo, whose spirit enlivens these pages, provided me with inspiration and strength during my stays. The path that led me to Badiraguato was guided by several people and I would like to express my gratitude to Anath Ariel de Vidas and Isabelle Rousseau in Mexico City, and to Arturo Santamaría, José Carlos Cisneros, and Guillermo Ibarra in Sinaloa. I am especially thankful to Ana Luz Ruelas for trusting me and welcoming me into her family in Badiraguato, and I hope that my portrayal of daily life in Badiraguato honors that trust. I would like to thank Patricia Figueroa for the vivid refuge she regularly offers me in her "Culiacán-Gotham City," and for sharing with me her deep-rooted indignation and friendship.

The research benefited from the advice, guidance, support, and friendship of my two thesis supervisors, Michel Naepels at the EHESS and Yerko Castro Neira at the Universidad Iberoamericana de México. Several colleagues and friends generously reviewed the manuscript at different stages: Martin Lamotte, Thomas Hirsch, Julia Burtin Zortea, and Leonor Gonzalez. I would also like to thank Sarah Carton de Grammont, Denia Chebli, Ricardo Ciavollela, Elisabeth Claverie, Gilles Dorronsoro, Nicolas Ellison, Pierre Gaussens, Jacobo Grajales, Thomas Grillot, Milena Jakšić, Éric Léonard, Françoise Lestage, Léonore Le Caisne, Dominique Linhardt, Claudio Lomnitz, Victor Louzon, Delphine Mercier, Julie Métais, Birgit Müller,

Caroline Perrée, Valérie Robin Azevedo, Sergio Salazar, Aël Théry, and Benoît Trépied.

Claudio Lomnitz's invaluable and constant support was key to translating my book into English, and this book would not have seen the light of day in the Public Anthropology series without the enthusiasm and support of Philippe Bourgois. I would also like to thank Fernando Montero and Alexander Aviña, who played an instrumental role in the publication of this book. My thanks to Henry Randolph for his care and perseverance in translating my text, despite my typically French overuse of the passive voice and a style that is particularly impervious to English translation. I am deeply grateful to Ieva Jusionyte and Kate Marshall for welcoming me to the Public Anthropology Series and providing me with their precious guidance throughout the publication process. Their sensitivity and insights have been decisive in the achievement of this book.

Several institutions financed and enabled this research. I have been fortunate to be part of the Laboratoire d'Anthropologie Politique (LAP) of the EHESS since joining the CNRS in 2022. The dissertation on which this book is based was funded by the Doctoral Fellowship of the Social Anthropology and Ethnology Department of the EHESS, as well as the EHESS Cultural Area Grant, the Labex Tepsis, and the Institute for Interdisciplinary Research on Social Issues (IRIS). The Harry Frank Guggenheim Foundation Dissertation Fellowship, the Institute for Human Sciences (IWM) in Vienna, a Fulbright Fellowship at the Institute of Latin American Studies at Columbia, and the Labex SMS in Toulouse allowed me to finalize the manuscript under privileged conditions. I am grateful to Gilles Dorronsoro and the ERC program "Social Dynamics of Civil War" (Grant Agreement n°669690), which funded the English translation.

Finally, Adam Baczko has accompanied me with gentleness and perseverance. Both the book and I are fortunate to owe him so much.

Introduction

AMANECIÓ A MUERTO, "dawn rose on a dead body," is what the inhabitants of Badiraguato say when they learn that yet another of their neighbors has been killed during the night. In kitchens, grocery stores, and on front stoops, this phrase initiates the conversations through which the neighbors deal with a new murder. It is an odd phrase in Spanish, as if to say the dawn acts on the corpse, revealing it by rising. *Amanecer* also means "to wake up": the corpse would rise dead with the dawn. For a corpse this seems to occupy a particularly active position. As for the dawn, it does not see the killer; and this is how the news spreads: without a killer. To say the "dawn rose on a dead body" is to be neither the person killed nor the one who did the killing. It means the survivors living into the next day sharing the bad news: when day broke this morning, someone had been killed during the night.

In this book, I explore the precarious lives of people who tried to survive, as best they could, in a context of armed violence and predatory capitalism. Badiraguato, a mountainous municipality (*municipio*) in northwestern Mexico's Sinaloa state, is one of many rural areas where access to jobs, services, care, education—in short, to desirable living conditions and horizons—is limited or totally lacking. However, during my fieldwork there starting in 2013, opium production provided a livelihood for many of its inhabitants, fitting into a transnational economy whose flows ranged from Colombia to Los Angeles by way of Malaysia and Europe. Several armed groups operated in the municipality, and their conflicts resulted in the forced displacement of thousands of inhabitants, leaving many hamlets deserted. Jointly with the US Drug Enforcement Agency (DEA), the Mexican army conducted operations that sometimes turned these dusty hamlets into battlefields. My interlocutors lived in their crosshairs because a spotlight shone on the municipality as the birthplace of the most notorious Mexican drug traffick-ers, Joaquin "El Chapo" Guzman[1] and Rafael Caro Quintero.[2] Badiraguato came to be regarded as "the cradle of drug trafficking" and "the base of the Sinaloa Cartel." Due to the high-profile trial of El Chapo in New York and two Netflix series, the municipality attracted exceptional attention and fig-ured as a profitable media industry construct.

The singular notoriety attached to Badiraguato concealed its inscription in a national context some of whose aspects were reminiscent of certain coun-tries at war. The hundreds of thousands of deaths in Mexico since 2006 exceed those from most of the twenty-first century's armed conflicts. This death toll was higher than Afghanistan's since 2001 and Iraq's since 2003, and has been surpassed only by the war in Syria since 2011 and Ukraine since 2014. Mexico exhibited traits like those that international law uses to catego-rize armed conflicts: armed groups, pitched battles fought with heavy weap-ons (machine guns, rocket launchers, armored vehicles, helicopter gunships), competition for territorial control, massacres, and millions of displaced peo-ple fleeing violence.[3] On the other hand, it lacked some of the salient features of contemporary armed conflicts, namely the application of international humanitarian law, recognition of refugee status for people who emigrate to escape the violence, and protection for internally displaced persons by the Office of the United Nations High Commissioner for Refugees. Moreover, fighting and violence coexisted with other dynamics: elections that resulted in political turnover, an economy attractive for foreign investment, a dynamic tourism industry, and a cosmopolitan capital where life was good for the well-off.

In 2009, I arrived in Mexico as part of a university exchange program and increasingly noticed the palpable tensions surrounding me: glaring inequali-ties, a pervasive military presence, affluent neighborhoods juxtaposed with impoverished regions plagued by violence. In 2010 and 2012, I carried out ethnographic fieldwork in a town of the sierra of Chihuahua, where the peo-ple I spent time with led a precarious life, haunted by past acts of violence and the ever-present threat of a morning raid in an area marked by two armed groups competing for local control. After completing my master's thesis on the protection practices of the inhabitants of this contested town, I decided to further study everyday life in the midst of violence in an area considered both violent and stably controlled by one group. The municipality of Badiraguato in the sierra of Sinaloa was the most appropriate place to do so, being both renowned as a violent place and as the historical stronghold of one of the most persistent groups in narratives about drug trafficking: the so-called Sinaloa Cartel.

This ambivalent state hovering between violence and stability has a long history.[4] It grew to an unprecedented scale following the election of Felipe Calderón (2006–12) in a widely contested presidential election marred by electoral fraud and scandals. In his inaugural address in December 2006, Caldéron made "reestablishing national security" his priority and declared a "war on drug trafficking." He used the slogan of the "war on drugs" that US Presidents Richard Nixon and Ronald Reagan had used to frame social and political issues in security terms. In the same speech, Calderón promised a "national accord" that would unite "civil society" against "organized crime," but whose landmark feature was deploying the army in cities and the countryside. Revealing his priorities, he pointed out that "it will cost a lot of money and also, unfortunately, human lives." By 2012, when he left office at the end of his six-year term, the official body count was sixty thousand dead and nearly twenty-seven thousand missing. His successor, Enrique Peña Nieto (2012–18), stepped up the use of the army; the next president, Andrés Manuel López Obrador (2018–24), proclaimed the war over but continued to militarize the fight against drugs. The record of these successive mandates is clear: since 2006, the years declared "the most violent" followed one another, so that by 2022 the death toll of this "war on drug trafficking" had climbed to more than three hundred thousand.[5]

As in other cases (organized crime, terrorism, gangs, or radicalization), state focus and increased funding fostered the emergence of an ad hoc field of study on drug trafficking.[6] Depending on the political context, researchers spoke first of "narco-insurrection" and then of "narco-terrorism," successively highlighting the "Cuban-Russian connection" in the 1980s, the obstacle the drug trade posed to democratization and liberalization in the 1990s, and the security risks it entailed following the 9/11 attacks. The common use of terms imported from the Colombian context—"plaza," "cartel," "capo," "sicario"— is emblematic of the discursive categorization work that lifts violence and armed groups out of their social context.[7] Beyond the crosscutting nature of its use—ranging from the discourse of public authorities to academic works—its political efficacy reflects the power of framing the drug trade as criminal. "Organized crime" is systematically blamed for killings and massacres—recall the disappearance of the forty-three Ayotzinapa students[8]—in the official discourse. Investigative journalists killed for uncovering corruption are regularly portrayed as "victims of drug trafficking."

Thus, the Mexican authorities deliberately use war rhetoric against organized crime and the violence of drug trafficking to criminalize opposition movements and cloak their repression.

The application of this interpretative framework to entire populations, such as the inhabitants of Badiraguato—and more broadly to the population of the state of Sinaloa—constitutes a brutal form of *otherizing* and depoliticization. Reduced to a subculture that is often stigmatized and sometimes glorified,[9] the inhabitants of these regions are portrayed as savage, barbaric, rebellious, and valiant, but always radically different—hence the talk of the transgressive character of "the Sinaloa man." This essentialization is accompanied by reductionist explanations of what motivates their actions: they are seen as criminals driven by the lure of gain and disregard for human life, which supposedly explains the prevalence of violence. This framing makes entire segments of the Mexican population incidentally responsible for the violence that they endure. Significantly, in some political discourses those involved in drug trafficking have been classed with indigenous peoples as obstacles to the modernization of the country.[10] Seen through the prism of "drug violence," people living in these areas appear as the new "savages."

INCLUSION THROUGH EXCLUSION

This book follows the people who were left out of the great criminal fresco: those who made ends meet despite the lack of jobs, who ran a grocery store, grew poppies on a small plot, or worked for the local government. The ethnography of their daily lives paints a different picture: a condition of vulnerability at the intersection of the local political economy, the threat of armed violence, and the constraints that inhibit articulating this experience.

The image of an integrated organization ("the Cartel") and the epic of a handful of outlaws neither render intelligible the historical structuring of the sector nor its productive organization, and even less its social and political implications. On the contrary, Badiraguato's exceptionalism and the infamy surrounding its larger-than-life figures are constitutive of its unique insertion into capitalist logics. This book blends the ethnography of an illegal economy with the perspectives found in works on agrarian transitions and social reproduction.[11] In this way, far from being contradictory or paradoxical, Badiraguato's two essential characteristics—socio-economic marginality and centrality in a transnational economy—are shown to be linked. The socioeconomic marginalization of a municipality like Badiraguato and its specialization in drug production are not the collateral damage of imperfect development, of lagging behind in the great march of progress, but the very shape that its integration into the global economy takes.

Exclusion thus appears here as a radical mode of integration into capitalism that exploits and reproduces a condition of vulnerability. It resides in the combination of geographical isolation, the lack of infrastructure, a dearth of alternative economic opportunities, the condition of little or no access to services, and the law—and it constitutes Badiraguato's comparative advantage in the global economy. This state of affairs owes much to governmental development policies and repressive activities, as well as to the processes of capitalist formation of a region that in effect straddles the United States and Mexico.[12] Indeed, a look at the socioeconomic dynamics that structure my interlocutors' living space and circumscribe their field of possibilities reveals a configuration structured by access, mobility, and the ability to move goods as a determining and unequally distributed resource.[13] Enclavement thus directly affects the possibilities of social and material reproduction and the ability of people to project themselves. And it is this play between opening and closure of the territory that fuels its lurid reputation—one mixing attraction and fear—occasioned by being the "base of the Cartel."

Seclusion thus benefits the few people here who possess the means of circulation at the expense of the rest of the inhabitants. Their predatory accumulation induces a pervasive armed violence in social relations.[14] Made more potent by the lack of recourse to the law, armed violence facilitates the appropriation of resources, and it ensures the profits of the few in the drug trade through the exploitation of smallholder farmers. This unvoiced and permanent threat shapes the daily lives of my interlocutors more broadly, creating a radical uncertainty for them. A key argument of this book is that violence made the most innocuous acts and relationships of my interlocutors objects of concern: it created an uncertain and confused life, requiring constant effort to avoid the perils of living amid pervasive violence.

As is the case in other armed conflicts, merely moving around, chatting with an acquaintance, cultivating one's plot, or, for a woman, dating a man, induced intense apprehension in daily life.[15] Rumors were both a key space for gathering information to protect oneself and a social activity that itself exposed one to violence.[16] The risk of once more seeing the dawn rise over a dead person led to an overriding need for protection, which exacerbated the material insecurity of the majority. It also meant that the most deprived people living there had no recourse other than to the very persons or groups against whom they had to guard.[17] These included both the state, which also exerted uninterrupted military repression, and the powerful locals who, moreover, appropriated the scarce resources through violence. While most inhabitants shared this vulnerability, it came with *differentiated* forms of exposure to injury, death, or deprivation—depending on gender, social position, and relationships. It therefore called for an ethnography describing the experience of violence and how it fitted into the relationships of predation, exploitation, and domination.[18]

In the confusion caused by this violence, the inhabitants developed skills, words, and narratives that let them grasp or integrate acts of violence into their lives. These daily conversations were the very place where the people concerned refined their interpretations and understandings of the situation in which they lived.[19] In Badiraguato, these allusive, fragmentary, and sometimes contradictory productions were enmeshed in two other framings. One framing, the media's, was of the drug-trafficking small town; the other was the institutional image of a "quiet" municipality, where "there is violence like everywhere else." On the one hand, how the inhabitants qualified their lives and the acts of violence happened in a context where men and women collectively were suspected of belonging to—or at least being associated with—the largest Mexican criminal organization.[20] How to grasp an up-close violence, inherent in proximity relationships, when it was commonly considered a fact of life, as an absolute and homogeneous evil, that of "the *narco*"? On the other hand, local governments, in a neoliberal logic, evaded the social and violent problems to which residents were exposed by dismissing them as individual responsibilities or even as emotional weakness.[21] This transmuting by local officials of the army's incursions into a "problem of low self-esteem," of violent kidnappings into "lover's quarrels," and the activities of armed groups into "household accidents," appeared all the more effective here because another considerable constraint affected how people formulated their condition: the threat of violence. Thus, in such a stigmatized context where explicit formulations were rare, in the following pages I pay particular attention to allusions, suggestions, and interpretations integral to the daily sociability of the people living here.

PORTRAYING A FAMILIAR WORLD

In a context marked by armed violence and repression of the mode of subsistence, essential questions such as "What do you do for a living?" were out of bounds. In such scenarios, many anthropologists advocate for distinct methodologies adapted to the difficulties of prolonged fieldwork amid violence.[22] In Badiraguato's case, however, not being able to ask questions about something as mundane as a person's job demanded an ethnographic investigation all the more.[23] "What do you do for a living?" loses its importance if, with the consent of persons who cannot be questioned point blank, you can immerse yourself in their daily lives.[24] This book therefore takes the classic approach dating to Malinowski: the village monograph.[25] In this context, I relied on the most quotidian and distinctive elements of the ethnographic approach: living in the place, immersing myself in interpersonal relationships, and favoring observation over interviewing.

This book challenges the otherizing of individuals living in regions like the sierra of Sinaloa by adopting an anthropological perspective that fosters a sense of familiarity through ethnographic investigation. During the eighteen months I spent in the Badiraguato *municipio,* its main town of the same name, in the town hall, and in the hamlets that dot the surrounding mountains, I shared the daily lives of a few dozen people who constitute the book's main protagonists. In following their daily lives, I resituate the experience of violence and illegality in the most ordinary aspects of rural life. Instead of thinking in terms of otherness or searching for hidden meanings behind actions, I seek to describe the material and discursive practices of the people I encountered.[26] I account for their experiences by focusing on the same acts that we all do in our daily lives (such as moving, being there, or pulling through), but in different ways depending on the context and the constraints (in this case, violence and illegality) that weigh on us.

This approach, which focuses on social situations,[27] emphasizes a deepening of the description to make the experiences of my interlocutors understandable and familiar to the reader. The conceptualization lies less in the application of a theoretical framework than in the accomplished description of the situation, which creates revelatory effects on the broader context and the manner in which they affect each other. This entails flushing out what is implicitly embedded in the situation and how the people involved contextualize and interpret it.[28] To make an action familiar, therefore, is to reproduce the scope of possibilities into which it fits and the constraints on it. To make a world familiar means following what is being played and replayed, accepting the confused way in which this world exists and thereby arriving at an understanding of the larger dynamics that shape it.[29]

I have chosen not to relegate my research methodology to an appendix, as I consider the way in which I conducted my investigation an inherent dimension of apprehending the context. The privileged access and the revelatory power that ethnography alone allows depend eminently on the relationships that ethnographers establish with their interlocutors. Because of its intersubjective character, the investigation produces knowledge that is necessarily partial, fragmentary, and situated, calling for caution, reflexivity, and restraint from the ethnographer.[30] The ability of ethnography to reveal the social world lies in embracing the limitations of a description that includes the conditions of the investigation and its fragilities.[31] I therefore intertwine the ethnographic material and its conditions of production: the investigation and its methodological dimensions pop into view throughout the book as the veil gradually lifts on fragments of Badiraguato's social life.

The book's structure follows this approach by ordering the ethnographic material according to seven fundamental logics of action.[32] It groups different situations analytically to illustrate and examine practices that are carried out in the same way, are commented on in a similar manner, or refer to like issues in the social context. Each chapter takes up a concrete practice and its local expressions to peel back the layers of historical, economic, social, and political issues. The logics of action constitute building blocks which, as I deal with each in succession, gradually outline both the insecurity the inhabitants share and its contextual conditions. The reader is thus introduced to their lives via the essential practices of movement and sociability that are indispensable for understanding their political economy and the way it informs property and gender relationships—and, ultimately, the exercise of violent and institutional power. Thus, the ethnographic material as a narrative builds layer by layer: first sketching in the lines and contours, then adding depth and color to familiarize readers with a situation until they themselves can detect what is surprising, what is funny, what confirms what we thought, and what is strange or absurd—as social reality sometimes is.

The first chapter deals with the uncertainty of "Moving Around." In it, I identify the stakes involved in my interlocutors' daily movements. It alternates between the material structuring of the territory and the difficulties of travel to and from the municipality. The second chapter, titled "Being There," dwells on the daily sociability of my interlocutors and the forms that self-protection takes in the face of violence, in close relationships, and in raids by the army. Through life stories and descriptions of the modes and the production relationships in poppy cultivation, the third chapter, "Pulling Through," analyzes the vulnerability of grower families induced by military repression and exploitation by the buyers of their crops. "Fencing In," the fourth chapter, chronicles the evolutions of land tenure (*ejido*), the logics of enclosure, and the constraints that weigh on land registry in illegal agriculture. It exposes the judicial cover provided for violent land grabs by imposing a "commons" regime.

The fifth chapter, "Stealing a Woman," starts with the abduction and rape of a young woman and frames this event through the experiences of my interlocutors. It explores how predation in gender relations fits into the violent political economy. Chapter 6, "Killing," recreates the social and political texture of homicides by putting aside the perpetrators' motives to describe how my interlocutors dealt with them. The point here is showing how homicides affect the social fabric in which they take place. The last chapter, "Administering," highlights how the municipal administration separates its actions from the context of violence, notably through the production of solvable problems and by setting a clocklike rhythm that immunizes it against the regular irruption of homicides. The institutional stability that coexists with armed violence is a defining feature of the Mexican situation and of my interlocutors' vulnerability. The book ends by "Returning Upstream,"[33] in a conclusion that invites reflection on the insights gained from the journey to Badiraguato by pulling the threads that run through the book: the insertion by exclusion into capitalist logics, the modalities of domination through uncertainty, and the various constraints that hinder the emergence of resistance and contestation.

ONE

Moving Around

"Don't get on the first horse that's going to throw you on the road!"

TEÓFILO

MOVING AROUND SIGNIFIES GOING by one means or another—depending on existing infrastructure—to a certain place at a given time to rub elbows with its inhabitants. It therefore involves setting foot in spaces that have a history shaped by the friendly, familiar, and commercial relations between the people who lived there in the past. In Badiraguato, moving around can present dangers that must be anticipated or defused. Everyone learns to feel their way, to ask questions, to listen, and to take precautions. It is a game at which not everyone is equally adept. Some are "unprotected" (*desprotegido*) when they move, while others are known enough by the people of the places they pass through to avoid peril—that is, provided that a conflict hotspot does not erupt to wreak havoc with what was already problematic.

"A DEN OF HUNDREDS OF BANDITS": THE CONSTRUCTION OF A CLOSED TERRITORY

That morning in December 2013, Ana Luz called me: she would not be able to take me as planned, but was sending me her fellow teacher, Diana, "a girl who knows how to move in Sinaloa." In the pickup truck marked "Universidad Autónoma de Sinaloa—Uso Oficial," the conversation was lively. On the road for three-quarters of an hour already, we were traveling north toward Los Mochis. On our right, the low hills previewed the mountain range we were heading toward. We talked about this and that, never mentioning the destination. Despite the pleasure of friendly encounters and the intimations of affinities that seemed to bind us with Diana, apprehension lodged in the pit of my stomach. I tried to neutralize it during a short silence by admitting to it, putting a brave face on it: "Ah, anyway, how exciting to be going to Badiraguato!" There, it was out, I had said it, but immediately I regretted it. My stomach tightened a little more thinking about the enormity it must be for a girl from Culiacán . . . my remark was sadly predictable coming from a foreigner. But, against all odds, Diana gave me a look of complicity that showed she was just as anxious: "Isn't it? I'm so excited, too!"

So, it was also a first time for Diana. A first, something out of the ordinary, because we were heading for a place charged with semantic intensity that was impossible to shake. All Mexicans know Badiraguato by name and reputation. During my years in Mexico, I heard about it everywhere, in all kinds of discourse. Movies and press accounts defined it as a place of drug trafficking, by its violence and its multibillionaire drug barons on the run. As we rolled through the desolate hills, this visual economy, this saturation of images and narratives, reverberated in the anxieties we both stifled.[1] The construing of Badiraguato as the epicenter of the "genesis of national violence" and the "cradle of drug trafficking" came in multiple forms: Mexican and international media articles, documents produced by national governments, expert reports, statements by politicians, popular songs, novels, films or, more recently, a Netflix series.

A 1997 article in *Proceso,* a magazine founded in 1976 by journalists critical of the PRI's one-party system, establishes the scene:

> In Badiraguato, Sinaloa, cradle of capos, drug culture is a way of being and thinking. Here begin the story and the legend. The poppy first, then the marijuana. This is the Mecca of gum growers (*gomeros*) and weed growers (*moteros*), the cradle of capos; not of all, but of a few, of the best. In this vast wild mountain range, the cultivation of poppies, the base for opium, supposedly brought by Chinese migrants who arrived in Sinaloa at the beginning of the century, was born. Here the gum trade flourished in the 1940s, responding to the demand for morphine from the United States during World War II. Hills and valleys were covered with green plants, the best weed (*mota*) in the world.[2]

In the classic book *El Cártel de Sinaloa: Una historia del uso político del narco,* Diego Osorno recounts his foray in the company of other journalists into Badiraguato in a military convoy:

> We find ourselves in the back of an assault vehicle that stops by the side of the road so that one of the commanders, riding in the back of a Humvee, can

coordinate with another officer before we enter the town of Badiraguato. . . .
Once the commanders have agreed, we move out again. In Badiraguato,
there is not a single official sign of welcome.[3] Not for anonymous motor-
ists, let alone soldiers. The Humvees of the Mexican army, accompanied by
journalists, enter this mountainous municipality that spawned Rafael Caro
Quintero, Juan José Esparragoza El Azul, Ernesto Don Neto Fonseca, the
brothers Beltrán Leyva and Joaquín El Chapo Guzman. From the pure
'Chief of Chiefs' [*Jefe de Jefes*,' an allusion to a popular song, a *narcocorrido*],
to powerful men, capos, the major operators—those known—of drug trafficking in Mexico in recent years. . . . As it is Sunday lunchtime, few inhabitants of the small town come out to watch the convoy of vehicles and olive
green uniforms that passes in front of them.

—It seems like people are looking at us with a lot of anger, I say to a fellow
reporter.

—No—he sets me straight—they look at us as if we were corpses.

—On the contrary—says another colleague—they are dying laughing at us
and at this performance in which we are participating.[4]

As reported by the US news channel CNN under the heading "code of
silence reigns in El Chapo's birthplace":

It's the kind of place where everybody abides by a code of silence. If you say
too much in Badiraguato, you may lose your life. Your family may be shot
and killed. This much is clear: If you stay silent, don't ask too many questions and mind your own business, you should be OK. It's the birthplace of
drug lord Joaquín 'El Chapo' Guzman, so perhaps it's no surprise that the
3,700 people of this town in the mountains of the northern state of Sinaloa
have kept their lips tight. Mexican media reported fifteen homicides in and
around Badiraguato last month. An additional seven people were killed in
November. Five men were ambushed, shot and killed in June. . . . Badiraguato
is also the gateway to the so-called Golden Triangle, an area where the states
of Sinaloa, Chihuahua and Durango meet and, more importantly for law
enforcement, where marijuana and poppy production thrives.[5]

Badiraguato gets a similar treatment in academic literature. For example,
the book *La narcocultura: Simbologia de la transgresion, el poder y la muerte*
[Narcoculture: Symbology of transgression, power, and death] underlines the
role of the media in building its reputation—which, to be clear, is well-
deserved: "Badiraguato. Land of 'violent and determined' men who con-
quered posterity by reason of increased production of drugs [and] the fame
acquired by certain characters of the region. With the decisive intervention

of the media broadcasts, Badiraguato is generally at the pinnacle of its stigmatization. . . . The borders of most of its vast and almost inaccessible mountainous territory lie in the cold heights of the Sierra Madre, adjoining the states of Durango and Chihuahua: the famous 'Devil's Triangle.'"[6]

Cultural production is no exception. The popular song "El corrido de Badiraguato" opens with these lyrics:

> Gentlemen, keep quiet and be very careful
> I'm going to sing a corrido from a very famous village.
> This village is famous throughout my Sinaloa,
> Because we are accused of growing [opium] gum here.
> I just want to explain that here we grow everything,
> And if you get mad about it, well, then get mad, so be it.[7]

Don Winslow's novel *The Power of the Dog* had to open in Badiraguato; the plot of Arturo Pérez-Reverte's *La Reina del Sur* hinges on "the warning given by a Badiraguato type." The name is dropped in primetime movies and is turned into the ultimate threat in Luis Estrada's *El Infierno*: "I'll send you a *cabrón* from Badiraguato itself!" Finally, the entrance arch to the main town, inscribed with "Welcome to Badiraguato," opens the credits of the Netflix series *Narcos: Mexico*.

Mexican politicians and officials regularly stressed its reputation, possibly to lament it, but never quite detached from it either. In the early 2000s COBAES (Colegio de Bachilleres del Estado de Sinaloa), the state government agency for secondary education, published a series of monographs on Sinaloa municipalities. The one on Badiraguato began: "Often, and unfairly, the name of Badiraguato brings to mind a black legend[8] that drops an obscure veil on a municipality condemned in some parts of the popular imagination."[9] Similarly, in an interview with the national press, Ángel Robles, the mayor of Badiraguato from 2012 to 2015, was quoted as saying: "I go to other parts of the state [of Sinaloa] and occasionally I am asked where I am mayor. I tell them, 'in Badiraguato.' And they cry out to heaven. I tell them: remember that sayings carry lessons and 'the lion is not as they say.'"[10]

These excerpts match: some claim and magnify the myth; others—the mayor, the *corrido*, and the COBAES monograph—respond with "the lion is not as they say," but, to defend themselves, alternate between fabrications and denials. "Badiraguato," then, seems to encompass a homogeneous territory imprinted by these discourses, a place difficult to think about freely without focusing on this matrix of signifiers that have built up around it. In that regard, Diana and I were no exception: you cannot go to Badiraguato the first time without this little medley running through your mind.

The discursive and visual economy that accompanies the name "Badiraguato" spilled out from movie screens. If the inhabitants struggle to recall whether the etymology of Badiraguato in the indigenous Cahita language would be "the river of many mountains" or "the place of swallows," in the rest of the country, other meanings were de rigueur: "inaccessible," "code of silence," "violent men," "cradle of the narco." Badiraguato's reputation was set in stone in the 1940s in the regional press: "Shootings are the order of the day, as are abductions, homicides and other blood crimes. . . . [Badiraguato is] a den of hundreds of bandits."[11] Its present exceptional status had its antecedents in the 1970s and 1980s, a period considered the "peak" of Mexican drug trafficking—but also of its repression during Operation Condor.[12] Badiraguato then debuted spectacularly in the role of the "place of origins."[13] And even the names of its hamlets entered the public domain.[14]

A huge volume of local, national, and international cultural production (musical, film, literary) built up the infamous leading characters. Often, their fame stemmed from being on the American DEA's list of most wanted fugitives, turning its fight against drugs into one of personalities.[15] Their names— Rafael Caro Quintero, Juan José "El Azul" Esparragoza, Ernesto "Don Neto" Fonseca, Joaquín "El Chapo" Guzman, the Beltrán Leyva brothers—stood for the phenomenon of drug trafficking on an international scale. The municipality's history was next reinterpreted in the light of its new role and propelled to the big screens in the national capital. In 1973 the film *Valente Quintero,* adapted from the *corrido* with the same title that tells the story of a 1920s duel between two men from two hamlets in the Badiraguato sierra, was the second-highest grossing movie in Mexico City theaters.[16] Los Tigres del Norte, the internationally renowned music group from Mocorito, composed and performed tunes of heroic figures who confronted, betrayed, prospered, faced torture, and died in the context of military repression.

Armed with Ana Luz's instructions, I've been on the road with Diana for an hour. In the distance, where the road branches off toward the mountains, a sign says "Badiraguato." We are in Pericos on a broad intersection that is surrounded by low-end buildings: garages, pharmacy, beer halls, restaurants, hardware stores. In the shade, they hawk coconut biscuits, peanuts, or ice cream. Ana Luz told us to stop at the Chuyita restaurant and have a coffee. We parked the pickup truck on the other side of the road and exited its air-conditioned cabin. The Chuyita was set back from the International Highway, which continued northward to the United States, and marked the beginning of the Badiraguato route. Between the terrace and the road, a group of young men were chatting. Diana and I passed in front of them, ignoring their sidelong glances as we took refuge in our conversation.

A broad cement roof sheltered many plastic tables and some slowly turning fans. There was no lack of choice: only two tables were occupied toward the back of the terrace, where we could guess the kitchen was located. We sat by the road, under a fan, ordered a coffee, and I lit a cigarette. The young men glanced in our direction and, now worried, we continued our conversation, but watching what we said. About twenty minutes later, we got back into the pickup's cab—now a reassuring sanctuary. We quickly concluded that the young men were standing lookout on the road.

During the remaining half-hour drive, the arid, shrub-covered plain gradually turned more rugged, and the road began to meander. In the midst of stunted deciduous trees, we drove through the hamlets of Camotete and Camichín. The road ran past dirt roads heading off to the left; then came a paved road to the right that led to another hamlet, Batopito. Soon, we passed under the arch that marks the entrance to the town of Badiraguato. We connected with Santiago, Ana Luz's father, in the store where he worked. We left the Universidad Autónoma of Sinaloa's truck at the town entrance and got into Santiago's pickup. As he drove, telling us several stories, we learned from him that "entry is monitored in Pericos, with the radios, they warn the higher-ups." He showed us around town, pointing out the school as recently having been "bunkerized (bunkeada) to ward off stray bullets." He asked me what I was after, what I am investigating, and clearly he didn't believe me. It is obvious, he told me, that I am investigating drug trafficking.

After showing us that there was "nothing to do in town," he took us via paved road to a nearby hamlet. He told us "if armed people stop us, don't get scared"; then, having scrutinized our worried look, he grinned, confirming my feeling of being on some kind of safari. As the road climbed, we passed white memorials, surrounded by railings. "Those are graves and what you're seeing there are cameras." We drove through the hamlet. The streets were paved for a short distance, then we passed through the three hamlets of Los Sitios (El de Abajo—literally "the one below"; El de Enmedio—"the one in the middle"; and El de Arriba— "the one above"), before turning around. Santiago explained that this was as far as we could go. Right here it's still ok, he said, because he knows the people, but *many places in the sierra are off limits to him. He told us that the municipality was "protected" beyond this point by people who were paid to keep out hostile groups. We drove back down to the main town, and I asked him if I could stay in his home should I return. With a still-half-suspicious, half-amused look he assented, and I took off with Diana again.*

My first visit to Badiraguato was not exactly how journalists typically went about it. They sometimes arranged their forays through fixers from Culiacán, generally through the municipality government, or they rode along with army patrols. However, in many ways, my first visit compared with theirs in the sense that all such movements represented incursions. Some inhabitants did not deny the difficulty of access highlighted by media and by cultural and political discourse; if anything, they dramatized it. From their point of view, the arrival of a stranger in the municipality was bound to be linked to an interest in narcotraffic. The guided tour that Santiago took us on lived up to this premise. In this sense, the reputation, often hyped from political centers (Mexico City in particular), was not simply a mirage, since it was played on in local practices. Santiago's tour highlighted the most picturesque elements: the "controlled entry into the territory," the school "bunkerized to ward off stray bullets," armed men who might materialize at any moment, marble mausoleums under video surveillance, and the "protected" municipal boundaries.

This staging did not mean that the controlled character of entry to the municipality was just pretense. The arrival of, say, military vehicles posed a threat to people who grew poppies or marijuana in the mountainous territory. The extremely rough terrain and infrastructure (a single road from the main town, the rest dirt roads in poor condition) made it easy to monitor the arrival of soldiers and thus to send early warnings upstream to people potentially threatened by their incursions. Similarly, attacks by rival groups in 2016 on La Tuna, the hamlet of the "El Chapo" family, showed that the need to "protect" boundaries was not imaginary. Sometimes, incursions were in fact attacks. But faced with these various phenomena ranging from journalists' visits to military operations and raids by rival groups, perhaps the inhabitants had many reasons for obfuscation and insistence on protecting their territory.

The course these incursions by visitors to Badiraguato took was therefore not designed to dispel the smokescreen produced by its reputation. On the contrary, they in effect reinforced the reputation as a closed and threatening municipality. Santiago held no positions in the local government and was not formally tasked with escorting journalists, but even he played into what he thought were our expectations: his tour picked up the discourse that emerged from between the lines of journalistic reportage and which I observed as municipal, state, and federal officials guided journalists on their visits. Rare as these incursions were, they contributed to building up Badiraguato's image. They constituted situations in which much of the discourses that they generated by portraying the municipality as "inaccessible" contributed to marginalizing it. The administrators in the town hall took advantage of these situations to position themselves as an interface between the reified place and its exterior (see chapter 7). In this sense, they were a feature of visiting Badiraguato, without, however, any relevance to the experience of the locals moving on this same ground. Once I had settled in the town, I would never again hear about the "bunkerization" of the primary school or the cameras guarding the mausoleums, which were very much a presence and which I would walk past many times.

These situations, in which the scenario of the gutsy incursion into an sealed-off territory prevailed, differed radically from those that caused the place's inhabitants to move on the same road we had taken. I therefore want to turn the focus to how life moved daily on this axis, and from there to the material structuring of Badiraguato's connection to the national infrastructures. Its history highlights the role federal and state public policies played in the municipality's isolation. Historically, Sinaloa was a frontier region, meaning there were issues of settlement, extracting natural resources, and being simultaneously connected with Mexico and the United States.[17] The state was accordingly structured around the road that runs the length of the coastal plain, from south to north, linking its three economic poles: the port of Mazatlán, the state capital Culiacán, and Los Mochis, close to the port of Topolobampo, constructed in one fell swoop in the late nineteenth century as an outlet for the ores mined in the western Sierra Madre.

The marginality of the mountainous regions in the center of the state, which include Badiraguato, was accentuated by the agribusinesses that arose in the coastal plain from the 1950s to the 1960s. The municipality was connected by the road that runs from the main town to the Pericos crossroads; it was not asphalted completely until 1974. As part of irrigating the plain, the Adolfo López Mateos Dam was inaugurated in 1964. Its construction heightened the marginalization of the mountainous area, which interested the

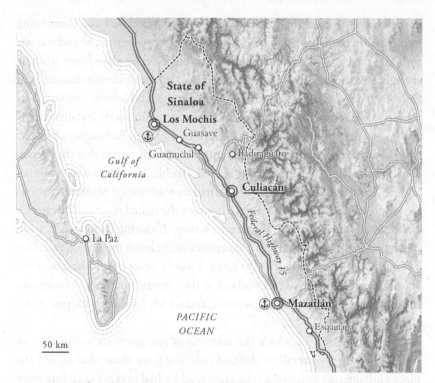

MAP 1. State of Sinaloa. Map by Alexandre Nicolas.

public authorities only for its water resources coursing down to the plain. The filling of a reservoir lake inundated several hamlets and displaced numerous inhabitants.[18] A substantial part of the municipality had its access to the coast cut off by the new lake, while the road that was to reconnect them to the main town would take nearly twenty years to finish. These public works deepened the isolation of hamlets and further concentrated traffic around the Badiraguato main town and its only road.

In the past, it was also possible to fly to Culiacán in small aircraft. But airstrips were periodically banned because of their use in drug trafficking.[19] In the late 1970s, a flight from the San Javier de Abajo area cost 25 pesos (10 dollars), and was therefore an accessible mode of transport for major travel, including medical care. In the mid-2000s, such a trip still only cost 700 pesos (65 dollars). Airfields were again banned after 2006, and some were dynamited by the army to render them unusable.[20] While the many remaining airstrips are no longer used for transporting people, they continue to be used for drug trafficking.[21]

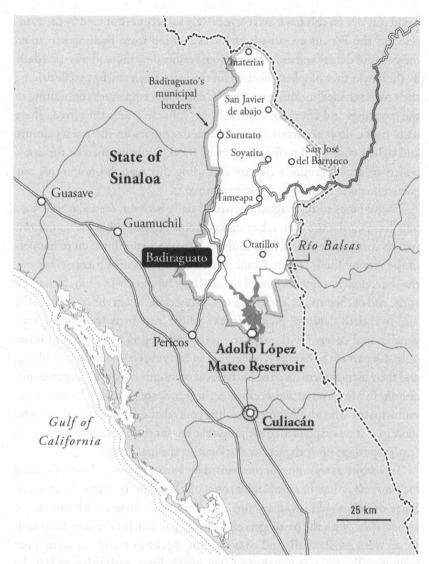

Vinaterias

Badiraguato's
municipal
borders

San Javier
de abajo

Surutato

Soyatita

San José
del Barranco

**State of
Sinaloa**

Guasave

Tameapa

Guamuchil

Otatillos

Río Balsas

Badiraguato

Pericos

**Adolfo López
Mateo Reservoir**

*Gulf of
California*

Culiacán

25 km

MAP 2. Municipality of Badiraguato. Map by Alexandre Nicolas.

The Pericos-Badiraguato road therefore funneled all travel into and out of
the municipality. The only anecdotes I heard conveying a certain degree of
apprehension about this route related mostly to its concentrating the municipality's broader issues—drug trafficking, violence, and repression—because
it was the only way into or out of Badiraguato. Thus, people marked for death
in the municipality could easily be identified and attacked on it. Open clashes

could play out on this road, and corpses were sometimes dumped by the roadside. At the Pericos crossroads, vehicles coming from Badiraguato town merged into denser and more anonymous traffic. But this road was used daily by the trucks that supplied the shops of the main town and by people driving their own vehicles, meaning mostly the municipal employees commuting in the mornings and afternoons, often from Culiacán where they lived. These daily traffic flows contrasted starkly with discourses on the town's closure and tightly controlled traffic. Barriers or checkpoints manned by the army, police, or armed groups were rare and using this road did not arouse any particular concern among my interlocutors.

Twelve buses to Badiraguato departed daily between 6:20 a.m. and 5:40 p.m. from Culiacán's central bus station. Some terminated in the main town (which they reached in an hour and a half); others continued on to hamlets in the mountainous region. Combined in the Lineas del Oriente company, the individual bus lines belonged to families who usually lived in the hamlet at the end of their route. These buses were descended from the *tranvías* of the mid-twentieth century, pickup trucks whose rear beds were fitted with benches and covered with tarps to protect passengers from the sun. Buses were still part of the hamlet economy, often carrying goods for their residents, and their owners were inserted in the local economic networks. For example, one day in March 2015, two weeks after the murder of a *pistolero* known in the municipality who also handled gasoline contraband ("that's why there is no more gas," it was explained to me), I saw the bus for the first time in many such trips stop to gas up at the service station near the main town.

Travel by bus was often accompanied by music, with the drivers favoring local *corrido* groups or *norteñas* hit songs marketed in the rest of the country. Some drivers would invite a young man from the village to belt out one or two *corridos*, with the passengers expected to pay him for the entertainment. Buses were usually full, and conversations between seatmates were quite common. The interactions showed that people knew each other, at least by sight. Drivers often knew their customers' stops without being told. When catching the bus at the Culiacán central bus terminal, passengers went from rather impersonal interactions at the ticket counter to immediate familiar relationships as soon as they climbed on the bus. At the exit from Culiacán, other passengers boarded at a regular stop that also served all the buses bound for the north of the state. Here, identities were indirectly verified even before getting on the bus: when waiting under the tarpaulins, the people managing boarding and checking tickets (selling CDs and soft drinks on the side at the same time) often acknowledged the people waiting by name. If they were strangers, they were asked their destination, what they were going for, or who they were going to see. I was asked whose daughter I was. Once on the bus, anonymity was impossible, as I would rediscover on returning to my field study in June 2016, after a year away:

I left the main town in a bus that arrived from a nearby hamlet. Next to me, an elderly man I didn't know gripped a radio wrapped in a cloth. He started the conversation: he explained that he was taking the radio to get it fixed in Culiacán. It's a good appliance, he said. It let him pick up the frequencies of the lookouts charged with watching for soldiers at the Pericos crossroads. During the hour and a half bus ride, unprompted, he regaled me with anecdotes about his past activities in the drug trade and organized violence. The entire time of the trip I was on my guard, making sure to show no interest in what he told me. I avoided tossing anything back at him. I was certain that I had never seen this man before; nothing in his attitude indicated that he knew me. So, I wondered, why would he take the risk of sharing this sort of information with me? As I made ready to get off at my stop, the bus entered Culiacán and I said adios; out of the blue he asked me if everything was fine at the university and if I'm pleased with how the book is coming along.

My unease and reticence during this exchange stemmed from a misapprehension on my part: I thought it would be possible to have an anonymous exchange on the bus. But the insertion of the drivers, the bus attendants, and the passengers in the social networks of the municipality was obvious. It was already quite apparent on arrival in the sierra, when they stopped to eat, pick up packages, and transmit messages for each other. But it was actually also a fact of life on the Culiacán-Badiraguato segment of the trip. This form of diffuse surveillance is found in most rural areas in Mexico, but in Badiraguato it appears to be more pronounced, due to the stakes involved in crime and its repression. Bus riders could be exposed to violent incidents: in July 2016, three armed men stopped a bus to kill a passenger before it reached the Pericos crossroad. Yet, this sort of incident remained the exception: strangers stood out easily, and the trips were marked above all by a free flow born of familiarity.

A "GOOD HORSE" AND A "SOCIAL PURPOSE": FROM
THE MAIN TOWN TO THE SIERRA

September 17, 1981

To the mayor of Badiraguato or to the secretary of this town hall:

After cordially greeting you, I would be very grateful if you would
be kind enough to help me with the following problem: I was on my way
to supervise the work at Ciénaga de Los Lara when my pickup broke
down; that's why I beg you to please send a car to take me to town
and then to Culiacán so I can get what is needed to make it run
again....

This piece of paper I turned up in the municipal archives brought to mind
the image of an engineer stranded by a dusty roadside. It spoke of the ever-
present vagaries of travel in Badiraguato's rugged terrain on primitive infrastructure. The municipality is one of the largest in Sinaloa, at altitudes ranging from 100 to 2,800 meters above sea level. Reports by agricultural
engineers in the 1960s and 1970s provided glimpses of the difficulties at the
time: they regularly dwelled on the impossibility of reaching a given hamlet
due to the weather, the poor state of the back roads, and how many days it
took them to make the round trip. Even during my stay, the journey to some
hamlets still took more than six hours and required a four-wheel drive vehicle
(ATV, 4X4, or pickup). The movement of state or municipal officials in the
sierra still occasioned many "mechanical breakdowns," and knowing how to
negotiate these steep back roads was an important attribute of the municipal
employees. As for the hamlet residents, they relished their misadventures.
One of my interlocutors from the sierra would tell me about it jokingly: "I
think it is a culture peculiar to them [the people from the main town] to
come unprepared."

Beyond the isolation of the sierra, driving up these back roads could mean
coming across men on ATVs, carrying automatic weapons, and with radios
attached to their vests. Moreover, the main source of income for the hamlets
that dotted the territory derived from cultivating poppies and marijuana,
both of which required intense measures of concealment and vigilance in
view of its repression. The centrality of the drug economy was also reflected
in the infrastructure. Thus, the construction of the main road crossing the
sierra was attributed to Rafael Caro Quintero, and the finished road was
regarded as having been taken over by the "government." According to the·

FIGURE I. The sierra of Badiraguato. Photo by the author.

former mayor, it was an "open secret. . . . Yes, it is true that at the beginning, in the 1980s, the señor [that is, Quintero] was moving around in the Badiraguato sierra. There is indeed a road that everyone knows was a personal investment by this señor. After the 1990s, the federal government took it over and started improving it in sections. And now it's a success for the state government and the federal government, because now the Badiraguato-Parral [Chihuahua] road runs a little over half the length of the western Sierra Madre."[22] Finally, symptomatic of the pervasive illegal economy is that it periodically attracts foreign visitors:

During a trip with the municipal employees, my companions tried to make the female owner of the establishment where we were having lunch understand where I am from. When they boasted "from France, can you believe it?," she disappointed them by responding without batting an eyelash: "Oh yes, bah, one time there was a woman from Colombia."

On another occasion, on a bus ride to a family I already knew, a young man started a conversation with me while the driver had stopped for his lunch break. He asked me if I had come for the Holy Week holidays and I settle for a "yes." He went on: "That's funny, how tourists love to come here. . . ." Noting my surprise, he told me about this man, "a black man from Los Angeles who often came by plane" to this young man's home hamlet. Apparently, the man loved it here because he'd say, "at home, you can't shoot [guns]. So, you'd say, he was enjoying himself here."

The origins of the two "tourists" and the unremarkable nature of such visits in the eyes of a restaurant manager and a young hamlet resident recalled the paradoxical insertion of this enclaved municipality into global commerce. The US and Mexican authorities accused especially the figures associated with drugs in Badiraguato of being involved in trafficking cocaine from Colombia. Since the 1980s, with the DEA monitoring the Caribbean routes used by Colombian traffickers more closely, Mexico had become an important route for cocaine destined for the United States. Los Angeles, from whence the man who liked to shoot guns hailed, was the destination of many Sinaloan migrants and one of the main nodes in the trafficking networks.

Beyond that, people from the main town reproduced the stigmatization that afflicted the municipality with respect to the hamlets. Thus, when the talk in town turned to the topic of violence, they would tell me that "people say 'Badiraguato,' but it mainly happens in the sierra," or "the people in the hamlets are uncivilized." This juxtaposing of a civilized territory with a wilderness inhered in a view of the mountainous region as homogeneous: you went "into the sierra" and rarely "to such and such hamlet." These stereotypical views affected people from the hamlets who came to settle in the municipality's center—a steady migration fueled by the armed conflicts that left many hamlets largely deserted (see chapters 2 and 6). In the main town, to say that someone was "from a hamlet" was a common and time-honored putdown. In 1981, a longtime resident of the town wrote this to the mayor about her neighbor: "You're going to say that these things don't concern you, but you have to put a stop to it. I don't know how to make him understand what he can and can't do. These are incomprehensible people who still think they live in their hamlet when that is not the case. Here they cannot live with the same freedoms as in the hamlet."

The stigmatizing discourse against the hamlet residents did, however, contain an element of ambivalence. If being "from a hamlet" *(ser de rancho)* referred to precarious material conditions, the sierra was also where prominent figures and their families originated, thus also eliciting admiring discourses. The registers may have varied, but this distancing from the mountainous expanse was common. Thus a state official stationed in Badiraguato told me that "the sierra is controlled by this sector" *(este gremio)*, the local term for armed groups and networks involved in the drug trade.

People working in construction and engineers employed by state agencies often made the trek to the hamlets from the main town. Among my interlocutors in the latter, those who had family and a vehicle also regularly returned to their native hamlets for ceremonies or parties. Although routine, these trips were not always uneventful. A resident of a hamlet I met on a bus told me he chose it as his mode of transport this day because his wife could not handle the fear that came with being forced to exit the car by armed men in the middle of the road. These buses served the two main sierra roads and stopped once or twice a day in the hamlets closest to the main town and one to three times a week in the more remote ones. They were mainly used by people living in the hamlets. In the main town, on occasion you would be told "as of now," the bus going to this or that hamlet was not safe because it had recently been stopped by armed men.

The to and fro therefore flowed more or less freely, could be more or less secure, and was more or less controlled, as the case might be. To account for these variations, two dimensions need to be addressed.

A man in a hamlet told me that many people refuse to come. I asked him, "Who?" His answer: "The aid workers, the engineers, the inspectors . . . we're always talked about as killers (matones)*, but no. Those who like weapons carry them and they can have enemies, but they don't hurt just anyone. And they're even less likely to do so if someone comes with a social purpose."*

Outside our respective rooms, I told my good friend and neighbor Teófilo—whom we will meet properly in the next chapter—that I would soon be going to the sierra with the aid distributors of the Family Affairs Department (Departamento de desarrollo integral de familia, DIF).[23] *Displeased, he retorted: "Don't get on the first horse that's going to throw you on the road!"*

"Social purpose" and choosing the right "horse" referred both to the objective and the mode of movement. Between these two conditions stretched a continuum from travel based on agreements to one where conflict was possible. Indeed, the purpose of the visit and the way it was made were the situational elements around which travel was negotiated. These issues figured particularly prominently in the journeys by the employees of the municipal administration into the sierra. While they shared the same status, they each had their distinct patterns and modalities of moving. In fact, a number were from one of the sierra hamlets. But they could go to a hamlet for entirely different reasons: either in the course of their duties or on personal errands. Based on their travels, I outline in what follows two situations with varying motives and modalities to highlight the very different degrees of vulnerability they experienced and the discriminatory dynamics of openings and closures of space that they might have to face.

At first, it appeared indeed as if certain motives for and methods of travel locked these civil servants out of an impenetrable territory.

I was hitching a ride with Juan José, the deputy director of the DIF (Desarollo Integral de la Familia) and also in charge of women's and minors' affairs. We were on the way back from a hamlet. He told me about his path through the various municipal departments and confided to me that of the two hats he currently wore, he much preferred the DIF as less risky. "The problem is that you wind up with a case of domestic violence, but you don't know what you're getting into; you are completely unprotected (desprotegido)." I asked him: "But how do you know that? Do you have a way of determining that?" He responded with a story: once a young girl came to see him because her mother regularly threw her out of the house; the girl asked him to intercede with her mother. When he asked his colleagues and friends if he should, they were quick to say, "Oh, don't even think about it." The mother was the mistress of an armed group's leader. "So, what did you do?" I asked. He concluded with: "No, well, no, I didn't go. Even agents of the state prosecutors with state police and everything, they don't want to go, so me alone? No, no, no, no!"

A few days later, in the offices of the DIF, I heard about the case of a young girl who had been raped in her hamlet and managed to escape. She was sheltered in a hostel in Culiacán and the state office of the Department of Family Affairs was requesting that her identity papers be recovered. Juan José, the deputy director, and Ivan, a psychologist in the Family Affairs Department, were assigned the case. Every time our paths crossed, I asked them about this case. Each time, they would tell me that they had not been there. On another occasion, an annoyed Ivan told me: "You don't know, but there's more than meets the eye here, with something like that!"

*Finally, one morning, I was present when he told the deputy director about their expedition the previous day: to begin with, they were not even sure where the hamlet was. Finally, arriving at the home of the town hall's local representative, he told of how it upset him to learn that even the rough directions and distances were wrong. He said they didn't trust them: "No, seriously, not like that! Me, I was all for turning back." The local representative sent her son on the ATV to show them the way, but eventually the boy stopped, then turned for home, abandoning them. They went on anyway. In a while, they entered a dark house with a man sitting at table, his gun prominently on display, drinking. Visibly anxious, in the ensuing exchange they learned that they were in the wrong hamlet. They went back the way they had come, because it was getting late, and asked the local representative to find the documents herself and send them directly to the main town. An employee, within earshot as the story ended, observed: "Yes, when you go and there is a drunken binge (*borrachera).....*" Ivan cut him off: "No, and especially given what we were after, we were completely unprotected (*desprotegido).*"*

The two stories are cut from the same cloth. They concern similar situations and the same term recurs: "unprotected." The two municipal employees went into a place where they had no family or friendly contacts. Moreover, since they were entering a hamlet on a mission involving domestic violence, the sierra back roads seemed to conceal themselves. As we shall see in chapter 5, and as Juan José suggested, gender relations often raised broader issues involving gun violence. Dealing with a domestic conflict did not qualify as having a "social purpose" but rather represented an intrusion, which could arouse hostility from the people they met. For Juan José, an area that "even agents of the state prosecutors with state police and everything, they don't want to go [into]" was also a no-go zone. Yet, state police forces would only go into a few places, and then rarely.[24] But if that appeared to him as a relevant indicator, it was because the stakes and the situation were similar. These municipal officials also lacked reliable contacts. In attempting to mix in domestic conflicts as part of their job, they took a significant risk: the purpose of their visit appeared similar to an incursion by the state police—the only difference, as it were, was that they went in alone and unarmed. That made them "unprotected," not personally, but situationally, hemmed in by the issues motivating their trip: "No, and especially given what we were after, we were completely unprotected."

On the other hand, most trips by employees in the Family Affairs Department were untroubled, even in areas controlled by an armed group.

Gabriel, Cristian, and I left at 4 a.m. on a DIF mission to distribute food aid in a series of hamlets on the municipality's northernmost road where Sinaloa borders on the state of Chihuahua. We started out so early because it would be a long drive and they wanted to return before nightfall. I had heard of a permanent armed roadblock where the road entered the area through which we had to pass. When I asked them about it they told me, "Oh yes, they charge 50 pesos for the road. You'll see, they're well-armed, and guess what: they wear uniforms like soldiers. It is their leader who asks for a contribution for the road, he has a machine [bulldozer] he uses to maintain the road and everyone pays." Gabriel and Cristian told me that they approved and gleefully added: "And there, everyone is equal (todos parejos)! When the mayor comes, he's treated the same, he has to pay. . . . On the other hand, when there are soldiers, they don't charge road tolls." When going to this area for distributions, the toll price was included in their expenses for the day. Then they explained to me that, by the way, they tell their manager that they have to pay 50 going and 50 more on the return. Once, one of their superiors (the Juan José mentioned above) threatened to call the pesado[25] to complain. Gabriel and Cristian panicked, but they ended up talking him out of it by saying that it would upset the pesado.

Around 10 a.m., my two companions alerted me that we were approaching the site of the checkpoint and, on rounding a bend in the road, they pointed to a rock. But no one appeared. We continued on our way, but in dead silence. A few minutes later, we approached a house. A mustachioed man wearing a uniform walked up to the van wiping his mouth. Greetings were exchanged; Gabriel and Cristian told him of their surprise at seeing the checkpoint was not manned. It turned out the men were busy at another site and it was this man's lunch hour. Gabriel and Cristian named the hamlets where they wanted to distribute breakfasts to schoolchildren. They paid him the 50 pesos and asked twice if it would be ok for us to come back through later around a certain time. The uniformed man nodded and as we were rolling again Gabriel and Cristian told me: "If you see these guys in the village, they are very nice, but now you see them being very serious because they're on duty."

This distribution journey involved an institutionalized practice of paying a toll to an armed group. Although endowed with aspects that a priori contributed more to the experience of uncertainty (because the man was armed and controlled who was allowed to pass), the roadblock appeared predictable enough to the people tasked with the distribution to let them devise a strategy. The systematic nature of this toll was even enhanced: for once, a certain equality prevailed, so that the mayor, a powerful figure, had to pay the toll just like everyone else who wanted to pass.

While uncertainty persisted (the drivers were spooked at not seeing the gunman at the usual spot that day), Gabriel and Cristian were perfectly familiar with the functioning of the checkpoint operated by the group controlling this part of the sierra. Conversely, the member of the armed group clearly knew all about the food distributions by the Department of Family Affairs. The pickup truck stamped "Desarollo Integral de la Familia" and the mutual acquaintance between the functionaries and the armed man were visible prerequisites for guiding the interaction and negotiation. These then played out in the jovial tone adopted by the drivers and their showing that they knew the usual location of the toll stop. While the exchange was not excessively warm, the insistence on the agreement that would reign between them was again staged for my benefit once we were under way again, with both telling me that "the guys . . . are very nice." In the end, a precaution had been made explicit: going over with the gunman which hamlets we would visit, estimating what time we would pass through on the return—all of it ensuring predictability for the rest of the trip.

These movements, whose stakes reside in the distribution of goods or subsidies, generally proceeded smoothly. On the one hand, they fit into the relationships of the residents with the town hall employees, who often were familiar with the hamlets—and might even come from them. Furthermore, the relationship between the municipal employees and the hamlet residents they met during these distribution rounds regularly provoked comic reversals that built a kind of alliance: in the course of organizing distributions in the sierra, the department's trucks can be counted on to break down, forcing the employees to seek help from the inhabitants. The anecdotes of such past setbacks often came up in exchanges between employees and the hamlet's residents during subsequent deliveries, creating a certain collaborative spirit. Moreover, the hamlet residents know that these are low-level employees since they are stuck with the most arduous of tasks: driving into the sierra. Thus, these movements take place in conditions of familiarity reinforced by repeated interactions.

Moreover, the reason for the movement here fell into the "social purpose" category. Once, in the late 2000s, a convoy distributing financial aid from a federal program in hamlets in the southernmost part of the municipality was attacked. This resulted, I was told, in a threat that "if it happened again, the distributions would cease." After that, the convoys were no longer attacked. The "social purpose," which meets the needs of a large number of people, is not a contentious subject in local social relations. Diverse and varied distributions (money, food aid, but also goods such as blankets) take place undisturbed.

Elections also illustrated these dynamics of the closing or opening of the *sierra*. These brought politicians and their campaign teams on frequent visits to the hamlets to organize rallies accompanied by festivities and the handing out of campaign collateral (t-shirts, caps, and so on). The hamlet residents would often remark how they only saw the municipal executives "during the campaigns," but these expeditions generally proceeded without any problems. However, this opening of the sierra roads to candidates was conditioned on their being belonging to the PRI, which almost all did before 2021. For example, during the 2018 presidential campaign, the opposition parties complained about the impossibility of "entering" the Badiraguato sierra.[26]

Travel from the main town into the sierra thus meant managing certain issues: dealing with people whose work involved concealment, and being susceptible to detention at any time by armed men, either soldiers or members of an armed group. The territory was not closed, but access was not always a sure thing and was rarely entirely untroubled. The factors determining how the journey went are revealing: while the purpose of the trip mattered, it also meant not going on random walks or seeking recreational opportunities in the sierra. Similarly, the trappings of travel, that is, its visible signs, were decisive, because the movements were never unobserved.

However, beyond motives and modes, the familiarity of the travelers with the hamlet's residents influenced what could be negotiated. The uncertainty surrounding access and the knowledge necessary for getting around it thus conferred a special value on being able to do so. People who "knew how to move" were in possession of a scarce resource.

In the office of Gonzalo, one of the municipal executives, I was chatting with one of his assistants who was telling me about his weekend festivities in a hamlet. He said he was a local; referring to my work, he exclaimed: "Hey, let me tell you!" He reminisced about a time when he was younger and lived in M*, about the "trolleybuses" (tranvías), how many times they came through each week, who owned them. He told me that his home doubled as a road house, since everyone *stopped to eat at his mother's. So he knew everyone: "I can boast to you that 95 percent of people know me well there. They take care of me. . . . When I go now, I bring the music, someone else has the beers, and we do it in spontaneous mode so that not everyone comes around and we avoid the confrontations (pleitos). . . . My house was the road house, when people had car problems, or the river was getting too high, they stayed overnight. I'm the one who harvests what my mother sowed. During the campaigns, I'm asked to come there. When I get there, I announce, "I am the son of doña Clara of M*!"*

His expression—"I'm the one who harvests what my mother sowed"—said it all. In the sierra sociability is a key resource, especially for political careers. Doña Clara's son did not hold an elected position. Despite his comment about the election campaigns, he did not "harvest" votes with his sociability; instead, he converted it into a resource for boosting his career as a local civil servant. It was a "harvest" because being allowed to come and go freely added value in many instances. For example, having someone like him on their campaign teams was an asset for candidates seeking elected office.

More broadly, as access to the mountainous territory is not a given, the trips made by outsiders (engineers, state officials, or journalists) invariably called for local people familiar with the sierra to get them there. Thus, I observed a municipal employee dissatisfied with having been assigned to escort a woman journalist from Mexico City into the sierra. The person he had brought the journalist to said, smiling, "But they don't send you for nothing, you know how to move around here." The employee replied, "Don't believe it. Look, if something would happen now in Badiraguato [the main town], I wouldn't even know about it." He downplayed having the know-how attributed to him, but not without acknowledging that staying connected with people was the key to "knowing how to move." These people in effect extracted value from their experience with uncertain pathways.

A PRECARIOUS FAMILIARITY: MOVING AROUND IN THE SIERRA

When pickup trucks coming from opposite directions met on the narrow sierra tracks, passing each other was tricky. First, as they drew nearer, one or the other or both vehicles had to come to a stop. Once they had pulled up next

FIGURE 2. A typical sierra dirt road. Photo by the author.

to each other, the drivers would roll down their windows, lean out, and ask: "All clear?" (*Está limpio?*) Meaning: you haven't come across any soldiers?

I accompanied Francisco Javier, a teacher and resident of a hamlet situated on the Chihuahua—Durango state border. He was embarking on a tour of the hamlet schools to recruit students to his own school for the next school year. He knew the roads perfectly, so the drive proceeded in a relaxed manner: he even called it a pleasure trip (contrasted with his work in his hamlet). Among the hamlets we visited, I recognized a school where I had been with Department of Family Affairs aid workers. On that occasion, things had turned tense, with many armed men loitering in the vicinity of the school. However, this time we entered it and the other hamlets without any difficulty. Francisco Javier talked to the students about the new school and, to break through their shy silence, called on some to give their last names and asked others he recognized: "Aren't you the daughter of (so and so) . . .?" He often guessed right and even found several members of his extended family.

So it went all day: we stopped in schools, in grocery stores where he knew everyone. Seven or eight times, on the dirt tracks between hamlets, he was asked: "All clear?" Toward the end of our tour, we stopped in the home and grocery store of a couple in their sixties with whom he was acquainted. We sat with them on a shady hillside terrace sipping on soft drinks. They told us that soldiers were on the prowl. In fact, while we were talking, a military vehicle pulled up and the woman quickly hid the wireless radio under her apron, between her breasts. As the soldiers stepped onto the terrace, she turned to me (putting us both on the sidelines), picked up a doily that she had embroidered, and launched into an innocuous conversation about the embroidered piece. Soldiers came and went on the terrace, leaning over to look inside the house. They asked, "Nothing there?," implying weapons and poppy gum, but did not search. A short time later, one of the soldiers told Francisco Javier they were lost and asked where they were. Then he asked him where this dirt road leads. Francisco Javier responded by naming the hamlets that the road runs through in each direction. They ended up leaving, and we did the same. Getting back in the car, Francisco Javier explained to me that the soldier knew very well where he was, but that he was trying to check if we knew and if he could detect any anxiety in his voice. Apart from this interlude with the soldiers, all day we blithely drove down back roads on which the municipal officials I had traveled with previously had been apprehensive. When I told him that the outing went very well, he clued me in: "Well yes, you see, I know everybody: this side [he pointed to his right], it's from my mother, that side [he pointed to his left] is from my father, you can bet on it!"

The soldiers sniffing around and the regular "all clear?" in the context of this day brought to mind what Francisco Javier's sense of ease tended to obscure: these were uncertain roads for people who, although acquainted, if not related by kinship, feared the soldiers and their searches and violence. The soldier questioning Francisco Javier as a tactic for checking what he knew effectively dramatized the protection that came from knowing the local geography. Nevertheless, a first decisive dimension in these journeys was the fear of crossing paths with the military. In 2008, soldiers had opened fire on a car, killing an entire family returning from a late-night party. Beyond the possession of opium and weapons, beyond familiarity, beyond the various protections that some might enjoy, moving around in the sierra meant first of all hoping that it was "all clear."

By also emphasizing the pleasurable nature of this road trip, Francisco Javier highlighted how it is possible, leaving aside the fear of the military, for experiences to differ depending on the degree of familiarity. He lived with his family and his brothers in a hamlet at a higher elevation in the municipality where the states of Durango and Chihuahua meet. On our tour we made a giant loop, passing through several hamlets inhabited on one side by his father's extended family, on the other by his mother's. Moreover, the back roads he followed were those he used when visiting his mother and driving down to the main town. He had known them since his childhood when he accompanied his late father on trips to restock the family grocery store. In other words, he knew his way around the back roads and the byways. He also had going for him that he was a schoolteacher, a member of a family well-known in the region, so that his movements around the hamlets did not target his activities for repression. All his brothers enjoyed this familiarity in areas that others passed through with trepidation. One of his brothers in particular, Enrique, went wherever he pleased, as I observed several times by accompanying him.

However, several days later, while traveling on a different road with Enrique, I discovered the limits of this familiarity.

I had known for several days that Enrique had to bring the engineer to the meeting of the adjacent ejido *taking place in Durango. When I told him that I would like to accompany him there, he initially accepted but, little by little, I sensed a resistance when I kept asking when we would be leaving. The day before the scheduled departure, Enrique suggested that I might not be able to come due to lack of room in the pickup truck. Finally, at one o'clock, he came with the engineer in tow and said: "Well . . . where we're going it is not secure. . . . Here it's ok, but when we go out, I know fewer people. I know some, but not so many. And there are isolated cases [of violence]. It doesn't mean something's going to happen, but just that sometimes, you know . . . I'd rather tell you." I saw the engineer was uneasy and asked Enrique if my coming would heighten the risk of insecurity. He answered no, so I confirmed to him that, if he agreed, I would like to attend the meeting.*

The day before he had told me that six people would be going, but when we left there were only the three of us: the engineer, Enrique, and myself. The atmosphere in his pickup was relaxed; we chatted until we arrived in a nearby hamlet. We stopped by a wooden hut in front of which several ATVs were parked. The engineer and I followed Enrique, who greeted David, a young man I didn't know. From their quick conversation, I understood that he'd be coming with us. The new guy was surprised there were only three of us.

We now all climbed into David's truck and drove a short way to a second wooden shack, where someone named Pablo joined us. We got back in: David and Pablo in front; the engineer, Enrique, and me in back. Only Enrique and Pablo spoke a little; David remained silent. All three kept their eyes on the road ahead. I could sense Enrique's tension next to me. As we crossed the Chihuahua state line, silence descended in the vehicle, and the heads swiveled as if trying to sense what would lie around the turns in the road. Gradually, we headed downhill. I learned that we were now in the state of Durango. We crossed green plains, surrounded by hilly pine forest. As we approached the destination, Enrique seemed to be relaxing. He explained to me that the hamlet we were heading for was complicated, that David had family there and that he rode shotgun with him every time Enrique had to go there. When we arrived, we stopped in a house where the flatland started. Enrique told me that this was the home of a loyal man who often worked for him, a man of trust.

The longer we were in the hamlet, the more astonished I was—given Enrique's elaborate preparations and the tension on the way—by his cordial relations with the people. Apparently, he had worked with them in the past. In fact, the precautions were primarily not for the hamlet itself but for a segment of the road. Unlike the other times I accompanied Enrique, the trip to this hamlet was intensely prepared for. The initial hesitation about my tagging along, the drop in the number of passengers going, and the mood swings in the truck were palpable. Enrique's reliance on David and Pablo and David's truck reflected a protective strategy for the journey. Enrique mobilized his network to compensate for a limited familiarity along the way: "Here it's ok, but when we go out, I know fewer people. I know some, but not so many." Not only was David familiar with this road, but he was also related to people from this area. Enrique would explain to me later that the road was patrolled by an armed group that it was better to avoid, even with David's presence and his knowledge, however limited, helping to contain the risks.

Echoing the response by Francisco Javier ("this side, it's from my mother, that side is from my father") and Enrique's relative assessments ("I know some, but not so many"), the familiarity at issue in these movements went beyond the knowledge of roads and people. We saw with the official who "harvests what his mother sowed" that this familiarity was part of more complex stories. When traveling in the mountainous area, the history of people's movements and of merchandise flows structured differentiated zones around networks of sociability and more or less close relations between specific hamlets.

Don Pedro and his wife, doña Lupe, lived in S*, in a house which together with two others formed an open square around the church. Don Pedro liked to tell *stories of his childhood wanderings in the company of his father. He recited the names of the hamlets, demonstrating his knowledge of "all that part there," and stressed the limits beyond which he never went. First his father and then he bought and sold cattle, the so-called "aventurero" profession. They roamed through the hamlets higher up, looking for people with a few head of cattle to sell. The higher they went, the less the animals cost, even when taking into account the expense, time, and effort of getting them to the coastal plain. In fact, it was first necessary to bring the cattle to S* so he and his father could fatten them for the drive to market and sale in Culiacán, a five days' trek. At L*, the mule track they used first crossed a road on which the* tranvías *traveled. They often over-nighted in L* (nowadays people stop there to eat). Then they again took the tracks leading to the main town, and then went straight down the paths at that level that took them directly to the coastal plain. Arriving at the lower elevations of the sierra (after Otatillos), they passed through the hamlets now bypassed by the roads and some that now lie at the bottom of the artificial lake formed behind the Adolfo López Mateos Dam, to finally enter Culiacán through the Tierra Blanca district. They would do this three times a year, always sleeping in the same people's homes. This is how he met his wife, who grew up in one of the hamlets on that mule path.*

Mule paths had long since fallen into disuse for long trips. Nevertheless, they helped form links between the inhabitants of some hamlets and specific eco-nomic flows. The journeys remembered by don Pedro highlighted elements that I found repeated in the stories of my interlocutors of the same genera-tion, irrespective of their activity. They were all of 1960s vintage, but the relationships built around the mule tracks persisted. In fact, the experience of walking these trails, besides calling for an in-depth knowledge of the ter-rain, implied the construction of particularly strong ties due to the time it took to walk them: spending nights, year after year, in the houses of the same friendly families led to building bonds of kinship, friendship, and solidarity. These links between travelers from one hamlet and families living in another hamlet gave rise to lasting sociability. As recently as the 1990s, even the early 2000s, hamlet residents preferred attending fiestas celebrated in hamlets connected by the mule paths their parents used to walk.

In the municipality's higher elevations, a study of the mule paths reveals two distinct zones, registered in different networks of interknowledge and relying on different economic and political intermediaries. The one further south connects the main town to the state capital of Culiacán; the other, northern one connects to Guamúchil on the coastal plain. The tracks walked by Pedro and his father joined up with those taken by the locals from many other hamlets south of the mountainous region. With the exception of some manufactured goods brought in by traders from Guadalajara (the Jalisco state capital to the south), all these mule paths, and thus the flow of goods and people, connected with Culiacán. In contrast, the mule tracks used by the residents of hamlets further up north in the municipality passed through different hamlets along the roads descending from the sierra through the neighboring mountain municipality of Mocorito to Guamúchil. In the early twentieth century, several mines operated in this part of the sierra and the inhabitants used the paths for transporting ore from them over the plain to Guamúchil.

At the municipality level, these flows of people and merchandise ended up structuring a territory that was much more fragmented than homogeneous, as it was commonly suggested to be. While the use of the same tracks by some hamlets had strengthened the links between their people, the reliance on separate paths and different economic centers made for less close relations between the two sets of hamlets in the municipality's higher elevations. Moreover, in this configuration, the area that depended for its supplies on neighboring Mocorito and then Guamúchil was more marginalized vis-à-vis the main town—which shared with the southern zone the same outlet to Culiacán and thus had many economic and political contacts in common.

Turning the trails into roads for use by motor vehicles (leading to the debut of the *tranvías*) saw many ups and downs and created two dynamics. On the one hand, the ensemble of these infrastructures affected the links that existed between the hamlets: by changing the modes of travel, roads transformed the uses and sociability centered on the mule paths; for another, the road now linked hamlets formerly bypassed by the trails whose residents had previously been more isolated from each other. Some of my interlocutors suggested that this created conflicts. Furthermore, at the municipal level, constructing roads reified and reinforced the dichotomy between the two regions. After passing through the main town, the road from Pericos split into two. One spur went north, the other south, dividing again at Soyatita with one segment stretching north to San Javier, the other east toward Huixiopa and San José del Barranco.

As built, these infrastructures repeated the economic and political structuring created by the mule tracks. Historically, the main path was the one

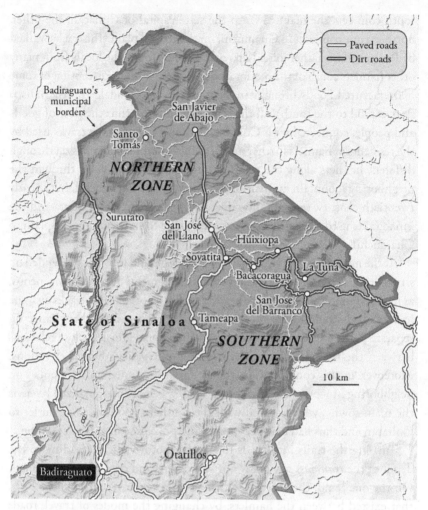

MAP 3. Heights of the municipality. Map by Alexandre Nicolas.

that continued after Santiago de los Caballeros and Soyatita toward San José del Barranco. The road now served the hamlets that depended on the same trails and thus preserved the networks that were built around the former mode of travel. The municipality council budgeted it earlier than the others (1964) and even if it had yet to be completed, its construction figured among the most important public works during each term of office.[27] In contrast, roads built in the area served by trails to Mocorito and Guamúchil fragmented the area. The road brought these hamlets back into the main town's lap. The segment serving Surutato was started in 1985 (the asphalting was

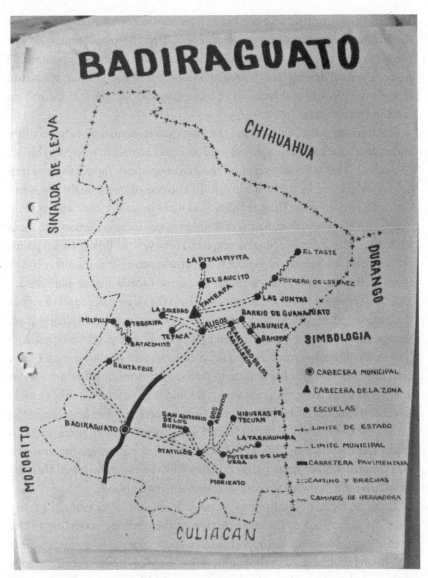

MAP 4. Map from the municipal archives, 1979.

finished in 2016–17, after my fieldwork) and specifically targeted an area whose main feature was stands of trees (a scarce resource in the municipality). The hamlets that lay north of Surutato and were connected by mule paths were now attached to the other road that went to the main town by way of Soyatita and Santiago de los Caballeros. It effectively severed their social networks and historical economic circuits, which may explain to some degree the lack of investment in this neglected area. That the armed group with an earth-moving machine mentioned earlier had taken charge of maintaining part of the road dramatized this region's isolation. A map I found in a carton in the municipality archives dating from 1979 did not show the northern road and its hamlets.

Road construction thus reified the historical structuring of the territory and accentuated its heterogeneity and unequal access. It was probably no coincidence that without exception the most important figures in drug trafficking originated in the area historically connected to the main town and Culiacán to the south. Their families, and more generally, the hamlets from which these figures came, had access to historical intermediation networks with the political elites of Sinaloa's capital. However, the link between political networks and costly investments in infrastructure was manifest in the town of Badiraguato. For example, in 2011 a former mayor published a "political radiography" of the mayors who held the office before and after him (see chapter 7), in which he wrote about a former mayor, originally from Surutato, whose rise he argued could not have been the governor's doing: "[The trail of the governor's sympathy] dissolves, since you, kind reader, are a keen observer and you have come to realize that once in office he did not benefit from the governor's support . . . for making the public works remarkable. Let us ask ourselves: by how many kilometers have they lengthened the Badiraguato-Surutato road (his home *sindicatura*)[28] after three years in office? DIFFICULT PUZZLE TO SOLVE."[29] The patronage dimension of road construction projects partly explains why the routes followed this historical division of the mountainous region into two zones.

Thus, the forms of familiarity illustrated by the travels of Francisco Javier and Enrique related to the construction of the territory according to the intensity of relations of kinship, economic cooperation, and solidarity. This structuring reverberated in the conflicts that erupted between armed groups organized along lines that mixed territory, sociability, and kinship. Some of my interlocutors identified these northern and southern areas as "opposing groups." For example, the Department of Family Affairs workers visiting a hamlet located on the northern road explained to me that it was forbidden to listen to *corridos* glorifying El Chapo (originally from the southern route), because of the enmity between him and the other area's chief. The dichotomy reported by these discourses simplified a more complex reality, as there were multiple armed groups in both areas and their hostilities were not systematic.

The fact remained that this division referred to groups whose practices differed[30] and that the inhabitants of one area definitely spoke of those "on the other side." The regions first outlined by mule paths and then by roads thus reflected easier alliances between groups of the same area, and more tenuous relations between the groups arrayed in each of the two zones.

A recent conflict between locals in a hamlet on the northern road (which I will call here N*) and a hamlet on the southern road (S*) illustrated this linkage. In hamlet S*, Tamara asked me if I'd ever been to N*. "There, where there are roadblocks of people dressed like soldiers who check (*checan*) everyone's license plates, papers, etc."[31] She told me that for a while she was seriously afraid to venture there. When they went with her family to her native hamlet in Chihuahua, they had to pass through it; they kept silent about being from S*. She assured me that, at the time, they really couldn't have said where they were from. One of her brothers, for example, had come to visit and they had arrested him. They detained him by the side of the road and threatened him. But, she explained, because she had a cousin who worked with them, with the N* people, he'd gotten out of it. The "soldiers" of N* verified that he was telling the truth by calling the cousin and asking each the first names of the other's mother, like this: to the cousin: "what is your mother's name?" and the brother: "what is his mother's name?" She added that "over there [N*], they are very strict. Now it's getting a little better, but it was a bad time, the people here couldn't go there, and those over there couldn't come here. And today, they still stay away."

The road control situation reported by Tamara occurred in the same place that I passed through with the aid workers from the Department of Family Affairs and put two differentiated experiences into perspective. The conflict that culminated in N* being off-limits to the people of S* began in 2006. I was told about it several times in S* but never in N*.[32] The version of the conflict that I relate therefore suffers from being one-sided. However, as I heard it: a man from S* had his ATV hijacked on the road by people from N*. In the course of the hijacking, this man called people from S* on his two-way radio. They came and killed two of the hijackers, but a third survived and spread the word. Then the people from N* avenged them by killing a cousin, the sister, and the mother of the man who had killed their people, and then the sister's fiancé, who happened to be the *pesado* of hamlet S*. The man initially involved was still living during my fieldwork; he was the hamlet's new *pesado* and the killing had stopped. But people from one hamlet were still given a hard time when they went to the other.

It bears noting that the conflict did not appear to be related to competition for control of poppy production. But it involved armed men operating in groups in historically connected areas with distinct commercial and relational flows. Tamara, married to a man from S*, and her brother were from a hamlet in Chihuahua. It was connected with "those in N*" and she traveled through N* to visit her family in Chihuahua. Tamara's brother's being detained involved two distinct elements: his destination and his kinship. Going to N* from S* fitted his movement into the current conflict, but thanks to the mother's first-name test, the situation constituted a kind of concretization of controlling for kinship.

These logics were crucial to understanding the difficulties Francisco Javier and Enrique had to grapple with in their travels. Enrique's exposure during the trip to Durango—explained in terms of "isolated cases" of violence and then by presence of an armed group—was linked to the entry into a neighboring area but in which sociability had been built around other mule tracks and other outlets: consequently, he "know[s] some, but not so many." Similarly, during another of my stays there in 2015, I journeyed into Chihuahua state with a person from the area to which we were en route, taking more precautions due to an active conflict between two groups located in separate areas, as in the case of the conflict between S* and N* in 2006.

In 2016, when I returned for a brief stay in the main town of Badiraguato, I saw how precarious these norms of kinship and familiarity were. Random external events that redefined the balance of power between competing groups, as well as the modalities of military repression, could call into question even the limited possibilities that still existed amid this uncertainty. When El Chapo was arrested in 2016, several people expressed their concern about rising tensions to me.

In the main town, by chance I met Damián, a young man from one of the hamlets my investigation had taken me to the previous year. From my stays in his hamlet in 2014 and 2015, I knew that he came and went between his hamlet and the main town, alone or with cousins and friends. The day after we met in the main town, we were standing on a doorstep when we heard a woman scream across the road. It quickly became obvious, because of the proximity of one of the town's funeral homes and the vehicle around which people were fussing, that it was a mother's lament for her dead son. I just glimpsed that Damián's eyes were red when he left to join her.

On his return, he explained to me that the young man killed was his compadre,[33] who had killed two people earlier. Damián told me that he had to return to his hamlet, but that he was barred from taking the road because, at the moment, there were complex road controls around the hamlet where the family of El Chapo lived. When I asked him what was going on, he said: "Only they know." The next day, I saw him again; he told me he was going to leave, but without trying to hide his sadness or his fears. I tried, to no avail, to persuade him not to risk it, but then could only urge him to take care. His reply: "When it's your turn, it's your turn. . . ." (cuando toca, toca).

In the space of a year, just like that, the character of a trip often taken was turned on its head. Damián's fears were a particularly poignant example of the fragility of the logics of predictability derived from the historical structuring of the territory. Two dynamics intersected and transformed a trip that Damián used to make quite readily into one where he feared the worst: "when it's your turn, it's your turn. . . ." On the one hand, road controls were set up in the context of conflicts that had been boiling for several months.[34] A few weeks after I had seen Damián, La Tuna, El Chapo's native hamlet, was attacked by armed men. The hostilities spread so that the inhabitants of many hamlets had to seek refuge on the coastal plain. Obviously, Damián knew more than he let on that day; his avoidance formula, "only they know," spoke volumes. The threat he faced was part of the temporality of a conflict in high places and reflected what people living in the region were exposed to. On the other hand, the recent assassination of his compadre put him in a personally precarious situation that affected his movement, despite the protection he generally enjoyed on this route. He feared being targeted by the people who had killed his *compadre*. The two dynamics intersected: a fixed checkpoint blocked the road to his hamlet at a time when he had to move as discreetly as possible. In this unique context, he knew that the protection afforded him by his familiarity was in question, turning the trip home into a risky incursion.

Thus, for people living in the mountainous part of the municipality, the ability to go to the main town, where the services were located, was shot through with uncertainty. As fundamental as being able to move around may appear, it could be complicated for my interlocutors by a constellation of forces over which they had no control.

One day in April, one of my interlocutors living in a hamlet discouraged me from going ahead with a trip that we wanted to make with his daughter: "Right now, it's tricky. You understand, between April and June, it's tricky, it's time for work [poppy harvesting], there's money, alcohol . . . September, October are also iffy, it's when the money runs out . . . well, and then comes December with the *balaceras* ["gunfire," but this includes celebratory shots]." He ended his sentence with a laugh, realizing that in reeling off the potential problems and their timing, he had ended up describing almost every month in the calendar as "tricky." By initially referring to the agricultural cycle, he formulated temporal hazards that I had already heard about in the course of my investigation. During the harvests, flows were considered more difficult to control because of the movements by the people coming to work in them. But, in doing so, he also concealed the magnitude of the difficulties involved in moving about.

Travel to and within the municipality was shadowed by varying degrees of uncertainty: being able to pass or not; dealing with obstacles or threats; being equipped or not with what it took to avoid trouble. This uncertainty could not be dependably mapped simply because these were not insecure areas in absolute terms. It arose above all from interpersonal and situational factors. Access was based on knowledge of roads and of the locals, the reasons for traveling, and in situ negotiations. The various degrees of knowledge and their formulations highlighted their inscription in a historical, economic, political, and institutional context. Through the modes of access to the economic centers in the flatlands, different areas within the municipality were emerging, comprised of more or less tenuous networks of solidarity and of armed groups whose relations were more or less confrontational. Thus, the situation of violence and insecurity made my interlocutors rely in their travels on a sociability that was particularly vulnerable in times of conflict.

The constraints that impinged on travel were delivered through a wide array of control modes—abundant discourse, an institutionalized armed barrier, an ingrained daily observation of everyone's comings and goings—making the identification of control actors particularly difficult. But these constraints also imbued access with its own intrinsic value as a scarce and unevenly distributed resource. In this regard, the municipality's isolation produced a negotiating space for the opening and closure of the territory according to persons and situations, representing either a serious constraint or an intermediation resource in the local political register. Paradoxically, while civil servants and local government would appear to have an advantage in these negotiations and possess an edge in accumulating the resource that access constituted, intrusive motives also emerged as constraints that were difficult to circumvent and set limits on the government's actions in the hamlets. Finally, the modalities of the municipality's isolation contributed to its insertion into global trafficking flows of its raw materials (marijuana, poppy), processed goods (heroin, synthetic drugs), but also cultural goods tied to its sulfurous reputation (music, films, novels).

TWO

Being There

"Do you know why the turtle lives to be 100 years? Because it doesn't stick its nose into other people's business!"

OWNER OF A TAQUERIA

YOU COULD RECOGNIZE GERMÁN by his nonchalant gait a mile away. Forty-five years old, he looked more like thirty as he roamed the town streets in baggy trousers and t-shirt. He wore his beautiful, slightly curly brown hair, which reached down to his prominent cheekbones, tucked under a cap. With this high-school boy skateboarding outfit, he stood out radically from the local male fashion. However, instead of high-top skate shoes, he did wear sandals (*huaraches*), the prescribed local footwear. He lived in one of the oldest houses in the center of the main town. In fact, his family was one of the "grand old time families," as people confided to me with a hint of irony: while his forefathers were influential, he, Germán "is not all there," they would say, invariably blaming it on too many drugs. He earned money running small errands for several people in the town, and he also had the newspaper route for the town hall offices.

We met at Santiago's house. I learned that he was also distantly related to Ana Luz, the researcher who had kindly opened the doors to her Badiraguato family for me. My presence seemed to disconcert Germán. He looked me up and down, and when I told him that I planned to live in town he became agitated. Immediately sympathetic, he blurted out: "Oh, Adele, you need to make connections!" When I found a small room to rent in the center of town, he was quick to offer me a pillow and even a stuffed animal. He couldn't let go of the idea of my moving to the town and kept coming back to me, saying, for instance, "No, here, alone, it's not possible," before taking off again. My move-in went well despite this concern; I made many new acquaintances from day one and so found myself oddly trying to reassure Germán. But he would not drop it. Our exchanges became more and more disjointed. They always ended up with him summing them up with one or another of these sentences that he repeated and switched among constantly:

"Oh, Adele, you have to make connections!"

"Oh, Adele, be careful who you talk to!"

"Oh, by yourself here, no. . . ."

"Oh, be careful of your relationships!"

Germán's agitated remarks conveyed a concern in the early days of my investigation that contrasted with the ease with which I met the inhabitants but also vis-à-vis their reactions, which varied from suspicious to merely indifferent. However, Germán gave voice to something that was not so much—or not solely—about my fieldwork as it was about sociability in the main town. Never formulated by my other interlocutors in this way, Germán's concerns would nevertheless emerge from their more discreet, more isolated, but no less cautionary remarks: being there in Badiraguato was both about "having relationships" and "paying attention to one's relationships." In other words, *being there* raised questions of self-protection in close relationships and articulating this was not without its problems.

Being there meant sharing the times, the places, and the ways of daily sociability: to sit in front of grocery stores, hang out in kitchens, and pause on stoops and doorsteps to meet my main interlocutors. Running through this chapter are two intertwined threads. On the one hand, being there was one of the key aspects of the ethnography.[1] It was by living in Badiraguato, in the main town and in the hamlets, talking with people, that the ethnographic material was produced. It means that I present the key people in my investigation, our meetings, the places where we communicated and how, and the stakes that came with our relationships. On the other hand, the portraits and scenes I will describe here introduce the pervasive dimensions of daily sociability. Indeed, being there also refers to the practices of the directly experienced social world, to the experiences of my male and female interlocutors in their daily lives. I studied with particular interest situations that confronted them with "relevant" elements, in the sense of Schütz's use of the term.[2] Some of these indeed involved mobilizing and producing a set of investigative operations to make taking necessary actions possible. The daily life of the inhabitants unfolded in the face of dynamics of violence that narrowed the range of things that could be "taken for granted."[3] By focusing on what they paid heightened attention to in their daily lives, I introduce the most relevant facets of their experience.

As Teófilo put it, "I don't believe in them [the newspapers]; here something happens, and they get it backward." Indeed, the production of knowledge by the main town's inhabitants in the course of their daily lives is largely based on their past experiences and exchanges. It is therefore by describing the past experiences to which these women and men refer and the different regimes of enunciation they mobilized in the daily exchanges—what was said, how they said it, and what they held back—that I try to highlight the production of knowledge that they mobilize in a given situation. In short, I account for the investigative activity of people living in a context of violence.[4] This is both because by mobilizing their "stocks of knowledge" they themselves contextualized the action, and because it was in their investigations that I ensconced my own.[5]

If the two threads—that of my investigation and of my interlocutors' being there—intertwine, it nevertheless seems to me they must be differentiated. My own insertion is relevant to describing their experience insofar as the openings, constraints, obstacles, and reactions of which I was the object revealed certain stakes in the social world in which I moved. Similarly, the changing relationships I maintained with some of my interlocutors, as well as the issues that cropped up, do fit in well with the texture of local social relations. Nevertheless, the parallel should not be pushed too far: the immediate experiences of my interlocutors were part and parcel of their past experiences. The interactions between these men and women that I participated in were part of longer stories that I could reconstruct but had not shared. Thus their fears, their worries, their interpretations were distinct from mine, each inscribed in our unique respective stories.[6]

UNEASY INVESTIGATIONS AND UNCERTAIN PROXIMITIES IN THE MAIN TOWN

Teófilo, Exemplary Investigator

During the very first days of my settling in, I stayed at the town hotel. Santiago had agreed to let me stay at his house, but my unannounced arrival on December 23, with his family about to visit him for Christmas, prevented him from following through. Instead, he dropped me off at the hotel run by doña Irina.[7] For a permanent place to stay, Ana Luz told me to contact don Nacho, a distant relative who owned a grocery store and rented out rooms. Don Nacho had recently celebrated his seventy-fifth birthday and it was his wife Blanca, about fifteen years younger, who usually tended to the store. The first meeting with don Nacho was cold. When I asked about the room, his

first response was a mumbled "No," and then "I don't know," before concluding, his back to the wall, "Come back tomorrow." He probably called Ana
Luz after that, because the next day he announced to me with a sly smile:
"Hey, you really arrive highly recommended!" Later, he and especially Blanca
got in the habit of pulling a small stool up to the table in the grocery store,
my cue that it was time for a chat.

Between my first and second meetings with don Nacho, I returned to the
hotel and told doña Irina, the hotel's owner, about my search for accommo-
dations. Hearing about don Nacho's room, she told me that I could do better,
but if I liked it would do: don Nacho's brother was at the hotel this very
moment to welcome one of his daughters who was down from the United
States for the holidays. She was surprised that I had not yet met him and told
me that he usually stayed in one of his brother's rentals. The next day, while
I smoked a cigarette sitting on the floor outside my hotel room, a pickup
truck pulled up in front of me. From my vantage point, I saw first a foot,
followed by a paunch, then a piece of straw hat with holes, which finally
resolved into a Falstaffian old fellow trying extricate himself from the passenger seat while muttering something in a kind of hoarse snorting. This was
how I first met don Teófilo who, in a way, is the hero of this book. If my
description of him seems unfair, let me quote as a retort how in the days to
come he would repeatedly recount his first impression of me: "I get out and
what do I see there? A little moron of a girl sitting on the floor fiddling with
something with her hands. . . . At first I thought she was a retard."

So that is how it came about that don Nacho agreed to rent me the room and
I happily became neighbors with don Teófilo. He regularly feigned mistrust and
tossed "you, you're from the DEA!" at me. But in fact he did not believe this
mock accusation, which several others would level against me in earnest at other
times. Very quickly, a strong friendship—and one rife with transference—developed between us. Don Teófilo would become a pivotal figure in my fieldwork
and my daily life in the town, and I would assume an important place in his own
life. As my investigation progressed, I realized that the security I enjoyed in the
main town was at least partly due to his relationship work. He never took credit
for this in my presence, since it would have undermined his parallel attempts to
"keep the little Frenchwoman for [himself]"—by warning me of the many dangers that awaited me and by therefore controlling my actions and movements—
which hardly made Teófilo the perfect research assistant. . . .

Don Teófilo liked to tell his own story—provided of course that he was
"inspired," as he generally put it. But as his neighbor, I was able to observe his

daily life, which appeared to be organized into two stages. First, there was the morning: after carefully sweeping in front of his door, he left for a long tour through the streets of the town. He would take off early but slowly. His gut weighed him down, and he took advantage of all the exclamations addressed to him in the street—"Hey, fats!" or "Hey, old man!"—to catch his breath. Then, after a few blocks, he would "get his second wind" and from that point on nothing could stop him. Breakfast took him to his brother don Nacho's or—the wallet permitting and the hangover demanding it—to the taco stand beside the boulevard where he would find someone to chat with. Before don Nacho suffered a heart attack four months into my stay, Teófilo could be seen standing, leaning against the wall, or sitting on a plastic chair, always watching the street in front of the small grocery store. With a toothpick between his teeth, he appeared to be guarding the entrance, while regularly turning to look inside to keep a disjointed conversation going with his brother. After don Nacho became debilitated, Teófilo would sometimes look after the grocery store for a few hours so that Blanca could attend to other things. And then you would hear about it in no time: how getting stuck in a grocery store exasperated him. Moreover, he would say, the people were unbearable: "Give me 10 pesos worth of cheese here, 20 pesos of tomatoes there . . . how do they want me to know that? I cut them a piece of cheese, I weigh it and they pay what it costs, that's all! Then there are also the ones who say, 'put it on the tab, I'll pay later.'"

He complained about people hanging out for hours in the small shop: "It looks like they're coming here for fun." That wasn't entirely off the mark, but when Teófilo did not have to mind the store, he was known to loiter there for hours himself. His morning tour could also take him to the town hall, to "the telegraph" (the Western Union office), to his friend Roberto's locksmith shop, and in front of every house where anyone hailed him. Discussions inside or on the doorsteps revolved around watching the comings and goings in the street. He would devote his entire morning to these exchanges; once the day turned hot, however, his tour was over. He knew just about everything that there was to know that day, so he shut himself in his room to watch baseball and soccer, then 1950s and 1960s Mexican movies. If the TV programming bored him, he would sit on an inverted bucket against the wall outside his room. He would take out his fan, tilt his straw hat over his forehead, and grunt while waiting for something to happen. In the evening, Roberto sometimes came by to pick him up, and they would swig a few beers in his pickup truck.

The Teófilo I met lived modestly (but with panache) in a tiny room thanks to the money his daughters sent him from the United States. But, as he told me and others were quick to let me know, his current state was not representative of his past life. One day, watching him walk by on the sidewalk in front of the hotel, Irina said to me: "Ah, quite a man, that Teófilo. Do you realize that? He who had everything, who was at the top, look where he is now. What a life!" This referred to a part of his life in the United States, where he had emigrated in his twenties. After working in a factory that closed, he got into the drug trade. During a drug deal in Los Angeles, he was arrested, his network having been infiltrated by the DEA. But when he talked about himself, Teófilo preferred to expand on the time before this US stay, when he was "young, beautiful, slender, and dashing," coming and going between the sierra hamlets and the bars (*cantinas*) of Culiacán. In one of his good moods, he relished the chance to reminisce about the time he accompanied a friend to a cantina where his pal obviously was not welcome. It wasn't long before a gunfight broke out. However, young Teófilo had not ducked— he was still standing in the middle of the cantina. When the guns fell silent, an old man praised his "courage," saying, "So, to you, hats off! You didn't move an inch!" Teófilo replied: "Ah, and why should I have moved? The tangle concerned my friend, not me (*si la bronca era con el amigo, no conmigo*)!" Laughing at the line that had earned him renown, he would admit, amused, that he had been paralyzed by fear.

Then there was the prison. "I used to tell the guys who were crying to see their folk when we were 'in college' [prison]. 'See that wall? Well, your life is between here and that wall. Get it in your head: the outside, it doesn't exist for you!' It's true, the guys were going crazy! I said to my people, 'Don't wait for me, I may not get out.'" He had a trove of unfunny stories and incongruous know-how as a result of his thirteen years in US prisons. He could cook anything—absolutely anything—in a microwave and kept his small room in perfect order. In these stories, he became "Mister Lopez," but also the one who was transferred to twenty-six different prisons, suspected of being a "heavyweight in the Sinaloa Cartel." When he went down, they took "all his properties" from him. From life at the "top," all that remained were the horizons that he was able to open for his children, as "being born citizens" (that is, they were American citizens by birth). His imprisonment motivated one of his daughters to become a lawyer so she could defend him. After his release, the DEA tried several times to turn him into an informant, but he never caved—episodes that must have taught him enough about the DEA that he could be sure I was not part of it. In 2004, at the age of fifty-nine, free but stripped of his US green card, he returned alone to Badiraguato.

Teófilo's everyday life exemplified the practice of producing and disseminating information in the town. Employed as a sweeper for the town hall until 2013 and jobless since, he organized the prime hours of his day around this exchange activity. On the one hand, the rounds he made in all directions in the mornings patently related to his searching for sociability in his somewhat lonely daily life. On the other hand, one of the key aspects of the exchanges was that they let him collect and produce information on daily life in the town. In these meet-ups, the people he interacted with in their workplaces or where they lived engaged with him in the same process of sharing snippets of information. In this sense, Teófilo's morning made manifest an activity that was not uniquely his own but collective, as well as the ways in which this activity took place. In these exchanges, the snippets of information that each party collected were correlated and triangulated, producing interpretations and—to the extent possible—anticipations. These exchanges always took place in private spaces and involved only a limited number of people—all of it frequently leavened by street-watching and systematically accompanied by a drink, a fruit, or other items invariably offered to the passer-by.

I witnessed many such exchanges in the town's grocery stores, kitchens, and town hall offices, sometimes with Teófilo and at other times on my own. As time went on, I was integrated into these situations where information circulated and was interpreted.[8] Understanding and reproducing the ways these things were done spoke importantly for being present for them, and it shaped, if not constrained, my manner of inquiry. As such, doorstep conversations would exclude direct questions. They took place between silent contemplations of the street, comments of a general order, and without expressing a particular interest in the snippets of sentences that intersected and seldom answered each other.[9] Information thus developed in a "minor mode" of exchanges, and an essential element of these was maintaining a detached attitude toward what emerged from them.[10] Santiago's wife Alejandra made plain the centrality of apparent indifference to what was nevertheless scrupulously commented on, identifying this attitude as a protective tactic in the exchange. Several months after starting my investigation, realizing that I was in trouble in a neighborhood relationship, she told me: "When someone tells you something, don't show interest, don't pay attention, because then if it comes out, then it will be said that it's Adele" who repeated it. In short, the mode by which information circulated and interpretations were formed was one of phatic exchange, that is, of small talk, while the statements themselves were localized, relevant, and precise.

In effect, these discreet utterances constitute a pooling of information and analysis to compensate for the indeterminacy evoked by the morning announcement: "Dawn rose on a dead body."[11] In the hours and days that followed, in kitchens, offices, grocery stores, and on stoops, the question of who died sometimes would be put but not often answered in so many words. Someone would observe: "they say" that it was such and such, the nephew, the compadre, the son of.... The dead person was first reinscribed in his kinship and possibly in his wider circle of acquaintances. After several silences, one or the other commenter would offer what "they say" about the place of the murder, what the victim was going to do, where he or she was before dying. Maybe someone would drop this truncated sentence: "for something" (*por algo*). She was killed "for something."

In chapter 6, I analyze in more detail what is being played out in the terms and phrases used to comment on homicides, but for now let it suffice to emphasize that these exchanges are discreet, indirect, disjointed, and always conducted with the air of being disinterested in the discussions that follow the news of a murder, as in those dealing with this or that person. The impersonal form "they say that" (*dicen que*) never raises the question "who said that?" However, even if I rarely heard any of my interlocutors wonder about the why of a murder, they all had a theory about it. Once they knew the identity of the victim or victims, their knowledge often spared them from having to dig deeper. Street-watching and what they knew about the neighborhood men and women were enough to make up minds. But in these exchanges following the announcement of a murder, there was never even a hint of assigning blame, a negative judgment: the "whodunit" question simply did not exist, and the strongest condemnation I ever heard was "it's ugly," dropped with weariness.[12]

While Teófilo's exchange activity was common among other inhabitants, the span of the networks from which he distilled information and wove interpretations was exceptional. To use one of his expressions, he was "better known than the common bean" (*más famoso que el frijol bayo*), an essential part of the daily diet. Like all the others, he was embedded in the sociability of his extended family and in political kinship ties through the *compadrazgo*. In his case, part of his maternal family was influential in the main town administration during the 1950s and 1960s, and he grew up in a hamlet in the lower sierra, a marginalized part of the municipality. For that matter, he had been a teacher in the upper sierra in his youth and continued to have long-standing relationships there. The family and friendly relations he maintained in the municipality were therefore socially quite diverse, ranging from "important families" to those he warmly called the "uncultured savages" of the hamlet in the lower part where he grew up.

Everyone knew his life story, marked by a remarkable rise and especially by the price he had paid for his loyalty. As a result, if many people constantly poked fun at him by calling him "old" or "fat" or "trash talker," among other gibes reminding him of his current marginal position, it was also a way of showing him a deep respect. Everyone else I socialized with in the main town expressed a great affection for him: listening to him was a delight for those who appreciated his repartee sprinkled with swearwords—a taste that is widespread in Badiraguato. As scruffy and sassy as he was, he circulated unhindered. This included both in what he ironically called "high society," meaning the members of the local trafficking elite (who always kept me at a distance but left me in peace, thanks especially to him, as I would realize later) and among the young armed men who knew him by reputation and never failed to greet him respectfully. Finally, he had lived thirty years on the "other side," in the United States, which let him cast an often distanced look at the town and lend perspective to certain behaviors with great humor. In short, the breadth of the networks from which he built his information store, the bonhomie with which he navigated them all, his unfailing daily participation in the exchanges, and the reserve with which he did so made him an outstanding gatherer of intelligence. The murders, like the vagaries of relations between armed groups in the vicinity of the main town, probably held even fewer secrets for him than for others—because his activity as an exemplary investigator took place in a town where daily life involved investigating and participating in the collective productions of information and interpretation.

On the other hand, the case of Teófilo, and in particular the extraordinary variety of his networks, manifested the unequal distribution of access to information and the modes of its production. The suspicion toward me was a tell-tale sign here: like Teófilo, who never suspected me of being a DEA plant, some people from well-off social backgrounds did not show me any particular distrust or reserve. However, it subsequently often became clear to me that one or the other of these people knew where I was going, who I saw, and what I was doing, including when I was in Culiacán. Whereas in the early days, I felt the state capital lay outside my field of investigation, their networks or recurrent stays in the capital let them quickly track my activities there, putting their suspicions to rest. Conversely, people from more disadvantaged social backgrounds with smaller networks did not let go of mistrusting me. Despite my explanations, lacking information for making sense of my presence and my comings and goings, these people resorted to various registers of distrust. Two families in particular would constantly alternate between periods when my presence seemed beneficial to them and others when I was threatening to them. At one point, having me at their house would appear to one of them as a positive in the context of the suspicions that attached to their family. At other times, more frequent, they would redouble their efforts to discredit me, starting a series of rumors that I was "a child stealer," "infected with Ebola," and, last of all, "a man stealer."

"The Chambers": The Threat of Violence in Close Relationships

Following my meetings with don Nacho and don Teófilo, I settled in what is known in Badiraguato as "the chambers" (*los cuartos*). A line of doors opened onto tiny rooms—with bed, sink, and a toilet for the most luxurious—at the end of a lot shaded by a few small trees. Don Teófilo enjoyed a privileged status as the owner's brother. Ismael and Adriana, a brother and sister from a sierra hamlet, shared another room. Ismael was a character: in the middle of this town dominated by hats and mustaches, his tight leggings, dyed mid-length hair, eyes outlined in kohl, and his various affectations looked totally out of place. The more don Teófilo maligned him, calling him a "dirty faggot" (*pinche joto*) and mocked him ("You can't wear hats like men?"), the more Ismael gave as good as he got ("Do you really think that you're the one I want to please?") and twirled his umbrella. Often, he could be seen outside the rooms doing fitness exercises. He lived from occasional odd jobs: swept up in a grocery store, helped in a friend's hair salon, and ran errands for soldiers at the military compound. Adriana, on the other hand, was not around much. She worked until late evening as a waitress in a restaurant on the road leading out of the town. A few months later, Yanitz, just twenty years old, also moved into one of the rooms, often accompanied by a young woman— letting fly quite a few gibes about her sexual preference. She worked in a clothing store in town, but she would not stay long, moving back home to live on the edge of the town with her mother. In a nutshell, these rooms were those of the marginalized, the few people who, for one reason or another, did not live en famille.

On the street side, a one-room open-work brick house with a tin roof partially closed off access to the street, forming a sort of courtyard with the row of rooms. It housed a small family. Rosa, in her early fifties, was a small, dry woman who moved quickly, in fits and starts. Depending on her mood, she would come to chat or she would walk around mumbling to herself, her head bent down, looking at her feet. At first, she seemed more or less indifferent to my presence; she would discuss everything and nothing with me, simply because I was around. But I had trouble explaining to her what I was doing—my attempts bored her so much that she walked off in the middle of my no doubt clumsy sentences. When I later started going to work at the town hall, she would repeatedly grill me about it. At first, when I told her about my difficulties with the new job, she told me she hoped I would be treated well. Then, later, she showed some resentment about my fitting into the administration ("All because [I am] French"), and then made sure that I passed on information about the aid programs to which she supposed I could help her gain access. Her daughter-in-law Teresa, with her five-year-old daughter, also lived in the small house. Teresa's repartee made the sparks fly with don Teófilo: both took obvious pleasure in their over-the-top verbal jousts while passing through the courtyard. She mostly stayed home to take care of the little girl, who was congenitally deaf. The girl had the run of the yard and was the object of the attention of all the residents. Although she initially showed some distrust toward me, Teresa and I had some good discussions, cemented by our shared enjoyment in making fun of Teófilo, notwithstanding that we loved him dearly despite all his foibles. Teresa's husband worked in a supermarket, and I only saw him when he went to wash up in the evening, as the family had to walk through the yard to use the toilet and the shower. He just tossed me a "hey" every time he passed—or on his good days, even a "So, neighbor, you scaring off the mosquitoes?," if I was smoking a cigarette. Rounding out this family was don Chuy, Rosa's father, who lived with them and never took off his hat. The old gentleman several times very kindly assured me that he found my having come to study Badiraguato a very good thing. On winter mornings, he went out to warm up "in the blanket of the poor"—the rising sun—and he, too, was highly amused by having a woman smoke in his company. The whole family lived quite modestly from the sale of Teresa's tamales, which were popular, and her husband's salary. Their *comal*[13] stood behind their house, and we all shared a tiny washhouse (except for don Teófilo, whose dirty laundry the owner of the town laundry picked up and returned clean). The tight confines of our respective living quarters found us living a good deal outside in front of our doors, making the shared courtyard a space of intense sociability.

In addition, the neighborhood along the street was also a mesh of close relationships. First, there was Joaquín, Rosa's companion (although they did not live together), who ran the grocery store across the street. Its shelves were nearly empty and he charged prohibitive prices for what there was, but with his merry eyes behind his little glasses and his good mood, many people stopped in to chat. A little further down the street, Gabriela and Jaime's family lived with their children—Gabriela often coming to spend time with Teresa, her *comadre*—and behind the courtyard lived Maria del Carmen, who was seen more rarely and prided herself on leaving her home as little as possible. Relationships—of love, friendship, or kinship—with the immediate circle constituted a network of interknowing characterized by a strong promiscuity and a relative social heterogeneity.

In fact, some of the men and women belonged to formerly influential families of the town, while others had settled in more recently, displaced by violence in the sierra. And, from the very beginning of my moving into the chambers, I was welcomed and surrounded by the daily exchanges of this network of interknowing. The sharing of several communal spaces and the activities of the residents and neighbors increased the frequency of interactions. With the exception of Adriana, Joaquín, and Teresa's husband, the members of this network of interknowledge lacked full-time jobs and lived from odd jobs, a symptom of the widespread underemployment in Badiraguato. When I told Santiago I had decided to live in "the chambers," he said, "Oh, that's great! The people in the chambers stick very close together." Indeed, the daily life in the chambers was marked by mutual aid for everyday things and incessant remarks alternating between jokes and sarcasm that denoted close ties of affection.[14]

However, as I gradually became part of these relationships, a second, just as pervasive, register emerged: calls for mistrust. Accusations of theft, warnings against gossip, cautions against violent personalities, or more or less veiled accusations of affiliations with any of the surrounding armed groups were peppered into these daily proximity relations. Inciting to mistrust could be done in the mode of the casual narrative in the same way as the exchanges described above. Sometimes taking me to task or as the recipient of a warning about one of our network, neighbors could nonchalantly evoke such and such story from the past, bearing lessons discrediting another neighbor; or, without spelling things out, present it as an innocent echo of a gossip that would circulate, implicating another neighbor.[15] On the other hand, only those with whom I had a more established relationship of trust explicitly told me of warnings or implications that directly related to the use of violence and to affiliation with armed groups. Of course, Teófilo took the cake in this regard. Trying to warn me against hanging around other residents or neighbors and seeing that I was turning a deaf ear, he would push the register to the extreme by claiming that I was putting him in danger. "What if they see you with them? Huh? You don't want that kind of trouble!" he said, before adding, "What if they mistake the door?" He was suggesting that, because his room was adjacent to mine, I also put him at risk by exposing myself to reprisals by armed men. Beyond Teófilo's ways of talking, which were not always representative of those of other neighbors, the link between gossip and the threat of gun violence surfaced many times in conversations.[16] Thus, Alejandra, Santiago's wife, would caution me on the same topic: "You have to be careful, here people burn you (*la gente te quema*). They talk bad about you, and a lot of people had to leave [town] in a hurry because they said this or that, even if it is not true."

Calls to mistrust were the subject of a recurring generalization: "Here you can't trust anyone." Letting on loud and clear that you remained on your guard in proximity relationships indeed fit a context where "being too trusting" (*confiada*) was a clear disqualification or criticism. For example, in the case of one of my interlocutors, her friends told me that she was "*confiada*" because she had a cordial relationship with a soldier. On another occasion, I was called "*confiada*" by the person with whom I had an appointment precisely because I had showed up as I had been asked to—when what I should have shown was mistrust. The expression therefore homed in on the fact of maintaining too varied a set of relationships with people one had to be wary of, or of being perceived as not being sufficiently on guard. In this sense, the effectiveness of this disqualification in Badiraguato was based on an agreement shared between my interlocutors: to be trusting is to make yourself vulnerable.

The expression of mistrust that was currency in the vicinity of "the chambers" is therefore a register that must be interpreted in a discursive and situational way: more than the expression of a psychic feeling or state, it was first of all a question of stating mistrust in the particular situation of the interaction. The many practices of mutual aid and solidarity that I witnessed invalidate the hypothesis of a generalized mistrust expressed by my interlocutors. It is therefore necessary to grasp the importance of the effect produced by these statements in a situation. On the one hand, it let people position themselves as non-dupes and therefore as canny. In a context where everyone is gathering intelligence, showing yourself to be on guard is a protective tactic. On the other hand, the abundance of disqualifying comments in a network of interknowing (here in the mode of the call to mistrust) is also a practice by which people belonging to this network affirm its existence, multiply their interactions, and express the conflicts that reverberate through the interknowledge group.[17] In the chambers, disqualifying statements were part and parcel of longtime relationships and linked to registers of social, economic, and gender differences. Thus, the accusations of backbiting tended to be reserved for women; those of theft for people with few resources in life. An insinuation that one of my interlocutors was prone to violence figured in a formerly conflicted relationship, linked to an inheritance dispute. Thus, these expressions, which were part of a continuum from mutual aid to mistrust, also provided opportunities for remobilizing past conflicts over love, property, extended kinship, or between armed groups. They were a manifestation, a management, in the interactions of everyday life, of the context of violence and of the indeterminacy it engendered.

Indeed, expressions of distrust also fit into a context of indeterminacy in people's affiliations, in one form or another, with drug trafficking and organized violence networks. While I met few inhabitants of the main town who claimed their participation in these activities during my study there, all of the people I spoke to counted one or more people among their family and close circle who were more directly involved. These links were brought up on a recurring basis as vaguely as possible, using euphemisms. Someone would say "I have a brother who acts like a hoodlum"; another would tell me that the brother in question "is a killer" (*matón*). Someone's cousin "is just a thug" (*malandro*) who, I would later learn, worked for an important *pistolero*. Another's father is a *pesado*, the brother of a different interlocutor "runs with the armed gang (*gavilla*) of X," the son-in-law of another is a "*pistolero*" for so-and-so, and on it went. Perhaps the most surprising interaction in this regard was my encounter with a woman who worked as a housekeeper and who enthused that "my son also travels everywhere," suggesting that he traveled like me, a French woman staying in Badiraguato. Seeing my surprise, she added: "Yes, you name it, he goes there. Malaysia, the United States, Colombia, the last time it was even Spain and Norway." I could only show my admiration for this quite impressive travel résumé and asked her— directly for once—what her son did.[18] With a coy smile and amused look, she said: "Oh, that. . . . Who knows. . . ."[19] More generally, because of the inter-knowledge networks, for arrests and killings in Mexico or elsewhere of the municipality's people involved in drug trafficking to become known often did not have to wait for newspaper headlines.

More pragmatically, these affiliations are also common currency because they refer to extremely varied forms of participation. I make the social anchoring of gun violence the subject of chapter 6, but it is essential to understand here that if affiliations were fuzzy, it was primarily because only some inhabitants participated in organized violence and drug trafficking. Moreover, while the vocabulary used (*gavillas*, killers, *pistoleros*) suggests a fairly easy identification of persons involved in gun violence and trafficking, the dynamics of these groups and activities were more fluid. At the town level, there were no strictly defined organizations that comprised all those involved in trafficking and thus made it possible to clearly distinguish the members of the so-called "cartel" from other locals. Some might be called "thugs" or "gangsters" because they were simply taking advantage of an opportunity (for want of others) to transport drugs and buy weapons without answering to a given status or network. However, the casual nature of their activity did not necessarily insulate them or their loved ones from the logics of competition and violence.

This indeterminacy therefore implied a significant degree of uncertainty in proximity relations. Being seen with a person who might be the target of death threats potentially exposed you to the same threat. "A lot of people had to leave [town] in a hurry, because this or that is said, even if it's not true," as Alejandra told me. Indeed, being the subject of gossip about one's acquaintances was a dangerous thing. In the space and forms of speech in the town, conflicts and enmities could end up enmeshed in the modalities of conflicts among armed groups. Moreover, these identification and interpretation issues were essential elements of daily sociability in a context where personal ascents through trafficking were both rapid and precarious, and the relationships between the different networks of people involved in trafficking were fluid. This made it particularly difficult to figure out who was targeted by threats of violence.

The need to know if such a threat hung over an individual belonging to extended kinship or neighborhood networks called for paying two kinds of attention. On the one hand, street-watching and scrutinizing the economic transformations experienced by specific individuals were essential ways of sensemaking. Ostentatious displays of economic status (of house, car, clothing, cosmetic surgery, skin-whitening) would be accompanied by showing off that let everyone see the change of fortune of a person who before had little. It involved parading gleefully again and again up and down streets in the city center in the new car, flaunting the newfound leisure, and possibly the new figure. On the other hand, participating in the exchange spaces in which information circulated and interpretations were constructed was decisive for identifying possible threats. However, this daily intelligence gathering took place in uncertain proximity relationships in which the affiliations of the interlocutors with distant relatives or friends could make speaking risky. This being the case, the daily exchanges on doorsteps and in grocery stores could also constitute engagement in a potentially ambiguous situation.

Thus, the same forms of exchange could be observed whether they were used to disparage neighbors or construct interpretations of a new murder: feigning disinterest in what was said, reporting elements in impersonal form, and not divulging one's sources. The daily exchanges in the main town thus combined three dimensions: interlocutions for producing the interpretations necessary to size up an indeterminate situation following a murder; a mode in which conflicts between persons were expressed while updating their reciprocal links and positioning themselves as not affected; and a space in which the discursive commitments of each participant comported with some degree of uncertainty, because taking part in gossip, as well as being its object, exposed one to violence.

Everyday sociability was therefore summed up in the lines that Germán kept repeating to me: "You have to make connections" and, along with it, "you have to pay attention to your relationships." One day in a taqueria, while I was having lunch with some town hall staffers, I heard the boss say about a recently killed person: "Well, yes ... but you know what they say. Do you know why the turtle lives to be 100 years? Because it doesn't stick its nose into other people's business. ..." I had to understand that the person killed had not followed this beautiful precept. Yet sticking one's nose into other people's business is the only way to build reference points and forms of protection in our daily sociability. You need to get information from your neighbors, while pretending to be indifferent to what you learn from them. It is also necessary to avoid placing blame, making accusations, or judging violent deaths in front of the people with whom you exchange information and with whom you nevertheless make sense of those deaths.

"Being there" in the hamlets of the mountainous area entailed entering into a form of sociability with very different stakes from those in the main town.[20] The rocky start of one of my stays in a hamlet revealed the forms and issues of this sociability. My going to hamlet Y* developed in the same way as on previous occasions: during my stint as an observer in the town hall offices, I met not one but two men from hamlet Y*. I told them I wanted to visit their hamlet after explaining to them that I was doing research on Badiraguato. They both agreed, so then I asked the food aid workers of the Department of Family Affairs to take me along the next time they made their rounds of this area. I would go up with them, and they would leave me there, just as we had done before. The appointed day came, at the end of which we reached Y*. In talking to the person receiving the food aid delivery, I learned that one of my two contacts actually lived in another hamlet at some distance and out of reach for me, and that the other one was away. The DIF people therefore offered to leave me at Eduardo's, assuring me that he was used to putting up town hall representatives on the campaign trail.

Eduardo and his wife Esperanza, both in their sixties, lived in the center of the hamlet in a tin-roofed adobe house. They lived off the help of their two daughters, one of whom had become a teacher in the hamlet school. The couple helped their son and daughter-in-law, who struggled to feed their own family with their earnings from growing poppies. Eduardo and Esperanza set up a bed for me at the foot of theirs. The next morning, on a walk through the hamlet, I came across a path. Following it uphill, in no time I found myself standing at the edge of a half-hidden poppy plot. I turned back immediately but, on the way, met a man coming up the path, obviously to tend to his parcel. I don't know which one of us was the more startled when we caught sight of each other. He asked me what I was doing there. I sputtered something about "just taking a walk," and he told me to stay away. The houses of the hamlet were widely scattered, and my attempts to meet the inhabitants on my stroll came to nothing, frustrated by the plots located between the houses. I tried to find the house of one of the two men I had met in Badiraguato, but at every turn I came across armed men watching me wordlessly from a distance. For the next four or five days, I ended up mostly stuck at Eduardo and Esperanza's, and all my attempts to go out ran into complications. To escape the close atmosphere of the house a little, I spent more and more time at the hamlet's small grocery store, run by Danae. Her uncle often visited her, and this gentleman invited me to his house, set slightly apart from the others. He brought in his nieces and nephews, who took it into their heads to have me discover the mountains and nearby hamlets. Through them, I finally got to meet other people who agreed to show me their daily life.

The difficulties I encountered in the first few days of my stay had nothing to do with hamlet Y*. They stemmed from the fact that Eduardo did not take the same approach as all my other hosts—thus revealing how much effort they put into it—by spreading word of my presence and directly or indirectly vouching for my person. Because of two-way radio communications, everyone pretty much knew by then that "the Frenchwoman is there," but, as in the earlier hamlet visits, my insertion nonetheless depended on being vouched for by a hamlet resident. This contrasted with Eduardo telling me three days after my first day's chance meeting with the poppy-grower whom I had startled that he was his brother, no less. He was highly amused by my having scared his brother, but did not seem to have tried to put either of us at ease. Without ever being malicious, and while showing me kindness, he did nothing to integrate me. Maybe he was suspicious, or maybe he just could not fathom how to help me. In fact, the effort invested by the people in the other hamlets required, in some respects, more explanation than his reservations, as logical as they were: he did not know me, the main source of subsistence in the hamlet was illegal, and no one important had asked him to look after me. The difficulties I encountered in Y* were therefore above all indicative of the stakes of disclosure—unevenly assessed by each of my hosts—that my presence raised.

But those few days in the sierra also hold interest for me for the insights they provided into how sociability was structured in the sierra hamlets. Unlike in the main town, the questions of identification linked to participating or not in a repressed activity were not at issue. Poppy production was the main source of income for the inhabitants and their daily lives required concealment in the face of repression. This implied that the vigilance toward others, the need to probe the activities of neighbors and relatives, did not pose themselves in the same way. Some hamlets might be built around two or three families while others incorporated several kinship groups, but the common nature of the means of subsistence suspended the forms of uncertainty that permeated sociability in the main town. The shared concealment from military operations accentuated the intensity of sociability within the same hamlet. Moreover, with the exception of a small grocery store in the most populous hamlets, there were no open places for meetings and exchanges.[21] The absence of a public square or a taqueria, as well as the disappearance of the inns in which people who traveled on the mule paths used to stop, drastically reduced the venues for sociability. Instead, it shifted to the domestic spaces, in more controlled and particularly gendered ways.

The modalities of being there in the hamlets thus partly suspended the uncertainty of proximity relationships; but this does not mean, of course, as we will see, that the social relations were consensual and excluded the use of armed violence. Simply, the attentions and inquiries of my interlocutors in the hamlets focused on threats over which they had little control: military repression and conflicts between the heads of trafficking networks.

The heavy reliance on sociability in the hamlets with regard to the incursions by the military was evident during the first fieldwork I did in Z*, thanks to my meeting Enrique. Fortyish, Enrique flashed a beautiful smile and made a point of making eye contact with whoever he talked to. I also met him while I worked in the Department of Family Affairs office in the main town. He had come from his hamlet to settle an administrative matter, and without much ado we agreed that I would try to make it there as soon as the food aid distribution schedule would allow. Two weeks later, my Family Affairs colleagues dropped me off in a nearby hamlet and one of Enrique's brothers came to fetch me. The brother took me to his house where his wife was just showing me the room where I would sleep, when Veronica, Enrique's wife, came on the scene and rather curtly declared that I would sleep at her house.

Slender and energetic, Veronica's face was dotted with small freckles and she wore her brown hair in a bob, tied in a ponytail and tucked into a cap. She often wore comfortable clothes and no makeup. And those were not the only differences from the other women I had met up to that point. From the very first days, Veronica drafted me for the housework. She did not particularly bother with smiles and manners; and even less with me, as I began my stay at her house by taking a seat at the table when it was the men's turn to eat. When she had time, she pulled on her high-top sneakers and walked with a quick and determined step through the hamlet streets with a plastic bag to pick up the detritus that people threw on the ground—and that too was unusual. As she said, and I observed, she "could not stand still." When she talked about Enrique, her eyes shining with admiration, it was to heap never-ending praise on him. At the beginning of my stay, I saw relatively little of him. When he passed by the house, Veronica did not stop what she was doing. While he took his meal, she continued with making tortillas, chopping wood, cleaning, cooking, even handiwork if necessary. In these particularly gendered relationships, here there were admiring glances on both sides. Veronica's "three men"—as she called Enrique and their two sons, aged three and eight—were her pantheon, and signs of her affection for them were everywhere. When I finally got to spend some time with the man I'd been hearing about for several days, and then only in hurried fashion, his questions were incisive. After watching me doing the household chores orchestrated by Veronica, Enrique lobbed some test questions my way: what did I think of the way they lived? What was my opinion on legalizing marijuana?

I had been at Enrique and Veronica's house for about ten days, and by that point was moving freely from house to house, when one morning, the impending arrival of soldiers was announced through the crackling of radios and by word of mouth. Indeed, that same evening they bivouacked among the scattered houses in the middle of the hamlet. Their arrival affected the whole of hamlet life: women no longer traveled alone, implying a readjustment of internal logistics in families: who took the children to school, who went to the grocery store, who dropped by the neighbor's to get something. One afternoon, a small group of us were walking with children up one of the sloping paths when soldiers appeared from behind the hillock we were climbing. It was as if they rose up from the ground little by little: first we saw their caps, then the weapons, and finally the men. The children with us screamed with fright and fell into a fit of tears.

The adults, reluctant to show their fear, focused on past stories. The presence of the soldiers that day was implicitly put into perspective with the modes of past repression. Indeed, people over the age of forty had lived through Operation Condor, and all had experienced its aftermath: a less violent but uninterrupted repression. The suppression of poppy and marijuana crops began in the 1940s and 1950s, but in a highly targeted manner, primarily as leverage in extortion practices. As in the rest of Mexico, army violence increased in the 1970s—for instance, in 1971, the military killed a dozen people in another Badiraguato hamlet at a baptism.[22] Starting in 1975, under the presidencies of Luis Echevarría (1970–76) and José López Portillo (1976–82), Operation Condor, carried out with the cooperation of the DEA, set out to eradicate marijuana and opium crops.[23] Badiraguato became the base for operations in the states of Sinaloa, Chihuahua, and Durango. One of the peculiarities of Operation Condor is that it was a cross between anti-drug trafficking and counterinsurgency operations against guerrilla movements in some regions. It was commanded by one of the generals responsible for the Tlatelolco massacre in Mexico City on October 2, 1968, and torture was routine. For example, in the state of Sinaloa, Operation Condor targeted both protest movements on the coastal plain and poppy and marijuana growers in the western Sierra Madre.[24] Numerous reports to federal authorities indicated the use of counterinsurgency tactics on peasants in the sierra.

Veronica did not like to dwell on difficulties—preferring to point out that she overcame them—but still, she told me about daily life in the hamlet during her childhood in the 1980s. Soldiers entered houses, especially at night, and beat, raped, and tortured the residents. She said all the men in the hamlets, including her father, would flee their homes every night to hide in the mountains. The women and children who remained in the houses suffered nighttime intrusions, rapes, and beatings, and lived in constant fear of not seeing their fathers, husbands, brothers, and sons return. The numerous complaints lodged by local representatives at different levels of the state suggested both how widespread torture was and the only means of protection available to the inhabitants: disappearing from the hamlets where they lived. For example, in December 1981, the local representative of the hamlet of Válgame Dios, high up in the mountains, listed the tortures to which the people there had been subjected. A few months later, when asked to conduct a census, he informed the town hall that he was unable to carry it out, as the residents could not return to their homes.[25]

The arrival of soldiers reactivated past experiences of radical vulnerability. The most common forms of the military's current incursions affected everyday life differently, leading the locals to distinguish between soldiers in the past and of today. Nevertheless, the search for certain infamous traffickers, including Rafael Caro Quintero during my investigation, went on in joint operations between the Mexican Navy and the US antidrug agencies.[26] The inhabitants thus got used to being surveilled with drones. On some occasions, incursions revived particularly violent military practices. In September 2014, for example, several helicopters landed in a hamlet, ripping off its tin roofs. Accounts by the victims of this raid told the story of the joint presence of Mexican and US military: after beating the local hamlet representative, the soldiers abducted a woman; they locked her up, tied her to a chair, and beat her for several hours so she would reveal the whereabouts of Rafael Caro Quintero.

Incursions by the military were therefore one of the main threats against which inhabitants of the sierra had to protect themselves in their daily lives. In this regard, some of the news that everyone gleaned took shape in the context of moving around which, as we have seen, involved maintaining links and sharing information with the residents of the other hamlets. But the essential protection asset was the two-way radio. The crackling and conversation snippets that usually sounded from the belts of all adults were a key element of the sociability soundscape in the hamlets. Radios were the only means of long-distance communication in the sierra, as the territory had no cell phone signal coverage. These radio waves hosted a complex jockeying between the military and the inhabitants, who monitored and warned each other of the former's progress, while the former listened in on radio traffic that they otherwise suppressed. My interlocutors explained the ban in these terms: "People talk trash about them [soldiers], that's why they don't want us to have the radios." Without covering all the issues inherent in this ban, this interpretation referred to the game of listening and reciprocal surveillance: the military would ban radios because, when they listened to the frequencies of their targets, they would not only hear their own movements broadcast, but also the nicknames pinned on them—at which they took offense.

Radios were subject to a complex prohibition regime. Banned by the authorities, they were the only way for sierra dwellers to communicate with each other and with the administration in the main town. Town hall employees often were authorized to have radios, unlike most of their interlocutors in the hamlets. In practice, the prohibition applied less to whether the radio itself was authorized than to where it was used: a municipal government employee originally from the sierra in possession of a prohibited radio had nothing to worry about in the town. On the other hand, in the sierra, radio relay antennas were periodically destroyed by the military, and anyone arrested in possession of a radio had it confiscated. This called for improvised tactics on the spur of the moment, like the woman we met in the previous chapter, who discreetly slipped her radio between her breasts after turning it off and who then managed to keep her back turned to the soldiers during their unannounced visit. As a result, people constantly fiddled with the volume on their radios, depending on where they were. And tellingly, one of my interlocutors who was actually authorized to carry a radio tossed it panic-stricken into the undergrowth when he saw soldiers approach.

The repression and surveillance of remote communication permeated the very mode of communication. The risk of being listened to required using multiple channels of transmission and thus objectifying the different solidarity networks in the hamlets: a frequency for all hamlets, another for a group of hamlets in an area, another for within the hamlet, one for a group of people working together, or even sometimes one just for family members.

Similarly, the inhabitants adapted to repression—as well as poor sound quality—by codifying the speaker announced at the start of the call, with numbers and codes assigned to a hamlet, family, or person, depending on the channel. They communicated tersely, utilizing a language that was not necessarily encrypted but was special. Beyond the nicknames given to plots, helicopters, and other elements strictly related to drug production and trade— some of my interlocutors insisting they were known to the soldiers and therefore useless—radio transmissions were rapid-fire and difficult to follow for anyone not used to them. Finally, the public nature of the radio communications required passing information selectively. Users would therefore have a fine feel for tailoring the message to the audience. I realized this when my comings and goings were the subject of radio chatter: on one occasion, when I stopped to eat, I understood that the lady of the wayside restaurant knew that I was on my way to such and such a hamlet; she then communicated my arrival on the channel shared by a large number of hamlets so that all the people I met later knew that I was coming, with whom, and around what time. Contrariwise, on a channel linking a small number of hamlets, including Y*, Eduardo, with whom I was staying and who was looking for me, explained to me why he had refrained from asking for my whereabouts on the radio: "If I ask where the Frenchwoman went, all these assholes (*cabrones*) will know that you are walking around God knows where."

Paradoxically, despite the encoding of the speakers, the careful word choice, and the reserving of specific channels, the use of radios illustrated the problems posed by construing Badiraguato as "the base" or "fiefdom" of the "Sinaloa Cartel."[27] In fact, their use cannot be considered as an indication of a hierarchical organization that integrated the inhabitants. Even if radio arrived in some hamlets thanks to an individual with the economic and political clout—in other words, a "*pesado*"—to have a transmitter antenna put up, radios were not handed out with it. Instead everyone bought their own, because they needed a means of communication. Similarly, setting the channels on each device was done by people with the necessary skills. During my fieldwork, it often still cost 500 pesos for setting up the channels; many people told me this changed because "all the young people know how to do it now." Above all, the way radios were used was inevitably enshrined in local social relationships, in which obviously the hamlet residents' only mode of subsistence had to figure. Thus, on the most-widely-shared channel, and provided their radio had sufficient range, people could alert each other about all sorts of happenings: an accident on a road to summon the Red Cross from the main town, or about the arrival of the soldiers three hours hence, or about a truck delivering construction materials. Access to radios was considered to have "saved many lives, given the lack of hospitals, of roads in good condition." On the hamlet channel, you could ask someone to bring tables for the new year's party or warn them about the military spotting a plot of poppies. Within a family, you could ask someone for a pickup in case of a flat tire and inform your husband if soldiers were about.

The intense and unceasing repression therefore permeated all daily practices. While the temporary and repeated incursions by columns of soldiers accentuated this vulnerability and involved other adjustments in daily life, forms of sociability were constructed, shaped, and reinvented in response to the many constraints that repression and marginalization imposed.

Another peril weighed on the daily life of the hamlets: the conflicts between the heads of trafficking networks. I observed the effects of this particular threat during my stay with Lamberto, whom I had met in the office of Gonzalo, an official from the same hamlet of S*. In his forties, Lamberto wore baggy, frayed jeans, sandals, and a thick shirt. He had come to town for shopping, taking the opportunity to bring along two of his neighbors to take care of some paperwork. When we met, I asked him if I could come to his hamlet for my fieldwork and stay with him. Without missing a beat, he agreed and even made sure that Gonzalo would alert me to his next visit to town so that he could take me back with him. The logistics of travel always being complicated, his thoughtfulness was particularly welcome.

He spoke with a slight lisp, but his tone of voice was warm. He drew on a thousand expressions to put me at ease about being welcomed and to indicate that I would have a good time with his family. And he was right. When we arrived at sunset in front of the little house, I got an instant eyeful of the tumult reigning in this large and restless family, with which I was lucky enough to have fallen in. On a little rise, several small tin-roofed houses stood on small terraces, one above the other. To reach Lamberto's from the dry wash that crossed the hamlet, we had to climb a path that took us past his sister's and mother's house, then past where his brother lived with his family, before we came to the house where he lived with Tamara and their children.

Tamara, thirtyish, small, rotund, and with very long hair that she combed through at night, was mother to five children. She was full of energy and had a great sense of humor. Nostalgia washed over her whenever she would talk about her family: she wanted to see more of her mother, her father, and her siblings who still lived in of the state of Chihuahua. As we saw in chapter 1, the journey, which normally took about ten hours, had become even more precarious after the conflict erupted between the people of the hamlets N* and S*.

Her favorite moments during her day were when she could spend a little time chatting with one of her sisters-in-law and other girlfriends in the hamlet. She would descend the steep path, her umbrella over her shoulder, on the lookout for a kitchen where one or the other of her relatives had time for a chat. But these moments remained few and far between. Although she took time out to laugh and chat, she was often overwhelmed. Despite her efficiency, her day was not long enough to do all she needed to do. This paradoxically proved to be a godsend for me. Veronica had made it clear to me that doing housework and scrupulously adhering to gender norms were both crucial if I wanted to be accepted into families. In this respect, my integration into the rhythm of Tamara's family was especially easy. With great pleasure and in the context of a relationship that would turn into a friendship with a woman of my own age, I tried to support Tamara. She took time to show me how to make tortillas and even went so far as to entrust the chore to me, at no small risk to the family's breakfast.

While spending some time at the grocery store in this hamlet, I met don Pedro and doña Lupe. They lived in a house that, with two others, formed a square. The tiny concrete patio slightly overhung one of the bends in the wash. The red tile roof of their house told you that it was one of the hamlet's oldest houses. A large front yard served as a shady corridor, lined with plants, and with a bench and chairs arranged on each side. Sitting with your back to the house, you could watch the comings and goings of people in the square, in pickup trucks, on foot, but mostly riding an ATV; they would always greet the old couple and their visitors. A large window open on this yard indicated that it was also a small grocery store, while at the back you could see the kitchen. Several people came by to spend a moment in the front yard's shade.

There were four of us on one Monday afternoon when doña Lupe volunteered: "They say X has been killed." This was weighty news: this X was a notorious *pesado* whose death would make the front page of the regional newspapers. The back-and-forth between doña Lupe and the two old men sitting on the bench turned into a succession of mumbled places and nicknames. They mentioned his hamlet, and up to that point I had more or less kept up with them. But then came the roll call of his family members (the son of ..., nephew of ...), usually by their nicknames, and now, despite my stay of by now several months, I was soon lost. This continued for several minutes and soon much of the family ties of the one killed and the people working with him had been inventoried. The commentators appear to have covered it all when a short silence set in. Then don Pedro, with a sullen air, let drop: "When the boss falls, the hamlet collapses." The others nodded in silent assent.

The departed *pesado*'s hamlet was not located especially close to where Pedro, Lupe, and their interlocutor lived. But their interest in the news stemmed from the fact that this death would affect people they knew and, more broadly, as in Pedro's maxim: "When the boss falls, the hamlet collapses." As we saw earlier, a conflict between armed groups could limit the movements of people from these hamlets. Similarly, these conflicts impacted the daily lives of the inhabitants of associated hamlets who would have the threat of reprisals looming over their homes. The disappearance of a "boss" or a "*pesado*" increased the vulnerability of the hamlet's residents. Many comments showed how prevalent this knowledge was. "You realize, if they hadn't killed X, this hamlet would be doing just fine," a municipal employee told me as we passed through an abandoned hamlet. The vagaries of the rise and fall of the "*pesados*" confronted the neighbors with two articulated dynamics. On the one hand, the economic opportunities offered by these figures who acted as middlemen (see chapter 3) would evaporate, at least temporarily; on the other hand, their disappearance potentially started conflicts stemming from internal competitions among the people living in the hamlet. More frequently, however, they were caused by another *pesado*'s attempts to take control of the resources produced by the hamlet's people. The disappearance of these depopulated hamlets was a central element both in the social geography of the municipality's mountainous territory and the relationships between the historical residents of the main town and the displaced people who settled there. The exchange in the small grocery store in S* was suffused by this experience of existential insecurity induced by the hazards that punctuated the lives of the powerful. Pedro's generalization made plain the serious implications that he knew a *pesado*'s death could have. His tone in making the point reflected how it weighed on their lives.

The way daily life unfolded in the hamlets clearly showed that two dimensions coexisted: on the one hand, there were the settled routines, socializing in houses, neighborhood relationships, and untroubled movement within the hamlet; on the other, there was the extreme fragility of this condition, threatened by dynamics that affected the hamlet as a whole. Just as the conflict between N* and S* directly affected everyday life, the death of a hamlet's *pesado* endangered its inhabitants, while occasional patrols by the military only called for increased vigilance. Uncertainty in the mountainous region mainly played out for people first around military repression and its timing, and second around the rises and falls, negotiations, and conflicts involving the powerful, who were at once protective and threatening figures.

Thus, in the sierra hamlets, as in the main town, probing into events was constantly woven into ordinary sociability. In different ways and in the face of varied types of threats, the people I met in the municipality deployed many information-gathering techniques that allowed them to navigate everyday life and anticipate threats. Their inquiries produced different forms of knowledge based on the observation of social dynamics; this intelligence let them identify places, periods, and situations that are more prone to violence.

IDENTIFYING THE THREAT

Santiago had been the first person to welcome me to the main town (chapter 1). Three days after my foray with Diana, I returned on the bus to meet him in the center of town. We crossed the square, passing through the streets that led to the river and to his house. Here I met his wife Alejandra, who was pregnant at the time and soon would give birth to Hector, and their son Aurelio, eight years old. They lived in the oldest part of a beautiful family home that you entered through a courtyard shaded by a magnificent mango tree. On the ground floor, this old, elongated building gave on a narrow shady porch with a few chairs. On the other side of the courtyard was another small house inhabited by Santiago's father and aunt.

During our first conversation, the fieldwork I planned to do elicited some curiosity in Santiago and Alejandra, but above all a lot of mistrust. Both were extremely welcoming and, at the same time, Santiago greeted all my explanations with an ironic smile. In short, while receiving me, he let me know that he was not fooled: I could say what I wanted; I was investigating the organization of drug trafficking. It would be flattering to think that I gradually managed to gain his trust, get him to lower his guard, but I do not believe I did. Santiago remained on alert. Without any prompting from me, he repeatedly told me, for example, that he would not take me into the sierra. In fact, this would be a theme in my relationship with a whole segment of his family: all showed me the same amused yet distrustful cordiality. Nevertheless, they invited me to their family celebrations and showed me several times that they considered themselves responsible for me.

On several occasions, there was talk about my settling with Santiago and Alejandra in their house, but when I did stay there for some days, it caused unexpected problems. At the end of the old building, on the side facing the street, they had recently built a small cinder-block addition. The ground floor served as a temporary storage area, but it had two small rooms on the second floor accessed by an external staircase. One served as a bedroom for Santiago, Alejandra, and Aurelio, and they offered to let me have the other. But a few days later, Santiago once again had to withdraw his invitation on the grounds that Alejandra and he would have to shuttle back and forth to Culiacán several times until January, so that they would only rarely be at home. He told me that they did not like the idea of me staying in the house by myself: "With the river right next door, we'd rather not leave you alone." Indeed, the back wall of their house and courtyard was the last structure of the town bordering a large wooded area that ran along the river. The riverside was hidden from view, and a place where people ventured rarely and then only by necessity; the town in effect turned its back on it. Alejandra also told me on this occasion that I would soon find that people did not go out at night, and they themselves made sure to lock up as early as 9 p.m. She carried up the evening meal, closed the large wooden shutters of the kitchen, and they remained in the small room locked securely behind a door of sheet metal. The two small rooms on the upper floor perched like a nest that the family avoided leaving after dark.

Alejandra and Santiago's general apprehension far outweighed their concerns about me. Alejandra told me about a time when Santiago had to leave before daybreak and she heard gunshots very close by. Thinking he had already gone out, she hurried down from the room in a panic, only to find him still in the kitchen. And, in fact, during the time of my fieldwork, three murders were committed in the vicinity. In May 2014, two men were found shot dead a few dozen meters from the house, which caused Alejandra to move up the time when the family locked up. Thus, the phrase "as the river is right next door" reflected generalized experience: knowing that a significant number of murders in the town were committed by the river, Santiago and Alejandra identified the place itself as potentially threatening. This formulation was particularly worrisome for them because of the location of their house, but I encountered it in more hushed tones from other interlocutors. A neighbor of mine told me, "I never go there," and Teófilo threw me the laconic observation that "they kill there."

I do not know if this labeling was unanimously shared in the main town, but what matters here is that the inquiries the inhabitants made—activities enabled by the collective exchange of information and sensemaking—led in some cases to identifying landmarks that helped them avoid threatening places. The same mechanism was at work in individuals establishing some kind of curfew for themselves. Apart from a few men who risked it, the vast majority of my interlocutors were emphatic about not going out at night. When it was punctuated by the sounds of gunfire, my interlocutors could distinguish celebratory shooting from shoot-outs, thanks in particular to knowing about any festivities planned for that time.

Some of the markers, the threatening places and times by which people oriented their everyday lives, formed part of a generalization of where and when murders tended to take place most often. However, other characterizations referred to more finely attuned ways of reading the social context, based on times, situations, and activities to avoid.

The hotel stood at the exit of the town where the road heads off toward the sierra—a stretch nicknamed "the boulevard." On the first day, with me in tow, Santiago walked into the hotel's empty courtyard, shouting "Rina!" Doña Irina eventually materialized behind the desk. She looked cross. Already not a little surprised at finding a hotel in the town, I was even more startled to hear doña Irina respond dryly to Santiago without looking at me that she was fully booked. Santiago insisted, explaining that I was a student "sent by Ana Luz," and that he had no room in his house. Doña Irina finally relented and let me have a room. Energetic, dry-voiced, in her fifties, in short order she had me settled in the room next to the kitchen. On the second day, doña Irina's manner seemed to be softening, and I discovered that I had landed in a female household: doña Irina lived with her eldest daughter and the latter's family, and with her middle daughter Elena, a former beauty queen, and her three children. After the Christmas Eve soiree I began to spend long hours over Nescafés with Elena or doña Irina. We talked about Paris, which Irina wanted to visit, her past and future travels, her daughters, and about good and bad marriages. Her hopes in this regard now rested on her youngest daughter, who, at the start of my fieldwork, was living with an aunt in the United States. In contrast to the somewhat dry exchanges at the beginning, doña Irina took me in at her own pace: we cooked together, and I was invited to the meals that follow Christmas. She put her trust in me despite the warnings by people in her social circle—people much better off than any of my other interlocutors—who advised her to keep me at a distance. One day, she invited me to a religious celebration where one of her friends confronted me with: "Someday you will not wake up. . . . Me, if I saw you, I wouldn't let you into my house. . . . They'll kill you over a misunder-standing." So, I would never be welcome in her circle of friends, but, in her own words, doña Irina "never closes the door to someone just because that's what someone tells her to do." She proclaimed this loudly and clearly, and even irritated me a little by comparing me to a soldier who had been stationed there and whom she befriended in spite of her friends calling her "too confi-dent" (*confiada*). This was the first family whose life I shared in Badiraguato.

On the third day, doña Irina's eldest daughter came into the hotel kitchen and announced: "I know who it is." "Oh, who's that?" replied her mother. The conversation cleared up the question: someone had been killed, she knew who he was. Doña Irina later told me: "That's how it is around this time of year . . . during the holidays, they kill a lot." She explained that people who had moved to the United States would come back thinking that the problems they had left behind unresolved in Badiraguato were forgotten, but that they were often mistaken. This new maxim, which came as a surprise to me, had the advantage of suggesting some exceptionality regarding the fact that six people had been killed in the first week of my fieldwork.

During the Easter holidays, it was Gonzalo who would pick up on the vacation theme. He was an important executive in the town hall, and I had first met him at Santiago's home before encountering him again once I started working in the administration offices. Always friendly, funny, and generous with me, he was the only politician with whom discussions around coffee cups ran pleasantly and who would open doors for me in his native hamlet. In one conversation with his colleagues, they talked about a murder that had just taken place at the start of the holiday. Gonzalo said this period was conducive to murder, going on to explain that the temporary return of emigrants resulted in score-settling: "There's no denying that the problem is that we hold grudges," and during the holidays some people "come back to settle scores."

Although punctuated by invocation of an essentializing suggestion ("we [the people of Badiraguato] hold grudges"), this explanation in terms of peri-ods of peak threat referred to a mechanism for generalization distinct from the remarks about the river and the night. Indeed, all my interlocutors had emigrant relatives who kept in touch regularly. Emigrants returning to Badiraguato during the holidays were a familiar social phenomenon which the inhabitants associated, beyond the pleasurable family reunions, with an intensified threat of violence. The knowledge that underpinned this recogni-tion seemed to be widely shared. Later, as the next Christmas approached, in the context of an ongoing conflict that had everyone's attention, one of my interlocutors worried: "And besides, the holidays are coming."

Thus, the identification of periods calling for special precautions resulted from generalizations based on past experiences and the analysis of transnational circulations. The outputs from these analyses translated into protective practices: the stakes mounting with the temporary returns of emigrants demanded increased attention. This was a period during which day-to-day facts had to be inserted into a special interpretive framework, that of indications of probable violence.[28]

These processes, which denoted a particularly detailed and in-depth knowledge of the social context in which my interlocutors lived, found other applications. These same analyses informed daily practices of self-protection, leading my interlocutors to generalize certain types of interactions to keep their distance from, avoid, or simply be more aware of. For example, the funeral vigils of homicide victims were identified as situations to be scrupulously avoided: "Even in my dreams, I wouldn't go there!," Teófilo confided to me. The vigil appeared to be a situation in which the threat of the violence that had been visited on the deceased could be perpetuated, an assessment that also related to knowledge of the dynamics of violent conflicts. Vigils were considered threatening because the killings possibly figured in a settling of accounts that rarely ended with this death and instead could fuel reprisals (chapter 6). In the sierra hamlets, the dances, organized by the important people, were also treated with circumspection. Beyond certain precautions ingrained in women attending dances (chapter 5), these festivities constituted prime spaces for outbreaks of conflicts involving the "*pesado*" who organized them.[29]

Finally, beyond one-off events or specific periods of the year, my interlocutors oriented their frequenting of social spaces according to what activities were better not to take part in or even attend. Alcohol consumption, bets involving money, or racing motor vehicles cropped up in the odd conversation. Thus, "don't go thinking that drinking is a good thing," an elderly lady in the main town told me once. An official told me all about his Sunday afternoon at a volleyball game and concluded with: "I left early, the betting was starting." Gabriela told me that her son got scared during a demonstration of controlled skids (*policiacas*) that was unraveling and where guns were pulled. She reprimanded him by telling me: "First he wants to go to the *policiacas* and then he comes back with his tail between his legs." My interlocutors never did spell out the common elements in these activities and situations: these avoidance tactics were the work of women, children, elderly men, and, more broadly, as in the case of the civil servant who skipped out of the volleyball game, of people who gave volatile situations characterized by the staging of competitions between (young) men a wide berth. Thus, against a backdrop of distinctive activity readings that mobilized attention and established avoidance practices, what came into focus was an unequal access to public spaces that women, children, and older men stayed or were kept away from.

THE IMPOSSIBILITY OF CHARACTERIZING CONTEXT

Observational and analytical skills allowed my interlocutors to read situations and interpret broader social dynamics. If they acquired this knowledge in the context of situated practices, particularly in trying to protect themselves, they also developed it through reflexive considerations on their actions. Paradoxically, these particularly in-depth analytical operations with respect to the context in which these women and men lived coincided with avoidance, even denial, precisely in the formulation of the context itself. While the characterization of the context may at times have appeared to be not "relevant"—in Schützian perspective, not necessary to carry out day-to-day practices—the deliberate disavowal of it reveals the constraints that weigh on its verbalization.

During the very first days of my investigation, while I was looking for don Nacho, I picked the wrong grocery store and got a dose of Yolanda's hearty laughter. "Rooms for rent??" Here was an idea that struck her as really funny! From behind her counter, she beamed at me. She asked me a ton of questions and all my answers made her laugh. At first, I failed to grasp why but just tried out other funny things to say on her. Her laughter bounced off the walls of her shop and enveloped me. While I found no room here, I would be wrapped in Yolanda's warm hugs, with her holding me really tight against her chest every time I came by and pretending to scold me for staying away too long.

In her forties, Yolanda liked to repeat that "the hours pass slowly." She confronted them with bright eyes in a chubby face on which played a constant expression of astonishment. I was introduced to her daughters and the little shady patio adjoining the grocery store. We would spend many hours there on plastic chairs drinking sodas from her store. There she welcomed "her little old suitors," starting with Antonio and Heriberto, both around eighty years old. She handled with a rare dexterity the *albur*—the practiced play on words and sexual double entendres that is usually reserved for men. She let the innuendos of her little old suitors fall flat, in a low key very far from her true best. Her girlfriend Fernanda, about the same age as Antonio and Heriberto, could almost beat her at it, but her credo was less about subtlety and double meanings than in-your-face provocation. She asked me many times if my "guy is any good" so that she could, each time, retort that she herself didn't like to make commitments, but that at least those she went with "can go the distance," invariably triggering Yolanda's resounding laughter.

We were just sitting in front of her grocery store when Yolanda suddenly said, "Hey, I'm going to tell you my story." Her tone of voice, playful as usual, held no hint of what she was about to tell me. She suddenly recounted that as a newlywed in her hamlet she had watched her husband get killed. After shooting him, the killers had turned their guns on her. She was running and shouting "like crazy," and her mother-in-law was trying to hold her back saying, "Stop, don't go, they're going to kill you!" She said her husband had been killed "for nothing, out of jealousy because he grew [the poppy] better." She told me that for the next few weeks, "I couldn't feel anything when I walked, I was like outside my body." She had taken refuge in the main town and had found work in a restaurant. Another marriage, from which her two daughters were born, went wrong, and she decided never to marry again. Her story was dense and continuous, from the murder before her eyes twenty years before to the opening of her grocery store ten years later. She let a silence set in before concluding with: "It used to be very quiet, not like now."

Yolanda's last sentence struck me as completely contradicting the rest of her story. In her account, Yolanda had not minimized her pain and horror at the violence she suffered and yet, with the phrase "it used to be very quiet," she incongruously seemed to describe this past as peaceful. The use of this anticatastasis (the expression of a situation diametrically opposed to reality) instructs us to consider its place in the economy of exchanges: it was a conclusion she drew, a way to close her narrative, to put it behind her. "It used to be very quiet" said that the story was finished for her, that it belonged to the past.

On street corners, in the grocery store, in the kitchens, as an afterthought to remarks about the heat and the wait for rain, it recurred insistently like an incantation:

"Here, it's very quiet."

"You've seen, it's quiet here, isn't it?"

"It's very quiet, right?"

These statements appear to propose a general characterization of the context or to invite a confirmation of this qualification. They were used regardless of the timing of murders during my fieldwork. In a week when three murders had happened in rapid succession, precisely during the school vacations and the returning of the emigrants, doña Irina's daughter said to me in a disjointed conversation: "It's very quiet, right?" These statements came out like a response, which would begin with an inaudible "but," an invalidation of a statement that was also left unsaid. Thus, these sentences should not so much be seen as valid or faulty descriptors of the context that is apparently being characterized. Of particular note is the internal tension in these statements (they negate what they assert) and the importance of verbalizing them.

The negation of violence was condensed into several ritualized formulas. "Here it's quiet" frequently rubbed shoulders with "there is violence like anywhere else." Of course, these various statements present nuances: in one there is no violence; in the other there is, but no more than elsewhere.[30] But all of these formulas share an essential characteristic: the way they are mobilized during verbal exchanges. These remarks were made to me on a regular basis by people I had just met. This could happen after my interlocutors had asked me how long I had been in Badiraguato, and if I liked it there. Invariably having answered with a "yes, very much so," I would then be told: "Yes, it's very quiet here."

I bumped into a kindergarten teacher in the street whom I had briefly met a few days earlier. She asked me for details on what I was doing in Badiraguato. I explained to her that I was doing fieldwork as part of my thesis and added that I wanted to stay in the village for at least a year. She responded with: "And you're not afraid to be here?" "No, it's fine," I answered—and immediately she said, "Look, here there is violence like everywhere else; if you don't get involved, there's no problem" (si no se mete uno, no hay problema).

This scene made particularly clear the role played by these utterances in the economy of exchanges. In this instance, our conversation had a break in it: her first question was a real question, an illocutionary act: she actually wanted to know if I felt no fear in the town. She engaged in our exchange in a warm manner tinged with curiosity. As for my part, accustomed as I was to meetings in the streets in town and to exchanges warm in form and basically superficial, I fell back on my stock answer that everything was fine. Without realizing it, my answer was a form of protection that I regularly adopted in random encounters in the streets of Badiraguato. But, in doing so, I thwarted her intent for the encounter. While she approached the exchange as the start of a real discussion and displayed curiosity, my attitude encouraged her to hide behind conventional phrases ("Look, here there is violence like everywhere else"), contrary to what her initial question implied. Violence denial is encapsulated in formulas whose meaning is not highly problematic since they allow limiting, reducing, or concluding exchanges at a lower cost: meeting and exchanging just a few words.[31]

To point out that these phrases intervened in exchanges with a phatic function does not mean that the statement itself is insignificant. Just as we can answer "I'm okay" without being so, these statements can mean different things depending on the situation and the speakers. Thus, saying "everything is quiet" or "there is violence here like everywhere else" can make reality acceptable by denying it, by telling yourself—in an incantatory manner—that you are not affected by violence, by communicating to others that you are cautious, or by putting an end to the anxiety or suffering that you have expressed. While it is often difficult to determine which of these psychic intentions or mechanisms are at play in the utterance, the fact remains that the utterance is never trivial. By this formula that generalizes their experience, my interlocutors glossed over, skirted, or denied the subtext of the analyses and sensemaking that marked their daily lives.

The importance of these statements went beyond the interactions of the inhabitants with me, the foreigner, and the desire to portray the town as peaceable. They surfaced in similar ways in conversations in which I did not take part and that took place in my presence in a setting where everyone knew me. Many studies on daily life in armed conflicts remark on the importance of these statements that contradict ordinary experience, raising issues, more or less explicitly, about the normalization of violence.[32] Through the narratives of the people of Huancapi in Peru (who say that their village was spared from war by St. Louis, King of France and patron saint of the city), Valérie Robin Azevedo perceived these stories as they related to the national discourse of the post-Truth and Reconciliation Commission, to the conflicting interpretations that this discourse encompassed, and to the restriction of the category of victim that it resulted in.[33] Similarly, it strikes me that the phatic nature of the contradictory statements on Badiraguato's tranquility must be put in tension with the very distinct way that armed violence is framed in Mexico's national context. Just as in Peru it made sense for Huacanpi's inhabitants to hush up the vagaries of relations with the Shining Path so they could find a place for it in the national narrative, in Badiraguato, protesting against the unstable and violent nature of everyday life did not elicit any recognition. On the contrary, the discourse on acts of violence in the region made them out to be of a criminal order and rejected their political or social dimensions.[34] In this regard, the euphemisms and contradictions of my interlocutors echoed the media coverage of violence in the national context. The print media were saturated with images of tortured bodies, with a mounting body count, but without ever dwelling on any of the violent acts.[35] In television programming, the decontextualized treatment of homicides in Mexico, where they ranked as miscellaneous facts, contrasted with the emphasis on armed violence that takes place outside the country.

In Maria del Carmen's house, we were seated in the company of her son and one of her neighbors in front of the television, while she prepared food a few meters from us. On the heels of the Iron Chef Salsicha culinary program (literally "Sausage Iron Chef"), the Televisa network broadcast a segment on a missionary from the Democratic Republic of Congo living in Mexico City, full of images highlighting poverty and the armed conflict. The missionary talked about his country's misery and the wars ravaging it. At one point, Maria's son said to me, "Hey, there's war all the time, isn't there? In every country in Africa, right?" While I mumbled an "Uh . . .," his mother broke her silence to say in a very assertive tone: "I say, only those who meddle in the affairs of others are killed. If you mind your own business, you'll be fine (bien a gusto)." When I asked her, "What do you mean?," she answered: "Well, see, here, if you don't go looking for trouble, you're safe."

Images on the theme of wars and misery in Africa are broadcast often on Mexican TV. Over and over, they show naked children, paramilitary convoys, abuses, and they run alongside a stream of unrelated violent acts in Mexico. At first glance, the situation in Maria del Carmen's home was characteristic of the forms taken by the diffusion of a hegemonic discourse: it is indeed difficult not to notice the linkages between media productions saying "over there everything is bad," and the abundant local discourses that repeat "here everything is quiet, right?," or "there's is violence here like everywhere else"—with "Africa" perfectly fulfilling the role of this radical otherness. However, Maria turned the game on its head: she commented on this violence, which is presented as extreme, and out of all proportion to the viewers' experience, with a locally accepted formulation that characteristically relativized the impact of violence in Badiraguato: "Only those who meddle in the affairs of others are killed. If you mind your own business, you'll be fine." She thus made the link between the violence depicted on television and that experienced in Badiraguato: "Well, see, here, if you don't go looking for trouble, you're safe." However, this turning upside down of the national framing did not involve an affirmation of the violent nature of her daily life, but operated by affixing the local statement of peace and quiet over violence in Africa.

Thus, "everything is quiet" sits at the juncture of the national framing and the local economy of the expressible and inexpressible—that is, making one's reality acceptable, not assigning blame, or presenting yourself as unaffected. Similarly, some statements that contradict experience can be found in formulating one of the least ambiguous power relationships: that between my interlocutors and the military.

"*Soldiers behave well.*"

　　　　　　　　　　　　　　　　"*When they're not there, the village feels empty.*"
"*They're doing their job.*"

Positive characterization of the soldiers cropped up reliably in many daily exchanges. It also appeared as a response to the emergence of critical comments which, by questioning the acceptability of situations, interrogated the relationship between experience and qualification.

In front of the grocery store, Yolanda, Antonio, Heriberto, and I were sipping our sodas when a military vehicle passed in the street in front of us. In that instant, the soldier positioned behind the heavy machine gun abruptly turned his weapon. From our vantage point by the side of the street, the soldier's clumsy movement made it look like he was pointing the weapon straight at us and that he was not in full control of his actions. Once the vehicle had passed, Heriberto and Yolanda laughed: "It looked like he was aiming at us, as if he was going to shoot. . . . We would have been scared to death!" Then, Antonio chimed in, saying that he didn't think it was right because "the government (el gobierno)

shouldn't parade around like that, aiming at people." He remained silent for a
moment, then added: "Really, it's not okay to target people like that!"

Heriberto cut in:

—And what do you want to do about it? It's like that everywhere.

Antonio turned to me:

—In your country, where you come from, the government also parades
around aiming at people?

—What do you mean?

—Well, that way. He's passing through aiming at people.

He pointed his finger to mimic the recent passage of the soldiers. I said "no,"
and he added:

—They kill like animals.

Yolanda immediately reacted:

—That's their job . . . and then it's normal for them to be scared.

The octogenarian Antonio designated the soldiers with the metonymy common in rural areas subjected to repression: "the government." Akhil Gupta
raises the problem that the "state," despite its translocal and multifaceted
character, is nevertheless understood by the governed from their interactions
with its representatives.[36] It is from this daily experience that my interlocutors construct the meanings contained in the terms "state" or "government,"
in this case the arbitrary nature of its violence: "The government should not
parade around like that, aiming at people." This naming of soldiers as "the
government" is thus trailed by a critical statement about the behavior of soldiers. But this verdict was immediately drowned in comments that humorously dispelled the fear provoked by the machine gun. In resorting to a comparison, "it's like that everywhere," those statements relativized the
unacceptability he perceived in the situation. Comforted by my answer,
which cast doubt on whether it is "everywhere like this," Antonio raised his
disagreement another notch: "They kill like animals." But Yolanda immediately disputed his point by fitting the behaviors and practices of the soldiers
into "their job" and justifying their violence: "And then it's normal for them
to be scared."

These (re)characterizations of situations involving the military cropped up
regularly. In Enrique and Veronica's hamlet, where the arrival of soldiers
disrupted the daily routine, most adults insisted strenuously on their good
relations with them: "They behave well," "they do their job." Someone who

hinted that they sometimes acted badly immediately added: "It's normal, it's because people badmouth them [on the radios]." These statements bracketed accounts of the torture that soldiers administered "in the past," and were emphatic even though I saw with my own eyes how fearful people were in the presence of the military. In a context where soldiers were a particularly serious threat, relativizing repression by portraying their actions in a positive light also appeared as a way for people to extricate themselves from the context. It was a way of pretending that it did not affect you, and of expressing, perhaps, the hope that indeed it would not catch up with you—an apotropaic formula.

The frequency with which these characterizations occurred underlined the importance of the situations that evoked them. They appeared, in fact, to be reactions through generalization to specific situations. In hamlet Y*, a detachment of soldiers had been destroying the surrounding plots and extorting money and provisions from the families of the growers for several days. While we were chatting in Danae's grocery store, they stopped by to charge their mobile phones. During the half hour they were there, the atmosphere was tense. We talked as little as possible. When they left, the discussion between Danae, her uncle and me turned to the fact that this time they did not turn the house upside down to search it. Danae's uncle concluded: "Think about it (*fíjate*), they are workers who live off the people's work. . . . If we didn't work [grow poppies], well, they would be out of a job."

His remark contained no hint of irony and must be taken at face value. In the context of utterances, it appeared to be a characterization that he would have liked to apply to the situation that had just unfolded. In Spanish, *fíjate* denotes a discovery, a truth hidden in the situation that is about to be revealed. It is lodged in how I was supposed to understand the relationship between the military and the growers. Living off somebody's work (*vivir del trabajo de*) can mean appropriating its fruits. In this sense, he did suggest that this was a predatory relationship, but the way he phrased it emphasized the normal nature of this connection: it fit into the order of things. Through the mention of "work," the uncle—like Yolanda and others who insisted that it was "their job"—enshrined the relationship in the order of needs: those of the soldiers, who wanted a good life, and those of the growers, who did as well, and who indirectly supported the soldiers. Thus, if the predation report was not entirely denied, insisting on needs naturalized it. The importance Danae's uncle attached to revealing the meaning of this relationship to me had to do with what he read into our interaction: the threatening nature of the visit became explicit when Danae recalled what might have happened, that is, if the threat of a search that was on everyone's mind while the soldiers were there had materialized. In this interaction, he understood that I was afraid of the soldiers and did not like their behavior. So he considered that, as a foreigner, I did not understand, and he explained to me that all this was necessary, normal, inescapable.

With a few exceptions, the explicitly critical comments about soldiers were made by older men, such as Antonio's "they kill like animals." Similarly, in another hamlet, an old man in an interview suddenly exclaimed, in a non sequitur to something he had said earlier: "Soldiers, by nature, can't be our friends!," as if responding to this incessant murmur of justifications for repression.

The positive assessments of soldiers, although elicited by a given situation, also have to do with mechanisms of generalization. An incursion by the military or an interaction with them gave rise to a blanket formula: "soldiers do," "soldiers are," etc. Just like the unceasing repetitions of "here it is quiet," generalizing the behavior of soldiers in positive terms could take on different meanings according to the situation and could be taken up in different ways by the speakers. But in either case, this abundance of positive labels was contradicted daily by the scale of self-protection efforts in the face of violent threats in relationships of proximity and repression. The sophisticated nature of the investigations, analyses, and interpretation of situations did not necessarily lead to the coherence of all these elements in formulating a general characterization of the context. As we have seen, exchanges between neighbors took fragmentary forms in an indifferent tone and avoided imputation or judgment. To characterize the context would involve formulating an interpretation, identifying causes to construct a narrative, and thus exposing responsibilities. Such a characterization would then be at odds with the ordinary forms of exchange marked by caution, by the implicit, and informed by the uncertain entanglement between armed violence and ordinary sociability. Thus, to speak of the context implies negating the murders, fears, sorrows, and repression: it is quiet and the soldiers are well-behaved.

The abundance of anticatastases reveals the difficulty in characterizing the general context. Like generalities or adages ("Here you can't trust anyone"; "Do you know why the turtle lives to be 100 years? Because it doesn't stick its nose into other people's business!"), my interlocutors sometimes devised cunning ways to highlight salient features of this context. In this sense, the witticisms that resided in the moment, in the possibility of ridiculing a situation, of having the implicit on the tip of the tongue, were a veritable local sport.[37] Here follow two examples:

I was talking with Santiago outside his house. A van pulled up and out jumped a young man whom Santiago obviously knew. They gave each other a proper hug and Santiago introduced him by his nickname "El Guacho" [derogatory: the soldier]. As we shook hands, Santiago added, teasingly: "If you are asked, say you are one of El Guacho's people." They laughed as I raised an eyebrow to try and show that I got the joke.

In this situation, in addition to the potential for pulling a foreigner's leg, Santiago trotted out a double-sided pun: on the one hand, in the local meanings of the turn of phrase "be part of the people of X," on the other hand in the nickname "guacho" that the young man bears, for reasons I was not privy to, but which is above all the nickname applied locally when talking about soldiers.[38] "Being part of the people of X" (*ser gente de X*) meant being a member of the armed group commanded by X. By telling me "if you're asked, say you're one of X's people," he twisted it to mean: claim this affiliation and the people will respect you, because X is known and his name alone inspires fear in people. But, through the common meaning of "guacho," this same mechanism is also mocked: the fear associated with the name of an armed group leader and its use to command respect. In short, his sentence said: if you are asked, say that you are part of "the soldier's" people. Obviously this was an unsavory claim in Badiraguato, but it also highlighted the army's power. His joke therefore worked on two levels: one that poked fun at my foreignness and passed the newcomer off as a soldier, and the other that used a turn of phrase normally referring to the power of a local armed group to make it depend on the designation of soldiers, that is, the power of the army. By doing so, he suggested that the army was just one armed group among many (as indeed he once told me), and he also derided the lesser power of local armed groups.

One day I met Araceli after school. She was one of the few teachers to actually come from the hamlet in which she was posted. When I bumped into her on the street, she was still caught up in her laughter: "I swear, kids, they come out with some real doozies sometimes. You shouldn't laugh because it encourages them, but sometimes it's hard not to." Then she explained what it was about: "You saw that my pupils often say, proudly, when the soldiers arrive, "there is control, there is control," meaning that a pesado *has made a deal with the soldiers so they would not destroy the plots. I nodded that I got it, so she went on: "Well, now we're trying to do a fundraiser for the end-of-year party, and there's nothing in the piggy bank. I pointed that out and they tell me they are broke. To annoy them, I say to them, 'Well, now, but didn't you say there was control?' And they came back with, 'No, ma'am, the only control here is the one for the TV!'"*

The joke that Araceli recounted relied on the homonymy between "control" and "remote control," both expressed by *control* in Spanish. Usually, when young people shouted "there is control, there is control," their words were not meant to be funny, but mixed relief and a boast: they and their families would not be bothered by the soldiers. However, Araceli's students flipped this term, which refers to the exercise of power, by reducing it to the control exercised over the television by use of the remote. This mechanism for ridicule aimed at the ambiguity and limits on the power of local *pesados* to protect against repression and played on the impact of repression on the hamlet's economic and social life.

These examples reveal the use of implicit and euphemistic forms for humorously diverting from a given situation. In local meanings of a turn of phrase, in the succinct application of associated ideas with another context, and in homonymic games, formulations were made meaningful by the constraints that weigh on the characterization of context. The ability to grasp a situation in a few words, to riff on the unsaid, and to instill ambiguity were in continuity with ordinary forms of exchange. The fluidity of affiliations with armed groups, the state's participation in these dynamics, and the dependence of the growers on the powerful were thus depicted and derided. In this regard, such circumlocutions should warn us against the temptation of presupposing that speakers bought into or internalized the positive characterization they proposed for the social and political context. The inability to verbalize the context did not mean that people subscribe to the labels they come up with. The fact remained that this did nothing to relieve them of the burden of not being able to say what was being experienced.

The daily life of my interlocutors was marked by intense information-gathering that was often carried out with bonhomie and the usual forms of sociability. The tactical use of tone and rhythms in ways of interacting and the mastery of specific enunciation regimes are the basis of an information-gathering activity. Abstraction, fragmentation of narratives, impersonal screens ("they say that"), and truncated sentences ("*por algo*") allow them to tell and inform, to construct a narrative about past events without ever delivering it, without imputing, without denouncing or criticizing. In this sense, the manner in which they conduct their inquiries highlights a demarcation between what can or cannot be said. In the course of their days, my interlocutors build and update analyses of the environment in which they evolve by relying on the constraints of enunciation in ordinary exchanges.

The enunciation regimes they put in place, like the dynamics they try to decipher, refer to precautions linked to the forms of the threat. In the main town, a socially heterogeneous space, daily exchanges exposed the inhabitants to a violence that permeated relationships of proximity, while simultaneously having to enable these for their protection. To be the subject of gossip was a dangerous thing: conflicts unrelated to drug trafficking could, as a result, be caught up in the dynamics of organized violence. Uncertainty, which permeated exchanges between neighbors, created a continuum between the expression of widespread mistrust, their use in the context of interpersonal conflicts, and a collective construction of information. In the hamlets of the sierra, where the identification of the activities of one and another is easy, the inquiry focused on the hazards that increased the vulnerability of all. Through radios and face-to-face exchanges, residents strove to keep track of and anticipate military incursions as well as the changing power relationships between leaders of trafficking networks and armed groups. All of these daily practices identified a spatiality and temporality of the threat, and characterizations resulted from the coherence and analysis of past observations, information, and experiences. Conversely, this intense activity revealed what weighed most on their experience: the army appeared as the chief actor in the sierra; conflicts between the heads of networks increased uncertainty; and the difficulties surrounding the identification of likely killers or people likely to be killed permeated daily life in the main town.

My interlocutors were highly reflexive, with some of them formulating their practices and what shaped them, that is, their context. However, general formulation of context was avoided: to make sense of and to narrate this context, the insecurity of their existence would expose them to imputations and an enunciation regime proscribed in threatening proximity relationships. The contrast between the sharpness of their information-gathering activities and the inability to characterize the context was an in situ definition of uncertainty: the impossibility of making sense of their own actions.

Thus, the men and women I worked with were astute investigators, and my own efforts in part consisted of grafting my investigation onto theirs. The description of the "being there" of my interlocutors led me to posit several thematic threads that emerged in the immediacy of their experiences. The remaining chapters follow these threads to trace the underpinnings of these experiences in social, economic, and gender relations, as well as the violent and institutional forms of exercising power in such a context.

THREE

Pulling Through

"It's under control, but it changes every two weeks."

MAURICIO

PULLING THROUGH (*SALIR ADELANTE*), a formula both recurrent and semantically rich, refers to what people do to provide for themselves. It indicates that their actions to that end are part of a quest to improve living conditions; and it suggests that this improvement is a horizon, a projection, because *pulling through* also says that supporting yourself is difficult in an unfavorable context. This expression therefore casts light on a logic of action that does not distinguish a specific activity or profession; instead, it can embrace all the issues of material reproduction in a precarious context. This chapter seeks to unravel the tension contained in this expression—that is to say, to relate the actions of people to support themselves with the socioeconomic structuring of the context in which they take action.

THE IMPOSITION OF POPPY MONOCULTURE

Gambusinos and Caciques: The Past Figures of Mining

The main economic activity around which the mountainous territory had been organized since colonial times was mining. Mineral resources were an attraction in the western Sierra Madre from that time on. Badiraguato had some veins that were mined, but the largest deposits were located farther south. In the late nineteenth century, the Badiraguato region was part of Mexico's "second mining frontier." Unlike colonial mining centers such as Taxco, Zacatecas, or Pachuca, which became important settlements, the regions exploited during the Porfirist period depended on foreign capital and were mining enclaves dedicated to export. Even though Badiraguato municipality had no major regional deposits, its few extraction areas were affected by the evolution of the concession regimes that, throughout the twentieth century, underwent a process of concentration in the hands of large companies.[1] I visited Alberto, an old *gambusino*, at his home in the hamlet of P*.

Alberto was proud to say that in 1955, the year of their marriage, he had paid Isabela's dowry with gold he had prospected for in the rivers. His father was "the stubborn man who got into it and worked hard at it." Self-employed, the father and uncle hired a few people and moved throughout the mountainous territory following the veins others had discovered. "You loved this job, you heard that in some place people were working the mines and that's where you would go." Alberto began to follow his father. They "worked the mines" in a rudimentary way, without any machines. These were the so-called gambusinos: *"people of little means, very little in terms of mining work." They prospected for gold, silver, and other metals but concentrated on gold because they knew how to process it and could sell it directly in Culiacán. He said the family was poor; he remembered many days without tortillas and that the work was hard.*

As for doña Isabela's father, he regularly went to work with different gambusinos. *His specialty was washing gold and sewing bags for transport. Alberto's father had hired him while his family remained in Revolcaderos (Chihuahua) where they had no land. After a while, he had brought his whole family from there, and that's how Alberto and Isabela met. Alberto recounted that when they started to open a vein and took out ore in those day, they marked them with* mojoneras, *piles of stones to indicate that the mine was being exploited by someone: "As if to draw a border, legalize, that no one would jump your claim." After his father retired, Alberto continued with his brother and then went on alone. He was still roaming the mountains in search of veins, but the "gringos" were more and more of a presence, they bought up the mines, and "did not even need* mojoneras" *because they were "in cahoots with the government." Today, there are no more* gambusinos.

The story of eighty-three-year old Alberto was tinged with a certain nostalgia. By accentuating the transition from small-scale prospecting to the gradual extension of concessions to a handful of foreign companies, his tale summarized the longer history of foreign investment in mining and its peaks and valleys,[2] but it also pointed to an essential transformation. The manual exploitation by *gambusinos* spawned a variety of trades, as when Isabela's father was hired to wash gold and sew bags. Condensed around the decline of understandings between people as materialized by the *mojoneras* and its replacement by agreements between the "gringos" and "the government," Alberto's story pointed to the gradual disappearance of livelihoods on the margins of the major concessions.

Juan Manuel also came from a *gambusina* family. Until the late 1960s, he worked with his father exploiting ore deposits by hand. Gradually, these opportunities dried up. When the Canadian company that bought up the concessions in their area set itself up in Juan Manuel's hamlet, it hired him in 1974 as a worker's assistant. To explain the arrival of the company and the expansion of its concessions, he said that they "came with ties to the power in Mexico City." For a while several of the sierra hamlets (San Javier, Tameapa, Surutato, Otatillos, Santiago de los Caballeros) benefited from this dynamic. Businesses setting up jobs there created jobs and spurred economic growth: they hired a few miners and cooks, shopped for supplies in local grocery stores, lent out their bulldozers. The boom attracted people from other hamlets. Until the 1980s the company near Juan Manuel's hamlet recruited some of its staff locally, but soon after it shortened employment contracts, gradually let the local employees go, and finally closed down the mines while still holding on to the concessions.

Nowadays, the arrival of people sent by mining companies to locate veins still raises hopes for a restart of mining. They are among those who can enter, stay, and leave the sierra without having the restrictions outlined in chapter 1 imposed on them, protected by the "purpose" of their coming. According to several people who housed or fed them during their prospecting, these men would always say that they would return to exploit what they found, but these plans usually did not pan out. At the regional level, mining remains active and has even increased since the early 2000s, mainly due to tie-ups between certain armed groups and the mining companies,[3] but my interlocutors insisted that it had declined in Badiraguato. Unlike other parts of the state of Sinaloa, the municipality had few active concessions, the sector no longer employed locally, and the process of capitalist concentration meant the disappearance of *gambusino* artisanal activity. The municipality's last ore processing and recovery plant was dismantled in 1992 as part of privatization policies. For example, in hamlet H* where Juan Manuel lived, the departure of the Canadian company was the final act in the drying up of job opportunities in the mining sector. One of Juan Manuel's daughters lived in the United States, and the other stayed and got married; she had a young child and her household got by on poppy cultivation. Of Alberto's children, three lived in major Mexican cities (Guadalajara, Culiacán, Nogales) and one other in Los Angeles; Alberto and his wife lived off their remittances.

The disappearing local forms of mining under the impact of concessions granted to large Mexican and foreign companies encapsulated the opposition between "gringos" and "*gambusinos*" that emerged from Alberto's narrative. Nevertheless, the history of local mining activity was also one of the small businesses of various types that played a role in ending the *gambusino* era.[4] Mining and its organization had been part of the business strategy of some local entrepreneurs who took advantage of the area's isolation to position themselves as essential local intermediaries. In telling me the story of his life, Edgar recalled his father's misadventures.

Edgar lost a lot in the closure of the ore processing plant. It ground the ore he wanted to sell before moving out without paying him for it. He recalled the story of his family's mining past. In 1942, his father Raúl had reopened a vein that had been abandoned for many years. His brother and an uncle helped him with the manual labor, but he could neither transport the ore nor sell it because he lacked resources and contacts. He therefore teamed up with Ramón, a cattle farmer, cattle dealer, and justice of the peace in his hamlet, who would transport the load over the mule paths to a place where "a rich merchant from La Lapara," Nacho Landell, would transport it the rest of the way and sell the load on Raúl's behalf for a share of the profits. The operation was set up and, after two years of work, the father watched his ore disappear down the mule paths. On his way to the main town to find out about Nacho Landell's sale, he was told that his ore got mixed with another load on the trip, making it unsaleable. Nacho Landell, who had probably sold the load, never gave him his share of the profit.

This account highlights the importance of intermediaries in the transportation and sale of minerals (to Culiacán or Guamúchil on the Sinaloa coastal plain, or to Parral in Chihuahua, depending on where it had been mined). The *gambusinos* needed means of transport and contacts for sales and therefore depended on—and were vulnerable to predation by—those who could supply them. The area's other decisive activity was livestock raising—cropland being scarce, of poor quality, and on rugged terrain. Raising livestock here and selling it on the coastal plain was an important activity in the organization of the hamlets and the traffic that connected them. Indeed, the ability to carry down and bring up goods, as well as the contacts to sell the products of the sierra to on the plain, constituted a niche exploited by the people who appeared in all the stories as the powerful ones of the times—Nacho Landell among them.

The Entrepreneurs of Marginalization

Until the 1960s and 1970s, Nacho Landell had his hand in all the economic activities of the sierra. In a recorded interview, Memo, his son, recounted it:

The son of a schoolteacher and a woman from a prominent local family, Nacho Landell was born in Huixiopa and met Memo's mother in the main town: "He came down from the sierra, he liked her, and he seduced her (la enamoró)." She was an orphan who had inherited a house in the main town but Nacho Landell "settled her" in a nearby hamlet. "When [Nacho Landell] wanted to set up his own business, he became a buyer of metal and, the story goes, also of [opium] gum. He bought the gold found in the river, which was called 'placer gold.'" In La Lapara, the hamlet where he bought the gold and gum produced by the inhabitants, he "became a womanizer and he stole another woman." From that point on, Memo's angry mother asked to return to the main town where she took over her family home. Nacho Landell gave her money to run a grocery store there and he returned to live in La Lapara with the other woman. Later, he again "stole" a woman in another hamlet very close to the one where he had settled with his second wife. "He would come, he would stay a month here, a month there and in La Lapara (hamlet of the second wife), there also longer, like five months."

Relations between his father's twenty-one children were distant. "He opened a grocery store for each of the three women; and he was. . . a bit like an administrator, he would come, he would check and if he lost money, he would put more in. And these were the first grocery stores. . . . He was the most important supplier, say; he took advantage of it and he made a lot of money. . . . He had a lot of land and cattle. . . . At that time, my family, people used to say, we were rich, one of the pioneering families. He was the first one to buy a car [to transport people], then two, and people wanted more."

Nacho Landell's grocery stores, the gum, ore, cattle, and transportation—all kinds of commerce—prospered between 1940 and 1960, when he also bought irrigated land on the plain. "Then, when machines started cutting holes [to build the roads], the grocery stores started to go downhill." When Memo and his brother reached school age, their father sent them to school in Guadalajara. When he returned to Badiraguato, Memo took over the livestock part of Nacho Landell's affairs and invested in the new political spaces: the ejido and the breeders' association, of whose creation Nacho Landell was in the forefront thanks to his friendships with successive governors. One of his brothers became mayor in 1975.

Nacho Landell's name comes up frequently in interviews conducted by Juan Antonio Fernández on the organization of drug trafficking between 1940 and 1977.[5] He bought the opium production of all the people who lived in and around the hamlets in which he had settled. His geographical coverage, anchored by family in each hamlet, positioned him as the middleman in a trade organized along lines of family ties and political kinship. But opium was only one of the goods he traded. The common denominator of all his activities (grocery, cattle, mines, opium, transport) was how he profited because of Badiraguato's isolation. He made himself indispensable for transporting goods and people between the plain and a part of the sierra. Nacho Landell's accumulation strategy resided in this interstitial space between an economic, social, and family grounding in the sierra and political and economic ties on the coastal plain.

This entrepreneurship of marginalization was also manifest in the profile of an even better-known figure: Melesio Cuén. In a more institutional manner than Nacho Landell, he too gobbled up the work of the *gambusinos*. In 1942, for example, miners denounced the federal government's award of the veins they had discovered and were exploiting to the Cuén Hermanos company.[6] Elected mayor of Badiraguato five times between 1920 and 1952, Melesio Cuén was said to have been the "founder" of the PRI in Badiraguato and to have appointed his replacements (sometimes bearing the same surname). He was (and his family remained) owner of much of the land in the main town, but he was simultaneously mayor, pharmacist, doctor, grocer, cattle farmer, head of the Cuén Hermanos mining company, and a grower, buyer, and seller of opium. Like Nacho Landell, but in greater measure, Melesio Cuén's accumulation strategy consisted of investing in multiple sectors, taking advantage of his position as intermediary with the political networks.

In different areas of the sierra, Melesio Cuén and Nacho Landell were part of a booming trade in opium, mainly buying and reselling gum.[7] The poppy, present since the turn of the century, flourished in the wake of World War II.[8] The common feature of those middleman positions was political support in the Sinaloa state government of the post-revolutionary period. The political elite inherited the military exploits and influence of Sinaloa's generals during the revolution.[9] In the organization of the growing poppy trade, this support was decisive. All the research on the history of trafficking shows both that the people who positioned themselves in the poppy economy were the most influential and affluent families, and that the state police in particular were heavily represented.

The poppy was then cultivated by a large segment of the inhabitants from October through May, the off-peak period for food crops. Poppy culture is described as collective and organized within the hamlets in logics of mutual aid between farmers taking turns to provide a certain amount of gum to the middleman.[10] Locally, the work was divided between the farmers, the "cooks" who turned the gum into heroin, and the middlemen. While collaborations based on the logics of kinship and proximity seem to have been structuring in the organization of production, the intermediaries took a large cut of the profits and their relationships with growers formed part of a broader relationship of domination. Beyond the major economic benefits they derived from their position in the marketing chain, the modalities of repression in the 1950s illustrated this latter dimension. On the one hand, the destruction of plots and the confiscation of crops hit the independent growers, while plots that were directly associated with middlemen were protected by agreements in high places and were spared repression. On the other hand, some of these intermediaries imposed themselves as *caciques* on the hamlet level, where their position let them instrumentalize repression for their benefit.[11] Thus, in a hamlet, a "*cacique* from before," Carlos, close to eighty years old, was now nicknamed by some "El Dedo" ("the finger") because he denounced anyone who produced better than him or with whom his relationship was bad. Carlos, for his part, explained to me that the power he wielded was linked to his political friendships in the main town. These allowed him to benefit from networks reaching all the way up to some officers from the army. Thus, following the "mistaken" assassination of his son in 1971 by soldiers, he had obtained the concession of "not seeing them here anymore"—that is, they henceforth would set up their camps exclusively in the surrounding hills, instead of in the hamlet as before.

Thanks to their intermediation, figures such as Nacho Landell and Melesio Cuén captured the profits of all the sierra's economic sectors by taking advantage of regional political links—while their go-betweens in the hamlets, such as Carlos or Ramón (who took part in the scamming of Edgar's father), reproduced similar mechanisms but at hamlet scale. The two men's descendants took advantage of this anchorage in the political networks of the state, inserting themselves in the municipal and state governments. After their studies in Guadalajara Memo and his brother commenced political careers in the municipality, the former in agrarian institutions (the *ejidos*) and the latter in the municipal government. Similarly, the descendants of Melesio Cuén still owned the land in the main town's center and became influential politicians, like Hector Cuén, rector of the State University.[12] He, too, is reputed to appoint his successors himself. He founded his own party, the Partido sinaloense, to win the governorship of Sinaloa, having tired of waiting for a PRI nomination that never came. The entry of these descendants into the political profession occurred in a context of the collapse of all economic activities in Badiraguato, except for poppies and marijuana, and of stepped-up repression of the drug trade, which made it more difficult to openly combine public duties and involvement in the local economy.

Irrigation of the Plain and Repression in the Sierra: The Final Act in the Imposition of Monoculture

Nacho Landell's activities peaked during the time when irrigation came to the Sinaloa coastal plain, starting the most decisive transformation of Badiraguato's economic structure. Dams built from the 1940s to the 1960s captured water from the mountainous area of the state to irrigate the plain, which saw massive investment. The rapid expansion of Sinaloa's agribusiness geared for export to the United States increased the disparities between the two major regions: the coastal plain—the setting of the Sinaloense version of the "Mexican miracle"—on the one hand and, on the other, the neglected foothills of the western Sierra Madre that attracted no investments and represented a frontier for Sinaloa's rising agribusiness sector. The coastal plain was part of the wider process of capitalist formation that structured upper and lower California and linked Sinaloa into the global chain of the tomato trade.[13] The gap between the two zones grew, turning the sierra into a territory whose comparative advantage was its inaccessibility, an essential resource for the cultivation of poppies and marijuana that had to be increasingly concealed. Badiraguato was one of the most difficult-to-reach sierra municipalities, and moreover had scarcely any arable land. In addition, the development of agribusiness depressed agricultural prices and made the sale of surplus food crops by the sierra dwellers uneconomical. Irrigation work on the plain marked the beginning of a rural exodus: masses of people came down from the sierra looking for work—including those displaced and looking for a place to live after their hamlets had been swallowed behind the dams. These migrants settled in the state's booming cities or went back and forth as seasonal workers. Food crops collapsed, poppy and marijuana became the rule, and the entrepreneurs of marginalization, some of whom had bought land on the plain before its irrigation, prospered.

Beyond seasonal or permanent migrations to Sinaloense cities, irrigation of the plains and abandonment of the mountainous land pushed many of the inhabitants to the United States. This migratory movement was further driven by the bracero program (1942–64), under the Mexican Farm Labor Agreement between the United States and Mexico. After World War II, needing manpower to turn around its economy, the northern neighbor cracked open its doors to immigrants from Mexico. Among Mexican states, Sinaloa was one of the largest suppliers of labor, and many people from Badiraguato also settled in the United States.[14]

Teófilo was born in 1945 in a hamlet in the lower sierra where his mother, originally from the main town, worked as a schoolteacher. The hamlet was one of those destined to be flooded by the Adolfo López Mateos dam. The Sinaloa government moved the expropriated residents into an ejido on the coastal plain. He followed his mother to her new school posting, before leaving because "there was too much killing." He was about fifteen years old when he was selected with two other classmates to take up a teacher position—yet it was unpaid.

A few months later, he returned to the main town where his family home and grandparents were located. The mayor, a friend of the family, offered him a real teaching job in the sierra. He occupied two posts in as many different hamlets. He recalls how everyone knew him in the main town and in the hamlets: "cousins, brothers, a whole brothel full." Finally, "bored," he took off for the United States.

His first job was in a factory in Los Angeles. From living there and making round trips to the border, he came across many people he knew from Badiraguato (family, from the places where he had taught, the ejido on the plain, etc.).

Contacts on both sides of the border and his presence in the United States led him to the drug trade, where he prospered until his arrest.

The collapse of the sierra economy pushed many people like Teófilo to take off for the United States. The migrant flows were concentrated around a few cities—Los Angeles, San Diego, Tucson, and Phoenix—where social networks were easily reconstituted. Teófilo's career was special in that he rose high, but it was also commonplace in being part of the massive departures from the area to the United States in a context of local economic opportunities drying up and the need for manpower "on the other side."[15] The only productive activity that survived in the abandoned area benefited greatly from the transnational networks fostered by emigration. Thus, transporting drugs, like migration, was organic to the networks of proximity and kinship spread on both sides of the border—material conditions and profits deriving obviously from where in the chain an individual was located.

Finally, the last act in the imposition of this monoculture paradoxically lay in the radicalization of its repression. It commenced with Operation Intercept in 1969 (quickly renamed Cooperation) and increased in intensity with Operation Condor in 1977. Operation Condor brought with it the massive use of defoliants to complete the destruction of plots complicated by the rugged terrain and their small size (often barely more than half an acre). Badiraguato was pegged as one of the main "critical areas" in this operation.[16] Accounts from this period are replete with systematic torture, killing, and rape, accelerating the exodus while defoliants wiped out what was left of the food crops.[17] These environmental crimes in Badiraguato recall "the ruins of capitalism" studied by Anna Tsing.[18] During this operation, Nacho Landell's son, who was then the mayor of Badiraguato, said that 30 percent of the population lived from opium and marijuana production. At the same time, the crackdown triggered an increase in poppy prices, expanded the cultivated areas, opened new transport routes, and led to better-organized trafficking.[19] A network was set up in Guadalajara (where the now more clandestine trafficking leaders had moved), some people experienced spectacular ascents, and all business operations henceforth involved a larger workforce to deal with the repression.

Gerardo's family was originally from the state of Chihuahua but forty years earlier had moved to a sierra hamlet because of the better land and schools there.

The father grew corn and beans, he "never liked the drug trade business. . . . He didn't raise drug crops, none of that, not poppies, not marijuana." His mother was the one who "struggled the most to find money"; she made breads and tortillas to sell in the hamlet and worked as a servant in the house of the hamlet's well-off family. Gerardo tried to go to school as long as possible, which he liked extremely. With the support of one of the teachers who paid his school fees, he continued on to high school while helping his father in the fields.

When his brothers and sisters left for the plain to find work, he stayed to provide for his parents. At the age of fifteen, he was hired by a public works company that was building roads near his hamlet, but this lasted only a few months. Very quickly, other opportunities presented themselves: "This was the time when Caro Quintero was at his peak, the hamlets were emptying, some left for what were called 'the control,' others were working with him." He explains to me what "the controls" were at the time: "We called it that because el señor [Caro Quintero] supposedly controlled the government, so we said: We're going to the control! We're going to the control [laughs]."

In the process, Gerardo and one of his brothers were offered several jobs cultivating large poppy fields in other states. But "us, they didn't let us go, my parents were not okay with that. . . . They said, 'You never know what can happen. . .' and we had to obey them." Later, one of his brothers, who had stayed in Chihuahua, made Gerardo the same offer. Gerardo was looking for money to "get married," that is, to run away with Leandra. So that is why he came around after all to learning how to cultivate the "little plant," the poppy. He sold his first harvest of one kilo and came to get Leandra. Later, the brother offered him another job, but this time it meant guarding a warehouse. Toting a weapon all night in front of this place, he felt that "it was not his thing, he was not made for it." He left for home and started planting poppies in his birth hamlet.

The repression and the ensuing reconfiguration of trafficking ushered in the golden age of the 1980s. The rise of trafficking and its clandestine nature called for a variety of surveillance, logistics, and protection tasks.[20] Whereas previously there were only growers, processors, and a few middlemen, small jobs that proved to be a boon for the sierra residents multiplied. The opportunities that presented themselves to Gerardo came mainly from expanding production to other states (Michoacan and Guerrero in particular) helped in part by workers from Sinaloa. Others (those who went "to the control") found their place in the myriad activities involving transport and the violent competition that grew up between rival networks. Although Gerardo refused the first offers, he was gradually pulled into an economy that became the only source of income in the region. The transformation of the regional economy precluded his mother from falling back on her subsistence strategies. Where before she could survive by selling buns, tortillas, eggs, and chickens in the plain, the tide now ran the other way: the people of the hamlets had to buy from the shops there, for which they needed cash.[21]

Participation in this sector in one form or another became the only possible horizon. For anyone unwilling to join in the organization of violence and lacking the resources to be a middleman, cultivation was the only option for making a living. The few success stories invariably were based on exploiting resources associated with the difficulty of accessing economic and political contacts in the plain. Ascending trajectories in the drug trade showed the importance of having invested in activities relying on transportation, including ranching and grocery stores. In addition to the money made buying and selling gum and marijuana, political connections allowed the upward movers to negotiate arrangements with the military and politicians and thus to cultivate vast fields without fear of repression.

Thus, the transformations of the sierra's political economy hinged on a few phenomena that gradually imposed the poppy monoculture. The sierra was caught up in processes of agricultural extraction and production typical of the "frontiers of capitalism."[22] The collapse of mining jobs and the coastal plain irrigation policy severely impacted the population living in the mountains. Emigration increased and some people enriched themselves by taking advantage of the area's heightened isolation, positioning themselves as middlemen in all economic activities. In this, they were aided by political relationships with state elites whose political weight upon emerging from the revolution had been affirmed with the rise of agribusiness entrepreneurs. Thus, these intermediaries became involved in what became the only form of legal economic accumulation: political careers that, in turn, benefited their descendants. In the contemporary sierra, legal jobs were scarce: a few positions for paid government representatives, some teaching positions that required pursuing a higher education in the plain. Joining the army was not a realistic option for the people of Badiraguato. For one thing, military service was generally associated with people from Mexico's south (and looked down on in a racialized way). For another, the long experience of repression, the humiliations endured in military service, and the possibility of profiting from the use of violence probably governed these choices. Thus, the few activities that persisted in the mountainous part depended on its isolation: a little livestock raising, the *tranvías*, grocery stores, and, of course and especially, the poppy.[23] Its cultivation has thus moved from a complementary activity in domestic economies to the main source of income. The people of the sierra have watched their children get caught between two alternatives: emigrate or participate in the poppy economy. In the remainder of this chapter, I focus on the experience of the people who stayed and, therefore, cultivated.

GROWING THE LITTLE PLANT

Getting ready to go to the fields meant first of all listening patiently to your radio. Often it led to not going at all. Otherwise, you would take the ATV, park it, and continue on foot on the trails, the radio charged and volume turned low. At the plot, you would weed around the flowers, giving them space and, above all, time. Sometimes to no avail. To be in the field you also needed to have an escape route planned—to know where to hide. Breaking down the various operations of poppy cultivation, often referred to as the "little plant" (*plantita*), lets me describe in what follows the local stakes around which this activity revolves. I therefore outline the production process based on my observations of the growers' daily lives, in that way highlighting the non-climatic vicissitudes that impacted poppy cultivation.

The landscape of the cultivation of the "little plant" was determined by state policies. It was said that they used to grow everywhere in plain sight in the hamlet in front of the houses. But now, from the paved roads, flowers were not visible in the surrounding mountains. It took several hours on bumpy dirt roads to reach fields of them scattered among the hamlet's most remote houses. Whenever possible, growers would try to work two or three plots, always small, in different places: a small one here, a small one there. If the military destroyed one, perhaps they would miss the other. This landscape revealed the social organization of production around small growers whose working conditions varied greatly depending on how often military patrols intruded. "Grower" did not necessarily mean "owner" and cultivating several plots implied having access to land. Among my interlocutors, two cases existed: some were locally recognized as owners of their land by their neighbors; others were in debt to another, the person recognized locally by his neighbors as the owner. Access to land will be the subject of the next chapter; for now, suffice to note that no one was ever a one-hundred-percent owner, and that some owed money to others following a harvest.

Surface area, location, and distribution of plots—how poppy cultivation was organized mirrored how it was repressed. The history of its concentration in the sierra has been naturalized: it is thus usual to read or hear that Badiraguato had the best climate for cultivating the little plant. It is also reported that the seed first arrived in the hands of a Chinese doctor practicing in the hamlet of Santiago de los Caballeros, implying that the priors of poppy cultivation in the municipality could explain its persistence. The rise of this economy in the region is also attributed to the supposed rebel nature of the Sinaloans.[24] In point of fact, however, plot layouts in the sierra mimicked locally the national and regional processes that confined poppy cultivation to marginalized areas. Until the 1950s, the small plant grew in the gardens of the Culiacánese and more widely throughout the plain.[25] Poppy flowers, needing little water and able to grow on rocky soil, could be cultivated almost anywhere.[26] The humidity index and soil quality affected the amount of heroin that could be extracted from the poppy gum after processing—according to my interlocutors, 1 kilo of opium gum would yield between 4 and 6 ounces of heroin. The poppy's progressive concentration in the mountains therefore responded less to climatic conditions than to the repression that sharpened the need for clandestinity and to the biases of state investments which, by promoting isolation in all its dimensions—economic, social, political, infrastructural, and juridical—facilitated concealment. This constraint conditioned a mode of production based on small growers whose forms of land ownership depended on local arrangements and everyone's relative social heft.

Going to your plot meant taking a separate path for each. On the other hand, upland, all shared the same practices: listening to the radios and keeping an eye on the comings and goings of the soldiers. Here follow some glimpses of this game of patience and mutual surveillance.

February 12—Some in the hamlet were already scoring the pods to harvest their gum, but not Lamberto. The day before he told me that he was going to go, but not just yet: "We are waiting for the soldiers. Yesterday they were in that spot," he said, pointing to the hills, "and a boy said they were coming, so we didn't go out." He thought he would go today, but the day was over: he had alternated waiting at home, radio in hand, and waiting farther down, perched on the ATV in company with the others. When he returned, he told Tamara, his wife: "The fields [of such and such] were reported."

February 13—This morning he told me it was safer in the afternoon, but in the afternoon the soldiers were in the vicinity of his plot. He did not go there.

February 14—This morning, he was gone. He wanted to take me, but in the end, this time he backed out: "Can you imagine the front page? A French woman caught in the poppy fields." We laughed. When he left, he took one of the radios and left the other with "the woman," as he called Tamara. I asked Tamara if she was scared when he left for the plot. She said, "Yes, especially when the soldiers are not far away like this, but then I hear him on the radio, and it's better." When Lamberto returned, Tamara told him: "Four plots have been reported, so they said on the radio."

During these few days, the soldiers rarely entered the hamlet from their camp in the surrounding mountains. But the rhythm of life in the hamlet was attuned to their movements, relayed by the radioed warnings of the neighbors. In the transcribed snippets in my notebook about Lamberto's repeatedly postponed departures, listening to the radio is geared particularly toward gleaning two pieces of information: what plots were reported and where the military columns were. These two pieces of information related to the operating procedures of the military and thus to the constraints around which agricultural work was organized. A parcel was said to be "reported" when the helicopter (nicknamed *el boludo*) flying over the surrounding hills hovered over a specific point. The inhabitants watched it from distance and guessed which parcel lay below it. So as not to identify the grower, information circulated by word of mouth or on local radio frequencies using only first names or nicknames. Once a plot was reported, it would probably be mowed down or torched by a squad of soldiers. The observation of the comings and goings of the troops made it possible to know which plots were being destroyed but also whether it was possible to access a given plot without risking a run-in.

On days like these the main activity therefore was the waiting game. Being a poppy grower then meant above all not being able to cultivate your plot. You stayed put, waiting for the troops to be seen at any moment in another part of the hills where they would jeopardize the plots of one while leaving the path free to the others. The waiting around, often formulated as a time when soldiers "keep you from working," was such a factor that analytically it should be integrated into the production process itself. During these moments of expectation, two things happened: on the one hand, the time on the plot, and thus the work of caring for the flower as it grew, was reduced; on the other hand, an anxiety grew that all growers shared. While the work on a plot was individual or perhaps familial, the waiting time was collective, involving the whole neighborhood. Based on the flow of information gathered by everyone, keeping watch on the troops and interpreting the helicopter's movements generated particularly sociable times. During the soldiers' patrols, many younger and older men hung out together; a few men might discuss the reported plots around two ATVs parked on the road side; or, in front of a grocery store, a group of men would be seen chatting. Outside of these particular times—when the soldiers "let them work"—neighbors might visit each other, but sociability out in the open was rare and mainly a pastime for the elderly.

How this information spread showed that everyone knew the location of each other's plots and that they worried about what might happen to their neighbors' plots. Thus, on his way home, Lamberto told Tamara that "the plots [of such and such] have been reported." Two days later, Tamara informed Lamberto that "four plots were reported, that's what they said on the radio." Still, production remained individualized and stories of harvest-stealing show that the cooperation between growers should not be exaggerated. Nevertheless, repression contributed to producing a common concern that also surfaced in the recurrent formulations of a shared diagnosis on the general economic situation of the surrounding area, such as: "many have lost their plots" or "the rain made the flowers rot."

If your plot had not been reported or destroyed, and the soldiers had been spotted elsewhere, then you could go to it.

I went with Lamberto and his daughter by ATV. Taking several trails, we rode about twenty minutes. He parked the bike and we continued on foot through the undergrowth until we came to a sort of clearing. There, surrounded by a fence, were planted poppy flowers with dried corn stalks scattered between them. He explained what he was about to do: pull out the bad plants that grow between the flowers so they have room and light. While he and his daughter busied themselves with that, he said to her, "See, my daughter? What do you think of your father's work? That's why I want you to study and so you can do something else yourself."

I asked him if he harvests a lot of corn. Very little, he told me, just enough to make "real tortillas" from time to time. But he also planted it to annoy the soldiers: if they should come to destroy the plot, they would have to mow it down. The flowers were fragile, they cut easily, but the corn stalks stopped the scythe. So it's perfect: not only did it throw a monkey wrench into the military's mission, but it might save at least a few of the flowers. He explained to me that this plot being more exposed, he hoped it would survive until the harvest next month, but another plot he owned had a better chance.

We moved out again and climbed the mountain in single file for about an hour. There was no marked path, but he led the way. As we hiked, we could hear the low crackling of his radio. I couldn't tell what was being said, and he explained that he kept it on just in case: if the soldiers had been seen in the area, someone would be sure to pass the word by radio. Finally, we arrived at the other, denser plot, only to see one of his worst fears realized: the plants had been attacked by rats. We stayed for a while as he surveyed the damage; he concluded that he would have to set out poison.

On the way back, still hearing the radio, I took advantage of the descent that had let me catch my breath to ask him again: "What would you do if soldiers approached?" He said he always parked the ATV as far away as possible. He would hike up; and for both plots, he had an escape route. If the soldiers got closer, he would head up in the opposite direction from where he parked his ATV, where he knew cattle were often grazing. That way he could claim he was looking after the animals. I asked him if he would warn the others; his answer was "no."

Plots were usually fenced to keep livestock left to roam free during the rainy season—which also marked the end of poppy maturation—from attacking the flowers. From the time the crop was put in, potential threats to it were factored in. In the case above, Lamberto cultivated two plots, of which he considered one to be more exposed to destruction than the other. The one at the lower elevation, located not too far back in the mountains, was relatively accessible, whereas the one higher up was only vulnerable "from the air," that is, from the army's helicopters. These calculations and the way he implemented the corresponding strategies contrasted with the rationalization discourse that Lamberto and other growers carried on about the repression. Invariably, they distinguished the current operations by the soldiers from past ones: before, they would destroy all the plots on which they chanced; now, it was only the ones that were reported. Left unspoken was the assumption that the soldiers would pass up an unreported field and only destroy the reported one. Some growers even said that because the soldiers knew that this was all they lived on, they sometimes would give them a break, telling them, "We're destroying it in eight days, harvest what you can." These discourses reflect a change in the forms of repression since Operation Condor, when the men could only avoid being tortured if they fled their homes and hid in the mountains. But the fact remains that the sensemaking underlying the distinction between the before and after, and the euphemizing of today's repression, conceal more ambiguous practices. It was with respect to the squads of soldiers on the ground that Lamberto considered his lower plot as most exposed and the top one as better concealed.

Lamberto's strategies revealed his perception of his work on the small plant as potentially vulnerable to actions by the soldiers. On the more accessible and therefore most exposed plot, he planted some corn. It contributed marginally to the family's diet, but his principal aim was to complicate the mowing of the plot. This non-systematic passive defense, feeble as it was, would make the work of the soldiers harder and take longer if they happened on his plot and decided to mow it down. His second plot called for a different strategy: less exposed, it was also less likely to be mowed, but because of being more difficult to access it was suited only for growing, harvesting, and accumulating small amounts of gum to carry down from it.

In addition, on the way there, the precautions preliminary to the work on the plot required planning routes of escape and the situational use of radios. Lamberto very confidently fielded my question about what he would do should soldiers appear in the area. Devising an escape plan was a constructed, reflexive, and therefore easily communicable strategy. At its core, it was about not getting caught red-handed on the plot and, secondarily, if caught away from it, about justifying his presence in the mountains ("looking after a neighbor's cattle"). Then there was the radio; it was our constant companion throughout our trek to and from the plot, with the volume turned low. This use, thought out in detail, solved the problem of how to keep track of the soldiers' movements while going to the plot when that bit of intelligence was needed most. Lamberto ventured forth after patiently waiting, listening, and observing, but once en route relied on the people back in the hamlet to continue monitoring the soldiers—especially on Tamara, who closely monitored the radio for him. However, radios, being prohibited, also increased the risk of being spotted. Lamberto kept the volume down and observed radio silence while at the plot. On one occasion, when I had gone with Lamberto's cousin to the latter's plot, we found Lamberto and Tamara in a panic when we returned to the hamlet. They asked the cousin what he had done with his radio; he then realized he had let the batteries run down so that it had gone dead. Lamberto and Tamara, knowing where we were, had tried repeatedly to alert us to a recent movement of soldiers in our direction. While the cousin and I did our best to reassure them and calm things down, Lamberto, an edge in his voice, reminded us: "No! There are rules! Check the batteries, have it always on turned down low, and listen!" The scene—and Lamberto's evident concern for me, a guest in his house—manifested the daily vigilance and especially the reflexivity that this work demanded.

Cultivating the growing little plant therefore required protecting it as best as possible from all hazards. While the plant was easy to grow, to ensure a good harvest required the classic work of weeding between the flowers, pruning it to concentrate the flower's energy, controlling rodents and infestations, and last but by no means least, being missed by the military's search-and-destroy incursions. In theory, with a good amount of water, the poppy could be harvested twice a year, but most people harvested only once: around March at an altitude of 1,000 meters and in April around 2,000 meters. Understandably, in view of the many threats to the harvest, the growers I met always invoked the traditional "god willing" (*si Dios quiere*)—said as if it was one word, "the-harvest-god-willing." At this time of year, the soldiers' sweeps intensified.

By the end of March, the number of plots reported and destroyed where Lamberto and Tamara lived soared by the day. It was also a delicate time because the incising of the bulb had to be timed just right: the petals would have dropped in the prior weeks and the maturation of each bulb had to be gauged by its color and texture. However, the rains that marked the beginning of the harvest also presented a risk: if they started too early, some bulbs failed to mature; if the rainfall was too intense, the flowers would rot on the stem.

Incision required precision: you had to circle the bulb, score it just enough so that it would release the resin during the night, but not too deep, so that a second incision could be made. Some growers fashioned tools to reduce the risk of cutting too deep, for instance, by inserting razor blades into a custom-made wooden handle. Tool-making workshops could be collective, with some growers being more skilled at the work than others. In front of one of Lamberto's neighbor's houses, the three neighbors, all growers, wished each other good luck in the harvest while prepping their tools. Because women were thought to have the dexterity required for incising, they would be sometimes be put to work on the harvest. Once the bulb had exuded its droplets of gum, a rounded-off plastic bottle was rotated by hand around the bulb to scrape the maximum amount of gum from it. During these intense days (every day, more bulbs were incised while others were already oozing their gum), every hazard cost the grower money: on the days of waiting around, the resin on the already incised bulbs could dry up or wash off with the rain. As a result, harvest periods required more hands. In the families I stayed with, the extended family (men and women) was marshaled for the occasion or family members took turns rotating through each other's respective plots if several of them were growers. When Tamara helped Lamberto, she also cut the leaves of the plant to cook as edible greens. The family dimension was on display in the protection practices associated with tending the plot, but it was even more evident during the harvest.[27]

SOLDIERS AND *PESADOS*: THE PROFITS OF UNCERTAINTY

The prominence of military operations in the organization of production, with every move and at every step, contrasted with the perennial focus of external discourses on the "Cartel" and the role of the high-profile figures of drug trafficking. Similarly, locally used terms conveyed the widely-held idea that local *pesados* benefited from agreements protecting them from the military—which is not in doubt—and, above all, that they would benefit small growers—which was less true. "Control," a concept that referred to the growing organization of trafficking in the 1980s, was now used to refer to agreements between a *pesado* and the commanders of military detachments that plots in a specified area would not be touched by the soldiers. However, like the joke by Araceli's students (chapter 2), the few times the word "control" came out of mouths of my interlocutors reveal its ambiguity and insecurity. So, when Mauricio, a young grower, told me about the large number of plots destroyed in his area, one where I thought this device was in play, I asked him: "But is it not under control there?"[28] He replied: "Yes, yes, it's under control, but it changes every two weeks."

The rate at which military detachments rotated in and out varied by area. In hamlets near a military post, the same soldiers would be on a mission for about six weeks. Where access was more difficult, they rarely stayed for longer than two weeks in temporary encampments. Where these arrangements with the on-site military shielding the growers of an area were in force, the "control" was therefore necessarily of short duration and the protection particularly precarious.

But the word "control" also covered a more complex dynamic. Thus, while I never got a look at existing agreements and none of the growers I visited benefited from them, my interlocutors talked about past forms of "control." In several hamlets, I was told that in the past "controls" were concluded at feasts when the detachments arrived. But the soldiers tended to "get out of hand." Someone told me more explicitly what others had only hinted at: "Before, control meant feasts, so we would kill cows and there would be boozing, but the soldiers forced themselves into women's beds. We preferred to put an end to it; now we just pay them." In another hamlet, I was told that the feast only sealed the deal that was made in cash and that it was stopped for the same reasons. The term "control" thus suggests an agreement, or even a power relationship in which the *pesado* would control the soldiers. Yet the elements that constituted the "control" and its failures showed that it served the military more as a predatory device for extorting food, alcohol, and money, or even for raping women with impunity.

In this sense, "control" lies exactly where a formulation by growers of a protective relationship with the *pesado* intersects with military predation. Unlike the classic case of mafia extortion, which is draped in the "protection" euphemism,[29] the relationship here is threefold: the *pesados* are deemed to control the military and thus to protect small growers from its predation. However, examination of one of these extortion seasons reveals an entirely different dynamic.

A Season of Extortion

Regardless of the use of the term "control" and how the grower families I worked with explained it, their daily lives appeared to me to be directly under the yoke of repression.

During the harvest in a hamlet at a higher elevation, the soldiers bivouacked twenty minutes from the hamlet. All the residents followed their comings and goings and warned each other by radio.

On the evening of April 9, Ricardo arrived at his parents' house. He was furious. He announced that the soldiers had just destroyed his plot and explained to me that he had no money to pay them off.

On April 10, Ricardo came to his parents' house to beg them for all the eggs from their chicken coop. Her mother gingerly filled a bucket with all the eggs. He told me he would be taking them to the soldiers' camp. Seeing my surprise, he told me how the day before the soldiers had destroyed a large part of his plot but left a little piece untouched, telling him they could work something out for what was left. Today, they asked for the eggs.

On April 14, while I was in the hamlet's grocery store, the detachment of soldiers arrived. They bought thirteen kilos of corn flour. When I returned to Ricardo's parents in late afternoon, I found the corn flour on the table: the soldiers had left it for the son to make tortillas and bring them to their camp that evening. For three hours, the three of us, the mother, the wife, and I, were kneading the dough, flattening the tortillas and cooking them. When I let loose that I found it abusive, the mother replied: "Well, that's how it is, it's the cuota (toll or contribution)."

In this case the soldiers availed themselves of Ricardo's goods and labor force—which he transferred to his family—during the harvest season. His household (he, his wife, and their infant son) lacked the cash for buying them off. By leaving a small portion of his poppies standing during the harvest, the soldiers leveraged Ricardo's hopes of earning some income and, through an open-ended "arrangement," extorted him in kind, cumulatively, and with no set value in the end. The detachment of soldiers corralled Ricardo as a way of upgrading their everyday fare at the camp with fresh eggs and warm tortillas. In this process, since Ricardo's home also did not have the products in kind and the necessary work force, he relied on his parents' household to pay his "toll." The part played by women in several stages of production (harvesting, monitoring the whereabouts of soldiers while the men were in the fields) was evident in the management of the extortion. All the goods they produced in the domestic economy were deployed to that end.

I returned to Lamberto's in late March only to learn that his most hidden plot, the one higher up, had been reported at the beginning of the month. This happened before Lamberto had started incising the bulbs. The family therefore agreed to pay 2,000 pesos (100 USD) to the soldiers to keep them from mowing down the plot. In the second half of March, with his uncle who came to help, he had started harvesting and bringing some of the gum home.

On the morning of March 29, we were making tortillas with Tamara at the back of the house when we saw soldiers approaching right above us. Tamara alerted Lamberto and walked back around the comal: continuing to make the tortillas, we watched them walk away slowly, then come back just above the embankment by the house. Meanwhile, Lamberto disappeared into the house and came back out again. His nephew also went in and reappeared. After a while, four soldiers showed up in front of the house. Saying little, they peered inside. Tamara stepped up to the front, and when they told her they wanted to enter and look around, she said "Okay, but you put everything back the way you found it, I just cleaned up," and referred to a previous search. The soldiers entered, one by one, looking around; Tamara followed them on their rounds; they didn't touch anything.

When they left, all the family members gathered and congratulated each other. The nephew retrieved the pistol he had hidden in the bag of corn; the father retrieved the gum. We spent an hour just talking; the atmosphere was light. All congratulated Tamara for her attitude, and she started telling me about other techniques she had used in similar situations.

In the ensuing days, the harvest continued, marked by rain and troop movements. Some days the gum was lost, other days it was harvested successfully, but every day the tension in the house was high. By the time I left, Tamara and Lamberto had made back the money extorted from them. In the hamlet, a large number of people could not cover the sums extorted from them because the rain spoiled their harvest. Lamberto and Tamara were among the lucky ones.

Dodging the search mobilized every family member's repertoire of interactional skills. Thus, it provides a snapshot of the fear the soldiers instill and the uncertainty inherent in extortion practices. The detachment of soldiers showing up that day was different from the unit Lamberto had dealt with less than a month earlier. Despite the fixed sum of the payment, the costs and benefits of extortion from the perspective of the family budget is difficult to determine. The payoff from a family's investment in the extorting soldiers in March, shortly before the harvest, can only be assessed at its end, at the time of sale. It is a short-term gamble, in a risky enterprise: the detachment that received the 2,000 pesos would not destroy the plot, but the next one might do so before the harvest ended, or it could search the house and seize the hidden gum. This dynamic applies to all small growers, although not all detachments of soldiers operate in the same manner: some would mow down the flowers without any warning; others would spare part of the plot on condition of being compensated; some would confiscate gum in houses; others extorted a considerable sum without guaranteeing anything. In the end, the repeated soldiers' incursions on the same plot and the same family seal their loss.

In Mexico, the word *"cuota"* can refer to road tolls or a fixed levy. Its use in this context, as well as the characterization as "nice" of soldiers who practice it—as opposed to those who destroy wordlessly—put on display a naturalization of extortion that the grower families must cope with. The frequency, forms, and amounts of extortion are too variable to be rightly labeled "tolls." On the other hand, what remains constant—and thus justifies the "toll" metaphor—is definitely the threat behind this extortion and the uncertainty it spells.

Insecure and Indebted Household Economies

Uncertainty hanging over the harvest determined the family budgeting. The degree of dependence on poppy cultivation varied from one family to the next, but the fluctuations that characterized this income, by being integrated within the modalities of constructing household budgets, permeated relationships within the hamlets to produce a debt economy. It is within the families that the uncertainty and social implications of integrating this debt economy into their local relationships were managed.

Poppy harvesting fit into family budgets in different ways. Alán said that "you make a living on the condition that you have no vices." He regarded himself as "doing well," given that poppy cultivation allowed his family to live and, indeed, some of the neighboring growers were far more insecure. A quick look at his family budget makes it possible to assess a little more precisely the place this resource occupied for a relatively well-off grower family. They had three small plots for a family of five children, one with a chronic illness requiring medical care. They collected school financial aid payments for three of them, part of which they spent on school supplies and contributing to the rotation system the mothers of the hamlet had set up for preparing lunches for middle school students. Five years before I met him, Alán had been made the town hall's local representative for three years, which came with a 3,000 peso (150 USD) monthly salary. Thanks to this extra income, three years before my arrival they had been able to add a second room to their house; before that, the entire family of seven had slept in one room. The year before my stay, harvest proceeds paid for one of the girls' first communion party, with help from the extended family in purchasing food, drinks, and the dress. The family hoped to use some of the income from the harvest to build a fence around the house and keep animals away from the few plantings that grew in front.

The sale of gum was the main source of income for grower families but would not suffice for any of them, even Alán, without the small but predictable supplemental cash inflows. In another hamlet, the Velázquez family had only one dependent child, since the two older ones were already tending their own plots. The three households combined to form one economy. They supported each other daily: both of the grown-up brothers' families ate at the parents' house and bought the groceries. Still, the father got a small job as a helper in a local business to supplement the budget. More broadly, young households that did not have these supplementary incomes, making them totally dependent on the uncertain harvest, regularly fell back on the resources of the extended family. In all cases, public and family assistance filled gaps in the budget: federal grants, money transfers from children working in towns on the plain, and occasional remittances from emigrants. In another family, a young man worked as a *pistolero* for a *pesado*, sent money, and sometimes had jobs for family members—who refused out of fear. For the lucky ones, the 150 dollars monthly that compensated a local representative position in the municipality boosted the family's income. These additional income sources were nevertheless limited and poppies remained the main source of income, while also being the most uncertain. Thus, contrary to what Alán said, "not having any vices" helped, but was not enough. To make a living from cultivating the poppy, subsidies and money transfers remained essential.[30]

Uncertainty surrounding the gum crop—and the money they made from it—often saw families struggle to make ends meet in the months leading up to the harvest, forcing them into debt. In the hamlets, "asking for loans" (*pedir fiado*) meant turning to the grocery store owners, a practice that was unheard of in the supermarkets of the plain or of the main town. On several occasions, women would talk to me about their "decision not to borrow against this money"—"this money" meaning what they expected to earn from the harvest. Faced with a hole in their cash flow, due to extortion followed by a poor harvest or the destruction of the plot, they "decided" that the family budget would no longer rely on this resource. By them "deciding" not to rely on these advances, the women were also commenting on social relations within the hamlet. Generally, they were the ones who had to apply for the loan and had to bear the embarrassment of facing the grocery store owner.

But, practically speaking, the families could not survive without them. Although the local grocery stores charged higher prices, people continued to shop there, even in hamlets well-served by roads. The grocers knew that they were the only recourse in the months leading up to harvest and that their niche was based on this indebtedness. In one hamlet, a grocery store owner had even taken advantage of his neighbors' insecurity by charging them interest. Moreover, sometimes the owner of the grocery store was also the one who would buy the harvest—the hamlet's *pesado*. It was that much easier for him to extend credit when his source of repayment was the crop he was going to buy. This forced indebtedness within close relationships thus partook of the insecurity of the growers, but also of a relationship of dependence vis-à-vis the *pesados*.[31]

Exploitation by Subcontracting

The repression and extortion practiced by the soldiers created the conditions that let buyers exploit growers: the former generated added value by forcing selling prices that were barely enough for their workforce to survive. The uncertainty that weighed on the growers was decisive in their relations with the middlemen who monopolized processing and transport. This system kept growers in the precarious state of being captive subcontractors in a transnational production, transport, and sales chain.

The buyers set the selling price for poppy gum. During the 2014 harvest in the area where Lamberto lived, it was 23 pesos (1.50 USD) per gram of gum, which was considered a good price. The existence of a price, determined in advance of the harvest and known to all, was evaluated by the growers as either "good" or "bad." But the growers' room for maneuver ended with these comments: the price was nonnegotiable. The growers often commented on the price in light of changes in consumption in the United States. These modes of interpretation were rooted in experiences from past changes in the market and referred to macroeconomic processes over which growers have no control. Indeed, the cultivation of marijuana was still underway during my investigation, but already shrinking. The share of income that Mexican growers derived from marijuana plummeted as a result of its legalization in some US states. They lost out to competition from US agro-industrial companies, which selected better seeds, had access to better land, and applied productive farming methods. Moreover, their logistics were more efficient and, above all, they did not have to factor military repression into their production process. The increase in hemp production in the United States had directly affected the selling price in Badiraguato to the point of wiping out all profit for local hemp growers. In a conversation between several growers in a hamlet, the older ones recalled that debacle with concern. Could the price of poppies ever fall to the same extent, they wondered? The youngest among them, an immigrant from the coastal plain who had recently moved in with his uncle to grow poppies, reassured them that while they should indeed give up on marijuana cultivation, they could depend on the poppy. It was a sure bet: the "gringos" would always want it, would never legalize it, and certainly would not ever grow it themselves.[32]

These comments ignored the extraordinary increase in value—largely because of prohibition—between the raw poppy gum and the final product, heroin, sold in the United States.[33] This difference between what the growers received in the Badiraguato sierra and the revenue "on the other side" never featured in their comments on price increases and decreases. The exclusive focus on assessing consumption trends in the United States reflected a belief in market forces: their income would depend solely on changes in the demand for their product in the United States. Paradoxically, the problems encountered here by growers in Badiraguato were at one with those most farmers faced, regardless of legality of their activity. As Birgit Müller points out, faith in market mechanisms leads to an invisibilizing of players who directly determine the local selling price, in this case that of poppy gum.[34] Like Canadian grain farmers when they fail to factor in Monsanto's effect on their condition, poppy growers did not associate pricing with an action, never mind a strategy, by trafficking middlemen. Thus, they failed to take into the analysis of their livelihood difficulties the local power relationships in which their production was embedded. Badiraguato's growers were actually caught up, for better or for worse, in a global supply chain indirectly regulated by the prohibition policy.[35] However, seeing that the transnational nature of the drug economy remained the only reason they adduced, it is worth looking into its effect in this instance: the growers, by buying into it, naturalized the profits that intermediaries reaped from their uncertainty.

My interlocutors all sold resin, not heroin. Their means of production, if they owned any, consisted of only those needed for cultivating poppies: land and tools. A large part of the inhabitants produced gum; only a few individuals had the wherewithal for turning resin into the high-value heroin. This operation usually was performed in one or the other sierra hamlets.[36] It required a discreet location, armed men to protect it, as well as the transport and delivery of chemicals, and a specialized workforce for the chemical processing. These different operations then necessitated manpower, weapons, political connections, and money to finance the whole operation. Moreover, the growers all sold their gum in the vicinity of their hamlet, usually to the same *pesado*. Laboratories operated on the coastal plain and, in theory, growers could have sold gum at a better profit by taking it down there themselves. However, like the processing, transporting the gum involved labor and the various political and economic costs of protecting it. The vast majority of the people in the hamlets could only dream of possessing the means to carry out these operations. Those who actually did command them would commonly be called *pesados*.

The importance of adding value through processing and transport here highlights one of the ways in which access is profitable as soon as it becomes a scarce resource. In this regard, the repression and violence of the *pesados* accentuate the effects of geographical isolation. They recall the instrumentalization of inaccessibility in the Amazon, as analyzed by Christian Geffray: there, exploitation relies less on owning the means of production than the means of circulation.[37] Similar to the Amazonian "bosses," having a stranglehold on the means of transporting opium and heroin is what distinguished the entrepreneurs of marginalization who constitute the contemporaneous *pesados*. In the cases I know of, the people who owned these resources also grew poppies—sometimes by employing farmworkers—but derived most of their income from buying the harvest of all the small-time growers living in their area. However, in the terms of this transaction lodged the texture of the social relations that bound growers to the buyer, and thus the place that their work occupied in this unequal economy.

In effect, from the start the transaction was conditioned by a set of upstream constraints. Lamberto, like my other interlocutors, always sold his crop to the same person. He knew that transporting his unprocessed gum to the coastal plain would indeed yield a better price, as many laboratories were located in or around town. But taking those risks, he told me, would be "something else," an approach he refused to take, preferring to be "here to look after the family." The different nature of this "something" lay in the conditions that transport implied: he neither had the address book nor the money it would take to see this operation through on his own and under conditions of acceptably limited risk. In other words, carrying out this operation with the economic and social resources at his disposal would have exposed Lamberto to a radical uncertainty, vastly higher than the risks he faced in producing gum from growing the poppy. So he continued to sell to the local *pesado* in small quantities. His stated "preferred" method was to sell whenever he had accumulated 200 grams of gum. Others would hold out for a little more, but this estimate was already an attempt at risk minimization: having no more than 200 grams at home meant never losing more than that to military confiscation. The timing of sales was therefore also constrained, revealing the extent to which repression structured the sector: small-time growers could not store and sell gum whenever it suited them, and so prices could not fluctuate at the local level. Thus, while only the value of the gram of gum was the subject of comments and concerns expressed, it was the very existence of a fixed price that appears to have been decisive. The price was fixed because the buyer had a monopoly position over the growers—they were in effect captives of the buyer because of the danger involved in transporting the gum. Finally, because of their exposure to search-and-destroy operations, the growers could not accumulate the harvested gum and time their sales to impact the price. It was through this set of constraints that every market fluctuation in the United States was passed directly back to them. Thus, with sales constrained, with growers captive to a seller who could exploit them, the latter could shed any responsibility and act like he was merely buying the crops from people who entered an international market on their own initiative.

The Lexicon of Domination or the Illusions of Reciprocity

Local formulations of the relationship between growers and their buyers mobilize the lexical fields of freely consenting choice, solidarity, and reciprocity. This emerged clearly in a conversation with Daniel as he reluctantly answered my questions. At first, when I asked him about his plot, he explained that it was "loaned" to him by Rafael Caro Quintero. I asked him, "Just like that?" He then confessed, almost regretfully, that he "gives him something in return." I kept digging: "Is it gum or money?," and he answered, "It depends, but mostly money." Hoping to get the amount, I asked: "Is it a lot?" and he replied: "Not just a little, I give him something just so he doesn't say: 'Ah, and this jerk, I lend him and then nothing.'" I thought it wise to stop at that point, thinking I'd been nosy enough. But, in a later conversation, I got confirmation that the "gift" in question was rent, since, as he explained, when Caro Quintero was arrested, it was one of his relatives who assumed "the responsibility" for receiving payment for the parcel.

The terms of the exchange were part of a relationship marked by Daniel's respect and admiration for Caro Quintero as a benefactor to those around him who had been hunted down. Daniel sounded a similar note in another case: like others, he always sold his gum to the same *pesado*. When I asked him if this buyer was his only option he told me that no, he had a choice, that "there are many people who come to buy," but that he "gets along very well with him." However, without being able to go into detail, I knew that his relations with the buyer in question were not good, so that in actual fact he had no choice but to sell him his gum. Thus, he formulated a relationship of captive sales as free, consensual, and based on mutual regard.

Numerous studies have highlighted these unequal transactions in relations that are formulated as reciprocal in rural contexts of precariousness. Indeed, the *pesados* who actually lived in the hamlets participated in the local social life, in the networks of sociability and kinship: they paid for parties, sent their children to the hamlet school, and sometimes their children married a neighbor. Their rise to this particular status was at times recent—for example, following the death of the previous *pesado*. As a result, growers would have witnessed the rise of someone they considered to be part of the same set of circumstances as theirs: the one who bought from them appeared to be one of them who had "made it."

If access to local positions of domination implied the mobilization of other resources—something that was not lost on anyone—the fact remained that the lack of other economic opportunities made the *pesados* the only role models of success within sight. "I've never seen anyone get rich legally," an elderly man once told me. People talked about their courage, their know-how, and stressed that they had risen to these positions even though they came from the local area. Moreover, the resources which let them capture the added value were obtained by recruiting workers for transport, protection, or cooking during harvests on large plots. The lack of other economic opportunities gave them the status of providers—that is, the rare people who could provide jobs—at little cost. Growers generally had several people in their extended families who in some fashion relied on jobs related to the *pesado*'s prosperity.

The fact that a large part of the hamlet's economy depended on the *pesado*'s activities was voiced on some occasions—for example, when a hamlet's residents were preoccupied with how they would fare following the assassination of a powerful man. In the case of the most well-known figures, while they may have been less present, the formulations in terms of solidarity and reciprocity were reinforced by the weight of the media framing. Some among them stood out for a few charitable acts—electrification of a hamlet, building of a church, paving a road—and the help they rendered to some people was regularly mentioned. But, above all, the way they were tracked down (with drones, the raids from the air involving US law enforcement personnel) aroused a feeling of a shared repressed condition and therefore of strong empathy. Daniel, who regularly saw drones overhead in his hamlet, openly sympathized with Caro Quintero for the hardships the latter had to endure in his clandestine life.

Thus, the expression of reciprocity and friendly relations was part and parcel of the hamlet's economic dependence on *pesados*. In addition, the place of gum sales in the daily lives of growers played an important role in how they characterized this transaction. By intervening only at the time of purchase, the powerful saved the various costs of protection during production. Indeed, each grower held his plot (even when "loaned"), cultivated his flowers, and faced the predation of the military as a family. The sale, in this respect, was the happy denouement to a long year of hardship. The family organization and the absence of the powerful in the production process relieved the latter of any responsibility for how it ended: they could not be legitimately blamed for the failure of "controls" or the lack thereof. Thus, not only did they save the costs of protecting production, but they were still recognized as providers, reaping the associated symbolic benefits. They got credit, too, for another type of protection: that involving the competitive relations between *pesados*. The takeover of hamlets following the death of a strongman that left some of them deserted constituted a feared scenario. And as we will see, for a significant number of problems (property, stealing women), the protection that proximity with a *pesado* brought was decisive. The registers of solidarity and friendship in the relationship between growers and buyers therefore captured just how deep some of these relationships could be.

However, these formulations should not obscure the fact that all of these relationships were extremely constrained: each person's position in the relationship was ensured by armed violence—the military's and that of the *pesado*'s hired guns. Selling your gum in one place rather than another, to one buyer over another, at one place instead of another, was governed by the fear of violence. As we will see later, assassinations of growers over transactions gone wrong do happen. I observed the same dynamic with regard to the jobs *pesados* provided. For example, a young man responsible for transport for a recently murdered pistolero explained to me that he had to find another employer to continue the same work because if "you don't work for a boss, people start to fuck you up (*chingar*)." The euphemism "people start to fuck you up" meant that they might kill you. The use of armed violence was not confined to competitive relationships but also intervened in hierarchical relationships within the same network. The word was that the *pistolero* in question had been killed "by his own people." Similarly, the possibility of violence also existed within dependency relationships. In this sense, the relationships around the buying of the harvest and their characterization should be understood as happening in a context in which the *pesado* is threatening, and in which the context itself, the violent economy of prohibition, constitutes a threat, with attempts to circumvent it exposing one to death.

This lexical field of reciprocity—in relationships where the precarity of one made the wealth of the other and the threat of armed violence fixed the relative positions of each—should not be seen as a nuance of the relationship of exploitation but as a constitutive dimension of it. Claudio Lomnitz proposes a redefinition of Marshall Sahlins's "negative reciprocity," which is characteristic of the most impersonal relationships,[38] to think about the dynamics of exchanges caught up in close relationships marked by predation and violence.[39] Indeed, he criticizes the evolutionism that underlies the theory of exchange through the common premise of strong reciprocity in the closest ties and weak reciprocity in loose relationships. The relationships between grower families and local *pesados* seemed to illustrate particularly well what Lomnitz defines as "asymmetrical negative reciprocity." Indeed, entry into the relationship was constrained by coercion, but the relationship took on the trappings of reciprocal obligations in which flows remained always one-sided: from the one who had the least to the one who had the most.

Thus, Daniel, struggling to support his family, considered himself obliged to Caro Quintero, who took over the surrounding land before renting it to him. Similarly, he was obliged to the buyer of his gum who had taken over this monopolistic position in a context in which this position relied on the possible exercise of violence and the summoning of political contacts. In this sense, these discourses that emphasized choice and friendship were part of a relationship of exploitation constrained by dependence and armed violence. They revealed both the experience of a relationship in which debts to the powerful were never paid off, and the difficulties of questioning this situation.[40] In this regard, it is worth remembering that these transactions brought families for whom the repair of a sheet metal roof was an uncertain investment and mobilized projections for a year, face to face with people whose wealth was difficult to estimate, but who showed off their imposing villas and gleaming vehicles. And it was in this context that the former considered themselves freely obligated to the latter.

The economic transformations undergone by the municipality in the second half of the twentieth century were stamped by the imposition of poppy monoculture. Mountainous Badiraguato was a frontier of capitalism in two respects. On the one hand, mineral extraction saw the attrition of small-scale production as concessions were concentrated in the hands of large companies. On the other hand, the insertion of the coastal plain into a transnational agri-industrial supply chain was reflected in the sierra by an economic and infrastructural isolation that state policies only accentuated. These larger developments created an enclave whose resources—labor and poppies—were inserted into the same transnational circuit as the tomatoes grown in the plain. Military repression completed the transition to monoculture by destroying the rest of the food crops, making the poppy more profitable, and indirectly multiplying employment opportunities in drug transport and protection. With these transformations came the entrepreneurs of marginalization. They took advantage of the place's isolation to enrich themselves and to establish themselves as unavoidable political intermediaries. For the rest, these processes led to shrinking possibilities, and the exhaustion of subsistence strategies based on a plurality of activities.

This history is crucial to understanding the context in which my interlocutors pursued the only available subsistence strategies: poppy cultivation or emigration. For the small-time growers, the modalities of repression increased the insecurity that is inherent in any agricultural enterprise, with harvests offering uncertain prospects at best. However, if the practices of destruction and extortion by soldiers were the most visible constraints on the daily lives of grower families, their insecurity lay ultimately in the exploitation by the *pesados*, that is, in the opportunity that the repression furnished the latter for buying the work of captive growers at low fixed prices. Uncertainty conditioned the profit margins of those who held the means of transport and processing, placing them at the start of the extraordinary added value offered sequentially by the illegality of the production chain. In short, the predation exercised by the army allowed the exploitation of growers by the *pesados*. These relationships were all the more crushing as the context provided the latter with the comfortable positions of protectors and monopolistic suppliers at little cost.

FOUR

Fencing In

"The problem, if you want, is that the law, it is made there, and the problem, it is here."

DON CHUY

THE EJIDO BUILDING IN THE MUNICIPAL SEAT, *which proudly displayed over its entrance the slogan "the land to the one who works it,"[1] was jammed with nearly seventy people on October 26, 2014. Word of mouth had spread that on the agenda this day was the land of the ore processing company. In 1978, the ejido had entered into an agreement with a federal agency (Fomento Minero) to lend it land on which to build an ore processing plant. But in 1992, when the plant closed for the last time, instead of returning the land to the ejido as stipulated in the contract, the organization sold the company and the land for its own benefit to one of its employees. Strangely, the original loan agreement then could not be found; the agrarian administration responded to successive requests from the ejido authorities by claiming that the agreement had been "burned," "lost," "waterlogged," and then simply that it had "disappeared." The employee-turned-owner of the plant (let us call him "Entrepreneur A") continued to operate it before abandoning it in the 2000s, when he moved some of its machinery to the neighboring municipality of Mocorito. Then, in 2014, another contractor ("Entrepreneur B") from the hamlet near the land in question expressed an interest in taking over the plant. Suddenly, Entrepreneur A stated that he too intended to restart the business. And miraculously, the 1978 agreement reappeared in the hands of the commissioner, the ejido's elected representative, by way of a politician member of the ejido, Miguel Ángel.*

On this day, the various parties were here to do battle. Entrepreneur A was there with his lawyer. The ejido's representatives were supported by several important figures in the ejido assembly: the politician Miguel Ángel, Hector, his sidekick, and Memo, the ex-commissioner. Miguel Ángel and Hector also seemed to have a certain affinity with Entrepreneur B. For his part, the latter loudly called attention to his supporters—"the people who accompanied me here"—pointing to a group of men standing in the doorway. They looked sinister and defiant, with the bodily attitude of people letting on that they are armed. Everyone else was seated on plastic chairs and the cement benches that lined the walls of the room. The atmosphere was tense. One speech followed another: Entrepreneur A asserted that his certificate from the Procede reform (the ejidal rights certification program) of 2001 made him the legitimate holder of the ejidal rights; the prominent figures of the ejido *questioned the validity of the certificate; Entrepreneur B pointed to his good relations with the residents living near the factory and appointed himself their defender on this occasion, arguing that they had been defrauded by Entrepreneur A. The speeches were met by a variety of reactions in the room: someone moved in his chair, sometimes there was applause or muffled outrage. When Entrepreneur A's lawyer took the microphone, the atmosphere in the room was electric. He seemed to want to stay above the fray: "Well, need I remind you that you are not owners of your land, you are only usufructers. . . ." [He looked around the room and appeared visibly discomfited by the reaction.] "Uh, that is, yes, you are the owners . . . but the real owner is also the* ejido." *Clearly, he had made a gaffe. . . .*

The lawyer's equivocation perfectly captured the confusion I could not dispel in the early days of my investigation: trying to figure out what rights the people of Badiraguato had to their land was a real headache. As elsewhere, this confusion arose from the tension at the heart of the relationship between legal recognition of use and possession, on the one hand, and social relationships bearing on access to the land, on the other.[2] In Mexico, this issue often crystallized around the *ejido*, a "social property" enshrined in Article 27 of the 1917 constitution. The *ejido* is recognized as a legal person and its members, the title holders, enjoy use rights on land protected by the state. Collectively, they form the assembly that constitutes the *ejido*'s supreme body and elect one of their numbers as their representative or commissioner (*comisario*). The *ejido* simultaneously designates the assembly (like the one in which the above-described scene played out), the local authority, and the legal regime governing the land (the one invoked by the lawyer in asserting that "the true owner is also the *ejido*"). In Badiraguato, the problem of access to land was all the more complex because the *ejido*, in all three senses, coexisted with the *cerco* (literally "the fence"), which designated both the physical fence itself and the fenced-in parcel.

The tension stoked by the lawyer that day revealed itself on several levels during my fieldwork. First, it was rare to hear about land and *ejido* issues in the same conversation. The two subjects were informed by distinct and often contradictory justifications, practices, and resource regimes. On the one hand, *cerco* referred invariably to the land as a place that was worked, as a means of production, and as a landscape, so that talking about land or accompanying someone to his *cerco* rarely led to mentioning the *ejido*. On the other hand, the *ejido* was the subject of a narrative about the revolutionary epic. Those who now or in earlier times had held important positions in the municipal offices or agrarian administration mobilized the grammar of the post-revolutionary national narrative: after "the victory of the revolution," landless peasants were encouraged to band together to petition the state for land grants that redistributed land seized, if necessary, from the great land-owners under the defeated Porfirio Díaz regime.

Finally, if, in principle, fencing-in is not excluded from the ejidal legal regime (the area endowed to an *ejido* combining both communal and individual uses), the nature of a person's rights to land differs depending on whether you are talking about *cerco* or *ejido*. As elsewhere, Badiraguato's *ejidatarios* were "usufructers" or "possessors" (*posesionarios*, the ownership term applicable to the *ejido*), but people with *cercos* were considered to "own" these. The owners of *cercos* and the *ejido*'s usufructers did not form two mutually exclusive groups, nor were they identical, but there was some overlap: some *ejidatarios* were owners or tenants of *cercos,* others were not; and some—but not all—owners of *cercos* were *ejidatarios.* Nor did the distinction between the two reside in the land in question: *cerco* rights and *ejido* rights could refer to the same spaces.

To grasp the ambivalent links between *ejido* and *cerco,* I therefore adopted an approach that reversed the strategy I normally employed in observing the protective and productive practices of my interlocutors. Instead of merging into my interlocutors' intelligence-gathering, I regularly provoked the interaction, drilling down with serial questions so as to elicit reactions and stories. The uncomfortable silences, and sometimes confessions, this approach yielded contributed importantly to my study of the modalities of land access.

This complex situation manifested itself in the great linguistic uncertainty surrounding the characterization of a person's land rights. Queried about their *cerco,* my interlocutors did not hesitate: they were "owners" (*dueños*). But when asked about how the *cercos* related to the *ejido,* either they constantly had to correct themselves—"the owners ... uh ... possessors"—as they concentrated to respond to the interview, or they switched back to "owner" as the conversation went more easily. In the former mayor's interview with the online daily *Sin Embargo*, a similar confusion had emerged. Speaking of the construction of a school in El Chapo's birth hamlet, where his mother still lived, he stated: "She is a good woman. . . . *She even donated the land.* I do not know why it surprises people. . . . I cannot say it because I am not the authorized spokesman, if I had the title deed, I could say so. So far as I know, *the San Jose del Barranco's ejido where she lives donated the land.*" (My emphasis.)

One day, returning from the sierra and driving past the hills near the main town, the former commissioner of an *ejido* located in the lower part of the municipality—who was also a municipal employee—tried to clear up my confusion: "Well, you see these hills? Let's say they're X's . . . in fact, they really are his (laughs). Well, if X wants to sell his land, he sells it, but he still remains an *ejidatario*. He retains the rights. It is the rights you can't sell." The ex-commissioner clearly articulated here the practical distinction between ejidal rights and access to land: being an *ejidatario* was a status which—in Badiraguato as in other municipalities—had little to do with owning a plot.[3] The confusion of my interlocutors effectively stemmed from the fuzzy relationship between legal statutes and land access practices.

"THOSE WHO HAD EVERYTHING AND THOSE WHO HAD NOTHING": CONFLICTING TAKES ON HOW *EJIDOS* WERE FORMED

Understanding the workings of the *ejido* and its place in access to land in Badiraguato was impeded by the many fragmentary and piecemeal narratives about it. This difficulty in reconstructing a history of how access to land was formalized was fed by the social issues underlying the communal regime and the ejidal institution in Badiraguato. To begin with, any inquiry about the past and present functioning of the local agrarian institution always first elicited an answer about the revolutionary epic. With a little persistence, I managed to collect the stories of people involved in creating the *ejido* and those who knew its history. My attempts to consult the archives were often thwarted by my interlocutors. The *ejido* authorities claimed that they did not exist, or that they had been lost. The staff of the Culiacán agrarian archives, for their part, insistently assured me of my "right" to consult them, while keeping me from doing so.

By using the archives of National Agrarian Register in Mexico City in 2016, after concluding my fieldwork, I finally was able to make some headway.

I then returned to Badiraguato, eager to reconcile what I had learned from my archival work with what the people there had told me. If I hoped to cross-check and triangulate these different narratives to trace the *ejido* story, the reactions of my interlocutors—they were flummoxed to learn that I had "dug" in the archives—kept me from pursuing this avenue further, but it did clarify for me that the contradictory readings were an essential feature of the different *ejido* narratives. The piecemeal, fragmentary, and contradictory nature of the statements concerning the formation of the ejidos is therefore where I need to start unpacking this history.

The interpretations conflicted in particular when it came to how the main town's *ejido* was created. On this topic, the discourse and archives were most abundant. While they agreed on some points with the versions offered by my interlocutors, they also diverged on some key aspects. The process I was able to reconstruct from the archives went like this: In 1938, in the context of a national land distribution policy,[4] a group of people would petition for an allocation of land to "benefit those who, until today, have not been able to obtain a piece of land ... to support a family"—in other words, "landless peasants," the classic figures at the center of Mexican land reform. The application for an endowment, processed by the agrarian administration, impacted primarily the eight large landholdings situated within the seven-kilometer statutory perimeter around the town. For two years, the petitioners, with the support of the League of Agrarian Communities and the Peasant Trade Unions of Sinaloa (linked to the ruling single party), and the potentially "affected" owners, supported by the mayor at the time, bombarded the Joint Agrarian Commission with their written arguments.[5] Their missives typically focused on three key issues: accusations of threats, "hostilities," and sabotaging of fences; questioning the surveys carried out by different engineers; and differences over who qualified for the categories created by the national agrarian distribution narrative ("landless peasants," "Porfirist landowners").

In 1941, after two years of intense back-and-forth and visits by three engineers, the last letter from the petitioners requesting a provisional allocation seemed to have remained a dead letter, at least judging from the archives. Then there was a twenty-year gap in the archives until, in 1962, a letter from the Agrarian Commission retained another engineer in Badiraguato. He was tasked with visiting the main town to check if the original petitioning group from twenty years ago still existed and, if not, to constitute a new group. This time the process went smoothly and quickly: the technical work that had been repeatedly contested in the past was ruled to have been valid and, with the requirement for a new census having been met, the "provisional endowment" was granted.[6]

The documents from the two eras (1938–41 and 1962) contained several contradictions. In 1938, the first engineer noted that the land concerned was "generally of very poor quality" and recommended the endowment more with the rationale of "unification of the inhabitants of the village around the agrarian cause" than for the subsistence opportunities offered by the land. "Calculating all the arable land," he wrote, "we come to the conclusion that it is not enough to meet the needs of the 30 percent of the inhabitants who appear in the census carried out [in 1938, 137 people] as eligible to claim land rights." In 1962, although pastures were also called "poor quality," they were nevertheless considered likely to "satisfy the needs of the nucleus," now comprising 519 people. And while the conflicting process of 1938–41 noted the importance of properties that were at risk of being seized for the *ejido*, in 1962, with regard to the same area, the report stated that new technical work was unnecessary, but pointed out "that according to this study on the ownership regime of these lands, these lands are free, considered to be the property of the nation which have been occupied by petitioners since time immemorial." With that ended the confounding archival paper trail.

The story of the *ejido* that my interlocutors told began with the 1960s. It credited one of the marginalization entrepreneurs, Nacho Landell, with having "created the *ejido*" and spoke of threats to the "land of the inhabitants." In a recorded interview, Nacho Landell's son Memo, a former *ejido* commissioner, told the story in these words:

> Forming the *ejido* was the wish of the governor at the time, Gabriel Leyva Velázquez. It was the time when the dams were built, of the irrigation work on the plain. They opened the hills, cleared them for farming, dug canals, drainage, all that. And so, many people in the valley who had like 1,000 head of cattle, started saying that they were going to drive the cattle into the sierra, up here, with us. So, the governor, who was a friend of my father's ... an acquaintance, told him to organize his people to set up the *ejido*, so that the *ejido* would keep out the cattle from the valley, because otherwise they would lose all the pastures. So, my dad was one of those who organized the formation of the *ejido*.

The stories of my interlocutors invariably portrayed the *ejido*'s genesis as a protection story featuring local strongmen and their political contacts at the state level. The *ejido* narrative here stressed the legal protection it offered— "so that the *ejido* would keep out the cattle"—to preserve a status quo by replicating the existing land distribution and so avert the potential threat to the sierra from the transformations taking place in the plain.

The archival accounts and those of my interlocutors diverged on the conflict of the 1930s and 1940s. On my return from my Mexico City archive dive, I presented the story I had pieced together in broad strokes to them. It caused them to adjust their narrative: Miguel Ángel and Memo now subscribed to the story from the archives of an agrarian struggle that failed—but they changed the cast of characters, turning the powerful men of the 1960s, who were not mentioned in the archives covering the 1930s, into the losing petitioners of the agrarian struggle of the earlier decade. Both men being related to these people, they recast themselves as inheritors of a peasant mobilization. The dissonance this produced was twofold. Not only did their new narratives differ from the archives, but they also contrasted with those they had proposed two years earlier, namely that their powerful ancestors, backed by political contacts in the Sinaloa state government, had set up the *ejido* in the 1960s. Moreover, neither the accounts of my interlocutors nor supplementary archives sufficed to fill the lacunae I encountered in the agrarian archives. In the end, I was therefore unable to trace the evolution of the power relationships and the distribution of land holdings between the opposing groups of the late 1930s.

Nevertheless, in their fragmentary nature and contradictions, these narratives echo the paradox of the *ejido* and the *cerco* that runs through my ethnographic investigation. Just as the discourses on *cerco* and *ejido* intertwine and oppose each other, two distinct and contradictory figures traverse these historical narratives. On one hand, there emerges the romantic and legitimate figure of agrarian struggle, that of landless peasants now protected by the inalienable nature of the lands they would have the use of, the figure of "land to the one who works it." On the other hand, there is a legal device for reproducing a land structure, a protection whose conditions were summarized in the governor's advice to Nacho Landell to "organize your people!" In that guise, the *ejido* appears as the cooptation by the elite of an institutional regime of distribution.

This tension lodges in the wording of the 1962 report: "These lands are free, considered as the property of the nation which have been occupied by the petitioners since time immemorial." In the 1938 archives and in the accounts later proposed by my interlocutors emerged the figures of the struggle between, as Miguel Ángel put it, "those who had everything and those who had nothing." The designation of the elites changed from the "Porfirist owners" in the archives to the "friends of the revolutionaries" in the accounts of their descendants. But the justifying principle remained constant, recurring as an agrarian struggle against an elite that was monopolizing land resources.

Conversely, the manner in which time and silent archives obscured the conflict of the 1930s and 1940s echoed the oral accounts of an organized allocation between local and regional elites. The rough-edged process of the 1930s and 1940s disappeared in 1962 with this characterization: lands that included private property were now called both "free" and "occupied since time immemorial by the petitioners." Those identified as the "Porfirist owners" of 1938 were included in the 1962 census and thus considered eligible to claim land within the framework of the land distribution. That way they became *ejidatarios*. Nacho Landell appears in the archives as president of the *ejido* in 1962, and Governor Leyva Velázquez was present for the provisional allocation act. In short, within the dissonances between the narratives and in their piecemeal character emerged an image: that of a grammar of agrarian struggle inscribed in the modalities with which the elite co-opted the instrument of land distribution.

On the contrary, it should be noted that the allocations of the sierra *ejidos* were not the subject of nearly as many narratives. The presidential resolutions creating the four *ejidos* on which I focus here dated from 1962 to 1968[7] and, despite differences in the dynamics that went along with their allocations, they shared several common traits reminiscent of Salvador Maldonado's "paper *ejidos*" in the state of Michoacan, or the "fictional *ejidos*" in Huasteca about which Frans Schryer wrote.[8] To begin with, there were archival traces antedating the chronology that the inhabitants shared with me. With the exception of *ejido* 2, where the institutional process is documented through local correspondence, the other cases showed a gap in the chronologies: according to the archives, the *ejidos* were petitioned for and then even allocated, but my interlocutors from these *ejidos* dated their establishment to much later.[9] In these cases, the agrarian archives turned out to be particularly fragmentary: on paper, representatives were indeed elected following the allocation, and a few signatures adorn scattered documents, but the residents, including those listed in the census, insisted that the *ejido* did not exist by then.

Second, the scenario of a threat to the residents' lands was repeated: in one case, the formation of a neighboring *ejido* in the state of Chihuahua triggered the allocation; in another, the allocation was linked to a mingling between the border to be established with an *ejido* (itself allocated on the border line with another *ejido*) and a state-funded road construction project. The notion of the *ejido* as a kind of protection is therefore found in all these *ejidos*. The land is always referred to as "free, considered the property of the nation" in the agrarian documents and the names of the prominent families of each area appear in the *ejido* census. There is therefore no evidence to support the thesis that lands had been distributed or allocated to people who did not possess them.

"WHAT IS YOURS IS YOURS": THE POWER OF THE *CERCO*

The technical, legal, and political issues of land access and the ejidal system are complex in themselves, and the answers I gathered during my investigation were often contradictory. So, I persisted in my questioning: how do you join the *ejido*? What are the powers of an *ejido* in the sierra? How was the 1992 land reform implemented? I had been inquiring into all this for several weeks already when Gonzalo, a senior official in the municipal offices, finally explicitly formulated one of the keys to the problem.

On a trip into the sierra, with me peppering him with questions, Gonzalo ended up asking me why I was so interested in the ejido. *His question was highly relevant because it seemed to me by this time that the* ejido *would allow me to approach the practical issues around land use and the organization of agricultural production (including of the poppy) from the angle of a legal institution and therefore, I imagined, less controversially. Although the* cerco *cropped up all the time in discussions from the start of my fieldwork, for a time I was rather distracted from what was happening "in the mountains" (el monte) where most of the issues played out around cercos and therefore poppy plantings. Thus, I had backed off on asking questions about the* cerco *and concentrated instead on asking about the* ejido.

So, I answered Gonzalo that the ejido *struck me as being central as a local authority in the hamlets and, more broadly, in a municipality where most people lived from agricultural activities, and that I wanted to understand how access to land works. After a silence came his reply, which took on a confessional if not concessional tone:*

—Well, let's say . . . in reality, there's something stronger than the ejido . . .
See that cerco? *[He asked me while we were driving on a dirt road fenced on
both sides with barbed wire.] This* cerco, *it belongs to someone. And that's all
there's to it! I don't get involved (*no me meto*) simply because . . . no!*

—Ah, but then what happens for example if someone has this cerco *and
someone else interferes or comes and fences it in turn?*

My question seemed to take him aback for a moment.

*—Uh . . . well . . . in theory the agrarian court is there for that. . . . You file
a complaint and it takes its course. . . .*

—But . . . and in practice?

*—Hmph, look here . . . if they kill each other over a simple look . . . you can
imagine it for a* cerco! *And then that way no more enemy.*

Originally from a hamlet in the sierra, Gonzalo was a senior civil servant, but
he was not an *ejidatario*. His discursive premise of a spontaneous and easy
recourse to violence marked a social distance from "them"—the owners or
tenants of *cercos*. Nevertheless, his primary intention—generous in the
Badiraguato *ejido* maze—was to let me know that if I wanted to understand
how access to land was regulated I was on the wrong track by concentrating
on the *ejido* side. In this revelation, he juxtaposed and prioritized *ejido* and
cerco: "in theory" the *ejido* applied but, in practice, the *cerco* was the "stronger"
and ruled because, unlike the *ejido*, it came with a coercive guarantee. He
thus suggested that official justice—"agrarian courts"—did not offer an
avenue for handling a dispute and therefore was not germane.

Such frankness was rare when land was the topic. My interlocutors frequently related the *cerco* to an earlier form of regulation, an authentic and
peaceful past "of the time when a man's word was his bond"—whereas "now
it might as well be air," as the saying went (*antes la palabra valía, ahora se la
lleva el aire*). On other occasions, the *cercos* were presented to me as latecom-
ers that threatened the *ejido*. "They are putting an end to the *ejido*, everything
is fenced!!," the president of the main town's *ejido* told me, before asking me:
"Where you come from, too, do they fence in as they see fit?" Between a
mythical past and a threatening future, the *cerco* condensed several problems.
Before we can grasp the "strength of the *cerco*" in relation to the *ejido*, we need
to sort out the two distinct logics that operated in the local uses of the term
"*cerco*" and of the fence made of wooden stakes and barbed wire: the *cerco*
fence and the *cerco* enclosure.

First, the *cerco* is a fence that corresponds to the local productive organization. Stockmen and farmers fence land, respectively, to keep livestock and to protect crops—previously food crops, later replaced mostly by poppies. Cattle-raising organization was decisive: toward the end of the dry period, around the month of May, the herders drove their cattle up into the mountains. Depending on the year, the release of the animals coincided with the end of the poppy harvest and, possibly, the start of planting food crops; the plots where they grew had to be protected by a fence. Thus these *cercos*, usually located near the hamlets, were the corollary of a wider use of "free mountains" (*el monte libre*), so-called because they were unfenced. Each cattleman had his pen (*cerco*) and also kept a place higher up, called the *querencia*,[10] where he habituated his cattle to go for watering, grazing, and resting. In times when cattle were released, herders knew which way the cattle would move and could find them easily in the vicinity of their *querencia*. This *cerco* was therefore linked to a shared use of the mountains, where the *querencia*, maintained individually, constituted a form of appropriation by use, a diffuse possession ("*mi querencia*") without stakes or barbed wire.

A variant of this productive use of *cercos* came closer to the second logic, that of the enclosure. In fact, the concealment required for growing poppies and marijuana involved fencing in isolated parts of the mountains where the animals typically grazed. However, some poppy fields were huge because they belonged to a *pesado* who had the means and political contacts that let him make stable arrangements with the army. These fenced-in spaces already differed from the productive organization of the *cerco* fence closer to the hamlets because the barbed-wire fencing in the mountains served also for marking it as property. Thus, it was a form of grabbing the so-called "free" part of the mountains that was all the more obvious because armed men generally guarded the plot. These *cercos* therefore corresponded to a dual logic, the productive function of the fencing-in accompanying the enclosure of large areas of communal (or at least unappropriated) land.[11]

Second, the recurring formula "when people started to fence in" was unambiguous: in parallel with the productive use of *cercos*, it was a process of enclosure in a given period, and it was more specifically around these practices of appropriation that the conflict of norms with the *ejido* emerged, that is, being opposed by "the force" of the *cerco*. When asked about the effects of the allocation of the main town's *ejido*, Memo, in the interview conducted in his *cerco*, associated the formation of the *ejido* with the fencing:

Then people started to fence to keep out the cattle [coming up from the plain because of the irrigation work]. For example, in a hamlet, let's say where the Rivera family lived, they fenced in so many hectares to keep out cattle. And so, when the *ejido* was formed, my dad also fenced in four or five [plots] . . . and hey . . . there you have it . . . when the *ejido* was formed . . . you can see that every time, when you form an association or whatever [the *ejido*], if there are rules at the beginning, there's always a smart guy or two who say: 'Ah, we need a couple more rules, right?' So, they added other rules, saying that the mountain that was still free was not to be fenced. So, the one who already had a fence, we left it up, but the one who wanted a new one . . . well . . . well, they continued to build fences, but out of mistrust, fear of disputes, threats, all that.

Two aspects of his story surfaced in other enclosure situations in the municipality. On the one hand, it associated *cerco* with a practice of securing land in a context of uncertainty over access. Memo explained that fencing went hand in hand with the allocation process: *cerco* and *ejido* were two sides of the same coin, two forms of protection against the threat posed by the changes in the plain. Thus, Nacho Landell, at the forefront of the institutional process, obtained other lands in parallel by way of the cercos, which in many cases was nothing more than a form of land grabbing. Paradoxically, the two modes of security differed in the face of the same threat: where the *ejido* would protect by formalizing a common possession, the fencing nibbled away at the commons; and, by fencing off spaces dedicated to a variety of uses such as the *querencia*, it protected one at the expense of others through an individual grab.

But other cases showed that fencing was not a practice complementary or parallel to the creation of the *ejido*. Instead, beyond a reaction to the threat of cattle from the plain, the *cerco* enclosure was primarily a reaction to the *ejido* itself. The process of formalizing the rights represented by the creation of the *ejido* created uncertainty and an urgent need to fence. In *ejido* 2, the local impact of the allocation process could be seen in particular around complaints about new fences that cut off access to paths or to water sources used by everyone. In the rest of the sierra, fencing especially increased during the Procede reform, intended to solve the problem of formalizing rights (see below). This was one of the prime facets of the phrase "*cerco* is stronger than *ejido*": the former was a way to protect oneself against the latter.

On the other hand, by mentioning "a couple more rules," Memo formulated one of the tensions surrounding fencing which, depending on the situation, opened either the possibility of legal recognition of a possession or of exposure to violence and uncertainty. Defining a particular moment shifted the *cerco* from security to uncertainty. In this story, the "smart guys" devised an arbitrary rule: prohibition on fencing land not yet appropriated. This rule enrolled enclosure practices in an uncertainty: "They continued to fence, but out of mistrust, fear of disputes, threats, all that." The paradox of the fence that secured and the fence that created uncertainty was prominent in the formation of the *ejidos* and the Procede reform that gave rise to a wave of fencings. In the Procede reform especially, this dimension was explicit since it provided for regularizing de facto possessions. Thus, it represented a window of opportunity beyond which the threat of violence would hang over fencing.

Like any formalization process, the recognition of certain land uses through the *ejido* implied the exclusion of others.[12] As we saw, the *ejido* justification regime mobilized protection against a threat to land use: the risks presented by livestock coming up from the plain (specifically to the area of the main town and the *ejidos* of the lower part), and by the formalization processes underway in neighboring hamlets that involved drawing boundaries, road construction, and mining concessions. However, if the *ejido* was supposed to ensure a status quo, in practice—by presenting an opportunity for formal recognition in a limited timeframe—it created an urgency to mark off individual possessions in that space. The compressed timeframe sharpened the competition for land.

The *cerco*, as both a corollary to and a reaction against the *ejido*, was primarily a local usage and as such referred to a form of regulation, of definition of the access rights to land:

> ADÈLE: Well, and when the *ejido* started, you started holding meetings how often? How did the themes relate to each one's *cercos'* function?
>
> MEMO: Well, it's that . . . Here traditionally what is yours . . . is yours. And us, we did not allow one law or a . . . something . . . want us to . . . to take something from us by decree, you know, the right of a person. So, here it has been said from the beginning that we will respect all those who have a *cerco* . . . we said we'd respect everyone who would have a possession. Here it has been said from the beginning that we will respect all those who have a *cerco*.

Here the *cerco*, which he later rephrased as "possession," was "the right of a person" that the *ejido* regime, once enacted, was likely to threaten. *Ejido* was a "law" or an intervention "by decree" that had to be kept at a distance or handled in a way that would keep it from jeopardizing a local definition of "what is yours." Thus, through the existence of a subjective right, to which it gave a universal character (that of an undefined person), the *cerco* was presented as a regulation, whose customary character was that it opposed to the "laws" of the state. *Cerco* was a standard construed by and applied among the people of Badiraguato. This discourse was heard regularly. When I asked another *ejidatario*, don Chuy, whose parents worked for the Cuén family, about the same problem, he replied: "The problem, if you want, is that the law, it is made there, and the problem, it is here." This was a second aspect of the concept "the *cerco* is stronger than the *ejido*": the *cerco* possessed the power of custom and rootedness against an alien law.

The definition of *cerco* as "the right of a person" that prevails over the *ejido* therefore reduced the question of access to land to that of the ability to fence it. The waves of fencing in practice amounted to individual grabs of land set aside for collective use. In this regard, the insistence on collective dynamics (such as the protection of Badiraguato stockmen against those of the plain) should not conceal the exclusion of the uses and possessions of some people for the benefit of others. Behind the general discourses about "when people started to fence" and the "right of a person" hid an economy of *cercos*—an economy in the sense of involving the distribution of a scarce resource. The following story of the Ortiz family, who grew poppies, offers a summary of the resources that were required for benefiting from the *cerco* and the dynamics to which they gave rise.

The Ortiz family moved to hamlet W* in 1969. It was introduced by the father's uncle, who had settled there years earlier, and by Tomás, the eldest son's godfather. The family was looking for a place to live where there was land that they could cultivate. Tomás, originally from the hamlet, had fenced a plot on one of the hills near the hamlet, a small part of which, on a flat, was suitable for planting crops. When Tomás decided to emigrate, he sold his cerco *to Ortiz senior. But Raimundo, the local* cacique *and a livestock breeder, also president of the new* ejido *and political intermediary for the municipal government, seized the* cerco *sold by Tomás to the father. Although cheated, the father "wasn't the type to argue, he didn't have it in him." The family then learned that Tomás had died in the state of Sonora, eliminating the possibility of his returning to testify about the sale and help them recover the land. As for Raimundo, he still held on to this* cerco, *but also to many others—so many that he was unable to tell me how* *many* cercos *or hectares he owned, just "really a lot." The Ortiz sons say they* *know that Raimundo had taken the* cerco *knowing full well what he was doing,* *since they recently had heard him again referring to it as "the* cerco *of Tomás."* *Meanwhile, in the mid-1980s, Rafael Caro Quintero, from another hamlet,* *bought many* cercos *in the vicinity of hamlet W* (but none of Raimundo's) and* *fenced another part of the surrounding hills. Through the uncle, Ortiz senior* *gained access to a* cerco *of Caro Quintero's, who let him rent it cheaply so he* *could support his family.*

The various transactions involving these *cercos* highlight the type of rights associated with the fencing: Tomás sold the plot he had fenced in on "free" land; Raimundo grabbed that *cerco*; Rafael Caro Quintero bought, fenced, and rented out other land. Regardless of whether it involved fencing land or a change of ownership, Tomás, Raimundo, and Caro Quintero appeared as full and complete owners of their *cercos*. The linguistic blur that surrounded the qualification of status ("owners ... uh ... possessors") was not related to a distinct use of the word "owner" or failure to master a legal vocabulary: *cerco* clearly did convey effective property rights despite the legal regime in force on these lands. However, like Raimundo, who lost count of all his *cercos*, there was no limit to expansion other than having the means to do so, such that economic, social, and violent resources made the *cerco*.

Economic means were indeed the key. Materially, a *cerco* was primarily made of wooden stakes and barbed wire. It therefore involved a real cost including labor, especially when it concerned several hectares during the fencing waves. The two people in the story who fenced, Rafael Caro Quintero and Raimundo, clearly could afford it. The letters regularly addressed to the mayor complaining about a neighbor's new *cercos* often referenced the grabbers' economic resources when closing off the commons, which, for example, ended free passage for the inhabitants or access to water. Beyond the material cost of the fence, the wholesale grabbers were usually already the most endowed people (such as Raimundo) or those with rising economic fortunes. Rafael Caro Quintero, who fenced at the height of his ascent, was a paradigm: the enrichment of some people in the context of drug trafficking was not irrelevant to the dynamics of fencing. On the lands near the main town, land speculation dynamics were one result of this linkage between rapid accumulation and fencing. In this regard, the fluidity between livestock raising and the drug trade was crucial. Many *pesados* went into trafficking using the political, economic, transport, and commercial resources built around livestock. This favored the blurring between the *cerco* fence and the *cerco* enclosure: on the one hand, herders expanded their *cercos* to include all the land on which their cattle grazed; on the other, those who had stable agreements for their plots fenced large areas in the previously "free" mountains, closing off access to the *querencias* of the others.

Another key element was the respect accorded to the marking of possession. Indeed, Ortiz senior bought a *cerco*, but his lack of social recognition—especially by the local *cacique*—prevented him from asserting his ownership. The social capital possessed by Raimundo and Rafael Caro Quintero was as much a feature of the *cerco* as the wooden stakes and barbed wire. It was based on the recognition granted to the person as the owner of the plot. A fortiori, the recourse to an external institution for redress, a court for example, was out of the question. It would have extracted them from local social relationships: in Gonzalo's words, such recourse was indeed "theoretical." The characterization of Ortiz senior as someone who "wasn't the type to argue" mostly concealed the fact that he could not afford to challenge the grabbing of his plot. Important owners could thus unequivocally express the importance of having their rights respected by neighbors—"here, people respect mine." This recognition was all the more central because it was so fragile in other cases. Indeed, like the "solution" to Ortiz senior's problem via Rafael Caro Quintero, many people got access to a *cerco* thanks to a powerful man's protection. Access to land for small growers therefore required patronage logics, since they depended on the respect paid to the one who guaranteed their rights—and, as we have seen, it was common for a *pesado* to be killed or, more rarely, to be arrested.

The final implicit dimension in the narrative of the Ortiz family was that the social capital invested in the recognition of a *cerco* was often linked with the ability to mobilize armed men. If the land purchases and grabs by Rafael Caro Quintero, an outsider, were respected by Raimundo, it was because Caro Quintero had the coercive means for meting out violence. Gonzalo's observation, "if they kill each other over a simple look . . . you can imagine it for a *cerco*," was part of the essentializing narrative of the triviality of violence in Badiraguato. However, in practice, episodic violence ran like a red thread through *cerco* stories. Some periods of intense fencing were locally referred to as "dirty wars." In an *ejido* in the municipality's northern part where I did not spend much time, fencing was said to have caused a large number of deaths (as many as seventy people killed in two or three years, in a hamlet of about eight hundred residents). When I did go there, I tried to meet *ejidatarios*. Two of them agreed to talk but seemed puzzled by my questions about the *ejido*. When I asked if they had *cercos*, they laughed and said no. Then they explained to me that the vast majority of the land actually belonged to one man who was not an *ejidatario* "but [who] has a lot of weapons," which other people corroborated.

Memo's formulation—"Here it has been said from the beginning that we will respect all those who have a *cerco*"—was therefore falsely neutral; it related to this political economy of the *cercos*. "What is yours is yours" depended on economic, social, and violent resources. As the owner of several *cercos*, including ones inherited from his father, that is to say inherited along with the respect accorded to his father's *cercos*, he naturalized his dominant position in the relationships that make the *cerco* by suggesting a universal right: "the right of a person."[13] However, it was precisely in the concrete modalities of fencing, in the inequalities that it assumed, that the "right of a person" resided, a right that the *ejido* could not threaten. Thus, when other *ejidatarios* in hamlet W* spoke of Raimundo, they would say: "He has a lot of power and *cercos*." This was the third aspect of the phrase "the *cerco* is stronger than the *ejido*": the economic, social, and armed strength of those who fenced. The *cerco* therefore appeared as the material expression of the domination at work in the economic relations described in the previous chapter, and the expression of these relations was particularly pronounced in times of instability stirred up by a process of formalizing rights.

THE PROFITS OF THE *EJIDO*

The dynamics of actual ownership in Badiraguato raise the question of how meaningful the *ejido* assembly and land tenure system are. If the *cerco* prevailed over the *ejido* in the domain that precisely constituted the latter's jurisdiction, why would people invest themselves in the institution to begin with?

The first answer to this question is that people often did not get involved. In *ejidos* 1, 2, and 3, the assemblies never met. The *ejidatarios* explained to me that they could be summoned if necessary but that there were no regularly scheduled meetings. In the absence of regular assemblies, representatives were duly elected, and their names appeared in the agrarian archives, but the *ejido* lacked a space for deliberation and collective management.

By contrast, the main town's *ejido* and *ejido* 4 did meet. The former met the last Sunday of every month. The room seldom got as crowded as it did during the conflict I described between the two entrepreneurs at the beginning of this chapter, but people did attend, even a few women (although I never saw any of them take the floor at a meeting). According to the ejidal authorities, some thirty people (out of two thousand *ejidatarios*) regularly attended meetings. *Ejido* 4 held assemblies every two or three months. As the date of the meeting approached, I met a lot of resistance when I tried to negotiate my attendance at it. I thought that the reluctance related to the subjects dealt with, but I found out it was because "we do not want women to come here; if they do, the others bawl," and when the time came, I was indeed the only woman in the room.

In either case, the functioning of the assemblies shed light on what participation in the assembly signified. *Ejido* 4 represented a revealing exception in this regard. It was by common knowledge the most active *ejido* in the sierra. The *ejido* authorities dated it back to its "reactivation" in the late 2000s under a contract signed with a consulting firm specializing in grant applications. For a fee, the company advised and assisted the ejidal authorities with their applications, through which this *ejido* qualified for many funding programs. For example, it received aid under a soil erosion control program funded by the Ministry of the Environment. Despite the scarcity of inspections but under the impetus of the president of the *ejido*, very sensitive to the preservation of "his native mountain," crews of *ejidatarios* actually built abutments.

The various programs and grants received by this *ejido* let it acquire a vehicle and an ATV for successive ejidal authorities and obtain the expensive permit for a radio frequency transmission antenna. The soldiers still confiscated the radios, but they no longer destroyed the antenna. In this sense, at least, the *ejidatarios'* involvement in the institution helped them solve everyday problems. This *ejido's* activity also made it possible to raise awareness among *ejidatarios* about problems stemming from production practices—for example, by training fire watch teams to contain fires started by stubble burning in the plots or slash-and-burn practices. Paradoxically, in a context of local government competition for public financing, the deviation from *ejido* logics (they were supposed to shield land from market forces) by subcontracting a private company led this *ejido* to achieve a rare success. Landing numerous grants let it finance activities specific to the *ejido* and to reward the *ejido's* membership through agricultural aid or with pay for participating in collective activities. For precarious domestic economies, access to subsidies, however meager, was one of the few opportunities for legal sources of income and, as such, was crucial.

While this case is exceptional, it reveals the reasons underlying the activity of the other *ejido* that met regularly. The size of the main town's *ejido*, its location, and the political clout of some of its members also gave it access to outside funding. As the most populous *ejido*, located in the main town of one of Sinaloa's eighteen municipalities, it was much better connected than the sierra *ejidos*. Comments about the elected authorities often focused on how well they competed for grants and how they distributed the resulting aid among the *ejidatarios*. The importance of these activities took precedence over other issues that could be addressed at the meetings. In fact, at times the need for access to programs was cited as justification for sidestepping practical issues related to *cercos*. Thus, at one meeting the main town's *ejido*'s commissioner announced that he was negotiating to have part of the *ejido* classified as a "nature preserve," a designation that would make it possible to access specific programs of the Ministry of the Environment. But he immediately clarified that his initiative might not succeed because of the *cercos*: "People have to stop fencing without permission [. . . because] the problem is that people use them for the [poppy] business." Associating *cercos* with poppy plantings let them be disqualified, thus fostering the illusion of two distinct groups existing in the assembly: the honest *ejido* citizen vs. the criminal *cerco* owners. Relegating the *cerco* to the role of obstacle to the activities of the *ejido* avoided discussing questions of effective ownership in the assembly. In *ejido* 4, assemblies also were not places where discussions flowed freely and where issues related to *cercos* or productive organization of the *ejidatarios* were dealt with. However, such discussions could take place on the sidelines of the meetings or after them. Thus, one of my interlocutors learned on returning from the meeting with another *ejidatario* that the latter was about to release his cattle next to the poorly maintained fence behind which he grew his "little plants."

Moreover, in the case of the main town's *ejido*, the fact that some of its active members also held administrative or political positions at the municipal and state levels was crucial for its ability to obtain outside funding. These dual positions were not disqualifying due to conflict of interest; indeed, these individuals usually were the most vocal in meetings. For example, Miguel Ángel prefaced his speech at an assembly with a reminder to the members present that he was coordinating two programs at the State Ministry of

Social Development (SEDESOL) where he held an important position. He stressed that he had obtained an extension of a deadline "especially for [them]" and urged them to apply quickly, concluding with: "Then I don't want to hear: 'Ahhh... Miguel Ángel, you were at SEDESOL and you forgot about us.' No, I want to be able to come back to this *ejido* whenever I can and always with my head held high." What he was doing was putting his political clout at the center of the *ejido*'s concerns and responding to the expectations of the ejidatarioship, despite these programs having nothing to do with the *ejido*. Miguel Ángel's was a common strategy; the main town's *ejido* appeared in this regard as one of the spaces where political careers were built. Together with the municipal and state governments, the breeders' association,[14] and PRI-linked associations, the main town's *ejido* was part of the local power games. It was one of the places where specific political networks consolidated around the chance of channeling and converting economic and electoral resources. Politicians excluded from this space because they were not *ejidatarios* for their part criticized "the policy of those *ejido* people." Involvement in the assembly by politicians who were also *ejidatarios* helped them consolidate their local electoral base, especially when, like Miguel Ángel, they had trouble being nominated for the municipal elections (see chapter 7).

Thus, a former ejidal commissioner in the lower sierra underlined the dynamics of *ejido* functioning on the local level in this way: "*Ejido* is actually a good thing, it's just that people are not trained to take advantage of it." On the one hand, being a member of an *ejido* sufficiently "trained" to attract a few subsidies and so generate additional income—even if it meant outsourcing—conferred status. Although assemblies did not function as debating societies, as most of those in attendance never rose to speak, they remained a space that some attended (and others did not) and where they were updated on procedures, obtained subsidies, or kept up their social contacts. On the other hand, the "trained" people in the main town's *ejido* built their local political careers, a logic of political instrumentalization that the Procede reform applied to the sierra *ejidos*. The potential benefits of the *ejido* were limited and they omitted—if they did not exclude outright—consideration of land access and agricultural organization problems.

Finally, as a statutory entity the *ejido* sporadically served as a local interlocutor for state and federal governments. A former commissioner of the main town's *ejido* told me: "We have not been able to valorize it, we only use it for the legal things." The *ejido* being legally "the true owner of the land," the assembly was supposed to play a key role in managing certain issues related to public works concessions: road construction, mining, electrical infrastructure, the establishment of military bases, the construction of schools, etc. In practice, with no actors from outside the municipality present, its authority was regularly bypassed. The issue of roads was highly revealing in this respect. In theory, planning and maintaining roads fell within the competence of the *ejido*, but in many cases the work was done by others. For example, as we saw in chapter 1, in hamlet N*, an armed group charged a 50-peso tax to anyone who used the roads running through its area. The tax was justified because the members of the group maintained the roads with a bulldozer owned by the local *pesado*. In this case, managing the roads remained outside the *ejido*'s purview, which left it without a reason for meeting. Conversely, in cases where a company or a state or federal government intervened in the work, the *ejido* did enter into the equation. The case of the municipality's main road, now called the "Badiraguato-Parral" road, perfectly illustrated the process. A section had been built by Rafael Caro Quintero (ignoring the *ejido*), but once the road was "repossessed by the government," lengthening it involved passage through the *ejido*'s concessions. The completion of certain roads had been a recurring promise of the various authorities, including municipal, state (Badiraguato-Surutato), and even federal in the case of the "Badiraguato-Parral," because it was an interstate road. Accordingly this issue mobilized the *ejidos*, which had to grant the right of way for the work to proceed.

In practice, therefore, the implication of the *ejido* depended less on its legal competency on a given topic than on the parties involved. Similar to the roads, the involvement of external actors, especially at the state level, created the ad hoc need of having the legal entity represented by the *ejido* act as an interlocutor. In this regard, the fact that almost the entire area was subject to the ejidal regime allowed for the production of legal formalities and therefore created, in an ad hoc way, the illusion of legibility for the state or federal levels.[15] When an organization needed a contact with recognized legal status for a matter concerning the municipality's mountainous territory, the *ejido* would do—in some cases this was even the only occasion for such interaction to exist. The dynamics of *ejido* creation, often involving initiatives from state levels, were partly driven by this need for ad hoc legibility.

These situations involved the institution in a special way. To fulfill the role of legal interface for which it was sporadically called on, the signatures of the *ejidatarios* reified the *ejido*. For example, when the Federal Electricity Company wanted to electrify a hamlet, it required the written consent of the *ejido*'s members for installing and connecting the power poles. Enrique, a notable figure in the area, managed to convene the assembly, at which, however, no negotiations were conducted. Those actually took place upstream because they involved Enrique, with his large address book of people who owed him favors. His success was concretized by the presence of the *ejidatarios*, who attended only to affix their signatures. This moved an older gentleman to exclaim: "Signatures! Signatures! Why do you want my signature while you always do what you want?"

Likewise, the dispute over land for the ore processing company reflected similar modalities of the *ejido*'s existence. As explained earlier, the company had been invited to the meeting of the main town's *ejido* on October 26, on which occasion the company's lawyer reminded the members of the *ejido* that they were not the "real owners" of their land. The conflict actually began outside the ejidal arena, between the two entrepreneurs, Entrepreneur A, to whom the federal agency sold the land previously loaned to it by the *ejido*, and Entrepreneur B from the nearby hamlet, who wanted to take over the land and the factory. The latter had the support of Miguel Ángel, who was not only a senior official in the state government, but also the chief string-puller as the *ejido*'s commissioner-elect. It was he who miraculously made the loan contract reappear, and it was this document that brought conflict between the two entrepreneurs into the *ejido*. The assembly of October 26 attracted far more *ejidatarios* than usual, and its proceedings made it possible to describe the issue as "an agrarian conflict" consequent to the *ejidatarios* voting for it after all the speeches. However, from then on, the assembly was sidelined: when an inspector from the agrarian administration arrived, the *ejidatarios* were left in the dark about it. Miguel Ángel admitted that negotiations had moved to the phone and informal discussions with the management of the agrarian administration. In the end, the commissioner simply informed the *ejidatarios* at subsequent meetings that the conflict was "ongoing." Paradoxically, while essentially entangled in external issues, the conflict's evolution into the ejidal realm made the *ejidatarios* part of an agrarian struggle. By claiming land that "belongs to the *ejido*," as elected representatives meeting in the assembly, they constituted a local authority that enforced and defended "social property," that is, what an *ejido* is supposed to be. Thus, while the ultimate objective of Miguel Ángel, Hector, and the *ejido* commissioner was to award the land to the second contractor, some *ejidatarios*, excluded from the behind-the-scenes negotiations, wanted to "fight for the land" in the hope of "recovering" it.

The life of the *ejido* as an institution thus painted a nuanced picture. Although detached from practical considerations related to access to land and respectful of the regulations imposed by the *cerco*, the *ejido* provided access to modest but predictable aid. And for those who mastered the legal arguments and could mobilize, bypass, and manipulate the *ejidatarios* in the assembly, it turned into a decisive political resource.

THE PROCEDE REFORM: GRABBING THE "COMMONS"

The reform of the Constitution's Article 27 in 1992 profoundly transformed the ejidal system, marking a break in the social pact between the PRI and the peasant sectors. During an economic liberalization drive led by President Carlos Salinas (1988–94), this reform declared an end to agrarian redistribution and treated the inalienable nature of land rights under the *ejido* system as a hindrance to the country's progress. It aimed to promote integrating the land into the logic of the market by promising access to bank loans, associating farmers with private companies, and democratizing ejidal assemblies.[16] Land reform did not completely destroy the *ejido* regime, but unraveled it. Its centerpiece was the Procede (*Programa de certificación de derechos ejidales*, the "ejidal rights certification program"), which consisted of issuing individual certificates. *Ejidatarios* were no longer just an assembly of people enjoying a given area of land on which they organized the commons portion and the individual holdings. With the Procede implementation came several formal options, some of which were particularly recommended by the administrators charged with carrying out the reform. Parceling out would make the members of the assembly individual holders of certificates indicating their respective plots. This was the most popular option, and the one the agrarian administration officers advocated in discussions with the *ejidatarios* unless they would agree to exiting the ejidal system entirely and becoming full owners of their land. In cases where they availed themselves of neither option, they had one other possibility—which the agents tried to discourage—of keeping the land as a common regime for use by all.[17]

The importance of the Procede reform was evident in the abovementioned dispute between Entrepreneurs A and B.

At the meeting on October 26, Entrepreneur A oriented his defense to the rights conferred by his Procede certificate and asked the assembly to correct it: it appeared to have been issued in 2001, at the meeting that marked the end of the Procede reform, but the first name entered on it was incorrect. Miguel Ángel objected to correcting the certificate, arguing, "If we decide to correct this gentleman's certificate here, then we will have to regularize all those who have fenced without permission. And clearly, we're not ready for that!" He and the others who pleaded for taking the conflict to the agrarian courts questioned the certificate's validity; on the street in town one of them explained to me that the first name was incorrect because "the friend is a bit of a mafiosi"; another said aloud at the meeting that the certificate was "crooked" (chueco); Miguel Ángel and Memo in private and then at the meeting of November 15 (in the absence of Entrepreneur A and most of the ejidatarios) assured everyone who would listen that they had not seen this person at the extraordinary meeting where the certificates had been distributed.

On November 15, during the visit by the agrarian inspector, he explained from the stage that he was "there to let the law be known" while tapping on the binder on the table before him. He recalled sternly that the purpose of the Procede was precisely to ensure legal certainty through certificates. He went on to explain that the certificates were particularly "strong," while the loan contract was "old." He added that Entrepreneur A would have no problem correcting his certificate without going through the meeting. In his view, it was legitimate to accept the amicable agreement that A proposed (which would have awarded part of the disputed land to the ejido). He concluded his speech by recalling the advantages of moving to full ownership, insisting that this possibility was always open and that the ejidatarios should think about it.

The certificate that Entrepreneur A brandished was one of those issued in 2001—at the end of the Procede reform application process in the main town. The reform was presented at the national level as a time for demonstrating "realism," for taking into account customary practices, and for updating the legal framework accordingly. One of the main arguments was to provide a legal certainty that was flawed in the previous system. In this sense, implementing the reform was opportune for opening possibilities[18] by potentially reconfiguring the relationship between *ejido* and *cerco*. The implementation of the reform and the choices made on that occasion thus shaped the current conditions of access to land.

To begin with, regularizing de facto possessions grappled with a key issue: expanding the number of *ejidatarios*. That was the specter Miguel Ángel raised to win their support: "If we decide to correct this gentleman's certificate here, then we will have to regularize all those who have fenced without permission. And clearly, we're not ready for that!" It was a misleading argument, because correcting the name on a certificate was different from reopening a process for regularizing *cercos*. However, it effectively reminded his audience of the increases in the number of potential grantees during the Procede reform—and thus the prospect of cuts in the individual shares of grant money. Such increases seemed to have occurred most often in the sierra *ejidos*, but they went unnoticed where there was no functioning *ejido*.[19] Inflating the number of *ejidatarios* reflected two forces at work: first, the often confidential nature of the first censuses during the initial formation of the *ejidos*, and second, the demographic shifts within the sierra based on migration from neighboring states (Chihuahua, Durango). Thus, in *ejido 4*, a large number of families from Chihuahua had settled in the hamlet. And in this *ejido*, Raimundo, the one who grabbed the *cerco* sold to the Ortiz family and who had lost count of how many *cercos* he possessed, who had presided over the *ejido* from day one, and who was pleased to have been its main intermediary with the municipal authorities for many years, now was unhappy with the reform: "The *ejido* was misinterpreted, [. . .] they brought in people who were not from here." It was not surprising that, in this *cacique*'s view, the opening up of the *ejido*, originally conceived as a way to "protect" his control over real estate, stemmed from a particularly damaging "misinterpretation."

Beyond increasing the number of *ejidatarios*, in practice, implementing the reform involved negotiations on how to go about it, the choices to be made, and their implications. In the main town as in the sierra, the reform initially met with resistance, suspected of being a "government strategy" designed to "take their land." Especially for the fictional *ejidos*, the reform led to a confrontation between the state and the *ejidatarios* over its terms: they appeared unclear to the latter, who already considered themselves to be landowners. Hence, they were suspicious of the motives of the agents from the agrarian administration.

Negotiations therefore involved a translation process.[20] In the main town, Miguel Ángel and, to a lesser extent, Memo, both *ejidatarios*, were the main contacts for the agents of the agrarian administration. It was due to their central role in the reform twelve years earlier that they could suggest that the certificate of Entrepreneur A was falsified: if he had obtained it in the normal process, they both would have known it. In the sierra, on the other hand, the implementation was not confined to face-to-face meetings between some *ejidatarios* and agrarian inspectors, but mobilized facilitators. Miguel Ángel and Gonzalo (the municipal executive who earlier had explained to me "the strength of the *cerco*") were among the intermediaries who guided the negotiations, interfacing between the agrarian administration and the sierra *ejidos*: before the arrival of the agents of the agrarian administration, they explained the reform, then introduced the agents to the *ejido* meeting. This approach put them into the sweet spot of the local, state, and federal political competitive dynamics. Miguel Ángel was an *ejidatario* in the main town but facilitated the reform's implementation in his capacity as a state official, and above all as a candidate for mayor. Gonzalo, who was not an *ejidatario*, was involved as a municipal executive and also as a candidate for mayor. It was therefore through their respective political affiliations and from the perspective of electoral competitions that they applied themselves to this reform task.

Both narrated this period as one of many ways of trying to "bring things to the people of the sierra." This particular mission was part of their relationships as intermediaries with certain residents of the municipality. They operated in hamlets where they maintained a political clientele, and their intermediation had encouraged the expansion of the number of *ejidatarios*. Thus, in a success of sorts, in one of the *ejidos* where I worked, Gonzalo was considered by several of my interlocutors as the one who "brought the *ejido*," the reform being regarded as the birth of the *ejido*. In another *ejido*, the nomination of Miguel Ángel as the PRI candidate was hoped for, since he "cares about us." Moreover, in the context of the negotiations they overcame local resistance, using a strategy that was replicated elsewhere. Faced with the reluctant *ejidatarios*, they presented the reform as opening the door to new agricultural subsidies. It was a game-changer in the negotiations, and with this inducement the *ejidatarios* fell into line. The process was all the more rewarding for the facilitators because, by paving the way for the inspectors and then shepherding the negotiation, they came to be regarded as the purveyors of the subsidies in question.[21]

Moreover, in addition to tending to their political clientele, Miguel Ángel and Gonzalo also positioned themselves as intermediaries vis-à-vis the state and federal authorities. The agrarian inspectors were under pressure from their superiors, and that made Miguel Ángel and Gonzalo ideal interlocutors for them. This directly benefited their political careers, determined from above through the PRI nomination (see chapter 7). Their strategy of instrumentalizing the reform thus exposed the *ejidal* spaces even more to the logics of competition between the party's state currents.

The decision adopted in Badiraguato, which reasserted the overlap between the *ejido* and the *cerco*, made it one of the exceptions in the application of the reform.[22] Of the municipality's thirty-six ejidos, only that in the main town and four in the lower part of the sierra were parcellated, and their *ejidatarios* indeed had their individual plots recognized. The rest went through the Procede process and implemented its reforms, but made the choice—a rare one, given the pressures—of the common regime. However, it would appear that this option was largely forced on them. Once the basics of the reform's implementation had been accepted, the choices offered (private property, parcellation, or commons) seemed to distill into a preference for recognizing the individual use grounded in the *cerco*. Parcellation appeared to be particularly interesting for people whose possessions depended more or less directly on being protected by a *pesado*. This dependence was compounded by the insecurity associated with the frequent deaths of *pesados*, which opened the threat of a challenge to their use. Thus, Gonzalo conceded that many *ejidatarios* had expressed the wish to have their *cercos* recognized.

However, parcellation equated to a land registry, which had profound implications for poppy growers. Holding a name certificate indicating each person's *cerco* exposed them to repression. Growers' protection strategies rested on not being caught red-handed on their plot, and land records would reduce this slim bit of maneuvering room, since merely locating a plot from the air would suffice to incriminate its owner. Whether or not they grew poppies, *ejidatarios* could not enjoy legal recognition of their uses without exposing the economy of all the inhabitants. To me, Gonzalo claimed he had taken these factors into account: "I told them, if you want to you can parcellate but ... everything will be locatable." It was with this negotiation of arrangements between institutional pressures and local interests that Gonzalo and Miguel Ángel added full value with their intermediation.

In the end, opting for the commons regime provided cover for violent land grabs. Institutionalizing the commons ended up endorsing and normalizing the demise of the shared uses. The legal system as an instrument of formal regularization promoted the two dynamics: the cooptation of the economic and political resources of the *ejido* by political entrepreneurs and the violent land grabs by *pesados* and other entrepreneurs of marginalization. In the context of a reform offering "regularization of de facto possessions" and "legal security," adopting the commons regime sealed the reproduction of these inequalities by anchoring the issues of access to land in local social relations and well out of the "theoretical" ambit of the agrarian court, in Gonzalo's words.

"HERE I AM RESPECTED, BUT NOTHING PROTECTS ME": THE OPPORTUNITIES IN UNCERTAINTY

In recent years, Jorge had fenced and bought several cercos. He showed me one he had just purchased. He answered my question about whether he bought it from an ejidatario with: "No, from someone who owned it, because the land belongs to him who works it, right?" Reviving that post-revolutionary slogan to explain that owning a piece of land, working it, and being an ejidatario were quite distinct things was replete with irony. He went on to explain that this land used to belong to a family that grew poppies on it. The son who handled the sale had been threatened with death if he did not get out of the area quickly. The family rushed to leave and sold their cerco at a fire-sale price to Jorge, who already owned many cercos.

In the ejido where his cercos were located, part of a road section was in the process of being negotiated, but it would pass through the ejido of which he was a member. The ejidatarios had already signed on the dotted line and granted the right of way. Jorge followed the evolution of the intended route and influenced it when he could so that it would pass through "[his] land." But then he clarified what he meant by "my land." "Well, it's mine, the people here respect that it is, but it's not really mine, nothing protects me (nadie me lo ampara)," he said, using a legal term.

Jorge wanted the road to pass through "[his] land" even though he would get no compensation through the ejido, which had already granted the concession based on the common regime. But what he was after would happen during the construction work. While the construction company may have gone through the ejidal institution, its employees would still have to stay in the sierra. He explained that he would make investments in his property (put up structures and raise food crops): builders who had to stay in the sierra roamed by armed men would not destroy a local's property without negotiating.

In Jorge's story, all the forces that structured the social relationships tied to access to land and to the *ejido* intertwined. First, land acquisitions mobilized all the intricacies of the *cerco*, its "strength." His social profile let him liberally fence in "free" land so he could then use it to the exclusion of anyone else. It was effectively his property because it was respected as such by "the people here": his reputation guaranteed the plots were his *cercos*. At the same time, the manner in which he acquired one of his *cercos* illustrated how violence ruled in getting access to land: the family of a small grower required protection by a powerful man to safeguard its ownership. The conflict over a sale signaled the end of this protection and the purchase at a modest price therefore appeared to be doing the seller a favor.

If Jorge distinguished between "the people here" respecting his *cercos* and the law not protecting them, it was because not only did he own the resources to make the *cerco* possible, but he was also "trained" to "profit" from the *ejido*. The story played out in an *ejido* that rarely convened unless it had concession issues to deal with, on which occasion it functioned as ad hoc resource. His position allowed Jorge to take advantage of the configuration created by the Procede commons, to keep on top of the concession from the *ejido* side, and to make himself indispensable thanks to the *cerco*.

Jorge's strategy was highly revealing of the texture of these social relationships around property and *ejido*. As instituted, the Procede common regime reinforced the dichotomy between the resources of the *ejido* and those of the *cerco*, which found a strong echo in the opportunities offered to an elite due to its usurping an instrument of agrarian distribution from the start. The institution of the commons coupled with the practice of the *cerco* set up a precarious situation for most of the inhabitants. Like the family dispossessed by threat, one of my interlocutors found himself in a highly vulnerable state following the assassination of the *pesado* who had protected him, not only in selling his crop but in holding on to his property. Particularly in cases like these, being cut off from institutional remedies enshrined in the common regime increased the insecurity of the domestic economies. However, it was in this context marked by uncertainty that Jorge's moves took on their full meaning and measure: he invested! This same configuration around the subtle articulation between *ejido* theory and *cerco* practice gave him, a man of power, enough predictability so he could invest. The constraints on the mass of inhabitants thus became opportunities handed to a few.

• • •

These dynamics highlight the need to think about *cerco* and *ejido* together, despite being seemingly distinct modes of regulation. As we have seen, the enclosure of "free" areas was linked to the modes of implementing land reforms. Similarly, the functioning of the *ejido* was embedded in the social relations surrounding the *cercos* that the *ejido* had to constantly extract from its assembly. Both truly formed a single configuration. Thus, if the *cerco* well materialized many local norms distinct from those of *ejido* administration, considering their presence alongside the state agrarian law as a situation of normative pluralism seems to miss the essence of this configuration. The practical regulation to which the inhabitants were subjected is that of the—violent and predatory—*cercos* in their linkage with the institutional common. I agree here with Boaventura de Sousa Santos's criticism of "the romantic biases of many of the reflections in terms of legal pluralism."[23] The *ejido* does not comprise a parallel offer of norms with which residents could practice "forum shopping" in negotiating their access to land.[24] On the contrary, what the *ejido* does in practical regulation is to exclude access to other remedies. It is not juxtaposed to the norms of the fence. By encompassing enclosure and land-grabbing within the legal concept of the commons, it constitutes a central element in the reproduction of the violent and predatory regulation of the *cerco*.

FIVE

Stealing a Woman

"Well yes, but you can't feed soup to one and refuse it to the other."

TEÓFILO

ADRIANA LIVED IN A ROOM next to mine, which she rented with her brother Ismael. Like she did every night, she was working at the restaurant outside Badiraguato when six men entered, carrying automatic rifles. They forced her into a pickup truck and drove away. She was beaten and raped twice by the person holding her, who then temporarily let her go. Her abductor ordered her to get her belongings: whether she liked it or not, she would come and live with him. When Ismael entered their room, he found his sister, crying, lying on the floor. She managed to explain to him that her abductor would be back, and so he helped her get away to a family in the town who were friends of their father. They hid Adriana until her father came down from the sierra to pick her up. Hidden under a blanket in her father's pickup truck, she was taken from the town just ahead of her abductor and the other armed men looking for her.

All this I learned from Ismael when I returned to Badiraguato: "They stole her (se la robaron)." I had been in Culiacán when the abduction happened, and Adriana had been hustled away the day before I returned. Standing outside our rooms, Ismael told me that the night before, the man had come armed and aggressive to this very spot looking for Adriana. As Ismael gave voice to his anger and worries about what lay ahead, another neighbor, Imelda, joined us. She told me that she also saw the kidnapper looking for our neighbor and how the thought of him coming back terrified her. After Imelda left, Ismael confided to me that he had asked Imelda for help in hiding Adriana the day before, but that Imelda was too scared and refused. Like the other neighbors, Ismael knew that Armando, Adriana's abductor, worked for a pistolero close to one of the most important families in town. Armando already had a wife, which only stoked Ismael's anger, which he gave vent to repeatedly as we spoke. He pictured himself confronting Armando, but everyone warned him not to. When I asked him if his sister was safe in his father's hamlet, he answered "yes," because Armando's men "can't go in there." He added that, in any event, reprisals by his father and the men in his hamlet could not be ruled out.

Ismael then explained to me what he thought motivated the abduction: at the village's founding celebration, two days before the abduction, Armando had spotted Adriana and sent Ivan, another of our neighbors, to ask her for her phone number. Ismael was with her at the time and said that his sister politely refused, saying that she was engaged to someone who commuted between Badiraguato and the state of Chihuahua. So, end of story. But two other neighbors, also sisters, were at the celebration and knew all of the parties involved. According to Ismael, the day after, one of them visited Adriana in her room and caught her there with a man. According to Ismael, she tattled to Ivan: "Tell Armando that if Adriana is not interested in him, it doesn't mean that it applies to others."

These were the conditions for Adriana's abduction as provided by Ismael and the neighbor. Indeed, when Teófilo returned that evening to the rooms, he seconded their story. But he summed it up with, "Well yes, but as I told you, you can't feed soup to one and refuse it to the other!," before adding that this was not the first time Adriana had gotten herself into this kind of trouble. He recalled another episode in which an armed suitor had made a scene outside Adriana's room. He said that he had personally ejected the man from the courtyard, fearing that it might turn out wrong for Adriana, whom he liked a great deal. But he insisted that in fact "it's her fault," and that there was nothing to be done. Moreover, he, Teófilo, was not sure about the likelihood of the father's revenge as predicted by Ismael; according to him, the father "is not heavy enough."

A few months later, Adriana was still living in her father's hamlet. Rumor had it that she married an associate of her father's, and that she might be returning to the town. After I had returned from a stay in France, I moved to another part of Badiraguato. One day, I visited Imelda and asked her about Adriana—whom I never laid eyes on again. Imelda told me: "Oh yes, supposedly she was abducted." I was deeply surprised because we had followed the events together and had shared our fears for her: "Supposedly?" Imelda explained to me that she too had worried, but then she learned that Adriana "had already spent time with him (Ya había tratado con él) . . . and it's not the same if a guy becomes infatuated with a chick without ever having spent time with her. That is different. As for Adriana, it's as if she had been his girlfriend, something like that. He kidnapped her, sure, but hey, it's not like they never spent time together."

In the immediate vicinity, the hours and days following Adriana's flight were marked by the processes that I had observed in the wake of all the acts of violence that took place in the town. The act itself was framed in a narrative with precedents and sequences that gave it meaning. These efforts to make sense of events confronted two problems posed by a new act of violence: first, it might be followed by others and, second, it reminded everyone of the insecurity that hung over their heads. In this way, at the same time as they contrived a narrative or interpretation, the commenters simultaneously anticipated the sequel and warded off the sense of vulnerability instilled by violence. Everyone's characterization of Adriana's abduction derived from their assessments of the likelihood of reprisals by her father; and Imelda's proposed recharacterization took place after the outcome of the conflict was known. These dynamics were also present in how homicides were apprehended, and I return to those in the next chapter. Here, I am interested in the justifications and argumentative logics that the neighbors marshaled to make sense of what Adriana had gone through.

That this armed abduction followed by a rape became transformed into a couple's quarrel appears to be a particularly brutal and lurid version of the "continuum of sexual violence." Liz Kelly developed this concept in the 1980s to emphasize linkages between various forms of violence, from sexual harassment to assault to domestic violence.[1] In line with feminist works of the time,[2] Kelly rejects the distinction between private and public, letting her conceptualize gender relationships and the system of domination that encompasses them through these different forms of violence. The concept of a continuum of violence is an analytical and theoretical device for bringing seemingly distinct phenomena closer together, the better to reveal the mechanisms they have in common. The successive situations around Adriana's rape collectively bring into play, in a single located configuration, all the phenomena captured by the continuum. Indeed, in this instance, the continuum manifested itself as a social practice: Adriana's rape and abduction gradually came to be described by the neighbors as a private quarrel.

Shocking and brutal as it may seem, in Badiraguato, this practice of recharacterizing violent events was not the exception. It fitted into a context in which the same category—"stealing a woman" (*robo de mujer/muchacha*)—was used to talk about situations that ranged from armed abductions to marriages portrayed as consensual. The gender relations[3] exposed by Adriana's abduction and rape were entangled in the relations of production and domination.[4] In a feminist materialist approach, and inspired by the work of

Nicole-Claude Mathieu in particular,[5] I examine how my male and female interlocutors made sense of these relationships, while reflecting on the issues and constraints, in which they—the women above all—were caught.

"IF A GUY LIKES YOU, DON'T THINK HE'S GOING TO ASK YOU FOR PERMISSION": THE CONTINUUM OF ABDUCTION AND RAPE

"Woman stealing," the expression alluded to by Ismael and Imelda, repeatedly surfaced in the external discourses on the municipality and those of the residents of the main town on the sierra. When speaking of Badiraguato in Culiacán, the state capital, I regularly heard that "over there, they steal women." This was sometime supported by a specific case: "I have a friend who is from Badiraguato, but she lives here because, when she was fifteen, her father made her leave to keep her from being stolen." However, to grasp what is playing out in "woman stealing" or "girl stealing" requires examining the diversity of situations captured in the expression *robo de mujer/muchacha*. Unambiguously, what happened to Adriana—kidnapped by six armed men, raped twice, and then told to go live with her abductor—is woman stealing. However, "runaway lovers" (*fuga de novios*), meaning an action purportedly undertaken jointly by a man and woman, may also be lumped in with this category. In this regard, Imelda's proposed recharacterization is interesting, because reading the situation as a couple's quarrel does not disqualify it as "woman stealing."

"Woman stealing," because of the variety of situations to which the term can refer, actually describes a continuum. As such, this radical scenario hides others and thus conceals a more structuring dimension in gender relationships that are shadowed by the threat of armed violence. To begin with, violent kidnappings are common occurrences, as my interlocutors testified. Zeica, a thirty-year-old working as a cashier in the main town, was abducted when she was seventeen. The man forced her to go to Mexico City where she knew no one, and from where, pregnant, she managed to escape. In opening up to me about it, she observed: "You know, that's how it is in the sierra; if a guy likes you, don't think he's going to ask you for permission." Here "stealing" implies rape. But retrospective comments on abductions often obliterated the issue of consent at the moment the act transpired.[6] Thus, Laura was stolen by an important *pistolero*. The term is apt and she used it, but having spent several years with him, the stealing aspects seemed to have dimmed.

The man, who also had a wife in Culiacán, took Laura with him wherever he went, and she spoke sorrowfully of the day he was killed, leaving her alone with their son. Her sister had also been stolen and was still married to the man who had abducted her.

Other stories of stealing seemed to involve different dynamics. When Rogelio stole Yaheli, he told me that he "was civilized about it." He said that they were already seeing each other, that he already knew her parents and, especially, that she was in on it. She knew what was going to happen. But to respect tradition, he told me, you have to go with one or two friends. The three of them entered the house armed to pick her up. Yaheli's mother still talked about it with a laugh and got along very well with her son-in-law. As for Tamara, she told me about her union with Lamberto, saying that she had noticed him when he went through her village once or twice a year, and that she had her eye on him until the day he "finally" came to "steal" her. Her sister-in-law, Leandra, worked it out with her abductor that she would be stolen on the road, but for her father and brothers it came as a shock. In an interview, Gerardo told me that the first time he sowed poppies, he harvested a kilo of gum that would let him "take off with the woman," speaking of Leandra, who was there with us. The ambiguity of the terms of the unions that I had recorded during several months of inquiry at that point caused me to make a faux pas in asking him "did you pay for her (*la pagó*)?" Gerardo stiffened and I corrected myself: "Uh . . . I mean . . . You asked for her hand in marriage (*la pidió*)?" He said, "No! Are you kidding, I stole her (*No! Como crees, me la robé*)!" Leandra, next to us, laughed. Both my slip-up and my correction missed the mark: it was the stealing that made the union.

One of the subtexts of "girl stealing" referenced the taking of a girl from her family. But in the relationships that are built around this practice, in the way the men and women who lived together mobilize the term, "stealing" seemed to register in two additional ways: on the one hand, as an old-fashioned way of speaking, tinged with a local romanticism, a manifestation of staging and narratives of violent masculinities and, on the other hand, as an eminently cultural practice, an imaginary that is obvious in the popular expression "marriage according to the three laws: that of the state, that of God, and that of the mountain." The last term here was a reference to the theft. It would therefore involve theater and narratives that would simply reflect local ways of being joined together.

However, the difficulty lies in differentiating cases of violent abduction from those reflecting ritualized forms of marital commitment. An account by

Horacio, the school principal in a sierra hamlet, testified to this. Originally from the state of Zacatecas, he had settled here as a physician's assistant some thirty years ago, then opened his own middle school that was later accredited by the state government. In our interview, he discoursed in learned fashion, adopting a distancing tone toward the "local culture" and seemingly eager to let me know that while he lived there, he "never mixed." He also had this to say about "woman stealing": "You know, here girls and boys have spent time together (*se tratan*) since kindergarten, and it's in school that couples grow close. They say they steal them, but it is a way of speaking; in reality both are consenting.... It's really about saving the expense of a wedding. They take the girls (*se las llevan*) to another hamlet for a few days and, when they return, the parents can only acquiesce. That's how people do it here, but both are in on it."

Horacio was the only one of my interlocutors to point out that "stealing" raised the question of consent, only to conclude—significantly—that consent was always involved. In his remarks, however, the subject of the action appeared clearly: "They take the girls" (*se las llevan*). Later in the interview, he told me, "Before, they would steal them by force, sure.... Well, now it is in school that you have to watch out. We see them and keep an eye on them. Boys often stop school before girls do, and when they stand there outside the gate looking at girls, you have to be on guard." The past and the present merged as he talked; one minute Horacio developed a scholarly discourse on "local culture," the next he discussed his specific practice as a school principal. In the former, school was the setting where couples might bond, in a community where people have been around each other since kindergarten, which would involve peaceable relationships and, despite the term "stealing," would imply consent. For the latter, school was a time for being on guard to keep young men—looking at young girls in the schoolyard—from abducting them after classes let out.

The case of Teófilo is particularly instructive for the continuum ranging from violent abduction, to "spending time with each other" (*tratarse*), and even to marriage. Indeed, he confessed to me that he had stolen a woman in his youth (which he referred to unfailingly with the formula "when I was handsome, slim, and dapper"), introducing the story in these words: they "were already seeing each other" (*ya nos tratábamos*) for some time. Then along came Joaquín, who lived in the United States and came home for the holidays, tinged with the aura of one who henceforth would move on to other spheres. One night, the girl agreed to dance with Joaquín. "In a fit of anger," Teófilo decided to take the girl by force: he dragged her off by the hair and took her on a mule into the mountains all night. He said that was all, and then he brought her back. He agreed that it was "not very nice" on his part. But he added that the girl's father eventually saw the humor in it and that her brother still does. The father jokingly called him "my son-in-law" and even told him that he had been in the right to do it. The social texture of "stealing" here is on full display: as a moment of gender relations crystallizing, caught up in the competition between men over appropriating a specific category of people: single women.

"BEING ALONE" (*ANDAR SOLA*): A VULNERABILITY BLAMED ON INDIVIDUAL BEHAVIORS

As we have seen, the commentaries on Adriana's abduction fit the act into a series of other actions that would explain it, that is, attribute causes to it. Confronting Armando's interest, Adriana replied that she was already in a relationship with a man—although effectively in absentia. Through a combination of circumstances and the malevolence of jealous neighbor women, Armando learned that she was nevertheless seeing another man in the village. The intervention is crucial here: the story is framed to suggest that, had it not been for this episode, Adriana would not have exposed herself to being kidnapped, raped, and carried off. Teófilo's maxim, "Well yes, but as I told you, you can't feed soup to one and refuse it to the other!," as terse as it is explicit, merely distilled the moral subtext that the other accounts mobilized to explain the rape: Adriana's promiscuous ways were the key issue, and because she transgressed social norms, she suffered the consequences. This logic obscured the fact that the stealing continuum was not about behavior, it was about condition: Adriana was above all a single woman. If the question of consent did enter into categorizing the "stealing," it was because it was inconsequential from the moment that a person belonged to the particular social group of women who did not belong to a man other than their father.

"Stealing" appeared again and again along with "spending time with each other" (*tratarse*). Adriana could not complain because she had previously spent time with Armando. The girls in middle school were necessarily consenting and stealing was only a "way of speaking," according to Horacio, since girls and boys had been "spending time together" since kindergarten. Teófilo was within his rights as he was spending time with a girl who started dancing with another man. "Spending time with each other" meant becoming the object of a man's attention as a single woman.[7] In this sense, the insistence on having spent time together concealed that the real issue at stake was precisely that of not belonging to a man outside her family. Thus Rosa, my neighbor, in trying to get me to understand that as a single woman my spending time with Teófilo made me the subject of gossip, told me: "It's that here people, as soon as they see that a woman is alone (*anda sola*), they talk a lot." She explained that after her husband's murder eighteen years earlier, she was alone for seven years. "It was unbearable, people were gossiping, they were saying I was with so-and-so, and then with so-and-so." Now, she and Joaquín (the fellow who long ago danced with Teófilo's acquaintance), were a couple. The gossip endangered her by the same logic as in Teófilo's saying. Once gossip attributed relationships to her, her preferences and choices no longer mattered. But, as she pointed out, these comments arose solely from the fact that she "was alone."

Moreover, the threats weighing on a single woman do not always involve gossip. Another neighbor, Maria del Carmen, in telling me the story of Teófilo's female cousin, who was shot dead by the man who "courted" her, drove home the point—exceptionally—about men's behavior, saying that "they get carried away" (*se vuelan*). But her story, which she returned to several times, was intended for me in a specific context: to warn me and urge me not to hang out with Teófilo—in short, to watch my behavior as a single woman. "Spending time together" and "stealing" went hand in hand because being a single woman meant being caught up in gender relationships marked by men's predation—and regardless of their behavior, what mattered was their condition of being single women. In this sense, "spending time together" was the modality by which a man tried to grant himself exclusivity over a woman who, because she was alone, was exposed to the predation of others. Such a situation could only be concluded, in one way or another, by stealing—at any given stage of the continuum.

This vulnerability was particularly rife among young girls, whose sociality was stamped by a profound uncertainty. Entry into this condition of being exposed to threat corresponded with turning fifteen years old, which was celebrated in a particularly big way with the quinceañera.[8] Parents dealt with fears about their sociability in a number of ways. For example, Lamberto and Tamara planned to send their daughter Patricia to the coastal plain. Avoiding stealing and earning a living went hand in hand: an abducted girl would not have access to "a better future than her father," a prospect which Lamberto and Tamara wished for their children (chapter 3). The resolve to see Patricia move to the city was part of an intrafamilial agreement with Lamberto's brother and sister-in-law, who lived in Culiacán and had a daughter, Maria, one year older than Patricia. The two families agreed that Maria, then twelve, would move in with her uncle and, once school was finished, Patricia would move in with her cousin Maria and her parents. This mutual aid arrangement for the two families allowed them to share the costs and support each other materially, Maria's parents coming up to the sierra every two months with supplies. It also let Lamberto and Tamara budget for and negotiate Patricia's departure for the plain at the end of high school. The terms of the agreement made particularly visible two key dimensions of these types of protection strategies. On the one hand, they showed the difficulties of knowing just when the threat of stealing became imminent. On the other hand, while the protection against stealing and the opening of future prospects for Patricia were entwined in the parents' reasons for acting (the way the agreement was set up incidentally allowing the first reason to be submerged, for a time), hosting their niece Maria as part of this arrangement would bring the threat of theft to the fore.

For Maria's parents, the decision was explained by Maria's "loose" character, her academic difficulties, and the bad influences she would have been exposed to in the city. Shipping Maria to her relatives in the sierra when she was twelve was therefore justified as a teaching experience: she would learn from the precarious material conditions of the hamlets and also be under the close social control of the hamlet of origin. As it happened, Maria was quite happy with her stay there. She said that in Culiacán her mother was very strict with her, that all her brothers and sisters were out of the house, that she was sad and lonely. She said she enjoyed living with Lamberto and Tamara's large family, where she felt surrounded and could look after her little cousins. She was well integrated into the school, had made many friends in two years, and had improved her grades.

The agreement seemed then to be going well, especially since Patricia was a particularly diligent student, very interested in studying and with a dream of going to the university. But by the time I met the family, the two cousins were fourteen and fifteen years old and were in their last year of high school. Maria's parents had gradually become particularly anxious and were constantly threatening to bring her back home before the end of school year, which could jeopardize the agreement that would allow Patricia to move. The explicit fear was that Maria would be stolen, although this was also framed as the risk of her being "seduced." For the past year, Maria's mother's relationship with Tamara had become complicated. The former put the responsibility for what might happen to her daughter on Tamara's shoulders, urging her to make sure that Maria had no involvements before she finished school. This situation also caused stress for Tamara. She faulted her sister-in-law for being too hard on her, but also worried because the risk of stealing was indeed quite real. She complained to me of her powerlessness, lamenting the burden it created for her: "How does she want me to do it? She has to go to school, her daughter." She escalated the precautions she took, forbidding the two cousins from going out, especially to dances; ordering them to come straight home from school; and lecturing them beforehand.

The agreement as worded effectively euphemized the threat of being stolen: it was above all to be about access to studies on the one hand and the effort to instill tighter discipline on the other. But the ambiguity of the benchmarks for when the threat would become pressing (the quinceañera or graduation) foregrounded as a daily concern the vulnerability of the girls while in Lamberto and Tamara's care.

In the room where I slept with Patricia and Maria, this issue haunted much of their nocturnal discussions.

"Some receive visits."

"There are several who have left."

"There's a girl in my class, they say she's been raped, but I don't know. . . . She doesn't look unhappy."

In the darkness, over the course of several discussions, they worried about the blurring of the line between a young man's "visits" to the house and stealing or rape, and about their powerlessness to define a threshold which, in reality, depended on the goodwill of men.

The threat of stealing was a constant concern for teachers, as it was for the middle school principal mentioned above. For example, in my fieldwork at a school in another hamlet, the female teachers expressly asked me to "set an example" by talking to the girls about my studies. Teachers reproached them for being "easily swayed" and accused them of "letting themselves be seduced." After some time in the hamlet, I realized that they were agitated over the recent abduction of two young girls from their school. The teachers saw stealing as a problem, but their action (asking me to "set an example" for young girls) still framed the problem as one of the girls' behavior: that is, that they were showing themselves to be available.

Dances escalated these tensions in gender relations. Many families refused to let their daughters attend or forbade them to dance with anyone. As it happens, at the one dance that I went to, I was caught up in a situation that illustrated the constraints that existed on a woman's room for maneuver. It was prom night at a school where I had spent three weeks in 2014 and then again in 2015 and where I consequently knew several students. It was a family atmosphere, with some teachers, students, and a few other young people from a nearby hamlet also in attendance. Some of the young men were armed and let the pistol grips protrude from their belts. Several couples were dancing, and chairs were arranged in a semicircle against the walls of the room, most of them occupied by young women—me included. Several times, I was asked if I was going to dance and I said no, that I would think it over. But, at one point, a high school student who had attended my French workshops and whom I therefore knew well invited me to dance. So, I accepted; we danced, I thanked him and sat down again. A little later, another young man I didn't know planted himself in front of my chair and asked me to dance. Not really keen on dancing with an armed man, I gave him a thin smile and was about to decline, when my female neighbors and the female professor rushed over to me, amused by my faux pas, but nevertheless dead serious: I couldn't dance with one only to turn down another—"you can't feed soup to one. . . ."

In a municipality where many young men die violently, marriage only temporarily exempts women from the condition of being single. In this environment, stealing does not refer exclusively to the taking of a young girl from her parents' house. Many women in the main town were widowed at a noticeably young age. The majority of my interlocutors found themselves in this situation and, more generally, "my husband was killed" was one of the phrases I heard repeatedly in Badiraguato. Elena was widowed, with two children, when she was twenty, Laura at age nineteen, and Vera as an eighteen-year-old. Others were widowed later in life, but the remarkably high mortality of young men made widowhood a widespread condition. Yolanda, who lost her first husband at the age of eighteen, remarried in the main town. Her second husband beat her, then left without a word. From that day on, she vowed never to enter into a relationship again. She knew that so many women shared her situation that, in her words, they constituted a real social subgroup: "Those who are widows." "I see them all, those who are widows and who run around; nooo, I take care of my children, that's all." Yolanda no longer wanted to be one of the widows who "ran around," went with men, and set themselves up again for being stolen, if not raped. This forty-eight-year-old single woman's disparagement of others' behavior highlighted the existence of this social group with which she did not want to be identified.

"Being a widow" meant being placed in the same position of vulnerability as a young single woman. Rosa suffered under gossip in her widowhood until she took up with Joaquín. The age difference of some couples and the predation of older men on young women was striking in this respect: young men died and their wives were left alone, at the mercy of those who remained.

The most intractable problems I encountered during my investigation were dominated by this condition of my being a young woman alone. Very quickly, I pretended to be married.[9] I had understood right away that having a beer was beyond the horizon of my possibilities, because it meant hanging out with men and therefore giving the impression that I was available. However, more than any other suspicion (DEA officer or informant, Interpol or Mexican government), it was extricating myself from the social category of prey that would cause me the most problems. I was not at risk of armed abduction, probably protected from it by my nationality. Nevertheless, a digression through my experience during my fieldwork is revealing: for if, when it came to the experiences of social and material uncertainty and the protection issues experienced by my interlocutors, the ethnography gave me only partial and mediated access, I was somewhat less spared by the reality of gender relations. I experienced in daily interactions the manifestation of common gender relationships—a dimension that it would have been difficult to draw from the discourses of my interlocutors, so much were they normalized—and marked by a predation dependent exclusively on this condition of being a young woman alone.[10]

When Diana and I visited the town on my first "incursion" (chapter 1), we asked Santiago to recommend a place where we could eat before hitting the road again. He pointed us to a comida corrida[11] *where we then stopped in. Next to us, a man in his fifties gave us the third degree (who we were, what we were doing there, and so on). In a balancing act (we were not on familiar enough ground to have the luxury of telling him to take a hike), we avoided most questions, but we let slip that I might be coming back. As soon as I returned, I had the displeasure of crossing paths with him many times, and my sense of fear grew as I ran into him everywhere. He went so far as to follow me, driving his car at my walking pace, offering to take me wherever I had to go. I ended up being ruder by refusing interactions with him and my bad luck seemed beyond doubt when I saw him wearing a municipal police uniform. In the meantime, I'd met Teófilo. In the first days after becoming neighbors, he took me around to discover places of* interest that he selected: the taco eateries by the road, the cemetery, the place where "the plane of death" crashed,[12] all places that had us walking together through town. Systematically badgered ("Hey, Teófilo, did you wake up warm this morning?" "Wow! Look at the old man!" "Hey Teófilo, where did you find her?" "Hey, did you wake up married?"), Teófilo did two things: he presented me as an anthropologist "reading the stones" (here exploiting the confusion with archaeology and referring to petroglyphs),[13] and he maintained the innuendos by exaggerating the air of one who struts with his conquest. My attempts at denial remained unheard and the first of many quarrels with Teófilo did not change anything.

On these walks, we ran into my municipal policeman a couple of times. He eventually would greet me from afar, but he no longer accosted me—I'm guessing that Teófilo's reputation had something to do with him keeping his distance. The next time, when I was alone and came across him in the square, he approached me with a bad mien: "And so where is he, your papi"—papi being a diminutive for papa, but which he was using in a suggestive way to mean "your man." Another time, he'd say, "He left you, your papi?" Little by little, during my subsequent meetings in the town, it dawned on me that for many people I was the protégé of Teófilo, a highly respected character—and even so I failed (as yet) to understand if, and if so how, people thought that I was indeed the lover of someone whose advanced age was plain as day.

A few weeks later, I was negotiating my participant observation in the town hall. The officials I met with knew that I lived in the "chambers" and all tried to get me to move, telling me that this was no place to live. The mayor told me to find a "decent place," the secretary of the town hall offered to rent me a room at his house, and another senior executive, Jesús Alberto, told me several times that he would find me another place where I would be settled comfortably "in the homes of good people." Teófilo rarely came to the town hall, and when he did the executives ribbed him. In short, this part of the fieldwork inserted me into a more affluent social environment, the town hall officials belonging to the local elite.

The first time I was allowed to attend a meeting involving several municipal services, Jesús Alberto came to me and told me that there was something he absolutely had to show me, which was "both very important for your study and on which the town hall may need your opinion." I did not feel at ease with him, so I tried to get out of it, but then ended up accepting the offer anyway. When he picked me up in his car, I was so on guard that I had a knife in my pocket, trying to convince myself that if he jumped on me in the car, I could defend myself. On *the way, very quickly he told me that I was "confiada": "I am surprised that you accepted . . . a young girl . . . alone, like that . . . But you did well, I see you as my own daughter." I swallowed my disgust and discovered what he wanted to show me: a petroglyph!*

In the months that followed, the mayor kept telling me that he "wants to marry me," that "I have to get married," that "we are going to find you a husband." The other executives persisted in wanting to kiss me every time I saw them (which was not customary) and some crossed the line by touching my mouth, until I made an angry gesture. So, I avoided the mayor, the executives, and the kisses. Once I was settled in among the employees of the Department of Family Affairs, this situation changed. In relations with the staff members, who came from a much more modest background, the social distance with "the French woman" overrode the gender relationship. In addition, Teófilo was "better known than the common bean" (como el frijol común) in this environment and persisted in "coming to see [me] at work." He insisted on visiting me during office hours, until I had to chase him away publicly—which only fueled the gossip about our relationship, especially since little by little a routine took hold where I made lunch for him every day, the fact of which he repeated to anyone willing to listen. In addition, I would help load cardboard boxes for distribution outlets in the sierra, which transgressed gender norms. From that moment on, the many trips to the sierra, in the cab of the truck where I was the only woman in the company of several men, turned into moments of camaraderie and none of the staff gave me any problems.

A few months later, I encountered the brutality of gender relations in the daily life of the "chambers." I was trying to set up a recorded interview with Joaquín (who fifty years earlier had danced with the young woman that Teófilo had "spent time with"). Joaquín was always very friendly, I knew his children very well, and we often chatted in his grocery store, which was right in front of the "chambers." We had been talking about doing an interview for several months. I had explained to him on one occasion that it would take conditions a little quieter than the grocery store, where people came and went all the time.

When the appointed day came, I was going to join him at his house, but he picked me up in his car, telling me that it was an opportune time for him to show me his cerco *that I had asked him about several times. When we got there, he opened the back of his van and, proudly pointing to a cooler full of beers, he said: "I prepared us a picnic." The vague feeling that I had been repressing since we had left now was confirmed: I had foolishly fallen into a setup. I refused the beers and*

I conducted the interview in a shack at the top of a hill while keeping my distance. So far so good, but when the interview came to an end, I had to insist that he take me back to the main town. Finally, I exploded in anger when he asked me to "at least kiss me." On the way back, I did my best to smooth things over, not allowing myself to part on too hostile a note. The next day, I forced myself to stop by his grocery store to test the waters, just in time to be caught in an argument between him and his partner, Rosa. When she saw me, in a fury she called me a "shameless man stealer."

This episode opened the most complicated period of my fieldwork. I felt guilty for letting myself be trapped, and Rosa would stay mad at me until I left eight months later. My attempts to mend our relationship came to nothing, and when I tried to talk about it with others, they told me that I should not have gone to the *cerco* and that I had better avoid Rosa from now on, because the men in her family were "killers" (*matones*). That the only conflict in which I was personally caught in the main town stemmed from my status as a single woman is significant. Although I exploited the few solutions available—pretending to belong to someone, transgressing gender norms where possible—this threat did not let up throughout my time there.[14]

The manner in which predation dynamics exerted a hold over women contributed to blaming this all too common condition on individual conduct. The formulations focused on behavior and obliterated the fact that this experience was primarily specific to the status of a woman who did not belong to a man. However, these innuendos, far from being the preserve only of men, constituted an important element even in how women related to each other.[15] Thus, Imelda's inclination to reclassify Adriana's rape in hindsight hinged on a condemnation of the victim's behavior. As a married woman, she felt swindled ("supposedly") when the violence done to Adriana heightened her own sense of vulnerability at the prospect of Armando's revenging himself in her yard. She was afraid, yes, but "it's not the same thing. . . . It's as if she'd been his girlfriend, something like that." Similarly, Yolanda's critiquing of the widowed women's behavior must be viewed from the perspective of her repeated experience as a woman alone running the risk of rape.

This vulnerability could not be warded off by formulating and apprehending it as a condition bereft of any notion of being able to do something about the uncertainty. The predation women endured was made of singular experiences, yet the latter all shared a naturalization of their vulnerable condition.

Zeica's formulation made this dimension obvious: "That's how it is in the sierra; if a guy likes you, don't think he's going to ask you for permission." Nevertheless, violence did not drive out desire and love. Thus, the young girls' doubts about whether or not their raped schoolmate was "unhappy" touched on the ambiguity of the situation they faced. Happy to have recently celebrated their debut as young women, their questioning highlighted the difficulty of dealing with this threat of violence in their dreams of being the object of attention and being in love. It highlighted the extent to which affects were caught in the vise grip of the economics of gender predation.

SINGLE WOMEN: THE STAKES IN A VIOLENT COMPETITION AMONG MEN

Following Adriana's abduction, the owners of the restaurant where she worked were at a loss as to what to do. They warned her brother Ismael but, since Armando worked for an important *pistolero*, Ismael, his family's friends, and Teófilo had their hands tied. Ismael, as if to compensate for his powerlessness and anger, fantasized to me about confronting Armando. But some friends—Teófilo among them—urged him to refrain. When Adriana managed to escape, they hid her until her father fetched her home to her native hamlet. Her father owned several *cercos*, regularly hired workers for the poppy harvest, bought the crops of neighboring families, and kept armed men. He therefore had everything necessary to be a *pesado*, and that is how he was considered by some. But, according to my interlocutors in the main town, he was a smalltime local *pesado* who lacked political and economic connections on the coastal plain. They suggested that he did not organize transport of his processed opium to the plain, which a better-connected network handled. Teófilo added that Ismael's being gay did not help his father's affairs. Adriana was therefore safe from Armando's men in her native hamlet; according to Ismael, "they can't come in there." Still, despite Ismael's predictions to me of possible reprisals by their father's men, Adriana merely stayed several months in her hamlet, eventually returning to the main town, but only after marrying one of her father's associates.

Adriana's abduction, Armando's "infatuation," Adriana's rape, the "protection" she received, its terms and limits—all were part of violent competition among the men. In this game, Adriana had little room for maneuver. When Armando asked her out, she tried to invent a protector by claiming to be in a relationship with a man who shuttled between Badiraguato and Chihuahua state. The subtext of her answer, mentioning these areas, was that this fictional fiancé was an important man in the production and trafficking of drugs. She displayed a keen knowledge of her position in these relationships and of the underlying logics: not only did she depend dramatically on a man's protection, but the efficacy of this protection was a function of the cards the man in question held in the violent social game. Her position was negotiable only to the extent that she would belong to her father, or to her imaginary companion, to her abductor—or to the man her father had her marry.

Like land ownership, woman stealing was an aspect of the economic and violent relationships revolving around the production and sale of poppies that determined who stole from whom. Thus, it was quite common in stories of armed abductions for the perpetrator/future husband to be a "*pistolero*," a "*pesado*," someone "who works for so-and-so." In this regard, abduction was only one of the practices around which the local political economy was materialized. Like pulling through and fencing in, stealing a woman depended on your resources in the predatory capitalism specific to the local drug economy. This homology highlighted the place allotted to the subjectivity of women in this context. The phrase "you can't feed soup to one and refuse it to the other" and the ways of behaving imposed on women at dances indicated the modalities of their inclusion in these competitive relationships. Whether through the injunction to close off any availability (not giving soup at all, i.e., not dancing with anyone) or that of a non-discriminatory opening (accepting all propositions), the central issue lay in the suppression of women's choice in the violent competition of which they are the object. These norms ensured that women avoided taking a part in social relations between men, that their capacity to act was annihilated, and that they were enjoined to remain neutral in the face of predation and thus to play no part in the competition.

Adriana's availability in the violent game therefore was linked to the stakes for the various men around her who, at one moment or another, appropriated her. This dynamic, like the local understanding of abductions, raised the question of the ability of fathers to provide protection. In this respect, Adriana's case was highly revealing: the expectations of reprisals were based on varied but always detailed assessments of her father's resources. However, these were chiefly linked to the observation of an obvious fact: all his resources could not protect Adriana in the main town. Thus, passive protection by fathers—that is to say, one that eschewed taking specific actions—

was not for everyone. Fathers with lower status had to take specific actions, such as arranged marriages. Thus, Adriana's father had his daughter marry his associate after the abduction. A frequent alternative move was to send your daughters to the coastal plain towns, where they were thought to be less exposed. This was the strategy Lamberto and Tamara's family followed. But it was based on a premise that undergirded the tensions between Maria's parents and Patricia's: the two girls were not assured of Lamberto's protection, because he lacked the resources necessary for deterring a potential abductor with a credible threat of reprisals. This lack of resources was part of the incentive for Lamberto and Tamara to conclude the agreement with Maria's parents. And in the fraught time during which the young girls were exposed, it fell on Tamara's shoulders (herself having been abducted by Lamberto when she was seventeen) to devise the few protective tactics within their means.

Stealing therefore placed women in relationships of dependency and made stakes of them in the competition between men. But, conversely, this imposed passivity did not render them immune to the fallout and hazards that accompanied violent competition. Thus, the conflict between two men from hamlets N* and S* ended up killing the mother and sister of one of the men. Similarly, the case of Beatriz, who was stolen by a *pistolero* from a hamlet near the main town, illustrated how little being deprived of the ability to act in the competition precluded becoming a victim of it. He took her with him to Tucson, where she "lived the affluent life" before returning to live in Badiraguato while he came and went. He then got caught up in a deadly conflict in the main town which kept him from returning to Badiraguato. Beatriz, who lived with her parents in the main town, began getting death threats from the rival group gunning for her husband. Teófilo looked after her every day, shepherded her everywhere, and controlled her doings to keep her out of harm's way. Beatriz finally had enough of it, saying to him, as she later told me: "Look here, Don Teófilo, if they want to kill me, you know very well that they will kill me no matter where I am." But she also told me that his emphatic presence, his reputation—and the reputation of her sister's late husband—might also have been instrumental in keeping her alive. Regardless of how a man appropriated a woman, as an extension of him she then endured the modalities of the violent competition into which she had been dragged. And the relative appropriation staged by Teófilo made plain that protection came by way of a man's hold over a woman.

The "protection" accorded to Adriana says a great deal about the material conditions of many of my married female interlocutors. Following her abduction in the town, she was taken back to the hamlet that she had until then managed to avoid except at harvest time. Protection against the abductor returned her to the family fold, that is, to the familial setting where the value of her work first benefited her father, head of the family. Thus, when she made food for the farm workers, she spared him the need to hire a cook. But this was a temporary situation whose eventual outcome was her marriage to the father's associate. In the framework of household economies bound by poppy cultivation, the configuration from house to house was in fact similar. For example, Tamara started her workday at 5 a.m., chopping kindling and firing up the *comal* to make tortillas. She was on the go the entire day without a break; a good day for her was when she could take a little time off in the afternoon for socializing with the neighbor women (while looking after the children or preparing dishes for celebrations). The contingencies of working the poppy fields being what they were, her husband could be around for much of the day (sitting and waiting on a plastic chair, looking at the hills and listening to the radio) or, on the contrary, he might be out in the field. On days he was home, he sometimes played with his preschool children; when he was not, radio surveillance was added to Tamara's duties. The tasks remained well separated, as well as the meals: Tamara routinely ate after all the family members had finished their meal, she cleaned up after everyone, and she did the dishes—in short, all the classic features of a patriarchal organization wherein the production relationships between men and women makes the latter's work invisible by integrating it into the man's earnings.[16] Only the husband was considered to be a representative of the family and only he participated in the external social spaces of negotiating and valorizing work. However, my study of poppy production patterns and constraints in chapter 3 showed that the whole household was a producer and that wives, since they managed the budget, were on the front lines of uncertainty.

The entangled logics of armed violence and gender relations continued to weigh on the experience of married women. My experience with the families I observed did not reflect the pervasiveness of domestic violence. I never witnessed physical violence in the houses where I lived, and some of my interlocutors would tell me that their husbands better not lay a hand on them.

Nevertheless, even the fact that the women talked in the negative about it indicated that this was a significant phenomenon. As a matter of fact, the local newspapers were full of stories about women murdered in their homes. A front page that circulated during my fieldwork headlined an article with "*Callada a balazos*," which roughly translates as "she was shut up with bullets," making armed violence a response to a common stereotype: women who talked too much. Many of my female interlocutors hinted at past experiences with or fears about abusive husbands. Yolanda's second husband—the one who was not killed—beat her, and Gabriela was afraid of Jaime when he came home drunk. The modalities of "spending time together" and the exercise of the same violent practices (including the use of firearms) afforded a glimpse of how armed violence spilled over into domestic spaces.

Moreover, the ever present violence also indirectly weighed on the experience of women in domestic settings. In all sierra families, when a man and a woman got married, the woman left her hamlet (however distant) and moved into the husband's house. Just as the husband owned the property, the couple lived surrounded by his extended family. This virilocal organization, which cut women off from their past sociality and inserted them into the husband's, was further reinforced by the context of violence. Leaving aside that none of my married female interlocutors owned a vehicle, the ability to move around—which, in the context of uncertainty, depended on her familiarity with the area and her social capital (chapter 1)—was strictly gendered. Few wives enjoyed a broad enough social network to let them move around alone. Thus, Veronica could not visit her family without her husband because it meant traveling through areas where he alone would be recognized. Without his familiarity, the journey would become unpredictable. This was also the case with Tamara, who greatly missed her family in Chihuahua and was terrified that she would one day lose her mother without having seen her again. But, since her marriage, she only managed to visit her parents every other year. Sociability in hamlets was also gendered, with women largely confined to the domestic sphere. In particular, women avoided the public places where young men hung out and that were often associated with violence. On the other hand, the federal *oportunidades* program, a monthly welfare assistance specifically for mothers, provided an occasion for all women to get together for several hours in the hamlet's center while they were waiting for the convoy.[17]

The inclusion in the husband's extended family, the restriction on movement, the confining of sociability to domestic spaces, and the burden of children made separations particularly critical. In talking to me about domestic violence, the psychologist from the Family Affairs Department mentioned a recent advance, a so-called "express divorce" (*divorcio exprés*) that did away with the husband having to give his consent.[18] He added, however, that the measure was rarely resorted to. In addition to all the constraints on women in that situation, separating from the husband meant returning to the state of vulnerability attached to being single. Something of this helplessness played out in front of me in one of the most emotionally-charged moments of my fieldwork.

During the Easter holidays, members of Lamberto's extended family arrived for a visit. This year it was Erica, Lamberto's cousin, who came with her husband and children from the coast to spend three or four days. In the days leading up to the holiday, all the women in this family organized the Easter Sunday picnic. On this day of celebration, nothing could be cooked or heated, the comal *should not be lit and, as it was a feast, you should eat a lot and eat well. So, in the days before, in metal cans converted to wood-burning ovens, the dishes and sweets for the coming Sunday followed one after the other: the sweet breads, the turnovers stuffed with caramel (*empanadas*). Close by, they prepared the* capirotada[19] *and the* sopa fria.[20]

The meal preparation was a collective effort, with everyone running back and forth, as they still had to take care of their usual daily tasks. Meanwhile, the men were in a house drinking beer, and the women in another around the ovens, kneading the various and varied doughs, taking turns, laughing and chatting. It was a great moment of sharing, on both sides. The bread that needed to rise was the most delicate task. Lamberto's sister Nacha had said she would have prepared it, but she had her period and one could not make bread in that case. Erica, the cousin who now lived in Culiacán, complained she never got it to rise; it was Jimena and Tamara who stuck to it. In the discussions, Erica shared that she had just found out, a week before coming, that her husband was cheating on her. She had found messages on his phone and they had gotten into an argument. There was nothing she could do, but she could not just swallow it, she said. She wanted us to have a party on Friday night. She wanted to get beers and drink. Everyone was breathless with excitement at the prospect: Tamara and Jimena were enthusiastic, but immediately anticipated the negotiations with their husbands to make it happen.

As the days went by, discussions began and their results were shared in the kitchen. Tamara's husband, Lamberto, had said yes, but had reminded her that she could not hold her alcohol. Then he had joked about making the tortillas himself the next day; everyone laughed. Jimena said she didn't give her husband a choice. It was going well.

In the evening, the beers (Bud Light to stay slim) were there and we looked for a tape recorder and a microphone to do karaoke. Gradually, the party took shape: we settled hidden behind the house, between the back wall and the platform that marked where the house's terracing started. Erica sang rancheras, then came the classics, and it was just perfect: they were always about tragic love and betrayal. Tamara took a turn, and I did too. We laughed, we downed beers. As Tamara sang one tune after another, and downed beer after beer, we had fun imagining her the next day at 5 a.m. making tortillas. As the evening wore on, the next morning's tortillas became the subject of recurring jokes, and Erica's husband cheating on her guided the selection of the ensuing songs.

The next morning before daybreak, through my headache, I heard the sound of the ax outside. I got up only to find a frisky Tamara chopping wood. As the day dawned, a certain hint of scandal was in the air. Jimena had yelled at her husband the previous evening when he had stuck his head around the corner of the house. In my recollection, he had just looked in on us, maybe he had laughed when he saw us, but whatever, Jimena said it made her very angry. Lamberto's sister Nacha, who had not attended our party, came the next day. To show her disapproval, she brought food to her brother's house and kept on harping on hearing the music until so late that she had suspected Tamara could not be depended on to do so after her little soiree. Although we told her that the tortillas were there in the morning, she repeated herself in a mocking tone.

This collective catharsis session illustrated the texture of negotiations that take place in domestic settings. There was the concealment out of sight—behind the house—in a space never dedicated to sociability, and the jealous protection of this rare moment of freedom expressed in Jimena's admonitions to her husband and Erica's full-throated anger; both put the ambiguities of interpersonal relations on full display. Jimena and Tamara's relationships with their husbands were marked by expressions of affection, love, and mutual concern. In the intimate setting, relations were more complex than just exploitation alone, and they incorporated ever-singular affects and relationships. Thus, Jimena was noticeably silent in public and showed an almost religious respect for her husband's word. At the same time, in the course of their daily lives, it was very clear that she expressed her opinions, withheld judgment, and that she was fond of her husband, who looked after her. The daily evenings at Tamara and Lamberto's house were of infinite warmth, marked above all by mutual affection.

To raise the dimension of domination did not mean reducing everyone's psyches and the relationships to the alienation of women in the domestic setting. This nevertheless implies fitting the affects into the material conditions they share and noting that the relationships between them are suffused with issues relating to their husbands, brothers, or cousins. So as a corollary of Jimena and Tamara's support for Erica we have the condemnation of their sister-in-law Nacha. The freedom they carved out for themselves that evening may have been poked fun at by the husbands—which sufficed to establish a certain illegitimacy—but the most explicit condemnation came from the sister-in-law. Stolen as a young girl, she lived alone with her daughter and was the subject of many comments from her brothers: her past relationships and her complicity in being stolen were thus recalled in a subtle but recurrent way. In return, Nacha sought to assert her current status any time an opportunity presented itself. Thus, by claiming at the end of the day that she did not have a moment to herself, when she saw Tamara with her umbrella coming up from visiting another cousin by marriage, she positioned herself not as a stolen and fickle woman, but as a particularly hard-working single woman. Without making assumptions about the intentions of each of them, it is worth noting that the condemnation she had to endure was part of complex family relationships, and the wives of her brothers bore the brunt of the situation. The totality of it showed the predominance of gendered domination relationships and the material conditions of each of them prevented the perception of a shared condition.

For the wives of men involved in the higher echelons of the drug trade, the "protection" of marriage and the dependence it induced took different forms. The bulk of the profits of the poppy economy that resided in transporting the goods meant the men involved at these levels were often away. While I never shared the daily life of these more affluent circles in the main town, I did on several occasions observe how dependent these women were on their husbands. When we first met, the wife of a *pesado* in the town proudly exclaimed: "Me, my husband supports me. Thank God I don't have to work." These women's quality of life might have been higher than Tamara's, yet their social status still depended on their husbands and it was generally the men's resources that played a role in their protection. Thus, Laura, when she was held at gunpoint with her father by the head of the municipal police for a parking violation, invoked her late husband, a highly placed *pistolero*, so that the policeman would "change his attitude" (chapter 6).

In this context, cosmetic surgery and fitness exercise, two characteristic activities, let these women claim a social distinction in the public space that translated into body work. Almost all the women who took the only exercise course in the municipality—Zumba—had in common the daily condition of being lone wives. Similarly, Beatriz, who hardly ever saw her husband, received money from him and had surgery three times in two years. Cosmetic surgery was common among women whose frequently absent husbands made a lot of money. The operation, visible and noticed, moreover provided the rationale for remaining bedridden for several weeks. To be afforded these privileges undeniably indicated that, even without a man by their side, they were not single women. In this environment, dependence on the status of men was linked to competitive relationships between women through commentaries, displaying their riches (cars, clothing), and body work.

Some women managed to transcend this context of violence and exploitation. Mariana was the daughter of a former *pesado*, from whom she was stolen by her husband in a legendary altercation (the man having threatened to drive his truck into a dance if the father did not "give" her up). Her husband, highly placed in the drug trafficking network operating in this area, was generally absent. She took care of the children and did the housework, but her daily life differed from that of most of my other female interlocutors. Once a year, she traveled with her husband to Guadalajara to buy clothes—insisting that she only bought what appealed to her—and used a room in her house to retail them. She sold men's, women's, and children's clothes, and locals frequented her shop almost every day. Next, she started making ice cream. Her home thus became an important venue for socializing in the hamlet, whether or not her husband was around. She also evolved into a full-fledged contact in the hamlet for municipal government officials.

What she achieved may have been enabled by her father's, and later her husband's, resources, yet the fact remains that her sociality and status were her own and her businesses contributed to her family's monetary income. Other women worked in the municipal administrative offices: a number of sierra women had been appointed representatives of the town hall in their hamlets, and the post of mayor had been held by a woman in 2016–19. It has to be said that the latter dynamic related to the way partisan organizations in the state of Sinaloa implemented provisions for parity through a blatant territorial division: the municipal posts in the rich coastal municipalities were held by men and the marginalized sierra municipalities were relegated to women. Still, it remained that some women managed to be dealt a hand in the game.

"THE PROBLEM WITH DOMESTIC VIOLENCE IS THE PRESUMPTION OF INNOCENCE": THE SIDELINING OF WOMAN STEALING

When Adriana was abducted, her employers and her brother briefly tossed around the idea of going to the local authorities, but at the time, the municipal policemen were in hiding because of the threat of reprisals against them (see next chapter). To help his sister, Ismael told me, he also thought he might call in soldiers he knew personally; but he told himself to forget it, because, as he said to me, "Had I done it, I would not be here to tell you." The treatment of Adriana's abduction illustrated how gun violence justified the disregard of gender relations in public action.

The secretary of the town hall told me that "the problem with domestic violence is the presumption of innocence." Seeing my surprise, he elaborated: "Yes, it is new in the country and that is a good thing. But it means that if I see that you're a suspect for example, well I can't do anything." Embarrassed, I asked him how cases of domestic violence came to his attention. He laughed: "I'm from here, word gets out." So I asked him, "And then, outside of your position as a civil servant, can you do something about it?"
—"Oh, no way! The problem is that you get killed if you get involved."

The discourse on the "presumption of innocence" referred to a common practice among local officials of washing their hands of one thing or another by citing legal provisions in an abstruse argument whose logic sometimes was difficult to follow.[21] The presumption of innocence would therefore be something new and certainly welcome, but with the unintended consequence of rendering the officials powerless to act against domestic violence. In applying it, the secretary of the town hall contrived a particularly important mechanism: he resorted to a generalization of individual cases that remained abstract. The terms of the public debate on "the problem of domestic violence" (*el problema de la violencia domestica*) made possible shelving them, first by legal constraints, then by the immediate threat of armed violence: "You get killed" (*te matan*). These generalizations and impersonal forms echoed the mobilization of a particular term among local officials: "the sector" (*el gremio*). Politicians used it regularly in alluding to organized trafficking and violence—allusive, but nevertheless signifying the idea of a centralized and institutionalized organization.

While the reference to the presumption of innocence was dumbfounding, it was the role of gun violence in gender relations and domestic spaces that appeared to be a more immediate obstacle for officials assigned to dealing with these issues.

During the meeting at the start of the office term that brought together all municipal services, each department outlined its objectives and priorities. Following all presentations, officials were asked to vote on an overall plan pulling together each department's specific priorities. The family psychologist (DIF) put "domestic violence" at the top of his list, but it came in last on the final list.

In speaking with the psychologist later, I learned about his disappointment with this classification, and I asked him if any women ever come to see him on this subject. He told me that it was very rare, because of a psychological process called "resistance." He added that there was a common conception that a woman who would come to him sent back a bad image. Then he said, "But you know, it's more complicated, too," and proceeded to tell me a story. The daughter of a pesado was stolen by a competing pesado. After being released, she was sheltered in a state DIF facility in Culiacán. In response, men stationed themselves every day in front of the Badiraguato DIF, putting pressure on officials. The municipal DIF called the state DIF, whose officials said to "ignore" them, and then sent the girl home to the precarious protection of her father.

A few days after our conversation, he learned of the case of another young girl sheltered by the state DIF.[22] The psychologist and the head of "Women and Minors" (two categories whose lumping together the reader should now readily understand) had to fetch her identification papers. Frightened by an armed man and the lack of cooperation by the people they met on the way, they turned back without having reached her hamlet. After that, he told me other similar stories: one was about a mother who came because her daughter had been kidnapped and raped by her former boyfriend; another involved a young girl whom her mother regularly kicked out of the house. Each time, the story ended in the same way: he and his colleague asked around if they could do something and the answer invariably came back as "don't even think about it," "she's the companion of such and such," and "she's the daughter of such and such." Thus, as we have seen, they both considered the issue to be one of the most dangerous in their work: "The problem is that you start with a case of domestic violence, but you don't know what you are getting into; you are completely unprotected (desprotegido).*"*

Thus, the shunting off by politicians of gender violence issues to "the sector" was reflected in the concrete constraints faced by civil servants in individual cases. In the latter's experience, all fathers, all husbands, all kidnappers were *pesados*, those "such and such" against whom they were powerless. The perpetuation of stealing, as a continuum, was thus ensured by the local power structure in which, once again, violent resources carried the day and avenues of recourse were few. Even the exceptions proved the rule, like an armed group in the north of the municipality which supposedly banned woman stealing. According to my interlocutors living in the area, its gunmen had even killed a man for stealing a young girl. While my observations on this group were too sparse to draw any conclusions about its behavior regarding this matter, this case nevertheless laid bare not only the relationships in which the possibility of violently taking a woman was embedded, but also what kind of position one needs to produce a discourse that would make rape and stealing beyond the pale.

· · ·

Stealing women merged all of the following phenomena: indifference to consent, violent appropriation of a single woman, objectification and being made the stakes in violent male-to-male competition relationships, domestic exploitation of women by men, and domestic violence. The logics condensed in the practice of stealing did not exhaust the description of unique experiences, emotional dimensions in marital relationships, and protection strategies adopted by women. But the violent appropriation of a social group was constitutive of particularly heavy constraints. It was also the cement of a common condition too often dismissed as an individual issue, that is, as the need to protect oneself from predation.

As in the case of land ownership, deferring to "the sector" with regard to dealing with sexual violence let violent social relationships define what was acceptable or not. Thus, it was the assessment by my interlocutors of the resources of Adriana's father that ruled their characterization of the situation as either Armando's unacceptable act or Adriana's fickle behavior. As we will see in the last two chapters, the weight given to individual responsibility was related both to the inhabitants' analytical work in confronting homicides and the broader silence of the authorities.

Killing

"Killing for a problem, a conflict, I don't say, but those who kill
for the hell of it.... No way."

TEÓFILO

THE DIFFICULTY IN WRAPPING your mind around the killings in
Mexico is that the media, public authorities, and many researchers a priori
put them down to an intentionality: either to criminal violence (the perpetra-
tor was seeking an illegal profit) or to political violence (he was aiming to
change the political order). To grasp the social issues around gun violence, I
propose instead to understand homicides by what they do in context. I therefore focus on the comments of people who were affected by these homicides
and who inserted them into their lives while giving them meaning. As we
have seen, my interlocutors intensively gathered intelligence in their daily
lives that let them identify places, times of day, and types of interaction to
avoid. In this sense, these men and women crafted a set of coping mechanisms, knowledge, and skills that let them deal with homicide.

I approached the murders and conflicts from the kitchens, the doorsteps,
and the corridors in which my interlocutors commented on them. While
these comments dealt with the circumstances and forms of a homicide,[1] what
interested me foremost was my interlocutors' work of qualification. It was
neither a question of me treating with suspicion their discourses, which were
sensible and appeared to be well informed about these murders,[2] nor, conversely, of using them as operators for describing the act of violence itself to
me. On the contrary, I took advantage of the heuristic effect of not witness-
ing the lethal interaction to leave aside the question of how exactly it was
carried out.[3]

I confronted the various discourses produced by my interlocutors on the
homicides and asked myself how they fit these killings into local social relations. My interlocutors' comments on each murder introduced references to
the dynamics outlined in the previous chapters; what they said constituted

the social texture of these deaths. Through daily information-gathering, the residents mobilized what they knew about ways of organizing poppy production and social relations in the hamlets and in the main town. Understanding the questions posed by the outbreaks of violence in the daily lives of these people therefore required familiarity with the social relations that made up Badiraguato's political economy.

"HE MUST HAVE BEEN KILLED FOR A REASON"

The murders that regularly punctuated daily life in the town intruded harshly on the lives of my interlocutors. These events, over which these men and women had no control, made themselves known early in the day, usually formulated as: "dawn rose on a dead body" (*amaneció un muerto*). The passive form and use of the term "a dead man" instead of "homicide," "murder," or "killing" manifested the indeterminacy and euphemizing that surrounded the news as it hit them. "Dawn rose on a dead body," and so the day began. The residents had to understand this, make sense of it—in short, to fit one more death into their lives. In the main town, they could be called on to make this effort about every three or four days, although sometimes a week would go by without "a dead man." There were also days on which several people were carried off. My interlocutors' immediate reactions always focused on certain elements of the killing, as illustrated by how the news of one of these murders spread in the offices of the Department of Family Affairs (DIF) on June 5, 2014.

It was not even 9 a.m. yet when Sergio's phone rang. He picked up the receiver, engaged in a brief conversation, "Oh well . . . ok," and hung up. Then he called someone in turn and, waiting for the other party to pick up the phone, told us, "They killed Luis." Talking into the phone then, he said: "There was a problem with Luis," and counseled staying away from the latter's house. Catching the sound of a woman's voice, I guessed that he had called his wife and that it was his neighbor who had been killed.

Word getting out about the latest death set in motion several urgent precautions. Sergio was warned about a quarter of an hour after his neighbor had been killed, and his first reaction was to protect his family members: the murder having just happened, being anywhere near it was dangerous because there was nothing to say that the incident was over. Sergio, who was among the first people to learn of it, immediately passed word on to his relatives and then to his various contacts during the day.

Unlike all those times when the dawn had simply "risen on a dead body," the news in this case broke with a name attached to it. More often than not, establishing who was killed was one of the first determinations to be made. With the most immediate precautions having been taken, the work of making sense of it usually began, often collectively.

After Sergio hung up on his wife, the rather desultory conversation revolved around the homicide. It was sometimes interrupted, sometimes revived by other employees who passed through the office. One after the other, they asked where Luis was killed and when it happened. Sergio's stock reply was "at home this morning." Everyone obviously knew Luis, the victim, whom they referred to by his nickname "the chicken" (*el pollo*). His house also was labeled "the club." They explained to me that nightly card games there often lasted until dawn. At one point, Cristian noted that "disputes over card games are classic." I asked if they thought the killing was related to that; the response was "who knows" (*quien sabe*)?

The interactions that ensued were in line with how news of a homicide was typically integrated into everyday life. As the morning progressed and the office routine resumed, Luis's death was progressively woven into the fabric of their daily life by the employees. Identifying where and when he was killed was part of an effort to reinscribe the homicide into the town's life. The women and men recalled his nickname, and the reputation of "the club" came up, quickly and casually, with an implication, in this instance made explicit by Cristian's remark.

Fitting the murder of an acquaintance, or even a loved one, into a storyline and explanatory framework helped to alleviate uncertainty and the sense of vulnerability produced by a death that was still fresh and risky. The indeterminacy that surrounded the news of a new death gave it a collective dimension: the whole town woke up to a new dead man and had to make sense of it. By attributing a history and a cause to the victim, my interlocutors put distance between themselves and the murder as a way to reassure themselves that it could not happen to them. When Cristian stated that "disputes over card games are classic," it was obvious that he did not play cards. His explanation attributed Luis's death to a vice, one in which Cristian did not engage, thus relieving his own sense of insecurity. More generally, these hints—Luis used to play cards until dawn, he was killed this morning at home—referred, as in the case of stealing women, to a frequent mix of bad behavior with violence. Gambling, but also and especially alcohol consumption and dances, were common contextual elements for explaining deaths. This register of vices was ingrained enough for my interlocutors to draw general maxims: "disputes over card games are classic"; "don't think that drinking bouts are a good thing."

Explaining murders using the victim's behavior was on full display in the sentence: "He must have been killed for a reason" (*por algo lo mataron*). It was the most repeated and succinct commentary, the one that simply gave a predictable character to the homicide, incorporating each successive murder into daily life: he was killed because he did something. Interchangeable with the adage "the turtle lives 100 years because it doesn't stick its nose into other people's business," several expressions that commented generically on violence kept popping up in my notebooks: "Only those who have pending issues get killed" (*solo a los que tienen pendientes los matan*); "only those who get into trouble are in for it" (*solo a los que se meten, les toca*). The essence of these phrases resided in the "only those who": by designating others, you exempted yourself and your loved ones. Another sentence pulled all these comments together into one lesson: "if you behave well, there is no problem" (*si te portas bien, no hay problema*). This systematic victim-blaming as a way of letting go of violent acts was part of an effort to set benchmarks that could make violence predictable. With more or fewer convolutions, details, and characters, all the comments served to (re)fit each murder into daily life in Badiraguato.

However, these references to the victims as responsible for their fate left room for considerations of injustice or disproportion between the assigned cause and the fact of being killed for it. Thus, in talking about a murdered man in December 2013, my interlocutors said that he "paid the bill for his sons," who had fled from the town after killing someone—the idea of death as unavoidable payback. With this expression, however, my interlocutors suggested that murdering a father because of what his sons did, while understandable, was unfair. Similarly, the death of a young man accused of committing several robberies was commented on by one of my interlocutors in these terms: "He'd stolen a tangerine here, poor guy. We knew about it, it was kid stuff, so we didn't do anything. But then he robbed in a hamlet, then [an important local business], so they killed him."

If my interlocutors stressed the victim's behavior to make sense of killings, they also voiced concerns that indicated that the confidence they placed in this approach had its limits. As we have seen (chapter 2), the funerals made this point unmistakably: behind "a dead man" probably hid networks to which both the killers and their victims belonged. These considerations and the broader understanding of the issues raised by each homicide heightened the sense of vulnerability.

*That same afternoon of June 5th, a woman from town came to the offices of the family affairs department with that subject on her mind. She said, "It's easier to get into trouble than to get out of it." She wanted to go to the wake because she knew the victim's godson well, but she would not go. "You never know, for going to the wake . . . for merely being seen there . . . it even gets scary . . . we can no longer go there" (*uno no sabe luego, por ir a un velorio . . . nada mas por verlo a uno ahí . . . hasta da miedo . . . ya no se puede ir).

Violent deaths of relatives were always complicated by the question of whether to attend the funeral or not. This woman explicitly formulated what was often implicit in the avoidance tactics most of my interlocutors adopted. Just as the murder scene was to be avoided in the ensuing hours in case the killers returned, attending the wake was also dangerous. If Luis was "killed for a reason," there was no way to be sure that his killers would not take advantage of having all his relatives in one place to murder them or select other targets, "for merely being seen there." Thus, the funeral processions, where they started from (one of the two funeral homes that did a thriving business in Badiraguato), and the cemetery where they ended up also had to be avoided. If the mechanics that underpinned the avoidance of these spaces were common knowledge, they did not make the grieving process any easier. Indeed, the ceremony was often notable for the relatives who were not present.[4] Conversely, the only two wakes following nonviolent deaths that took place during my investigation (a lady who died of natural causes and a painter who was accidentally electrocuted in a building) saw an impressive crowd, all the neighbors attending several times on wake days. One day, Teófilo told me of how he resented some of his family for not coming to mourn his murdered son-in-law: "Okay, he was a thug (*malandrino*), but they didn't come. Don't you think it hurt me?"

Being exposed to occasional but regular homicides gave rise to practices of generalization. While they may have zeroed in on the victim's questionable behavior ("don't think that drinking bouts are a good thing"), the frequent homicides dotting their daily lives also elicited more general reflections on "violence." Thus, in one hamlet, one of my interlocutors made a distinction between "here" and "there": "Over there, its hostile groups that kill each other, but here it is just because they are drunk (*por borrachos*)." She meant the main town in this instance, but another time she drew the same distinction for me regarding another hamlet in a different part of the sierra. And in turn, in this other hamlet, a woman in whose house I was staying told me exactly the same thing: "There, it's for drug trafficking, here it's the drunken binges." These mechanisms thus deflected some causes of violence among neighbors and picked on others to contrast with home. The inhabitants thus took up national discourses of disqualification and depoliticization of the social dimension of gun violence on the margins. Gambling and alcohol were linked to spontaneous use of violence. They formed part of the essentializing discourses about the residents of Badiraguato, the "land of violent men" with "hot blood," to use the title of the book by a former town politician.[5]

Moreover, in the Mexican context, "narco-trafficking" was an absolute evil. In Culiacán, an old woman telling me about the young people of a modest family in her hamlet close to the Badiraguato sierra assured me that they were "good people," "very nice," and that they owned "laboratories" for making synthetic drugs in several states. Then she asked me, sounding worried: "But that doesn't make them *narcos*, does it?" Similarly, in Badiraguato, I heard repeated praise for President Felipe Calderón, despite his policies that resulted locally in stepped-up repression, because "something had to be done to stop drug trafficking." My interlocutors, however immersed they were in the social issues surrounding drug production, its trafficking, and armed violence, thus invoked official discourses that invisibilized their experience in making sense of the homicides that suddenly intruded on their daily lives.

These explanatory registers were part of the institutional and media treatment of "criminal" violence. In Sinaloa, and in Badiraguato in particular, the police generally did not investigate murders. According to figures from the Mexican Institute of Public Statistics (Instituto nacional de estadística y geografía, INEGI), in 2012, 99.2 percent of homicides in Sinaloa went unpunished.[6] Furthermore, under an agreement reached in 2005 between the regional media outlets following the murders of several journalists, the outlets stopped looking into the killings and published only the information fed to them by the public authorities.[7] The lapidary articles followed one another with the same information: where the body was found, possibly whether or not it was "in a bag" (*embolsado*), and the time between death and the arrival of the police on the scene. Victims might be named or anonymized. The number of bullet holes routinely would be specified, as was the number of cartridges found at the scene. The photos that accompanied the articles typically anonymized the victims.

This coverage of bodies dumped by roadsides fueled the tendency of the media to blame the victims. They would trot out one or another of the rote explanations for the violence: they had either gotten mixed up in something or they were violent types themselves.[8] A caricature by the cartoonist Antonio Helguera in the newspaper *La Jornada*, reproduced in a book by journalist John Gibler, sums up the weight of these suspicions: in a landscape of graves in a cemetery, the names and dates of the victims on the tombstones are replaced by shibboleths like: "Who knows what he was messing with"; "What was he doing out at that hour?"; "She was a whore"; "She dressed provocatively."[9] If by blaming the victims for their killings the inhabitants of Badiraguato were engaged in a flimsy effort aimed at generating predictability, in the national context these discourses contributed to the phenomenon that Gibler called "anonymous deaths": fostering confusion about or even deflecting from the killings, to conceal the state's repression of protest movements and collaboration between state armed forces and non-state armed groups.[10] Indeed, the anonymous death without any history raises doubts, and the many victims of state violence are cloaked by the suspicion that hangs over those who die.[11] If the killers and the killed were "drug traffickers," those figures of otherness, the anxiety level dropped. The "scourge of drug trafficking that ravages the country" thus concealed the variety of violence and the modalities of repression by the state in Mexico. In Culiacán's journalistic circles, the government was sometimes dubbed "the devil in a cassock" and the consensus among many journalists was that covering drug trafficking was less dangerous than denouncing government violence and the links between the two.[12] However, covering drug trafficking without linking it to the state was pointless, so it was better just to count bullets and dwell on the crime scenes.[13]

"THOSE FROM EL RANCHO": THE IRRATIONALITY OF
THE DESTITUTE

While the dead men were usually held responsible for their own deaths, a violent conflict that had started a little over a year before I first set foot in Badiraguato appeared as an exception. As soon as I arrived, I learned that it had escalated into a wave of murders that ravaged the town. People still spoke of "killings every day," with bodies "found in the central square" day in and day out. My interlocutors told me that they found it impossible to make sense of the deaths that shook the town. These discourses puzzled me from the start of my fieldwork, as they clashed with what I was learning about everyday life there.

I had only been in town for eight days when Teófilo told me about a party the previous evening in a "high society" inner courtyard under a tarpaulin. The music was in full swing when it started to hail. The partygoers mistook the sound of the hailstones on the tarpaulin for the sound of automatic weapons fire. Everyone stayed where they were until the tarpaulin finally gave way under the weight of the accumulated hail and doused the entire audience. The scene made me laugh, but I still wondered out loud that the sounds of automatic weapons had not even spooked the audience.[14] Teófilo responded with, "Oh no, but it's just that here, you never know," launching into a story from last year of the murder of a friend of his that had taken place in the courtyard of our "chambers."

The victim used to park his van in the yard. One day, he had been threatened, but he paid it no mind. Several nights in a row, Teófilo and other friends had gathered around the man's van drinking beers. Then, one evening around 9 p.m., Teófilo was in his room, door closed and the TV on, determined to stay inside and spare his liver. He heard a "tatatatata"—but, he said to me, "look": he took a hold of his room's door made of sheet metal and rapped it loud and staccato, and then said: "You see, you'd think it was bullets, wouldn't you? . . . Well, I thought at the time they were knocking on my door, and I didn't go out."

An hour later, he saw that all the lights were on outside. He went out to find all his neighbors in a panic and his friend's body riddled with bullets. He said the killer had left through the gate of the last street before the river, that the neighbors had called the police who had refused to come, then the soldiers who were in the area but who at first also refused to move, before finally coming into the yard an hour after the incident. When Teófilo came out, the soldiers asked him who the dead man was and he said he didn't know. He imitated Ismael, who came to see him in a total panic and asked to stay with him.[15] He recalled his incomprehension amid everyone's panic and said, "I couldn't believe it. He was a good young man, but I never thought he would be killed."

"Why did they kill him then?" I asked.

"That ... we never knew ... some reason. From that day on, they started killing a lot, every day."

He regarded his friend's murder as the first in the ensuing wave of homicides. Despite a prior threat, the murder was represented to me as unpredictable, and would have remained inscrutable because, this time, the victim "was a good young man." Although Teófilo alluded to the possibility of "some reason" (*algo*), this murder was regarded as illogical, unlike other cases where the victim was systematically blamed for his own death. Afterward, to my growing astonishment, I encountered the same puzzlement in others among my interlocutors: many people had died without anyone knowing what for, or who had killed them.

The body count just kept rising, without anyone understanding why, until one day, of two people who had been attacked, one survived to reveal the killer's identity. It turned out to be Martín, one of the Gomez brothers from El Rancho, a hamlet not far from the main town.

Wrapping up the tale of his slain friend, Teófilo said: "And in the end the killer turned out to be the one you least expected." Then he mumbled something indistinct about the father and then mimed something by bringing his limp hands close to his torso and pouting. Trying to interpret what he was doing, I was torn between him imitating someone with a cognitive impairment or a man acting too effeminate for his taste.

Martín was regarded as the leader of a local armed band to which his brother also belonged. Yet, in stories and comments, finding out that it was him did not make his previous choice of victims any more intelligible. Indeed, just like Teófilo, in these always retrospective accounts, my interlocutors continued to insist that they could not figure out a motive for these killings. And discovering that it was Martín only shifted their bewilderment: he was "the one you least expected." The most common way my interlocutors described him was as a person "who was into killing," an expression that I had never heard elsewhere and which exclusively emphasized the act of killing for no apparent reason. As Teófilo put it: "Killing for a problem, a conflict, I don't say, but those who kill for the hell of it ... no way!" My interlocutors agreed on this point: the violence perpetrated by Martín and his accomplices made no sense.

Faced with this discovery—and in keeping with the idea that the El Rancho band's type of violence of was irrational and unfair—the main town's leading families launched a wave of eliminations. Now, the murders targeted "those from El Rancho"; "the El Rancho band (*gavilla*)"; or "Martín's men," as they were variously called. Martín managed to escape, but his brother and accomplice and many others were killed. Once again, many dawns rose on many dead, but this news was integrated into the daily life in the usual manner: the "reason" behind these deaths was punishment for the previous, still mystifying, deaths. Retaliation continued on two fronts: assassinations and messages slipped under the doors of some houses warning their occupants to get out of town. The scale of this operation and the two mechanisms employed left open the possibility that people were mistakenly targeted. So, when I had just moved to Badiraguato, Alejandra told me about the town, its daily life, the town hall, and in no time started in on the "gossip" (*chisme*):

"You have to be careful, here people burn you (la gente te quema). *They talk bad about you, and a lot of people had to leave [town] in a hurry because they said this or that, even if it was untrue." She continued: "There was one who was into killing, and a lot of people who worked for him. So they started looking for everyone who had associated with him and they killed them. And those who were less [involved], well, they were left with messages in the houses: "Get out or else" (se me van y ya saben). A lot of people had to leave, sometimes for no reason, just because they were burned, even if it wasn't true."*

Messages saying "get out or else" were slipped under many people's doors. These reprisals sowed doubt within the main town's interknowledge networks. The gossip, the suspicions that motivated the murders, and the threats all intertwined. Some families' temporary departures were interpreted in hindsight as evidence of their complicity. Thus, when they came back, suspicion of them continued to linger in seemingly innocuous daily interactions. In my immediate vicinity, supposed affiliations with Martín were the subtext for some of the expressions of mistrust I recounted in chapter 2.

This conflict and its aftermath continued to reverberate during my investigation. "They say that" Martín and his men returned to hide in El Rancho's mountainous surroundings and moved about heavily armed. One of my interlocutors confided to me that he had been threatened by Martín while he was out near El Rancho delivering materials for the company for which he worked. Since then he had refused to go back there. When another neighbor from the hamlet in question invited me to his house, Teófilo and Santiago strongly advised me against accepting. Many of the murders that took place during my stay grew out of this conflict. One morning in January 2014, two people were killed next to Santiago's house, and he blamed it on the "Martín gang." Three other people killed a few months apart in the hamlets near the capital were also considered to be Martín's accomplices. He, however, remained on the loose.

Finally, in October 2014, as I was returning to the main town from Culiacán, I heard *banda* music in the distance, guessing that it meant a procession. Indeed, I soon learned that Martín had been killed in Sonora (the state bordering Sinaloa in the north) and his body had been shipped to one of the town's funeral homes before it went to El Rancho for his relatives to look after. Teófilo urged me not to go "over there," by which he meant the funeral home, "in case the opponents come." While none of my interlocutors attended the ceremony in the main town, the atmosphere was particularly tense for some who would have liked to attend but chose not to as a precaution.

That same day and the next, the comments flew from all sides, including from people who had not spoken to me on the subject before. What the phrases "the one who was into killing" and "the one you least expected" emphatically suggested was that Martín was "bad" (*malo*). For all the other murders that happened during my field stay or that I was told about, the killer was never said to be "bad." However, here all the comments focused on his personality. For two days, everyone I met in town hammered away at this theory. Doña Irina bent down to me and, grasping my forearm tightly, gasped, "How bad he was!" Yolanda told me, "If you knew how many people he offended here!" Gabriela, vaguely: "Many innocent people died because of him." An old gentleman in a grocery store: "His wives [in Martín's family] must be at peace now." The puzzle about his motives turned into questioning his personal qualities. Blanca explained the conflict to me in these terms.

Martín's brother had lost an eye while target shooting. A sliver of wood took out his eye. When he came to the tortilleria, *she saw him, "with his hand on the gun constantly turning to look behind him, as if the devil himself were after him."*

As she was talking, she imitated a paranoid person, with jerky movements, as if unhinged. "After the eye," she said, "he turned bad, but his brother, the one they just killed, he was even meaner." I asked her how they knew they were the killers and why they killed. She replied: "People just knew, and as to why, that, the brothers alone knew. They were evil."

Martín's brother thus was thought to have gone "bad" after a self-inflicted eye injury. As for Martín himself, he was known to be even "meaner," although without bothering to specify why. Dwelling on the eye episode was part of trying to make sense of the killers' personalities: it operated as a root cause of their deviance, which in turn accounted for the series of homicides. These were murders whose logic, if it existed, would have been intelligible only to the deranged and pathological psychology of these brothers. Thus, the odd behavior of the younger brother in the street, first and foremost involved in a deadly conflict, in Blanca's account was unfounded and paranoid: "As if the devil himself were after him."

However, another narrative, which was not volunteered in these exchanges, surfaced in some houses. Gabriela reflected after Martín's funeral that his death was "very sad" because "already his father, his mother, his brother, and another of his brothers, and now he, had been killed." Those earlier murders several years ago had been linked to the father having stolen a poppy crop. I could not determine whether the family had worked a *pesado*'s plot or whether they grew their own and were obligated to a *pesado* at the time of sale. Regardless, it seemed that the family was caught up in the exploitative economy that characterized drug production, and that the family met its end in the context of these relationships.

Those who alluded to retaliation as playing a role did not invalidate the dominant framing of the surviving brothers' deviant personalities. All the same, Gabriela opined that "since their family had been killed, they turned bad." Without, of course, presuming to know the motives for the El Rancho brothers' penchant for violence, it sufficed to raise this source of tension in processing the killings. My interlocutors made an exception: while a storyline was available to them for making sense of the murders committed by Martín's band, men and women both discarded the logic—and therefore predictability—that they nevertheless attributed to the other homicides. Thus, Teófilo, imitating a deranged man, mumbled something about "the father," but declined to anchor the conflict he told me about in this story that he clearly knew. El Rancho is a hamlet located relatively close to the main town and, given the impact that the murders had on the town's daily life, it was highly likely that they all knew the history of Martín's family. The reading of settling a score was therefore available but not mobilized and, through a reading in psychological terms, these murders were excluded from the town's social life.

The people who discussed the murders of Martín's relatives with me belonged to the families that had been displaced in growing numbers from the sierra during the previous two decades. Gabriela's husband came from El Rancho, Rosa and Teresa from other nearby hamlets. Their accounts of leaving their hamlets dovetailed: some mentioned the lack of resources that made survival in the hamlets impossible, but all of them agreed that the time to leave came "when they started killing a lot of people." Rosa's father explained to me that her native hamlet ceased to exist almost twenty years ago: "Everyone was gone. They were killing each other and the rest [left] out of fear. . . . I had no reason [to fear], but hey, if they kill you just like that. . . ." He went to Sonora, then to the United States, before returning to the main town.

Some of these hamlets had only empty houses, no people. Former residents who still lived somewhere near the hamlet might keep a few animals there, caring for them regularly and working small plots of food crops. Others could not go back at all. Dozens of hamlets ended up deserted by their inhabitants following such episodes of violence. While displaced families from the sierra had often settled in the main town in recent decades, they now regularly sought refuge on the coastal plain, where they lived in dire poverty. The phenomenon had assumed such proportions that it became fodder for the politicians.

Multiple logics guided these population movements. Conflicts were sometimes attributed to "outsiders," to networks based in larger hamlets that had taken control of production; other times, they involved "the people of the place themselves" (*la misma gente de ahí*), conflicts between hamlet residents ("out of envy," "because some produced better than others"). In short, they were caught up in the competition over organized trafficking, and in particular in its manifestations in the more marginalized environments. The takeovers of certain populated areas and internal conflicts were linked to the changing balance of power and the fragility of others around the commercial and political intermediation that structured the production spaces.

The main town, with a large part of its population thus being from the sierra, was a socially heterogeneous space, in which the criteria of distinction were based on how long people had been settled there or how their places of origins ranked in the poppy trade. The relationships between my interlocutors illustrated this dimension. Beyond a simple difference of main town vs. sierra, they played out based either on membership in the town's great families (both old-timers and newcomers) or fragmentation along lines of origin from different areas of the sierra. Thus, the relationships of distinction expressed in terms like "people from a hamlet (*rancho*) without culture" (to use an epithet to which Teófilo was partial) concealed considerations that pertained to a social geography. Indeed, many areas of the sierra were, on the contrary, socially valued by the main town. As the chorus of an El Kommander song proclaims, "Yes sir, I come from a hamlet" (*Si señor yo soy de rancho*); some forms "of being from a hamlet" were actually a source of pride. Some of the sierra hamlets were associated with the "great" ones: in particular, La Tuna, home of "El Chapo" and the Beltrán Leyva brothers, La Noria of Caro Quintero, and Santiago de los Caballeros, a historical place also associated with many great figures. Conversely, other places—which partially crossed isolated areas in terms of infrastructure—were marginal in the organization of trafficking.

When I told doña Irina that I was trying to get to and stay in a hamlet in one of these areas, she, as a member of an important family in the main town, said to me with a grimace of deep contempt: "There is nothing to do there apart from packing marijuana." Marijuana no longer represented a substantial source of income since its legalization in parts of the United States, so these hamlets stuck in this now unprofitable activity justified the more general disqualification she shared with me. She counseled me to go instead to other areas that she named that were better supplied with poppies and great men.

It goes without saying that Martín, his brother, his family, and others from El Rancho were on the wrong side of these leverages of distinction—between the main town and the sierra, but also between the sierra of the big names and the sierra of the destitute. This also applied to those among my interlocutors who eventually would bring into the discussions the violence suffered by "those of El Rancho" antedating the conflict in the main town. Moreover, the way in which the many messages left under the doors of houses in the town heightened the insecurity in the daily relations between the inhabitants also formed part of these same social issues: the people I knew who were targeted by the letters and those who were suspected of complicity were among the marginalized.

In this context, the term used to refer to the group formed around the El Rancho brothers—"*gavilla*," an armed band—spoke to the linkage between these social distinctions and the use of violence. The word *"gavilla"* can be applied pejoratively to mean a group of criminals. Thus, Santiago, who was very critical of the abuses visited on the area by the army, told me: "Me, I tell the people in the sierra, imagine that the soldiers are just another *gavilla*, only they're from the government." In the main town, the term was generally used to refer to groups associated with the more marginalized areas in the sierra. My interlocutors often thought that *gavillas* were at least partially independent—that is, not reporting up in a hierarchy—and that many homicides resulted from frictions that played out between or within these groups. They also conceded that there were more powerful networks that could bring some *gavillas* to heel.

Similarly, my interlocutors who belonged to important families called armed men from marginalized backgrounds *"matones,"* *"malandrines,"* or *"maleantes,"* which meant at best killers, with shadings more toward thugs, scoundrels, rascals, mobsters, or crooks. Conversely, killers in areas associated with big men, as well as those of dominant families in the main town, were often simply not tagged with this moniker. For example, no one talked about the gunmen of La Tuna as a *gavilla*; possibly they might say "El Chapo's people." Often my interlocutors would refer obliquely to them by using the passive voice or impersonal formulas that omitted the actor's name. If one of these persons did have to be described (often when people were confronted with a case like Adriana's), the preferred term was *"pistolero,"* an armed professional, someone who was just doing his job when he killed.

Thus, the act of portraying the murders that started the conflict centered on Martín as irrational, as manifesting the pathology of those who perpetrated them, as resulting from a personality disorder. Formulating a moral condemnation, in addition to the wave of reprisals that followed, helped frame a narrative where the dominant networks were bringing the deprived young men into line. How armed men were characterized was therefore part of the social structuring of the drug economy, and in particular the existence of marginal armed groups that nevertheless remained independent of the most powerful networks.

These joint dynamics—independence in social margins and their susceptibility to being brought into line—echoed the ephemeral ascents of young men of modest means, captured by the local saying of "Going for a ride" (*hacer un viaje*). "Going for a ride" meant undertaking to transport a more or less large quantity of drugs outside the intermediation networks. Without enjoying the political and military protections available to the *pesados,* some individuals would "go for it" (*se avientan*) by transporting the drugs to the border, crossing it, and selling their load on the other side. They usually linked up with family or neighborhood contacts, a widely distributed resource due to the scope of emigration to the United States. But the ride constituted a "shot" and was risky, because it took place outside the exploitation relationships in which growers or young men working in transport were enrolled. Extremely dangerous, a successful "ride," and a fortiori several of them, represented access to considerable amounts of cash.

Thus, some stories were told of meteoric rises that started with a "ride." But while these ascents could quickly provide access to a lot of money and weapons, they were often extremely precarious. Thus, Beatriz, who "knew wealth" in Tucson for a time, found herself in a fragile situation, under threat of being killed while her husband could no longer come near Badiraguato. Also from a marginalized hamlet, he was one of the armed men accused of running with the "El Rancho *gavilla*." If, in this case, he managed to survive and could keep sending money to Beatriz, other stories that began with "a ride" could end abruptly. Then, too, there was the logic of bringing new entrants into line through homicides by the established networks that were invariably said to be linked to "a reason." Teófilo said that it was because these young people "do not know how to administer" the drug trade that they fall or get killed. In this regard, it appears that administering was not so much a question of "knowing how to" as of belonging to the more powerful, better connected networks.

Beyond the motivations behind the violence carried out by the El Rancho band, how this conflict was dealt with and how it affected the social life of the town involved relationships of domination. The framing by my interlocutors of the killings committed by the El Rancho band was an exception to the usual treatment of murders committed by the powerful. The irrationality and psychologizing lenses through which my interlocutors viewed these killings allowed them to describe it as gun violence by the marginalized. It turned these men into killers without a (legitimate) reason who dumped bodies in the central square, "the one you least expected." Like the distinct designations that men who killed received according to their social positions, the comments around the act of killing showed that the legitimacy and rationality accorded to violence depended on the position of the one who committed it.

The evidence surrounding the homicides following the discovery of Martín's identity pointed toward a particularly violent domination. In the passive form of "he must have been killed for a reason" lurked how the murders committed by the dominant networks raised uncertainty. The discourses aimed more broadly at the situation of armed groups in the municipality referred to these powerful elements: "They protect us from the bad guys...uh...enemies who want to enter the municipality"; "those here, they are friends, they do not kill for no reason"; "they don't extort...we are protected." My interlocutors rightly noted that the situation in Badiraguato differed from that in many other parts of Mexico where extortion or violent clashes between competing networks were rife.[16] Still, as the social texture of this conflict illustrated, it was through a permanent use of violence and threats that the powerful exercised their domination.

During Martín's funeral, it was rumored that a *pesado* had paid for the ceremony and the subsequent celebrations that night in El Rancho. There were reports of many shots fired into the air on the occasion in the hamlet. In a grocery store, an old gentleman and Blanca talked about what might come next. "Well, let's see if they won't rise up now. You know that they don't miss any chance to kill each other," said the gentleman. Even if this perspective just envisioned a superficial motive (a "chance"), it nevertheless put a finger on the central element of the relationship between Martín's group and the dominant network in the main town that brought the wild bunch to heel: "to rise up" invariably induces an armed action that challenges a relationship of domination. After the old man left, Blanca told me that Martín was killed because he was betrayed; there was talk of a phone call from one of his relatives and, she said, "it came from here." She added: "That's why we're just going to wait and let's see what comes next." Something seemed to have changed: a *pesado* paid for the burial and the idea of reprisals by Martín's band was now neither excluded nor irrational. This kind of reversal revealed what causes the "high periods," those in which my interlocutors increased their attention beyond the usual information that would lead them to declare: "He must have been killed for a reason." When a group had the resources to rise up, the fear of reprisal followed.

THE BRAVURA OF "EL GALLITO":
THE VIOLENCE OF THE POWERFUL

Another conflict that happened during my investigation helped me clarify how killings were processed. This one differed in two respects: on the one hand, it aroused particular concern among my interlocutors, the conflict being likely to provoke a "high period," that is, a wave of murders; on the other, it generated an abundance of commentary, due to the direct involvement of the police chief of Badiraguato's municipal police: José Guadalupe Guerrero Reyes, nicknamed "El Gallito" (the little rooster).

From November 23–26, 2014, the town of Badiraguato celebrated its founding with a festival. On Saturday the 24th, I returned to the main town from a hamlet in the sierra where I had been staying. Sunday afternoon I took off for Culiacán to teach some classes at the Universidad Autónoma de Sinaloa. Monday morning, I received a cryptic message from Teófilo: "You have a knack for never being around when you need to be," which I understood as a reference to my habit of being absent from Badiraguato when an event like the arrest of "El Chapo" went down. I later gleaned from local press accounts what it was about this time: the first headline announced "Three Dead During Badiraguato Founding Day Celebrations." Skimming through the few articles, I learned that "three offenders" had died in a "clash" with the municipal police. At the end of a high-speed car chase, the occupants of the vehicle, armed with a Kalashnikov, reportedly opened fire on the police officers, who returned fire, killing the driver and the two passengers.

Returning to the main town in the early afternoon, I stopped in Yolanda's grocery store where I found her with Antonio, settled as usual on the store's shaded porch. The atmosphere was gloomy. The pair were observing the street and put even less energy than usual into keeping up a conversation. We self-consciously ended up talking about the village festival.

ANTONIO: "In your lands [in France], do they kill?"
ADELE: "No, not like here."
ANTONIO: "Ah there . . . Here, they kill a lot."

He stared ahead fixedly, his hat tilted on his forehead. "Really, it's not possible, in the town square, it wasn't beautiful to see." The discussion moved haltingly, interspersed with silences. He talked about the stray bullets, the people they hit; pans of tamales and menudo overturned, panic everywhere, an old lady fell, she was shoved, trampled. Antonio punctuated it with: "No, I tell you, it's ugly. . . . Three, just like that (tres de un tiro). . . . No, I'm telling you, it's never going to end." I ended up having to ask, "But what happened?"

ANTONIO (*WEARILY*): *"Pfff, who knows, quarreling (pleitos), boozing (borrachera), money. . . . If you had seen the pans of tamales all spilled. . . . It's never going to stop."*

YOLANDA: *"It's been a while since something like that happened."*

ANTONIO (*SHAKING HIS HEAD*): *"Three, just like that, three young people."*

Gradually, as we talked, from bits and snatches of conversation I pieced together what had unfolded on Sunday night.

YOLANDA: *Their car hit the power pole at the intersection with the cemetery road, they killed two there in the car, supposedly they were still armed, that the other ["El Gallito," the police chief] was afraid. . . . Pedro jumped out of the car, he ran toward the cemetery. They say he had no weapon, he begged the chief not to kill him but he put six or seven bullets in his head anyway. Just like that, there in the cemetery. They say that he begged for his life."*

ANTONIO: *"Three, just like that."*

Antonio invoked the usual causes, which, as we have seen, simultaneously helped make sense of violence with minimal efforts ("pfff, who knows?") while also referring to the prevailing and stigmatizing ways of talking about it—quarrels, drinking, money. However, a different narrative emerged that departed from what the local press had already relayed. In fact, the circulation of the media narrative about the deaths of the three young people remained limited. Only two newspapers were distributed in the village: the one that broadcast the headlines by loudspeaker did not report the incident, and the other buried it in the inside pages, under miscellaneous happenings.

In the efforts to account for these new deaths, the discussions in the aftermath of the festival tried to reconstruct the night the three young townspeople died, but without the media discourse being mentioned, criticized, denounced, or contradicted. So, from the day after I came back, I got a different story—consistently from all my interlocutors. It diverged completely from the one I had gleaned from the local press. The train of events was as follows: on the second night of the village's founding festival, a gunfight broke out while the celebrations were in full swing. Among the activities on the program that evening was a beauty contest to elect "The Queen of Badiraguato" with a jury composed of the mayor and members of the Sinaloa state government, who had come especially for the occasion.

The event was staged on the recently renovated central plaza: a dais, seating, and at the back, in front of the steps of the town hall, a bar. The shooting broke out near the bar between youths from the village and the municipal police, injuring onlookers. Despite the mayor's attempts to calm things down, the incident ended the celebration. Police arrested four of the gunmen. Later that night, the police station was attacked with automatic weapons in an attempted jailbreak. The attackers and the freed prisoners fled in two cars. The ensuing chase ended at the cemetery road intersection when one of the getaway cars crashed into a power pole. The police riddled the car with bullets, killing two of the three occupants, all cousins. The surviving one, Pedro, fled to the cemetery, where "El Gallito" caught up with him. Unarmed, he begged the police chief to spare his life, only to end up with several bullets in his head.

This narrative included precise and detailed moments, such as the words exchanged in the cemetery just before the third man's death. Everyone knew the story by now, whether or not they had been in the square during the shooting, near the police station during the later attack, or by the cemetery during the execution. Beyond the consensus narrative, none of my interlocutors explicitly objected to what had happened. Still, the way they commented or dwelled on a particular sequence of events that night hinted at an unvoiced judgment. In front of the grocery store, Antonio and Yolanda, who had been present in the plaza, recounted in great detail the moments they had witnessed and could not shake. Yolanda, whose daughter was sixth in line to parade before the beauty contest judges, said the shooting began with the fifth contestant. The conversation then quickly touched on the attack on the police station, but Yolanda focused on the chase and its tragic outcome. She reported that Pedro had no weapons when he was killed, while Antonio repeated: "Three, just like that."

In another conversation in the courtyard of the "chambers," I rehashed the events with Ismael and Teresa. Ismael began by recalling the words of the mayor following the shooting in the square: "This jerk (*pendejo*), after the shooting, found nothing better to say than 'it doesn't matter, it doesn't matter, don't pay attention.' But how do you do that?! People were hit!" He then suggested that this little phrase was not to everyone's taste and also spoke of the pleading in the cemetery. In the same vein, Roberto focused on the shooting by taking exception to the location of the bar: "The bar in front of the door of the town hall! We've never seen anything like this!" In another grocery store, the conversation between a customer and Blanca that I overheard evoked the three young men's family ties and what else was known about them.

The choice of whether to focus on the shooting, the chase, or how the three youths met their ends, as well as how to talk about it, let me grasp which actions or sequences were questionable in the speaker's view. This was particularly revealing in the interaction between Teresa and Ismael. He reported the mayor's words, expressed his disagreement, and immediately clarified that he was not the only one who found what was said to be problematic. This last clarification—regarding the impact of the mayor's words on others—is important. In fact, it articulates that singling out a detail or action meant judging it. By specifying that the attention to the mayor's inanity was shared, he suggested that this was a widely-held opinion in town. Thus, Roberto relied on the same episode as Ismael to implicitly criticize the mayor—of whom he did not think highly—by suggesting that the location of the bar facilitated, or even provoked, the shooting. Yolanda would not outright express her outrage at the killing of the three youths, but dwelled on Pedro's pleading for his life and the fact that he was unarmed. Similarly, in Blanca's grocery store, by focusing on the three locally-known young people, she and her customer emphasized their roots in the town and its networks of interknowledge. They did so less explicitly, however, than Antonio, with his repetitive "three just like that" and "it's ugly." And in all the conversations in the days that followed, the episode in the cemetery gradually stood out.

As expected, Teófilo's reaction once again contrasted with those I had encountered. Arriving at the doors of our respective rooms on the evening of my return to town, he responded to my puzzlement and air of being a little undone by the day's conversations—during which I also had just learned of Adriana's abduction—with this: "Unfortunately, it is the fault of the young people." Seeing my surprise, he went on: "Oh, and if I come and shoot at your house, what do you do? You chase me and you kill me, that's it! It's the young people's fault!" By the radical contrast with the other snippets of exchanges, Teófilo's statement was revealing both in form and substance. It was no secret that he never shrank from expressing loud and clear what was on his mind. He was particularly in form that night because it was in the same conversation that he told me, "You can't feed soup to one and refuse it to the other."

However, his take on the deaths of the three young people differed from what I had heard so far. As Teófilo saw it, the attack on the police station justified what followed. He made the argument by analogy: him shooting at my house would equate to the three detainees' relatives attacking the police station; and my defense or the revenge I would exact by going after him to kill him would be equivalent to the car chase and the shooting of the young people by the police. He thus proposed interpreting the reaction of the police independent of their function, as if they were reacting in a private as opposed to a professional capacity. This perspective, about which Teófilo made no bones, also surfaced in others' reactions. But whereas he said that it is not right to shoot at a house, most of my other interlocutors felt that it is not right to kill an unarmed man begging for his life. Thus, when Teófilo used the word "fault" (*culpa*), he made crystal clear what was most often only insinuated in a lower key. Antonio's phrase "it's ugly" understated how wrong he thought what had happened.

A reading of this event as likely to trigger a cycle of revenge gradually imposed itself. It became more and more explicit in the ensuing weeks. My interlocutors opined that there would be "retaliation," that "it will never stop." In January, I learned that at the Christmas service, when "El Gallito" entered the church, many people walked out. While this could be interpreted as a gesture of disapproval, my interlocutors put it down to fear that his presence would trigger other violent acts. As for Teófilo, he said that "the hunt between the two sides continues." So, in all respects, these expectations fit in with the experiences in other conflicts, such as the one with the El Rancho *gavilla*, but also differed from murders that were only apprehended with "he must have been killed for a reason." This time, too, just as at Martín's funeral, it was "let's see what comes next."

These reactions naturally formed part of how people viewed the forces involved. On the side of the young men killed, some comments dwelled on family ties to a person described as a *pesado*, although the three young people seemed to have primarily run with a fairly minor band. In any case, they were not linked to the dominant main town network. On the other side, the profile of "El Gallito" was crucial. A member of the Federal Ministerial Police since 2010, he was first stationed in the port of Mazatlán, where he was ambushed. His armored car, which he still used, saved him. In 2013, he was appointed chief of police for Badiraguato, where one of his "women" lived. Described as a "*pistolero*," he personified the ambiguous distinction between state and non-state violence. Heavily armed and traveling through town in his armored vehicle, he earned his byname for other activities attributed to him. As *pistolero*, or henchman, he was reputed to take part in armed operations related to conflicts between trafficking network leaders in northwest Mexico. His local social status thus showed the entanglement between the power he derived from the state and his own as a powerful actor. The characterization by my interlocutors of the cases around "El Gallito" as "retaliation" was revealing: the violence he exerted as a state representative was above all violence carried out by a powerful actor. Far from justifying a possible anticipation of other remedies (for example, institutional or judicial), the understanding of these acts was eminently rooted in local violent relations. Conversely, it was possible to see a process emerging that was usually missing: a condemnation, however discreet and only hinted at, of the police chief's actions.

On March 22, 2015, at around 8:30 p.m., I received a phone call from Teófilo telling me not to go out, that "there's trouble brewing . . . you never know." I asked him what was going on, and he replied, "It is said they just killed 'El Gallito' in Culiacán. Can't you look at your shit (*chingadera*)?" He meant "check your smartphone." That evening nothing appeared, but the next morning, I actually got the headlines of the regional newspapers saying that "around 8:30 p.m. we learned from the hotline that a person had been shot by 'hitmen' (*sicarios*). He was the chief of the Badiraguato local police."

That evening and the next day, a process of storytelling and processing this death began again in the daily life of the town. First of all, even though it had not occurred there, it was related to the main town by my interlocutors starting on the evening of March 22. Laura told me that when she drove around town that evening "people didn't look sad." Teófilo, who by then was living in an outlying part of town where relatives of the three murdered young men also lived, said: "Around my house, it looked like it was the New Year!," referring to all the guns popping off in celebration.

The next day, elements were brought into the town's conversational forums that helped to weave a storyline around the police chief's death. In particular, two antecedents were suggested. On the one hand, they cited the death a week earlier of the brother of one of "El Gallito"'s November victims. This man, they said, had sworn revenge, and had been kidnapped before being killed—implicitly pointing to "El Gallito." On the other hand, a woman from the same family allegedly took the police commander to task at a public event, accusing him, insulting and threatening him. These discussions seemed to have two intelligibility effects on my interlocutors. First, it was a question of explaining why the homicide happened now, not two months before or six months later. They thus fitted the police chief's death into the events of November, that is, in what they had expected, anticipated, and predicted. On the other hand, it broadened the relevant elements needed for making sense of the new death: what had taken place in Culiacán that night would not have made sense without the events in the previous days in Badiraguato. Regarding how the assassination was carried out, the comments in the village were particularly focused on the presence of the police chief's children at the assassination scene. The salient detail for the commenters was that the assailants insisted on letting the children out of the car before gunning him down.

The apprehension of this new homicide, however, took place in a very different context. The discretion and modalities of the November media treatment contrasted with the media coverage of the death of "El Gallito." The news made the front pages of all the regional newspapers several days in a row and reached the national press. The official account presented the murder as the work of "hitmen" and underlined the police chief's courage—he was said to have died to protect his children. *El Debate* reported that, according to a witness, "he tried to defend himself, but, with his children present, he raised his hands in a sign of surrender, and then apparently exchanged words with his killers, two of them took out the three children and then we heard the shots."[17] Brave man that he was, he was therefore killed due to another of his qualities: that of loving father. The town's mayor, interviewed on the occasion, attributed the killing to "organized crime." Asked by a reporter if he thought the murder related to the work the chief had done in the municipality, he replied: "I don't think so. In truth, we always maintained close contact and there was no sign, no such threat." This narrative was therefore also based on a different logic than that of my interlocutors, namely one of dissociating the assassination from Badiraguato. However, unlike in November, this official account pervaded the town.

On the way to the sierra with two municipal officials, we stopped first in a taquería in town. They hugged the proprietor and we sat down at the table. As we were waiting for our tacos that his wife was preparing, he started a conversation about the death of "El Gallito" with Gonzalo, one of the important officials of the local administration. In no time, our host mentioned "the November thing," causing an obvious embarrassment for Gonzalo, who regularly turned to me, as if to check if I was paying attention. He replied: "Who knows?" Then: "He ["El Gallito"] must have had all kinds of trouble," concluding evasively, "Who knows where that came from?" Finally, he reminded his interlocutor that this happened in Culiacán. The proprietor jumped on this last point, saying:

"Yes, it was agreed, that it shouldn't be done here." The official, clearly even more embarrassed and temporarily at a loss for words, obviously wanted to let the conversation run out of steam. Left in control of the field, the owner ended with: "Ah, the grudge. . . . I knew one, they killed his father and he said he could forgive. Three months later, the other guy was dead." When we were back on the road, I was careful not to bring up the subject again. Gonzalo, however, still commented, in effect telling me that if the state government were to think that the "problem came from here" we ran the risk of a reinforced military deployment in town.

The *taquería*'s proprietor paid no heed to the problem that my presence posed for Gonzalo and that was obviously embarrassing him. Presumably, given the *patron*'s bluntness and Gonzalo's attention to my presence, the discussion would probably have taken a completely different turn had I not been there. It highlighted the situational stakes of this discourse. My presence, it seems, required Gonzalo to put on his hat as a municipal official and interpret the death of "El Gallito" as best he could to conform to the official line. With his last comment in the car he distanced himself from this discourse and staked out the town hall's overriding objective: avoiding a reinforcement of the military presence in the municipality.

This narrative weighed in with a contradictory effect. On the one hand, it came with a threat that all bore in mind: although "people didn't look sad," rejoicing loudly at the police chief's demise was not advisable and, because the inhabitants were quite aware of what "military repression" meant, caution was the order of the day. Thus, in front of me, some people were more cautious than the *taquería* owner and were more reticent in how they talked about the latest homicide. On the other hand, by virtue of being in the newspapers and known throughout town, this story challenged the residents' version and how they thought about it, sometimes forcing them to argue their point of view more stridently. In a way, in the face of the challenges posed by this new murder, my interlocutors did more than make it understandable: they appropriated it by legitimating it.

Thus, the inhabitants framed the story all the more firmly the more it was challenged, and in the process highlighted the critical questions posed by the act of killing in general. First, as the conflict over the El Rancho band showed, an important question—never formulated in this instance—was who did the killing. When the three cousins died, this question raised no difficulties: the fact that it had been "El Gallito" was not doubted by any of my interlocutors. On the other hand, the identity of his own killers was a subject of rumors. As implied by the words of the proprietor at the *taquería* that "it was agreed, that it shouldn't be done here," several of my interlocutors suggested that the murder had been planned for a long time and had been negotiated in high places. Armed men who were relatives of the young men killed in November were not necessarily the only ones behind the act. Even if a relative of one of the cousins was a *pesado*, it was understood that he was not enough of a heavy. It was rumored that an important personage had summoned "El Gallito" to discuss what had happened. By refusing, he would have crossed an additional red line, sealing his fate with the more powerful man.

The hypothesis circulating in town was therefore that a more important man had ordered the killing—and that is how the *Riodoce* regional weekly would report it later. The spread of this hypothesis, with many details left out of the narratives, demonstrated the importance in the eyes of my interlocutors of attributing this act to the powerful. The essential element of the proposed narrative—the victim had crossed another red line, forcing the powerful to punish him—is that the killing of an important armed man is necessarily the work of an (even more) important sponsor. The stories of powerful people who decided to kill someone (less) powerful or who ended violent conflicts through mediation were common and pointed in the same direction: the act of killing depended on the social hierarchy. Unlike the incomprehensible murders by the El Rancho brothers, who killed without being powerful, the other homicides showed that you had to already have power to be legitimate to kill.

Second, the expedient gloss of "he must have been killed for a reason" did not apply here. Given the issues raised by the death of "El Gallito," my interlocutors dwelled on why he got killed. Most notably, mentions of Pedro's plea in the cemetery surged the day after the hit on the police chief. Recalling the victim's entreaties was enough for "El Gallito" to deserve condemnation without the need to rehash all the facts. Antonio recalled on this occasion that "Pedro wasn't even armed," and Yolanda said: "Personally, I had no grudges against him. But hey ... those who did this had to know why. ... And the November thing, they say the other one begged." While in November the insistence on this episode was one of many forms of muted judgment, the victim's pleas had now become the main register of attributing a cause. The need to explain the murder led to a more explicit condemnation of the action in the cemetery. Most noticeably, a new formulation surfaced now: "He was the law, he should have stopped them, not killed them," as Laura put it. This argument was neither advanced in the wake of the November killings or in the months marked by the expectation of reprisals. Focus on his police status appeared to help further explain the death of "El Gallito."

Finally, in parallel with the cause attributed to the death of "El Gallito," the modus operandi of the attackers—how they killed—was raised and judged appropriate. The assailants' initiative to get the children out—a theme widely picked up by the newspapers, but in the reverse sense—contributed to this reading. Likewise, the manner in which "El Gallito" shot Pedro was grounds for condemning him and allowed the townspeople to reappropriate the police chief's murder. The attention paid to the details of the act was made explicit by the critical nature of the plea, but it aligned with the questions surrounding the "how" (where, when) that arose in the commentaries on the other murders. It represented the narrow margin of evaluation expressed by my interlocutors regarding these numerous logical, evident, and dominant murders: the right to assess how the act of killing was carried out in a given situation.

This focus echoed the recurrent figure of betrayal. Thus, Teófilo often lambasted the cowardice of subterfuge. His own son-in-law had been killed through a ruse: a friend picked him up with his car, telling him to leave his gun, and delivered him to his murderers. Similarly, one of the problematic aspects of Martín's death was that a relative gave him up with a phone call. The threat posed by the involvement of relatives in murders was perhaps one of the reasons why my interlocutors focused on how the killings were arranged. The figure of betrayal here expressed the difficulty of fending off the insecurity created by murders.

The specificity of the conflict around "El Gallito" did not reside in the modalities of making sense of homicides and therefore raised the question whether his status as chief of police mattered. The gradual condemnation he faced following the unarmed Pedro's murder reveals a concern over the manner of killing and the resulting "high period" of conflict.

In evaluating his murder, my interlocutors seemed to detach the chief's special status from it. However, this dimension was not dropped and the modes of judging these acts related more broadly to the margins of evaluating the violence ordered by the powerful. Indeed, the resources provided by his status (the uniform, the armored vehicle, legal legitimacy, political connections) were integrated into the fears expressed by the townspeople. Similarly, his role as policeman was recalled after his death around several themes: his uncompromising enforcement of parking rules and of wearing helmets on two-wheelers, his closeness to the *pesados*, and his character as a man deemed "*bravo*." Depending on the context, *bravo* can mean brave, ballsy, arrogant, violent, aggressive, or even ferocious. His status as an armed man was recognized—as a man working for a *pistolero* in the sierra told me: "If there is anything he is to be recognized for, it is that he was *bravo*"—and it was not incompatible with the fact that he "was the law." On the contrary, even, the reactions of my interlocutors showed that, unlike the case of El Rancho, the status of "El Gallito" did not pose a problem for understanding his violence. Thus, it was less the status of police officer that constituted the determining criterion for my interlocutors than his membership in the social group of those who have the power to kill, a status reinforced by the resources that came with his job.

. . . . .

Many murders followed, one after the other, that were regarded as isolated from each other by my interlocutors. This consideration, which defined "low periods," was accompanied by fitting homicides into their daily lives. Without feeling the need and without having the means for in-depth inquiries into each of the murders, these men and women assigned them causes. In doing so, they reduced the uncertainty and vulnerability that homicides introduced into their daily lives: "Only those who make trouble are in for it." However, the causal explanations they produced harked back to the media and institutional framing in which these attributions were made. Indeed, references to making sense of this threatening violence became available through the depoliticizing and exoticizing of the municipality, its people, and its economy. In this framing, the killers and the killed all were criminals, and all political, repressive, social, and gender violence was swallowed up in the illusion of a common and elusive enemy: drug trafficking.

The study of a conflict that eluded the causes usually grafted onto homicides revealed the issues behind this obviousness, behind the use of the impersonal form and putting the blame on the victim. The series of murders surrounding the El Rancho conflict revealed the extent of the destruction wrought by clashes between armed groups: areas under attack, hamlets deserted, populations displaced. The killings in Badiraguato therefore related to economic, social, and political dynamics. The characterization of the violence of the El Rancho band as irrational exposed the assumption on which the usual processing of homicides rested: it was the powerful who killed.

Making sense of murders was also compelled by the domination of those who wielded the resources to "administer" their trade—and the term "administer" matters, since it points to the centrality of political connections. This dimension emerged clearly from how my interlocutors understood the "El Gallito" murders. The questions this conflict raised were resolved by a paradox. On the one hand, the more sustained intensity of the comments highlighted the specific nature of the conflict invoked by the status of the chief of police; on the other hand, the elements that were considered as determining the judgment revealed those that lurked in the usual treatment of one-off murders: who, why, and how they killed were the questions reserved for violence by those who dominated, and in which lodged the anticipation of reprisals.

Thus, violent acts committed by the destitute tended to be viewed as pathological and irrational, while those by the dominant appeared as constitutive of a social order, a coercion that would impose sanctions on deviant behavior. Acts of violence intersected at the crossroads between self-protection and the unequal social relationships of predatory capitalism. Behaviors that were supposed to protect against violence defined what "behaving well" meant and, conversely, conduct that exposed you to violence was judged to be poor. Similarly, the assessment of whether or not the manner in which a person was killed was acceptable intertwined with the social positions attributed to those involved and in the evaluations of whether or not reprisals were likely. In this sense, qualifying a situation, positioning and judging it by inserting it into a storyline, were operations that remained eminently embedded in violent social relations. The confrontation between contradictory positions with regard to an act of violence that had just taken place was constrained by the possibility that reprisals would come to define a posteriori the past act as unacceptable. In short, that violence responded to criticism.

Paradoxically, when it came to "killing," the term "administer" appeared to refer less to state representatives than to heft in the drug trade, serving to distinguish the powerful who would know how to administer from the marginalized who would never get it. In the next chapter, I follow the trail of the local authorities' absence in the operations of qualifying violent acts to understand how the state's local representatives fit into this context.

SEVEN

Administering

"And when everyone will say, 'In Badiraguato, they wear helmets
and use seat belts', I will have succeeded, I will be satisfied."

THE MAYOR

TAKEN OUT OF CONTEXT, this statement by the mayor of Badiraguato
would be trivial: a mayor concerned with the road safety of his constituents.
Yet it is precisely when judged in context that this statement is remarkable.
Indeed, the preceding chapters reveal a paradox. On the one hand, state policies evidently structured the political economy of the municipality. Irrigation
of the plain, military repression, and the strategies of former mayors strad-
dling the poppy trade and political posts were decisive in the imposition of
poppy monoculture. Similarly, unequal access to land derived from state
actions: in the formation of the *ejidos*, in their cooptation, and, in a particularly accentuated way, in their translation by the political-agrarian intermediaries who set up legal cover through the common property regime. On the
other hand, in ad hoc interventions, officials kept shirking responsibility for
some of the most pressing issues, delegating them to abstract figures. Thus,
the municipal employee could say that the sierra was "controlled by this sector," another senior town hall official could maintain that the *cerco* is stronger
than the *ejido*, and a mayor could blame the assassination of his police chief
on the indefinite figure of "organized crime." Badiraguato offered a version—
perhaps more extreme and therefore more visible—of the apparent gap
between the context of violence and the routine functioning of government
services in Mexico. Politicians whose action was constitutive in configuring
social relations could nevertheless publicly sidestep key social problems.

Hence, in what follows I situate the day-to-day actions of local government in the context I outlined in the previous chapters by focusing specifically on the practices of municipal employees to gradually unpack the issues
these raise. The daily life of the local government concentrated several characteristics that make describing it particularly heuristic. First, the "free

municipality" (*municipio libre*) is the base unit of the federal structure, and it enjoys important prerogatives.[1] The municipalities were expanded as part of the decentralization that began in 1982 and the expansion of anti-corruption policies, with several hundred billion dollars primarily appropriated to the municipal level.[2] However, the local government was staffed by Badiraguatenses who lived there and who were thus also mired in the context of armed violence. The central focus of the chapter is the sometimes jarring inclusion of these governmental practices in uncertainty, repression, and predation, a configuration which we now know was intrinsically linked to federal policies. So, I deal here with the public administration in the Mexican state's most basic unit, a level that itself is caught up in the state's public policies. The inconsistencies revealed by the need for this distinction are crucial to understanding the paradoxical coexistence of a stable public administration and the dynamics of armed violence.[3]

I conducted an ethnography in the offices of Badiraguato's local government. As a participant observer, I worked for several months first in the Department of Family Affairs, then in the town hall secretariat (*secretario de ayuntamiento*), and finally in the Department of Social Development (*desarrollo social*). I immersed myself in daily office life, sat in on meetings, traveled with the civil servants, and pitched in at public events. My approach builds on the anthropology of the state and of development, describing the concrete encounters between the governed and the governing—the administration at the "street level." My other focus was on the local implementation of state policies and so, in what follows, I account for the bureaucratic reproduction and depoliticization that shaped the discourses and actions of the town hall officials, specifically in how they linked to the context of violence.[4] Thus, the central tension of this chapter stems from the reproduction of practices apparently disconnected from the context and what they actually did in context.

"BECAUSE I THOUGHT YOU WERE THE BOSS": A LOCAL POLITICAL GAME UNDER STRAIN

In the Department of Family Affairs, I inquired into the office employees' careers in the municipal government. Gabriel said he had been working in various administrative positions for eleven years. He was unionized, so he could not be fired, except for gross misconduct, but when administrations changed it got tricky—since he could be shuffled into harder or easier jobs and either get a raise or have his salary cut. Jorge, for his part, told me that he had been working there for fourteen years. I asked him, "Unionized?" "No, on trust" (de confianza), meaning that he was placed in the job by the current mayor and was therefore also extremely vulnerable during changes in administration. That surprised me:

—And no mayor has turned you out for fourteen years?

—No, but I have the playbook. Their problem with others is that they are in too much of a hurry and don't stick around. Me, I wait around to find out which is the right one.

—Waiting for the results?

—No, I am waiting to find out who the right candidate is. Because, you see, it's like the one who was [in that post] before Gabriel. He went to campaign for someone, there was a video, he got burned. As a result, when the other one [the new mayor] took office, he took revenge and threw him out.

Cristian reminded Jorge that his recipe was not foolproof, citing the case of a former colleague who campaigned for the right candidate but still did not get his job back. Gabriel retorted: "Yes, but that will always happen, no matter which mayor comes in, because he gets his orders from higher up, too: that the governor wants such and such a place for someone, that the compadre *wants a job, the first cousin also. . . . It's normal."*

The "playbook" proposed by Jorge and amended by Gabriel referred to the critical moment in the political life of Badiraguato. Jorge explained something that was common knowledge and unambiguous: picking the "the right candidate" referred to the PRI's nominating process for the municipal election. There was never a mystery as to the election's outcome: the candidate of what formerly was the only party—and that was hegemonic in Badiraguato until 2021[5]—was routinely elected. Being nominated therefore more or less made you a shoe-in come election time.[6] The real competition took place before the nomination, with individuals jockeying to let the higher PRI leaders know of their availability to be a candidate. This period, called the "pre-campaign," was marked by great uncertainty. The various candidates "running" for the nomination solicited municipal employees, especially those hailing from the sierra, to campaign for them and facilitate access to their hamlet. In this situation, the employees faced a dilemma: opting to work for a candidate early on and thus being among the earliest supporters meant possibly being rewarded with a (better) position, but they also ran the risk of suffering the winner's ire if the PRI did not choose the candidate on whom they had bet.

However, for Jorge, Cristian, Gabriel, and other municipal employees, holding a position in the administration was a rare privilege, it being one of the few sources of legal employment in the municipality. Even if the salaries were quite modest, such a position could bring financial stability. Cristian, in his fifties, had started a municipal job two years earlier. He had spent much of his life trying multiple subsistence strategies, ranging from emigration to the United States to seasonal work in the sierra during the marijuana harvests. His son had managed to get himself appointed as a driver for the town government and was unionized. But he was killed during the El Rancho conflict and, with the support of the municipal union, his position went to his father. Many of the other core employees had returned to Badiraguato from the United States, having failed to make it on the "other side." José had also emigrated, before returning and landing a job thanks to being related to one of the senior municipal executives. Getting into a unionized position reduced future uncertainty, but working conditions remained dependent on the ins and outs of mayoral mandates, and for the many "on trust" employees, at stake was a three-year horizon for a source of income.

It was therefore no surprise that following his inauguration as mayor, the anteroom of Mario Valenzuela López (2014–16) was jammed for several weeks. "On trust" employees of the past administration and people who could claim connections with the new mayor lined up hoping to get "something." The new mayor also had to deal with demands from the PRI leadership and from some of his defeated rivals who sat on his municipal council, as Gabriel pointed out: "The incoming mayor ... also has orders from on high: that the governor wants such and such a place for someone, that the *compadre* wants a job, the first cousin also." The losing candidates for the nomination sometimes managed to place some of their faithful, leaving some hope to those who had bet on the wrong horse.

Even non-supporters still clung to the hope of negotiating "something" during the new mayor's early days in the office. For example, Gabriela queued up seeking a job for her husband, a former municipal police officer. When Mario Valenzuela finally received her, he turned her down as she had feared: "And why don't you go see Lorena [Pérez Olivas]?"—a rival and ex-mayor of Badiraguato (2002–04) and, at that time, the local member of state parliament. The situation of Gabriela's family was indeed paradoxical: the husband was a distant relative of one of the most influential female politicians in the municipality, among the few to have experienced a substantial social ascent through politics. However, as Gabriela told me, they had missed the mark: "Had we supported Lorena at the beginning, we would be better off today." She only begged the new mayor for any junior position, just to get to the health insurance that came with municipal jobs. But Valenzuela, well aware of Gabriela's and her husband's situation, could not seem to get past their being related to his rival. To his provocative question "And why don't you go see Lorena?" she had proudly shot back, "Because I thought you were the boss." Her retort made her feel better, but the family's financial situation would remain quite precarious for the next few years. Gabriela's example reflected the linkage between the material insecurity of many of the inhabitants and their dependence on political networks whose stakes were largely out of their reach.[7]

Mobilizing support of the inhabitants during the pre-campaign was important because it could help candidates convince the party leadership to choose them. It would even appear that on three occasions since the 1950s, the party in effect consulted with activists on deciding between candidates in a primary. While these conversations did not go anywhere and remained isolated instances, local mobilizations nonetheless retained some of their importance; at least, they still figured in the strategies of several local politicians. However, during the period of my fieldwork, this strategy produced only losers. Thus, Lorena Pérez Olivas, the member of state parliament, was a clear favorite for being reelected mayor (to a second term) and conducted no visible mobilization activities locally. On the other hand, Miguel Ángel and Gonzalo, competing against each other, maintained considerable local patronage networks—for example during the implementation of land reform (chapter 4)—but their fate and that of the people who depended on them was sealed at the state level. Miguel Ángel had little chance of becoming mayor after betting on the wrong candidate in the contested nomination of the PRI candidate for the 1999 state governorship. While he did not hold down a municipal post, he nevertheless found refuge in the state government and continued—pending a reversal of fate—to be quite prominent in the municipality. Thus, the methods of the game in which people who tried to latch onto modest but legal incomes were embedded in the competition between local male and female politicians, a competition that, however—in Badiraguato, as in all municipalities where the PRI still ruled—was largely determined by state party officials.

My interlocutors were wise in the ways of this political competition, which Professor Praxedis Alarcón Valdez, a former Badiraguato mayor (1981–83), exposed in a book he published in 2012. I heard *Political Radiography: A Retrospective Vision* mentioned often when I started my investigation. One of my interlocutors then had told me: "There is one who has settled his accounts and who spills the goods on their internal workings." The author had retained significant political influence after his term in office and held senior positions in the municipal government until the mid-2000s. In his book, he denounced the control exerted by state networks over local politics, the doings of gray eminences at the state level who had more power than the elected officials, and the resulting monopolization of positions by a select group. Reflecting the real-life functioning of the municipal political system, he never mentions the election itself in his book, instead focusing on the internal PRI nomination process. Before delving into the deplorable appointment practices of recent years, he reviews the political trajectories of all Badiraguato mayors since 1954 and fingers the elements that allowed them to be appointed.

His work, written in a caustic style and replete with popular sayings (which the author puts in the mouths of the people mentioned), is certainly illuminating but also requires factoring in the author's personal and political motivations. On the one hand, his son's political career seems to have been ill-fated for two reasons. The first, which is blasted in the book, stemmed from the role that Praxedis Alarcón played in a competition between two municipal networks of the PRI: "the Teachers" (*los Maestros*), a group with which Praxedis Alarcón was affiliated, versus "the Laras" (after a powerful politically networked family). Each group was nicknamed in a deprecating manner. According to Praxedis, "the Laras" had put their thumbs on the scales for most positions in recent elections and municipal senior executives blocked Praxedis's son when he tried to become president of the PRI youth wing in Badiraguato as retribution against his father. Moreover, the son was a follower of Miguel Ángel, and his political fortune depended on the latter's clout over important posts. As long as Miguel Ángel remained persona non grata for municipal president, Praxedis's son had little chance of rising in the municipal hierarchy.

On the other hand, Praxedis Alarcón wrote during what he deemed a particularly calamitous time: multipartyism had perfidiously penetrated into Badiraguato! Worse, the PRI's own leadership had introduced this political Trojan horse! In point of fact, Ángel Robles Bañuelos, the mayor from 2011 to 2013, was at the time of his appointment neither a PRI activist nor a native of Badiraguato (although he had been an inspector of public education in the municipality for twenty-two years). His appointment by the PRI resulted from negotiations for the election of the state governor. Threatened by the National Action Party (PAN), the PRI concluded an alliance with the Green Party of Mexico (PVEM) and the New Alliance Party (PANAL) which required it to share the candidacies for certain positions with its new allies, including the post of mayor of Badiraguato. A member of the PANAL, Bañuelos was installed by the PRI, short-circuiting all the other local candidates who had been patiently "waiting their turn." This move appeared even more misguided to Praxedis Alarcón, as the PRI still lost the election for the Sinaloa governorship. It prompted him to write his book to highlight the history of Badiraguato's manipulation by state networks—but with the unfortunate fact that the whole story revolved around his party, which he wanted to persuade of his loyalty. As the dedication indicates, the book aimed to benefit the PRI, which was going through a historical crisis: "This book is dedicated to reflecting on people; the very people who have become identified with boundless respect and who make the struggle for the dignity and value of individuals a daily mandate to be fulfilled. They were the motivation and inspiration for the thoughts that I have formed into this simple book."

To account for the political scene in Badiraguato, he expounds on his own career and seizes on his own nomination, which he insists was unexceptional. He sets out the general lessons he drew from it as follows:

> As I will devote more space to the information that relates to my particular case, I want to clarify that I am doing so to avoid misunderstandings. . . . So I don't want anyone to think that I'm applying here the logics of popular proverbs like 'he who deals, takes the best part' or that of 'holding the frying pan by the handle,' although it is possible that there is something to 'wanting without wishing to.'
>
> Time has taught me that, in looking for and especially in obtaining a public or elected office, the circumstances of the times in which things happen matter a great deal; without neglecting, of course, the particular skills of the person who is fighting to be given things; and, by way of adding a little spice . . . a bit of luck. . . .
>
> Politics is a thing of friends and interests, or of both. All you need is to have one or more friends in or near the place where important decisions are made. It is only necessary for someone to lay his protective mantle on you, to recommend you, to reach out to you, and to save you; no matter how tiny the place you find yourself crammed into at that particular moment. Ah! but ultimately, being a beautiful man or woman, having enough money, and, at worst, having someone who covers your possible economic needs has become the more indispensable and recurring criteria to be able to aspire to a candidacy, whatever it may be, and a fortiori to those at a high level.

He proceeds to explain how his nomination as the mayoral candidate in 1980 was due to his "friendship" with the secretary-general of the state PRI. In his flowery prose, he describes how he learned of his appointment: "Amazed by the unexpected nature of such pleasant news, with a smile of satisfaction spreading across my face, I tell them [the two men who woke him up one morning]: 'Ay muchachos, and you apologize for bringing me this kind of news! . . . But I'll be waiting for you here in three years [at the end of his term as mayor] to wake me up again, telling me that I am the candidate for the position of local member of the state parliament!'"

This reflection thus underlines the extent to which the nomination to the (candidacies for) the two most-coveted positions in the municipality depended on a morning decision sent down from Culiacán. After being elected mayor in 1981, he had made his nephew Fidel Olivas Alarcón secretary of the town hall office, pointing out that like the mayors before and after him, "you can't deny a certain nepotism." In the pre-campaign period following his term, his nephew received the nomination. According to Praxedis, this plum was less due to his own support than to the nephew's "sincere and loyal" friendship with the former PRI president—as opposed, in his view, to opportunistic friendships referred to in the proverb: "One only visits the *nopal* [the prickly pear cactus] when it bears fruit."

Beyond the decisive character of insertion within state networks, several dynamics stand out in Praxedis Alarcón's recital of preconditions for being nominated, recounted in fine detail that my observations confirmed. First, the holy grail was the candidacy for mayor. Until 2014, this position was put back into play after a three-year term, since the Mexican Constitution drawn up after the Revolution limits to one the number of successive terms in office (the slogan in the campaign that pitted Francisco I. Madero against Porfirio Díaz was "effective suffrage, no re-election"). The "consolation prize," according to Alarcón, was being nominated as candidate for parliament. In recent years, this position had often been the stepping stone to the mayoral nomination, the local MP resigning at the beginning of the pre-campaign if he or she was anointed for the mayoralty by the PRI leadership. Competition for these positions was fueled by the considerable economic benefits that came with them. As in the rest of the country, mayors' salaries are not subject to fixed regulations and are established by the municipal councils. In 2013 the civic organization Iniciativa Sinaloa, founded in 2010, published the salaries received by mayors under the transparency law.[8] Ángel Robles was paid

92,569 pesos a month (6,000 USD), in a country where the average monthly income was around 300 USD; in 2013, Mario Valenzuela López raised the mayor's salary by 5 percent. Asked by the press in 2016 about the gap between his salary (among the four highest in the state of Sinaloa) and the fact that his municipality had the highest poverty incidence, he slammed the MPs for earning 200,000 pesos (13,000 USD) per month.[9] Being made mayor was more sought after than the local MP because the former position was free of regulatory mechanisms and oversight and the large sums flowing into municipal coffers provided opportunities for personal enrichment.

In addition, kinship ties, interknowledge, and a few shared traits combined in a social group that grabbed most of the political and administrative positions. Originally from Badiraguato, they built their careers in the municipality's political or trade union representation but often lived elsewhere. Many mayors were former teachers affiliated with the National Union of Education Employees (SNTE), a corporatist organization associated with the PRI. The PRI's municipal section and subsections (attached to the state equivalents: PRI women, the revolutionary youth front, the working-class sector, the agrarian sector) were the other gateways to political careers.

Although rarely taken, other paths were possible: "Nachillo" Landell, son of Nacho Landell, became mayor in 1975, boosted into office by the local breeders' association founded by his father. Affiliated with the State Association of Breeders, the organization offered him access to influential PRI figures at the state level. Antonio López (2005–07) was in some respects an exception because, although he followed the usual stages of political careers (notably the passage through the municipal PRI), he rose to these positions thanks to federal contacts he acquired during an agrarian conflict around the forests and sawmill of the Surutato *ejido*. These superiors imposed him on their state subordinates—much to the chagrin of the other politicians in Badiraguato, one of whom told me: "He couldn't even read." Despite its relative homogeneity, this social group was crossed by the many conflicts arising from its being structured into competing clienteles. Thus, the patronage networks maintained by Badiraguato's politicians depended, like them, mainly on the fate of state, if not federal, politicians. Between "pre-campaign" periods, the successive mayors took office, and if they were focused on issues outside the municipality, the fact remains that they also were in charge of Badiraguato.

A LOOKOUT AND MOTHER'S DAY: THE
TOWN HALL'S CHOSEN REPERTOIRE

The beginning of my investigation coincided with the new mayor Mario Valenzuela López taking his oath of office (*toma de protesta*). On this occasion, he ran through the major projects his administration would undertake. Following in the footsteps of his predecessors, he made upgrading the town center one of the priorities of his "municipal development plan." Two months later, the central plaza had been completely redone. The palm trees, benches, and library made way for a large pedestrian mall over which large pink, green, and white letters spelled out "Badiraguato." At his inauguration, the new mayor expressed his

> pleasure at having the opportunity to inaugurate this municipal Zócalo as a place, a physical area to give Badiraguato a center;[10] with the time that has passed and the works that mayors did during that time, twenty-eight years have gone by. Maybe it was appropriate then, but today the population has grown, the needs have increased. For the next *Grito* (Independence Day),[11] no longer will we have the problem of not enough space, we will celebrate the founding [of the town], we will do it here with the church as a backdrop; it just shows you that our administration is transforming Badiraguato. This can be seen in a number of projects. In two months, we have worked very hard. . . . For instance, the new poplars promenade (*nueva alameda*) where we are currently working on the zip line that we plan to inaugurate in fifteen days.[12]

Indeed, among the other major works carried out were the "new poplars promenade"—a riverside development—but also the "lookout" (*mirador*) on one of the hills surrounding the village, and a swimming pool to replace the stadium located at the edge of town.

These initiatives rolled out to an intensive public relations campaign and the "great works" were a talking point for the municipal government, which, however, the town's people had no trouble seeing through. Teófilo expressed it this way: "I don't know why they do this, but every time there is a new one, he undoes everything the other did before him." He also explained that the preceding mayor, Ángel Robles Bañuelos, owed his nickname "Ángel palms" or "Ángel speed bump palms" (*Ángel palmas topes*) to his having ordered the planting of a large quantity of palm trees in the town; some people said he was friends with the owner of a tree nursery in Culiacán. He was also responsible for raising many speed bumps and replacing the benches in the plaza, with ones made in his hometown, according to the same commenters. These were the trees and benches that his successor had no qualms about ripping out. Once the work was completed, commemorative plaques indicating the mayor's term in office and name were mounted, giving visibility to one of the stakes in this monument-building policy. These public works were in fact one of the main ways in which the administration asserted its presence: writ large, the mayor's. Not surprisingly, on June 29, 2019, the local press announced that the new mayor, Lorena Pérez, had decided to renovate the other end of "this plaza that was in dire need of it and now will become an additional space for tourists who visit us."[13]

As this strategy was explicitly part of the elected officials' repertoire, the residents in turn seized on the mayor's actions in this realm to express their judgments on municipal politics. Like those who pointed out where palm trees and benches installed by Ángel "speed bump palms" came from, the new mayor's public works drew criticism or praise according to how my interlocutors regarded his administration overall. Thus, Valenzuela's detractors regretted the disappearance of trees from the central plaza, which had provided shade for the benches and made it a place for life, for selling ice cream. His supporters, however, liked the renovated square because it allowed staging events the same way as before. Blanca—whose husband, Nacho, insisted that the mayor had been nice to them—said that she "liked the new square," but still acknowledged that "some do not agree," revealing how urban development divided the town.

While the many criticisms lobbed at the new mayor were related to how jobs were handed out—and the disappointments that resulted from this—the residents' way of expressing them focused on the work performed. The same mechanisms were in play where the poplar promenade and the lookout were concerned. Teresa admitted that "Me, I've never even seen the poplar promenade." Teófilo told me that its construction would jeopardize the houses on the opposite river bank the next time it flooded. Finally, the lookout was unanimously rejected in my circle of interlocutors. As we talked about mosquitoes, the dengue fever season, and the insecticides that the municipal services were supposed to spray, Rosa exclaimed, "Pfff, he'd do better taking care of this than making a lookout."

Administrators and the administered thus were in agreement when they made public works a criterion for evaluating municipal policies: for the elected officials it was a badge of activism, and the residents judged them according to their own lights. Nevertheless, this equation concealed a definition of these projects essentially as a function of outward appearances. The lookout was an obvious case in point. The top of one of the hills was bulldozed completely flat to set up the giant letters spelling "BADIRAGUATO," visible from afar, ostensibly creating a lookout point. This act of environmental destruction cost the town hall a fine from the State Ministry of the Environment. Among the negative reactions of my interlocutors, Teófilo's said it all: "A lookout for what? So we can see the hills? We see them every day! So we can see the town? We see it every day!" He concluded: "What's it going to turn into? [A hangout] only for thugs (*de puros malandros*)." He pointed out the critical element: many projects did not aim to improve the lives of the residents ("We see them every day"), and simply ignored the issues they had to deal with in daily life. Predictably, none of the people I knew went to the lookout. After I had left Badiraguato at the end of my fieldwork, I would learn from the newspapers that a body in a bag had been found on the lookout. Teófilo always was a bit of a prophet and above all a very good reader of what went on around him.

On the wide tree-lined riverfront, the "new poplar promenade" struck a more ambiguous note. It was designed as a leisure destination meant to attract tourists: it had a zip line, a suspension bridge, children's playgrounds, picnic tables, and barbecues. The municipal communiqué stressed the fact that it offered Badiraguatenses the opportunity to enjoy a "pretty place, with water and a lot of shade on the banks of the Badiraguato River, and [so] they don't have to go to another place for Easter week."[14] However, developing a leisure environment in this space was problematic from the outset. The riverside, which was regarded as dangerous by many of my interlocutors (chapter 2), had no lighting and was isolated, out of sight of the town. It served mainly for the entertainment of (young) men, who aroused the concerns of other residents who continued to shun the place.

Using an American-style playground model, the infrastructure installed by the town hall was designed to attract families, but it forgot about the modes of protection that local sociability induced. That said, however, the municipal public relations, which also posted about the project on the town hall's Facebook page, got a better reception for its work, mainly from emigrants living in the United States, who posted comments such as "How beautiful my Badiraguato is; I miss it!" By making tourism a priority, the city hall primarily designed these as attractions for people who did not live in Badiraguato, such as the emigrants.[15] It also helped burnish the administration's image among state officials.

In a more clear-cut manner, the other essential criterion for evaluating the municipal government, the organization of celebrations, put the elected officials at odds with the experience of its inhabitants. The attendance at these events was a demonstration of the mayor's popularity, and my interlocutors had this aspect figured out perfectly. Thus, in the same way that saying "Me, I've never even seen the poplar promenade" meant taking a stand against the mayor, Gabriela boasted that she went to a different Mother's Day celebration than the one organized by the town hall on the central plaza. Similarly, Teófilo, trying to convince me that this mayor started his term in office very badly ("this one is too pretentious with the people") cited as proof that, according to his information, the meal planned for Students' Day was far below expectations: "Sandwiches and soft drinks. . . . No, but what is he thinking of?" This affront, including the lack of *sopa fria*, would, in his view, only fuel the wave of discontent that ran through the town.

However, as signaled by the shooting that shut down the town's founding party in November 2014, the stakes in organizing a party attended by large numbers of people were high. As one town hall official explained to me, that particular episode had been all the more damaging because representatives of the state government had been on the beauty contest jury. The political capital of the elected official was therefore directly at stake, and the mayor tried in vain to limit the damage after the shooting by pleading "it doesn't matter, it doesn't matter, don't pay attention."

Mother's Day 2014 was a revealing example of attempts to anticipate threats of violence when organizing events. This celebration posed all the more risks as the mayor had decided to organize it as an open air event, namely on his new plaza: "He will throw a big party with impressive decorations like never before in the history of Badiraguato," the local press reported.[16] In the weeks leading up to the fiesta, he announced that "since this is Mother's Day, men will not be admitted" and jovially added that "for once, women will be served, relaxed and among themselves." The event turned out to be a great success, with many women attending. The square was dotted with tables at which women were served by male municipal employees; there was live music; the women danced and, remarkably, some stayed until very late at night. The photos of that day scrolled for several weeks on the screens in the town hall's waiting room. Over the next few weeks, in his speeches the mayor invariably reminisced about that day. In a hamlet where he came to close out a program, he addressed the women present with "You did not come for Mother's Day? Oh, what you missed. . . . The mothers were very happy! That day we stayed up all night (*ese dia amanecimos*), we were outdoors, the mothers danced all night!" The reference to having "stayed up all night" in the central town square cropped up in all his speeches from then on. In a context where people locked themselves in when night fell, this was the ultimate proof of a highly successful event.

The mayor could claim this as a victory by stressing "that day we stayed up all night"—unlike all the times when the dead were there at dawn. Thanks to the measures he took, he reversed the nighttime dynamics. In fact, Father's Day a few weeks later made it clear that the key to the success of Mother's Day had been the exclusion of men. In the aforesaid hamlet on the same occasion, the mayor announced plans for this newest event: "We celebrated the moms, now we're going to celebrate the dads. . . . For the sake of equality, women will not be invited." And he immediately added: "There will be security measures and searches at the entrance, they will not let any weapons through."

Thus, unlike urban development, the organization of events entailed a different understanding of the context of violence on the part of local politicians. The celebrations were a test of their authority and the absence of shootings the proof of their having taken charge. Events tested the administration's ability to reduce the uncertainty that accompanied festive frameworks. When events were announced, including in the local press, they always noted that there would be "security measures." And accounts of successful events often referred to the risk of violence in the negative—as in an article that appeared under the headline: "No death (*saldo blanco*) reported in the celebrations of Badiraguato's birthday."[17] During my participant observation fieldwork in the town hall secretariat, in the runup to Independence Day, I frequently heard the incantatory question: "People are going to behave, right?"

Planning for events forced the officeholders to take into account the context of violence. The mayor's strategies in that respect (excluding men for Mother's Day, confiscating weapons for Father's Day) demonstrated a keen understanding. If this expertise was not brought to bear in designing public works, it was probably because, whenever they could free themselves of this context of violence, their actions were geared to impressing the state officials who made or broke their careers. This same use of their understanding of the context for more effectively holding violence at bay manifested itself in the way the municipal government defined the problems that needed fixing.

"THE MANDATE'S AIM IS NOT JUST PUBLIC WORKS, BUT ALSO SOCIAL ORDER": THE MANUFACTURE OF SOLVABLE PROBLEMS

On May 27, I tagged along with all municipal employees invited to the dedication of one of the main town's resurfaced main streets. As at every event, red signs, with the municipality's logo and the occasion printed in white letters, were everywhere. The director of the House of Culture took the microphone to briefly describe the reason for the event to the twenty people or so standing around. He then passed the microphone to the director of the public works department, who quickly went through a list of projects underway and on the drawing boards. He finally handed the microphone to the mayor, who went back to the list to highlight the scope of the projects carried out by his administration and his personal commitment to continuing this work. He went on to say that soon the sidewalk curbs downtown would be painted yellow to deter parking "because the mandate's aim is not just public works, but also social order."

He then went over the main measures he planned to put in place. They related to parking, the wearing of motorcycle helmets, the enforcement of tinted window regulations, and seat belt use. In returning to the subject of the just-resurfaced street, he acknowledged the presence of the shopkeepers whose businesses lined this street. He assured them that the improvements being made in the center of the village were "for everyone and especially for you, the retailers, because when people come to take pictures in the pretty historical center of Badiraguato, it will be good for business. And when everyone will say that 'in Badiraguato, they wear helmets, there are no tinted windows beyond what's allowed, and they use seat belts', I will have succeeded, I will be satisfied." He concluded with: "This is what the law says, it is enforced in Culiacán, and soon it will be here, too."

The traffic safety measures the mayor dwelled on for the occasion were indeed among the priorities for his term in office. In his speeches in the months following his inauguration, the mayor repeatedly referred to the success of these measures and the "order" he had brought to Badiraguato. The "social order" at issue here stood for traffic safety and abiding by parking regulations, in other words, for applying the "law."

At an intersectoral health committee meeting I attended, identifying these priorities emerged from the many debates, one of whose stated objectives was "citizen participation." This particular meeting featured a representative of the state government who kept reminding the municipal officials that they had to focus on "achievements [aimed at their] publics and not [their superiors in the] state government," by which he mainly reminded people that the constraints on local executives produced the reverse. The Department of Public Safety made these issues part of its portfolio. Speeding, "controlled skids" (*policiacas*), and helmet wearing were singled out. On this last point, one of the department's representatives asserted that "here [in the main town] it is done"; to which the state consultant replied: "Yes, but let's not confuse this with paternalism, it is the worst enemy of citizen participation."[18] He then summarized the steps involved in implementing a public policy: "Remember: prevention, awareness raising, grace period, then punishment." The solution offered for solving the controlled skid problem was to confiscate the cars and force the skidders to erase the tire tracks they left on the asphalt.

In the ensuing discussion, participants frequently cited "lack of education" as the main source of the problem and as being at the root of many such disturbances. One of the attendants suggested that municipal police officers too at times lacked "civility." An employee of the public security department echoed this notion. She said that she herself had observed disturbing behaviors by police officers during arrests for parking violations in Badiraguato, "but also in Culiacán." Several discussions followed on whether to provide "public relations" training to municipal police officers. Someone floated the idea of organizing workshops to "encourage their active participation and to help them improve their relations with the public."

My interlocutors spared no words when it came to the new traffic safety rules and how strictly they were enforced. According to some, motorbikes were confiscated until their owner could produce a helmet, and others talked about a 600 peso fine (50 USD). Similarly, the yellow paint marking the no-parking zones that gradually coated sidewalks in the town center were a favorite subject. The municipal police chief "El Gallito" was in charge of enforcing the rules. All the people I spoke with about the new measures imposed at the start of the current mayoral term invariably added, "They say he is really hard-nosed." Parking enforcement and suppressing controlled skids were the two main areas in which he had distinguished himself for my interlocutors. Laura recalled how one day when her father had parked in front of their house to unload his trunk, a police vehicle pulled up. The police chief emerged from it, pointing his assault rifle at her father and telling him that he could not park there. The police held Laura and her father at gunpoint until Laura let "El Gallito" know that she was the widow of the late X, an important *pistolero*. As she recalled the scene, her anger surfaced again at their having been treated "as if it were a serious crime."

Perhaps for officials gathered at the abovementioned intersectoral committee, this kind of police conduct justified the idea of workshops for training police officers to "to help them improve their relations with the public." On another occasion, on the road from the top of town, "El Gallito" intervened to end a controlled skidding session. He arrived with several police officers and again held the people there at gunpoint. According to witnesses, the scene was particularly tense as men pulled their own weapons in response to the heavy-handed police tactics. After the police chief's assassination in Culiacán, the commentary on his record related to his strict enforcement of these measures. Some pointed out that he was overdoing it, others that "it is true that he had people toe the line a lot, but often it was for their good." The mayor told the press that "He created order for me in the main town; he ended the controlled skids, stopped the speeders.... He earned people's respect, sometimes by being strict, by enforcing the law, sometimes by being a diplomat."[19]

The intersectoral health committee meeting I attended showed me how problems were identified so they could be remedied. The "public disorder" category was linked in the committee presentation to the fact that "some people are not well psychologically." In another presentation, a slide captioned "the reality of our municipality" listed these problems: "Consumption of alcohol, tobacco, marijuana, cocaine, crack [with an arrow pointing to it], all associated with violent behavior in the family and criminal conduct in society." The presentation went on to cite these as root causes for "family breakdowns, school failure, lack of life plans, teenage pregnancies, following a pattern of behavior, car accidents." Addictions thus appeared to be at the root of many of the municipality's major social problems.

In my interview with the psychologist of the family affairs department who deplored his powerlessness to stem the violence against women (chapter 5), the way he hemmed and hawed was particularly revealing about the ways causalities were attributed in these types of meetings. When I asked him at the start of our conversation what problems he saw most in his practice, he cited "low self-esteem.... People here call it 'nerves' (*los nervios*), but they are forms of depression, of anxiety." How did this problem manifest itself? "Well, for example, they hear the sound of a helicopter and they start shaking." Surprised at the mention of what in the context of Badiraguato is closely associated with repression by the military, I asked if he meant people who had experienced violence. His tone immediately turned defensive: "No, well, yes, but in their intimate life. As you have had a chance to observe, here it is not as they say; it's quiet and you can have times like now when it is quiet, but then there comes a day when someone is killed in the square, or you hear the salvos, and that's it. . . . But as you can see, I didn't talk about it until you brought it up."

As shown by the immediate response of "low self-esteem," individual behaviors are the preferred register for formulating and deferring social and political problems. This mechanism is part of a national, and more broadly, global framework of normalization of neoliberal ideology, of the government of self and psychologizing of the problems that result from it. In the local context, it echoed the pathologizing of violence and pinning blame on the victims for their own murders.

Moreover, as his remarks and his defensive reaction to my question on violence revealed, the government's effort to prioritize projects was fully invested in the context of violence. Like the psychologist who admitted that finding corpses in the central square affected people but noted that "it's quiet," the speakers at the committee sprinkled in similar references. The doctor in charge of the health department stated that homicides had dropped that year from being the leading cause of death in the municipality to third place, which led him to conclude his presentation by congratulating "the public security department." This was actually the only time that I heard the drop in the "homicide" rate formulated as possibly linked to the local police. The public security representative who cited accidents and compliance with the traffic code as the main problems handled by his department put it this way: "The problem is that the officer gets out of his car and the first thing he hears is: 'I am the son of so and so, and you are nobody.'" This sentence, whose subtext is the limits to public action that were grounded in violent social relations, was then reclassified as: "All this, it's a problem of lack of education."

In setting priorities for their electoral mandate, the town hall executives used their knowledge of the social context. And the priorities they identified outlined the administration's effective prerogatives focused on traffic safety, addictions, low self-esteem, lack of education. However, despite their apparently disconnected nature, they were all entrenched in the context of violence. The emphasis on traffic safety in no way indicated a lack of awareness of, disconnection from, or indifference to the concerns of the residents with regard to the dynamics of violence. The fact that "El Gallito" was famed for his strict and coercive enforcement of rules for parking and controlled skids highlighted the seriousness with which these problems were regarded. It seemed to me that rather than a mere powerlessness of local officials in confronting the pervasive violence, administrative practices derived both from neoliberal public policies and how they were applied locally. The "social order" to which the officeholders and executives referred was in fact a mode of government in a situation of violence. They set priorities taking the context into account and produced problems whose very specificity was that they could be "solved."

A solvable problem was one that could be talked about publicly—for which one could stage workshops, develop programs, provide training, make measurements, and possibly print out or take pictures of. These solvable problems were at odds with those insoluble ones that the elected representatives and municipal officials consequently abandoned to other forms of control, for example to "the sector" (*el gremio*), the one imagined as a centralized organization for drug production and trafficking to which could be transferred the lack of alternative livelihoods other than poppies, the rape of women, homicides, or even conflicts around access to land. The design of a mode of governing relying on the construction of solvable problems was accompanied by ways of euphemizing or circumventing salient elements of the context. Like the psychologist eager to clarify that he did not talk about violence and who, on my pushing him, fell back on "it is not as they say, it's quiet," the municipal officials made a special effort to dodge the issue of homicides. The mayor, in his many speeches, never mentioned the murders that plagued life in the town—even though a dead man had appeared with the dawn just a stone's throw from the event over which he was presiding.

Homicide was even ignored when public policy explicitly targeted organized violence. A striking example of this was furnished by the implementation of the disarmament program in Badiraguato. Named the "Permanent Campaign for the Donation and Voluntary Registration of Firearms," it drew its inspiration from the many "Disarmament, Demobilization, Reconstruction" (D.D.R.) programs, jargon of international organizations intervening in armed conflicts for mechanisms rewarding the turning in of weapons for financial or material incentives.[20] In coordination with the Ministry of Defense, the town hall accepted firearms turned in on a voluntary basis in an auditorium from May 16–30, 2014.

The program launched on May 16 in the House of Culture auditorium was arranged in the conventional manner for public events organized by the town hall, except that this one came with a military presence. The mayor explained the program's importance and expressed his pleasure at being able to inaugurate it on this day. He continued: "The problem is domestic accidents with children. . . ." He explained that by having guns at home, you could never be sure that a child would not find it and be injured or even killed. "For example, myself I had some and now I don't have them anymore, I just have one that is of sentimental value." He went on to stress the great opportunity that this program, in cooperation with the Ministry of Defense, represented: it was a chance to make some money while also making this important gesture of "taking weapons out of our homes (nuestras viviendas)." He said: "If Badiraguato, where we've already had accidents of this type, comes out on top, the town wins a new police car." He explained that all the municipalities in the state of Sinaloa were competing to see which turned in the most weapons per capita.

He stressed that weapons would be accepted with no questions asked and paid for at 1,000 pesos (65 USD) for civilian-type weapons and 2,000 pesos for military-style weapons, either in cash or vouchers for computers. For the town hall's local intermediaries in the hamlets [sindicos, comisarios], executives, and employees of the town hall in the audience, he had this to say: "We have to promote this in the schools . . . we know the people in the hamlets, we go to see them, we know who has weapons, we will tell them that it costs them nothing and we must stress that we guarantee their anonymity." Then he called on a man, a sierra hamlet sindico: "Ah, you came to turn one in?" The other nodded, so the mayor asked him: "Big caliber?" The reply came: "Mmh, more or less, 9 mm". . . The people next to me smiled when they saw the "more or less" "big caliber" gun. The official photographer snapped away as the man handed it over.

Then another man brought up a small submachine gun so rusty that the soldier who had to check the condition of the weapons could not cock it. After a moment of embarrassment, the man took his machine gun and managed to show the soldier that it could be operated . . . by pushing hard. . . . To conclude the event, the mayor once more urged people to spread the word: "Get the guns out of our homes! And we'll win a new police car, God willing!"

When the event was over, I returned to the offices with the municipal employees. I asked them if people brought many weapons, to which they responded: "Mmh, not that much, only the ones that no longer worked or they didn't want. . . . Well, let's say that those for whom it is their job, they can't give them away, they'd be out of work. Can you imagine if a chief hitman (sicario) said to his people: 'Give it all up!'" Our small group laughed at the absurdity of the thing. Another adds: "And, besides, when they still work, it's more interesting to sell them to an individual, you get 10,000 to 15,000 pesos (650 to 1000 USD)."

On May 27, at the dedication of the newly asphalted street mentioned earlier, the mayor, seeing someone in the audience, paused: "Ah, Aurelio how are you?"

Aurelio, a sindico *from a hamlet with an armed group infamous for its excesses and unpredictability, returned the shoutout with a head movement, seemingly unwilling to respond any more emphatically in front of everyone. Thereupon the mayor said to him: "We have a weapons turn-in program, it's anonymous, and we can win a police car. You tell our friends over there, where you live, so they come."*

The way of communicating this program was emblematic of all the ambiguity and intense effort involved in circumventing the context of violence in its enunciation. In a bind because of the rationale for this policy and caught up in a hierarchical issue in having to execute a federal program locally, the mayor performed a real tour de force. He managed to present a program for combating organized violence in the guise of ending the scourge of "domestic accidents with children." And he doubled down: "Badiraguato, where we've already had accidents of this type"—strictly "domestic," of course. However, while in denial about violence and the fact that in Badiraguato armed groups owned weapons taken in clashes with the army or bought from soldiers, he nevertheless managed to present himself as a bold official by publicly proclaiming his knowledge ("we know the people in the hamlets, we go to see them, we know who has weapons") and by addressing the relevant people in the know ("You tell our friends over there, where you live, so they come.")

The mayor's nimble footwork on this occasion clarified the key issue in defining municipal priorities: how to manufacture solvable problems as a method of governing in the context of violence. Municipal public policies and the production of appropriate measures were defined using the traditional planning tools: PowerPoint, conference easel, legitimization by expertise, mediation models, training workshops, keywords ("citizen participation"; "civility"; "public relations")—successfully deploying their depoliticizing potential.[21] This mode of administering a violent context displayed another facet: the programs followed each other at a pace set at the state and federal levels that was impervious to the realities of daily life in the municipality.

RED SIGNS, SPEECHES, AND PHOTOS: THE PRODUCTION OF AN INFALLIBLE RHYTHM

The waves Edelia and Ursula were making in the office of the municipal Department of Family Affairs had Joselita on edge. In the air and office routine, the stress on both was palpable. Seconded from the State Department of of Family Affairs (DIF Sinaloa), they were here to set up the "economic kitchens" program in the municipality. For several months, they had been going to different "communities" (a developmentalist jargon term rarely used locally) to set up women's committees responsible for what in effect would become "economic kitchens" or "community kitchens" intended to "create social ties." Once a kitchen was set up, the women on the committee would be supplied with food products through the Department of Family Affairs at low subsidized prices. Members had to organize for preparing lunches to offer "the rest of the community," costing 10 pesos for adults and 5 pesos for children. Two days hence, a renovated community kitchen in a hamlet not far from the main town was slated for launch. The event would be coupled with the termination of the "block-making machine (bloquera)" program, which also benefited the people of the hamlet. These machines for making cinder blocks had been brought in three months earlier, and sixty families had been chosen for the program to let them build cinder-block additions to existing homes or build new ones.

The stakes were high for Edelia and Ursula, as their supervisors would be observing their work at the event scheduled in two days. So, Edelia was tasked with going to the hamlet to set up the event there. She was panicking: the kitchen was not ready, the building lacked windows and toilets; neither the water nor the sink drains had been connected. The meal slated to be served to the executives on the day of the event would have to be prepared by the inhabitants in their homes and then brought into the communal kitchen as if it had been prepared there. Agitation in the office was building: the tarp slated to be used as the backdrop for the event was not ready; they needed a picture of the kitchen to print on it "but if possible so you don't see that the windows are missing." Joselita tried to reassure Edelia and Ursula: "Stop already, there wasn't any money for windows; it's not your fault. Full stop!"

Over the next two days, the pace of the grand opening resumed. Program registration forms gave rhythm to the hours and twice during the day the word passed: "The presidency has called." This was the code for: Event! Everyone must go there!

In the morning, the launch of a vaccination campaign: red signs, speeches, photos. . . .

In the afternoon, another newly asphalted street is inaugurated: red signs, speeches, photos. . . .

The following morning Health Week launches: red signs, speeches, photos. . . .

In the afternoon, a celebration in support of the elderly: yes, more red signs, etc. . . .

The next day, the dedication of the renovated community kitchen is on the agenda. The municipal executives welcomed their guests from Culiacán in the Department of Family Affairs offices before departing with them for lunch in a restaurant. I went to the hamlet with the employees, helping them load the chairs and set them up in an outdoor basketball court at the event site. We arrived about an hour and a half before the event was slated to start. We finished the setup and people started arriving on the court as I stepped off to the side for a cigarette break. I met two sisters who explained to me that they had benefited from the "block-making machine" program. A young man joined us. He asked the sisters to support him in speaking up "on behalf of those who have been wronged." I asked him what he was upset about, and he explained that the machines were there but only one load of the promised cement was ever delivered. Several of the selected families signed up had not had a chance to make the blocks. They hoped to take advantage of the presence of municipal and state officials to demand the missing cement and additional time before the cinder-block machines were moved to another hamlet.

Some time later, the executives pulled up in their big SUVs. The mayor and his wife got out and mingled with the audience, shaking hands and calling people by their first names. The proceeding began, with the speeches following one after the other. Each speaker congratulated their department on the success of the "economic kitchen" and "cinder-block machine" programs, to the point that it became difficult to tell who was getting credit for what. Finally, the moment of the symbolic handing-over of a cinder block to a resident arrived. Photographers from the municipality and state governments got ready; a little old man was picked to be handed a cinder block by the mayor and his wife.

The photo session over, the mayor departed immediately. The mayor's quick departure pulled the rug out from under the young man who wanted to speak "on behalf of those who have been wronged," and he was given no chance to speak publicly. The rest of the event schedule took place at the community kitchen. While waiting for the meal to be served, the mayor's wife and the director of the State Department of Family Affairs headed to the swings, gathering children around for a photo opportunity with the municipal photographer clicking away.

Finally, it was time for the meal in the kitchen. Ursula had taped white paper on the freshly painted walls. Each depicted a hastily-drawn busy kitchen scene: one captioned with "assignments" had a list of three women's names alternating each day of the week; another named the five work themes assigned for each day

FIGURE 3. Town hall photographers taking a photo of the mayor as he symbolically hands a cinder block to a resident. Photo by the author.

FIGURE 4. Continuation of the photo shoot: municipal and state DIF female executives playing with children. Photo by the author.

("food security; health promotion; fostering education; home and community improvement; strengthening the family and community economy"). On the left of another sheet were written the words "brush your teeth well," and on the right side "every day consume foods belonging to the three food groups." A third photo shoot started when the two directors of the municipal and state Departments of Family Affairs sat down at the kitchen table where they admired the doilies embroidered by the women of the hamlet for the occasion.

The executives settled down to their lunch while the hamlet residents waited outside. Sitting on a wall near the kitchen, I heard my neighbor say to someone: "No, we can't go in." The community kitchen remained a VIP preserve, but one of the executives came out to beckon me back to my seat at the table: "Adèle, come and eat with us." The meal over, we put away the chairs, the last SUVs left, and the folks from the hamlet made short work of the leftovers. . . .

Daily life in the municipal offices was characterized by two overlapping rhythms. There was the office routine oriented around a never-ending series of programs and their administrative followup; then there were the events that could empty the offices several times a day. These two dynamics produced a time experience and a pace all its own for the administration.

At all times, the operative word in the Family Affairs Department's offices was "the presidency has called." No sooner did it come than the offices would empty of nearly all employees. This exodus took place daily in all the departments in which I was a participant observer (except for the town hall secretariat). The political stakes of attendance at events made obeying these summonses unavoidable, even outside working hours, as the elected officials sometimes demanded. On the occasion of "Students' Day," for instance, the word passed in the offices of the Department of Social Development that there would be consequences for anyone who failed to attend it the following weekend. The week after that, the weekend event "Government in Mobility" was even more significant. With the state governor expected to attend, all employees were not only ordered to be there themselves but to bring two other people along.

In the Department of Social Development office, Sarita, Juan, and Ivan were trying to think of someone to bring. Most relied on family members to hopefully give in to their entreaties. None of them would explicitly balk, but the weary facial expressions and the lack of enthusiasm suggested that they knew they could not get out of it this time either. Thus, if the number of people was supposed to show the popularity of the mayor, we must be careful not to read into it the extent of individual support.[22]

Once the audience gathered and the scene was set, the events unfolded in the same way: first came the speeches, then the photo op. Through multiple rhetorical tactics, successive speakers each would pat themselves on the back for the different programs. For the inauguration of the community kitchens, the mayor stuck above all to the cinder-block machinery program, thereby sidelining the State Department of Family Affairs, which had no role in it. The program was actually run by non-municipal development bodies, but their representative did not show up, which let the mayor claim it as his own. His speech combined the challenge of building homes with—as in all other events—the objectives of his mandate and how they had been met brilliantly. He concluded with the announcement of the upcoming festivities. Then, the director of the State Department of Family Affairs thanked her Badiraguato counterpart for "helping" to set up their community kitchen program, which she dwelled on at length, making only a passing reference to the "block-making machine" program. The mayor's wife, director of the local Family Affairs Department, thanked her state counterpart for the "support" rendered to her department in "her municipality's" community kitchen program before reciting the list of programs underway in her department.

If one of the issues of these jousts was promoting oneself and one's department as the provider of aid, the speeches were also part of the competition within the regional political field. Seen in that light, the sudden departure of the mayor before the meal in the economic kitchen takes on a greater significance. My interlocutors explained it by the fact that his wife was in fact trying to build her own career,[23] and the mayor's critics often pointed out the mistreatment he inflicted on his wife, who, unlike him, had "a heart of gold" (*un pan de dios*). Rumor had it that he not only cheated on her, but that he was taking a hatchet to her department's budget to undercut her career.

The second key moments were the photo ops that marked the different stages of terminating the "block-making machine" program and inaugurating the "community kitchen." The choice of the elderly gentleman with his cane for the symbolic reception of the cinder block was to be expected. The absurdity of the staging—the elderly person wobbly on his legs who obviously could not heft a cinder block—made people laugh, but neither of the two photographers paid any heed since they were after staged images for dissemination. Watching them do their work during several events provided insight into what they regarded as a good shot. Children with swings obviously fit into this framework; this was also the case for embroidered doilies that documented the activities of housewives in the rural sierra.

Similarly, at an event to distribute gallon bottles of water, a young woman who was the town hall's representative in the hamlet (*comisaria*) was asked at the end of a speech to pick up her infant—whom she had just handed to her mother so she could attend to the director of the Family Affairs Department, also the mayor's spouse. The photo was snapped with her surrounded by others, specifically pregnant women, children, and the elderly. Whenever the senior executives were on the move, especially in the sierra, the town hall's photographer trailed them everywhere. He staged pictures that showed their closeness to people through the care given to the "vulnerable," personified through the most obvious social and administrative categories (minors, mothers, seniors).[24] The photos then would be posted on the municipal Facebook page, which the official photographer managed, and they were also displayed on printed panels and video screens in the town hall's waiting room.

Gazing at the doilies and the infant suggested a closeness between women that bridged social gaps. Both for an external audience and for visitors to the town hall, the municipal communication sought to bridge the social distance between the executives and the people they met at these events. Most of the executives, who, as we have seen, depended largely on state networks, lived in Culiacán. The state capital was one of the first destinations for people who rose to high positions. It was a move even low-level municipal employees could appreciate: "They're doing this for the future of their children." The fact remains that they had to reassert and demonstrate the folksiness that is supposed to be the basis of political representation. Accordingly, the inhabitants of the sierra sometimes emphasized the instrumental nature of visits that took place only during events and election campaigns.

Beyond the photo ops, the actual implementation of "block-making machine" and "community kitchen" programs was ignored. Some of the recipients of the former had not received the necessary building materials and the kitchen was unusable, but neither point emerged during the event. On other occasions, executives would discuss the inefficiency of programs. I learned that they knew about supplies of food for the kitchens being resold at a small markup by the hamlet women enrolled in the program, a behavior they resented. The locals were also reproached for listlessly cleaning the kitchen building—out of order in any event—to make it presentable on food delivery days.

FIGURE 5. One more photo session: the municipal DIF director, also the mayor's wife, poses with residents during a water distribution in a hamlet. Photos by the author.

Beyond the pace of events, the daily town hall office life revolved around the multiple programs that the municipal services were responsible for implementing. Each program covered a specific theme, population, and timeline. Their terms and conditions were known to the citizens who came to inquire about and hopefully access them. For example, in May 2014, several people

FIGURE 5. *(Continued)*

showed up at the offices of the Family Affairs Department saying that they had heard that corrugated sheet metal was to be had for the asking. I watched with astonishment as one of the employees registered the people who showed up and another did not. On one occasion, a person came in when the department's director was in the office. The director explained that it was just a rumor, that there was no sheet metal program currently. Nevertheless, she assured the visitor that they were putting names on a waiting list, so that "if anything does arrive, we will give you the sheet metal." Her name was duly taken and the director took the opportunity to tell her: "By the way, at the moment we have life insurance for the female head of the family, and canes"—the two programs of the moment. The lady then came over to me, as I was in charge of registrations for "female head of family life insurance." After the cane distribution program came a "wheelchair" program. During my work there, no sheet metal programs were launched, but a program for pregnant women substituted for the wheelchairs.

The implementation of these programs involved a trade-off for the municipal employees: pressure to produce numerical results on the one hand, and, on the other, creating leeway for themselves for helping relatives and the more disadvantaged families. They had to register applicants despite sometimes restrictive eligibility requirements. Thus, the form for "life insurance for female head of family" in small print restricted it to "in the event of the death of a woman when she is the head of family (*jefatura de la familia*) and in a situation of extreme vulnerability, and after reviewing the file following the possible death, partial financial support for the needs of children under twenty-three years of age." A large number of women came into the office, and I learned from one of them that in the outlying neighborhoods and nearby hamlets, a municipal car drove around with a loudspeaker inviting "rich or poor, come and register for the program 'female head of family life insurance.'" I also occasionally saw municipal employees explain to applicants how to fill out the forms to help them qualify for and access certain programs. On other occasions, employees of the Family Affairs Department offered one-off assistance: paying for a bus trip to the hospital in Culiacán, help with state or federal administrative procedures, supporting hamlet claims against a teacher who didn't show up, etc.

This sequence of programs produced an internal administrative routine. The cane, sheet metal, and wood-fired stove programs each involved several phases: announcement, committee formation, launch, and closure. Similarly, each construction, renovation, or development of a building or road section went through its announcement, the actual start of the work—the "*bander-azo*" or flag-raising—and its dedication, with each of these events serving as occasions for speechmaking. These events provided opportunities for the town hall to demonstrate its management of municipal affairs, but always according to its own agenda. This routine could be disrupted by strife between public administrations that prevented funds from being disbursed or a program being implemented. The rhythm of the town hall therefore depended on the supralocal levels and taking on solvable problems. Consequently, it remained impervious to issues that were not solvable with programs: the murders, the attacks on hamlets, and the emptying of some of them.

In this sense, the context of violence, meticulously swept under the rug in governmental practices, had no effect on the town hall, which had its own temporal points of reference and staged them in the public space. Development programs thus produced a form of predictability of administrative action, through a regularity hermetically sealed from the vagaries of the context of violence. The production of a rhythm and its administration responded to the silence on killings, armed groups, and repression of livelihoods.[25] Thus, the town hall administered time by producing a consistent experience: it benefited the people who were integrated in it when they managed to occupy one of these positions, and it was staged for all others, some of whom chanced to derive some material advantages. It was a town hall run like clockwork in a town marked by uncertainty.

A POTEMKIN VILLAGE: SILOING BY ESCORT

Administrative practice in Badiraguato crystallized around mechanisms of detachment from the context of violence and avoidance of situations in which this context was at play. Make tourism the key economic objective when the daily movement of the inhabitants is unsecure; prioritize traffic safety when homicides are a constant occurrence; stage an infallible administrative routine when everyday experience is structured by alternating high and low periods of violence; stimulate "social ties" through development programs where the main source of income forces people into an economy repressed by another level of the same state; and do all of this without ever naming these dimensions.

This Potemkin village politics was a tour de force by the local authorities. They administered the context of violence by circumventing it, but at the same time were addressed as—and had every interest in presenting themselves as—the mayors of the "cradle of drug trafficking" and of the "fiefdom of the Sinaloa Cartel." This feat was made possible by the siloing of what happened in Badiraguato and what was said about it outside. This interface position between the municipal population and all others was an essential resource, making them indispensable intermediaries for both sides. However, the advantages of this position required maintaining—that is to say, reproducing—this internal boundary and thus reaping the benefits of monopolizing passage across it.

A few weeks after my arrival in the Badiraguato, I scored an interview with the newly elected mayor Mario Valenzuela López. The secretary of the town hall welcomed me. I handed him a letter of recommendation written for me by the University of Sinaloa's Ana Luz, a researcher and native of Badiraguato (chapter 1). Before I entered the mayor's office, the secretary, teasingly, said to the people present: "Yes, she's been here for a while. She was watching us from afar." As soon as I entered the mayor's office, he said, "So, you're a French journalist?" After I straightened that out, we had a brief talk: I presented my research interests, to which the elected official responded by talking up his municipal program. When I told him that I wanted to stay in the municipality for a while, he replied: "You want to go to La Tuna ["El Chapo"'s birthplace]? There is no problem with that. Besides, his mom was there for my inauguration, she gave me a basket of buns. Of course, the lady came without an escort, for obvious reasons, no one was going to do anything to her. It also seemed to me that Rafael Caro Quintero's wife was there. . . . An army helicopter is going to take aerial photos [of the municipality]. If you need them, we can share them with you. And if you need anything, we're here."

On the way out after the interview, I talked briefly with the secretary, who seemed to have a better understanding of what I was after and seemed quite willing to explain to me in more detail the various administrative activities and the corresponding services. Inviting me to come with him to the civil registry office, while we were driving in his car he let drop that he recently escorted some Dutch journalists who were interested in "the graves of the narcos," because "we have here the most expensive tombs in the world, with marble from Italy." In the parking lot, he told me that if I needed a car to get to the sierra, he would provide me with "a driver who knows people." He added: "There is no problem, we will take you, but it is better not to say 'French' because there people are suspicious of the DEA and Interpol. The less they know, the better. Or we just have to say that you're a journalist." I interjected: "But, then, [being a] journalist, isn't that dangerous?" "Ah yes, of course, journalist, it's more dangerous." I reminded him that I was a student and he exclaimed: "Oh yes, that's it! We just have to say that you are a student, in exchange with the university, and so on. . . ." And that is how he introduced me to every office in the administrative unit.

The request for permission to conduct an ethnographic study was an unfamiliar process for the mayor and his secretary. Our meeting was therefore one long misunderstanding in which they persisted in making my presence into something to which they were accustomed: the visit of journalists. As my interview illustrated, one of the hallmarks of local government was the mismatch between the discourses produced by elected officials for the attention of the inhabitants and those they addressed to the national and international press. In Badiraguato, Ángel Robles—a.k.a. Ángel "speed bump palms"—was thus the mayor of public works. On the other hand, Mario Valenzuela López was the *mano dura* ("heavy hand") for controlled skids, parking, and helmet use. But, apart from that, both remained above all the mayors of the cradle of drug trafficking, the stronghold of the larger-than-life figures of the "Sinaloa Cartel."

This identification was affixed to them by the media, but they also participated in producing it, even staging it, while claiming to have no part in it. In Badiraguato, for example, Mayor Mario Valenzuela maintained a stubborn silence on the November 2014 assassination of "El Gallito," but in the press he fulminated against "organized crime" as responsible for the death of his police chief. Similarly, in August 2013, Ángel Robles gave a long interview to the online newspaper *Sin Embargo* following the release of Rafael Caro Quintero. The introduction to the interview teased reader curiosity by stating that the town councillor "admits to knowing El Chapo's mother" and would talk straight. The mayor focused on the stigma on Badiraguato and the poverty that plagued it, blaming the municipality's reputation for wealth for unfairly excluding it from many aid programs. While playing up his closeness to the media figures of drug trafficking, he denied their importance. He discussed the repression of marijuana, stressing that the municipality had been very quiet during his tenure—never mind that this coincided with the increase in homicides in the main town in consequence of the conflict with the El Rancho gang. Some time later, while I was doing my fieldwork, a

Televisa crew was filming Mario Valenzuela on a tour of the sierra he presented as a "weekly practice" to feature in a program entitled "The Mayor in Your Community." The *Televisa* reportage trafficked in the same contradictions as the interview with Ángel Robles. The mayor displayed his knowledge of the history of the great figures while he was shown distributing blankets in the hamlets (a first, since normally the Department of Family Affairs employees carried them out), explaining against the background of *corridos* that the municipality was "very quiet and peaceful."

Every judicial development and its side effects drew the national media's attention to the municipality, letting the elected officials step into the limelight. If El Chapo escaped, a newspaper headline read: "Badiraguato celebrates El Chapo's escape"; if he was extradited, the mayor was interviewed; if he was he sentenced, "Badiraguato cries and prays for El Chapo."[26] The silence of the elected officials about violence when facing the local people was in contrast with their exploitation of the sensationalist coverage of drug trafficking by the media. These issues formed the background to my meeting with the mayor and the secretary and, despite my denials, they shoehorned my presence into the interest shown by the media in the great figures of the "Sinaloa Cartel." In this way, they reeled off the clichés they thought would satisfy the appetites they correctly attributed to journalists: hence, the name-dropping about "El Chapo"'s mother, with her basket of buns, and Caro Quintero's wife.

What the mayor and the secretary were telling me had the same aim: to transport me to this (even more) fantasized sierra (after the passage in the mayor's office). The escort mechanism he proposed appeared in all its ambivalence. For one thing, the proposal was about managing, being responsible for a foreign visitor's safety. For another, the secretary's quip "she was watching us from afar" also raised the issue of monopolization implied by being escorted. Indeed, escorting journalists played an essential role in preserving the distinction between the public works mayor and the mayor of the drug-trafficking center. By taking advantage of the difficulties of access—real and imaginary—escorting let the town hall channel the reporting by selecting certain interlocutors, situations, and places. Preserving this monopoly, and the intermediary role it provided, implied the need for consolidating the discourses on the dangerousness of their municipality, all while pretending to deny them. Thus, when the secretary of the town hall let me know that the people of the sierra were suspicious and urged me to keep quiet about being French, he reinforced the image of the high-risk incursion—and implied that he alone could guarantee security, thanks to his driver, who knew people well.

The benefits of this intermediary role also redounded to state or federal officials visiting hamlets in connection with aid programs or when campaigning. Thus, on another occasion, the town hall secretary congratulated himself on having responded to the "guys from Culiacán or even Mexico City" who suspected Badiraguato's elected officials of favoritism in awarding grants and managing programs: "In any event, you will only be able to enter the territory if it is with a car and a driver furnished by the town hall ... as a matter of safety." On several occasions, I observed how municipal employees led visits by their state or federal counterparts. Conversely, people in the hamlets were hard put to bring in state or federal personnel without support from the town hall. In addition to the need to have connections within these administrations, bringing them to a hamlet involved picking them up and taking them back to Culiacán—beyond the reach of most hamlet residents. Finally, the escort system was particularly advantageous during state election campaigns. Sinaloa state politicians, needing exposure in the sierra during their campaigns, depended on local elected officials for arranging access, which allowed the latter in turn to lobby and score points with important political figures.

Escorting as a practice thus touched on and participated directly in the political capital of executives, in the added value that they could assert vis-à-vis the heads of state networks on which their appointment depended. By consolidating the compartmentalization that has been backbone of local domination since the 1940s, they could play on this paradox: concealing violence and its implications when facing residents and staging it vis-à-vis the outside world to boost their careers. The escort was part of managing the Potemkin politics of the municipal authorities through a specific control of the territory: that of perspective. The escort served the drive for a monopoly on the production of discourses invisibilizing social issues behind a screen of media figures.

"A Topic That Should Not Be Treated in This Way, Much Less by a Mayor"

The mayoral media strategy of presenting themselves as mayors of the cradle of narcotrafficking did not only respond to what journalists wanted, but also stemmed from the need for conformity with the discourse at state and federal levels that considered violence and organized crime to be outside the realm of politics. To illustrate this point, I translate here in full an interview with

Mario Valenzuela López by the Spanish newspaper *El Pais* that appeared in February 2015.

"Without El Chapo, there are more thefts and more unemployment"

On the road, we see alternately cows and men wearing cowboy (*vaquero*) hats, perched on old mares, until on the horizon come into view gigantic letters arranged like the Hollywood sign on a hill: BADIRAGUATO. In this municipality of 32,000 inhabitants, located at the foot of the Sierra of Sinaloa, where the most astute peasants grow marijuana instead of beans, were born the best-known drug traffickers in Mexico's history.

The mayor is one of those ever-present politicians. The municipality has an administrative center, also named Badiraguato, and an infinite number of hamlets scattered in the mountain, some located on the summits a seven-hour drive away. This winter, Mario Valenzuela tours all these hamlets distributing wheelchairs, blankets, and messages like this to the inhabitants: 'I come to ask you to be responsible citizens. In Spain or the United States, they have laws just like we do, but there they obey them. That's the problem I have in Badiraguato and Mexico in general.'

Valenzuela's bushy hair, with roots that start almost halfway down the forehead, bears up under the relentless midday sun at El Sitio de Arriba.... His audience sits on the ground where the meeting takes place: women with children, the elderly. Before the interview, in which Valenzuela will talk about El Chapo, El Chapo's mother, the fugitive Caro Quintero, Caro Quintero's cousin, El Azul's non-death, he plays riddles with his constituents: 'Here's an easy one: what's the name of the animal that flies with its paws?' 'The duck!' yells someone in the audience.

• • •

QUESTION: What is the situation in Badiraguato one year after the arrest of Joaquín El Chapo Guzman?

ANSWER: The problem is one for the state (of Sinaloa). The arrest of someone of El Chapo Guzman's stature leaves many people temporarily unemployed. Until things settle down, there are new commanders, new hierarchies, we have new problems. Thefts have increased, there are more attacks....

Q: A year ago, you told me that you had some relationship with El Chapo's mother.

A: Yes... the lady (Mara Consuelo Loera) has lost weight these days. Last Wednesday I was at La Tuna (a hamlet in the municipality where the most wanted narco was born). She's calm, her condition is stable. As it happened, this time I did not see her, but the time before I went to dedicate a resurfaced road and the church to which she belongs (evangelical, built by El Chapo, although he is Catholic), and there I was with her for a while. She invited me to lunch, and we had a very pleasant meal. It is not her fault that her son embarked on this career.

Q: You believe that El Chapo's successor may be Dámaso López Nuñez, a.k.a. El Licenciado?[27]

R: I don't know. What is certain is that El Chapo has sons . . . there's *el Iván*, and then there's his brother Aureliano, and I believe it is they who must take control before El Licenciado.

Q: Have you seen the presence of other criminal groups who want to take control of this place that belongs to the Sinaloa Cartel?

R: No, the hierarchy of these people is not local, it is for all intents international.

Q: A lot of meth labs have been found in Badiraguato.

R: Yes, now the synthetic drug is manufactured here, and that's wrong because in the end it does more damage than marijuana. Synthetic drugs are fashionable, as the young people say. Is Badiraguato the cradle of drug trafficking? Yes, a lot of *narcos* were born here. The Lord of the Sky (Amado Carrillo, who died in 1997 during cosmetic surgery), El Azul (Juan José Esparragoza, an old-time capo who his sons claim is dead), who is said to have died but this is not true.

Q: His death is a trick to stop the authorities from pursuing him?

R: They checked with the family, which said no. For that matter, the remains would have been brought here, I imagine, his ashes or whatever, and that didn't happen.

Q: Mexican intelligence believes that Caro Quintero—who spent thirty years in prison for the murder of a DEA agent and was released lawfully last year—is hiding in his village, La Noria, very close to here.

R: It would be complicated to assert that, too reckless. That is what they say. In February, the Navy came with eighteen helicopters. They badly beat up my representative to the community, a first cousin of Caro Quintero. It is not his fault that he is a cousin. He told the Marines [Mexican naval infantry] that yes, it's true that Caro came here, he came, and he put on a barbecue. They went to greet him at La Noria, and they really enjoyed it. When Caro was free, he helped a lot along the way: he installed electricity, he built a very pretty church, he created jobs for people. Of course, it was a pleasure for them that a relative who had spent thirty years in prison was released. But that didn't warrant hitting them. There are a lot of hypotheses about Caro: they say he's working in the mines, he's helping people, he's sorting out the Cartel. I hear he's saying he'd rather get bitten by sierra mosquitoes than go back to prison.

Q: On the wall of famous Badiraguatenses that you are building, you will put there...?

R: Nooo, no way!? I'm not going to put El Chapo on it! For sure, then Peña Nieto would come down on me.

This interview succeeded in distilling the linguistic elements and key motives of Badiraguato's media discourse. The interview is a classic in many ways. Notably, the reporter had already interviewed Mario Valenzuela the previous year and had already heard the anecdotes about his closeness to the great figures. It is clear that, using this register, the executive scored a hit, since it got the journalist to reopen the topic: "A year ago, you told me that you had some relationship with El Chapo's mother." This is even his best hook: "The interview during which Valenzuela will talk about El Chapo, El Chapo's mother, the fugitive Caro Quintero, Caro Quintero's cousin, El Azul's non-death." The top people are all there, along with their little families; the teaser promises new scoops. The celebrity magazines will just have to catch up: *El Pais* beat them to it.

More broadly, we encounter a mayor full of humanity, close to the people in the staged handing-out of blankets and wheelchairs. The target audience being mainly Spanish, the interview is also introduced by an exotic staging: the sun is "relentless," and the mayor has put on his hat for the occasion. Again, Mario Valenzuela was on target; once the article is out there, he becomes the elected official of the place where one sees "alternately cows and men wearing cowboy hats, perched on old mares, until on the horizon come into view gigantic letters arranged like the Hollywood sign on a hill: BADIRAGUATO." All good things come to those who know how to wait: the lookout finally had its moment in the sun. We now understand what Teófilo had missed when he asked: "A point of view for what? So we can see the hills? We see them every day!"

The interview also touched on several intertwined themes that highlight what went on in the media game. The topic of infrastructure financed by Caro Quintero served as a leitmotif for successive mayors in their statements to the national or international press. Second, Mario Valenzuela knew that words about celebrities and their relatives are fodder for the journalists. The anecdotes of everyday life arouse an unbridled curiosity. In his reply, the wording shows how intent he is on projecting familiarity: "The Iván" he says, the article in front of the first name in Spanish denoting a certain closeness. Launched on this trail, he echoed—or even took sides in—a dispute over who would "succeed" Joaquin "El Chapo" between his sons and Dámaso López Nuñez, known as "El Licenciado." He then doubled down on the strategy of presenting himself as an insider in the public eye by claiming confidential information about the death, or lack thereof, of one of the oldest figures of drug trafficking, "El Azul." Finally, he seemed to address key aspects of the municipality's situation, dwelling on the economic impact of a figure like "El Chapo" (which the headline picks up) and the repression whose arbitrary nature he underlines: "It isn't his fault that he is a cousin."

All the more remarkable was that the mayor's words, surprising as they were, were given on the record to the international press. At the journalist's suggestion that he might set up a bust in tribute to El Chapo in the plaza of illustrious Badiraguato citizens, the mayor reacted with: "Nooo, no way!? For sure, then Peña Nieto would come down on me." Thus, he formulated a key element: by saying that this particular act would cross a line, he indicated that in his mediatization game he had to abide by certain implicit rules laid down by his institutional hierarchy. In fact, the interview earned him a slap on the wrist, since the PRI's state president issued this statement following the publication: "It seems to me that this is a topic that should not be treated in this way, much less by a mayor. I absolutely disapprove of his expressions." The press account reported that "she asserted that the mayor's comments were hardly constructive by any means," although she admitted to "not knowing the security situation in Badiraguato municipality."[28] Still, overall, the interview did not lead to political outrage or scandal, and the reprimand remained caught up in the usual repertoire of institutional competition. Thus, the same PRI state president had publicly disapproved of the provocative statements made by Mario Valenzuela López on the absurdity of the gender equality rules.

That the mayor made these remarks while remaining focused on the tacit boundary drawn by superior leadership is particularly revealing. His seemingly glaring statements about drug-related issues tested the limits of the permissible. Yet, it is noteworthy that they remained fully in line with the definition of acceptable speech established by federal and state upper echelons. The personalization of the drug trade around these figures left a wide range of permissible speech. The fantasy of clandestine bandits and their conflicts appeared inexhaustible and unlikely to bring armed violence into the political order.

Thus, while it was striking to hear the mayor comment on the episode of the eighteen Navy helicopters and the physical abuse inflicted by the military on the hamlet *comisario* because of his kinship with Caro Quintero, it must be clear that this was only more of the same siloing and way of governing that characterized the administration in Badiraguato. Six months earlier, in the weeks following the troops' raid, the silence from the town hall had, as usual, been deafening.

The government in Badiraguato was placed at the junction of two tensions: its own reproduction and a specific mode of government of the context of violence. Dependence on the state and federal levels significantly skewed the strategies of local politicians. Staying in power gave access to positions making accumulation possible, but also meant being part of the balance of power between competing state networks. It entailed maintaining local patronage networks and dispensing the available institutional resources caught in short-term program-based policies. But these strategies remained the work of the marginalized in this social group—the fate of each being ultimately determined by the state authorities. The real local challenge of staying in power resided elsewhere: in a government that kept violence out of the realm of institutional politics. By manufacturing solvable problems and establishing an agenda impervious to the events that punctuated the life of the municipality, elected officials put the management of some of the most pressing social concerns out of their remit. The "social order" they imposed resided in the treatment of issues that skirted local social relations, thus keeping themselves away from all that went into making up the context. This mode of government is thus constitutive in reproducing the violent context: by reproducing itself in this context, by ensuring its stability, it contributed to the reproduction of violent relationships.

The phenomenon of the "escort" and the media sallies by the town officials showed that government of the context of violence in Badiraguato was well integrated into the institutional hierarchies of the Mexican state. By trying to impose a monopoly on the discourse bearing on the municipality, they not only ensured the sustainability of this Potemkin village, but also depoliticized armed violence and its social, economic, and political logics. The articulation between the structuring of violent social relations by state policies (repression, isolation, intermediation) and the construction of public policies detached from social dynamics allowed the nonpolitical framing of armed violence and institutional stability.

Conclusion

RETURNING UPSTREAM

"Returning upstream does not signify going back to the source. Far from it. Rather it signifies a leap, a revival, a return to the undigested nourishment from the source, to a higher vantage point, upstream, that is to say, to the most marginalized place there is. To what end? Georges Bataille will tell us: 'This flight toward the summit (which, dominating even the empires, is the composition of knowledge) is just one of the ways through the labyrinth. But this course that we must follow from illusion to illusion, in search of reality, we cannot avoid in any way.'"

RENÉ CHAR,
Retour Amont, translated by H. Randolph

THE JOURNEY I SET OUT on for this book took me through the often vulnerable lives of people I met in Badiraguato. Along the way, I had to describe situations in which I encountered singular women and men taking actions, and in so doing delineate the distinct ways they performed these actions and the issues raised for each of them. In every case, I strove to describe these practices, highlighting the problems they posed and the contexts in which they took place. In sequential chapters, I sought to portray specific aspects of Badiraguato's social life and to gradually build an increasing familiarity with the municipality and its inhabitants.

On this journey, we learned a number of things. Examining my travels and those of my interlocutors (to the main town, from the town to the sierra, from hamlet to hamlet), it turned out that moving from one place to another entailed forms of negotiation, and that access was an unevenly distributed resource. Trying to understand the reasons for this led me to investigating the history of how the land was structured, as well as how the economic flows and the infrastructure fit into relationships with the regional elite. This historical detour highlighted the fragmented nature of the municipality's territory and of armed groups.

Then, after talking on doorsteps, in grocery stores in the main town, and in houses in the hamlets, I turned my attention to the daily manifestations of gun violence. In conversation with my main interlocutors, we learned that their intense information-gathering revealed their most pressing concerns: the entanglement between the threat and the proximity relationships in the main town, and, in the hamlets, the incursions by the army and the conflicts between *pesados*. Paradoxically, despite the abundant analyses of their environment that the inhabitants produced, they proposed generalizations that contradicted their experiences, including characterizing the place where they lived as "quiet."

By tracing the transformations experienced by the families of poppy growers and then describing their daily lives, I highlighted both the shrunken horizons that came with the disappearance of many subsistence activities and the uncertainty that permeated these family economies. Various forms of military repression weighed on every stage of poppy cultivation and conditioned how the *pesados* exploited the growers. Oddly, while the grower families alone had to face the military's extortion practices and the *pesados* leveraged their local monopoly status for profit, the latter were considered to be the former's benefactors.

By attending on the ejidal assemblies and questioning my interlocutors about their access to land, I analyzed the confusion that reigned and constantly emerged in their discourses. In describing how the *ejidos* functioned and analyzing the land enclosure waves, I pointed out the social, economic, and violent resources that governed ownership. Thus, a unique configuration prevailed in access to land: the legal cover provided by a common property regime for violent land grabs.

In reporting on Adriana's abduction and rape, her subsequent flight, the terms of her protection, and the comments of her neighbors, I exposed the continuum between marriage, kidnapping, and rape. Predation on single women ran through all gender relationships, depended on the same resources that made access to land possible, and thus formed part of the violent competition between men. Moreover, imputing responsibility for the violence they suffered to the women imposed a set of constraints on their capacity to act.

In the ensuing chapter I returned to the kitchens, the town hall offices, and the grocery stores in the main town; in these everyday settings I described the usual way of commenting on homicides. In considering two conflicts that took place during my fieldwork, I singled out the elements underlying the common understanding of the murder victims as responsible for their fate. In describing how homicides affected everyday life I elicited their social and political texture. The exercise of violence was not a form of social climbing but one of the means for reproducing relationships of domination. It emerged that when marginal people resorted to armed violence, it struck a discordant note: it was relegated to a form of deviance, a symptom of deranged psyches.

By observing the routines of the employees in municipal offices, participating in the events they staged, accompanying them on their travels into the sierra, listening to their speeches, and watching them implement a multitude of development programs, in the final chapter I was able to show how state institutions operated in this context. The modalities of political competition led to municipal policies that were essentially designed for meeting the expectations of decisionmakers at the state and federal levels. It caused the elected municipal officials and civil servants to develop a unique mode of government in the context of violence. They relied on manufacturing solvable problems in workshops and followed an agenda that sidestepped violent upheavals, homicides, armed conflicts, and the disappearance of entire hamlets. To stay in office and build their own reputations and careers, the administrators also, in effect, contributed to reproducing violent relations and sustaining the area's enclavement by stoking its virulent reputation.

This journey through Badiraguato's social relationships now allows us to return to the contextual conditions that underpinned the inhabitants' experience of vulnerability: the political economy that structured the place where they lived, the role played by armed violence in their social relations, and the impediments to their formulating a critique of their condition.

ENCLAVEMENT AND EXTRACTION: A POLITICALLY INDUCED CONDITION OF VULNERABILITY

A political-economy perspective shows that the usual focus on drug trafficking does not so much describe a place like Badiraguato as play an influential role in it. Indeed, the process of how a poppy monoculture was imposed on the municipality shows the impact of its historical and social structuring around exploitation of a resource whose value is set outside its territory. As such, the illegality obscured the continuities that existed between the classical extractive economy and the poppy monoculture, in particular the decisive role of the municipality's enclavement.

The progressive concentration of poppy production in the sierra and its disappearance from the coastal plain were both legacies of the access constraints that organized earlier mining and commercial activities. Exploiting the difficulties of moving around the region was the main road to riches for the people I have called the entrepreneurs of marginalization. The area's inaccessibility made movement a scarce and unevenly distributed resource; the production of poppies, requiring isolation, concealment, and armed protection, in this respect actually boosted its potentialities. These entrepreneurs of marginalization not only captured the profits from enclavement, they actively contributed to its maintenance, or even to its reproduction, through political intermediation and involvement in the drug trade. Thus, the area's lack of accessibility furnished the node around which constraints and opportunities crystallized: being in a position to take advantage of it or put up with it defined the field of possibilities. This is what the word "powerful" meant in the local context: the dichotomy between a few marginalization entrepreneurs and a mass of the marginalized.

Enclavement does not merely reduce to a geographical constraint, but first and foremost constitutes a process involving infrastructure, economics, institutions, law, and the media. Indeed, infrastructural isolation in frontier areas characteristically fosters concentration on activities with high added value— but with limited local dividends—and on forms of delegating authority. These peripheries are also favored spaces for practices lodged in the gray area between legality and illegality. The law played a pivotal role in marginalizing Badiraguato: the illegality of poppy cultivation legitimized a military repression that in effect criminalized all of the municipality's inhabitants and, besides, fueled a media discourse on the area's dangerousness, opacity, and inaccessibility.

The repression that fed on outlawing was decisive in the transition to monoculture from the 1980s on. In the early 2000s, it underpinned the nonrecognition of land ownership rights. Legal isolation through criminalization thus sanctioned the exploitation of resources according to relationships of economic and political intermediation. The way in which "the den of hundreds of bandits," "the black legend," or "the cradle of drug trafficking" moved to the center of the municipality executives' discursive productions for journalists contributed to reproducing the enclavement. It is clear here how the semantic field of crime and profligate use of the *"narco"* prefix contributed to the reproduction of Badiraguato's central resource—its enclavement—more than to describing a productive organization and the social relationships on which it rested.

Moreover, the mode of production—concealing the plots and organizing the work—stemmed from its repression. The sale price was in fact linked to the exploitation by local intermediaries of the constraints created by the army. The poppy economy was thus indirectly regulated by the Mexican authorities, which left small growers destitute vis-à-vis those who bought their crops, while offering a competitive advantage to large producers who could protect themselves from repression by making arrangements with the military. In this regard, military operations played an essential role in the balance of power, favoring the traffickers at the expense of the growers forced to sell their harvests bit by bit at a low price. Thus, military repression was more than a fight against the production of marijuana and the poppy: in effect, it meant that the Mexican state—along with the United States—was structuring the distribution of the added value throughout the sector.

Far from the image of an integrated organization projected by the term "cartel," the growers and traffickers were in a subcontracting relationship. The grower families had to deal with all the hazards associated with cultivation and the costs of extortion and selective destruction of plots by the military, while the middlemen only got involved when the harvest was sold. *Pesados* saved the costs of protection and regulation and thus were more like ultra-liberal entrepreneurs than the image of the paternalistic mafia godfather that is often attached to them. Ironically, Joaquín "El Chapo" Guzman suggested this in his interview with the American actor Sean Penn in which he tried to squelch the charge that he was running the "Sinaloa Cartel."[1] He stressed that the people who engaged in this activity did not "depend" on him. Indeed, the outsourcing of costs and the profits derived from uncertainty, two key elements of this productive organization, showed strong similarities with contemporary neoliberal practices, reminiscent for example of the "partners" on the Uber platform. This mode of organization reminds us that the production and trafficking of drugs, far from the exceptionality attributed to them, constitute above all a radical form of inscription in contemporary capitalism. In drug trafficking as elsewhere, the subcontracting relationship is based on an illusion of worker autonomy and the mirage of an escape from insecurity.

The local intermediaries realized considerable profits thanks to their monopoly position vis-à-vis the growers. As we saw, the most lucrative stages were those involved in processing and transportation, which required political connections and armed men. These activities were out of reach of the growers due to repression and the violent competition, which, for example, prevented them from taking their poppy gum to the coastal plain region directly and thus bypassing the local intermediaries. Therefore, at the municipal level, the sector consisted of a captive mass of subcontractors competing with each other for a small number of buyers. The limited incomes of the growers, their insecurity, and their lack of prospects precluded any form of accumulation and projection into the future. The depth of the exploitation was evident in the precarious economy of the grower family: uncertain sales of iffy crops were not enough to ensure the reproduction of the labor force and required not only supplemental remittances from relatives living in the United States but also state subsidies. Ultimately, this predatory accumulation and cooptation of the growers' work relied on sustaining that which let the intermediaries maintain their local monopoly: repression by the state.

Enclavement accentuated the economic and social efficacy of subcontracting, lending the exploitation practices of buyers the gloss of favors done for the municipality's poor. Given the lack of alternatives to poppy production and activities associated with this sector, the local intermediaries were regarded as the providers of the incomes of the majority of the population. Moreover, the neglect by state authorities let them occupy the position of protectors or even benefactors at lower cost. Compared to the profits they drew, the services they provided were paltry (and never really free): rentals—termed "loans"—of land, protection against the armed men of their rivals, stocking (lucrative) grocery stores, or building places of worship and road infrastructure. Finally, the collective nature of the media and institutional stigma fed the illusion of a shared condition between growers and the powerful involved in the drug trade. The use of drones and the violence of military raids in the hunt after the most wanted traffickers stoked an admiration for these rare local success models, whose modest origins the media liked to showcase—an assertion built on extrapolating their condition from the social and economic marginality of their place of birth, that ignored the fact that they belonged to the most affluent families, enriched precisely by the region's enclavement.

In 2017, the introduction of the illegal market for an opium substitute, fentanyl, induced a change in the economy of this mountainous part of Sinaloa.

Just before I set foot in Badiraguato for the first time, the legalization of marijuana in some US states had taken this resource away from the producer families. Poppies, on the other hand, were thought unlikely to be legalized and thus appeared to be a safe bet. But then came fentanyl, and it was a game-changer: it required no agricultural work, only the synthesizing of chemicals. Consequently, in two years, the price of the Mexican poppy dropped tenfold, threatening the livelihood of the majority of the municipality's inhabitants. However, the Badiraguato sierra still retained its competitive edge: its enclavement made it easier to conceal the laboratories. Before the arrival of fentanyl, many laboratories were already producing synthetic products, such as methamphetamines, and were processing opium into heroin. With the rise of synthetic opioids, drug traders employed a skilled labor force and therefore no longer needed to maintain a mass of destitute subcontractors.

These recent developments highlighted the insecurity on which Badiraguato's economy rested. The profit margins of the marginalization entrepreneurs were not threatened—quite the contrary—by these upheavals, the costs of which were mainly borne by the growers. The subcontracting relationship now stood out in all its brutality: in an almost pure application of the "law of the market," the drop in demand for opium justified the fall in the price and the consequent further impoverishment of growers without alternatives. Fentanyl showed in sharp relief what mining, the poppy monoculture, and the chemicals industry had in common: the added value resided primarily in transport, in other words, outside the municipality. In this structuring, it was not poppy cultivation that produced the value, but its extraction from the place. However, the Badiraguato area was structured by these dynamics: entrepreneurs could shift from one resource to another, unlike most inhabitants who just tried to get by and were forced from one insecurity into another. The changes in the territory induced by passing on the market shifts to poppy producers showed that their "choices" were extremely limited. In short, isolation and military repression underpinned extractive and externally-oriented logics and thus produced deprived and vulnerable lives.

THE CERTAINTY OF UNCERTAINTY

The predatory forms of accumulation and the uncertainty they induced were essential elements of the social context in which the people of Badiraguato lived during my investigation. Faced with the uncertainty in travel, sociabil

ity, and subsistence, my interlocutors adopted a set of self-protection practices. However, these women and men formulated part of this protection in
terms of "behaving well," making statements that paradoxically suggested
that armed violence was predictable and that following social norms would
keep them from harm. This insistence on conformity as an essential form of
self-preservation implied the existence of a local monopoly on violence that
would set clear norms and impose them coercively.

On the other hand, ethnographic investigation shed light on the existence
of different armed groups whose more or less conflicting relationships were
the object of great vigilance on the part of the inhabitants. The people I
worked with carried out an intense intelligence-gathering activity in their
daily lives. Through information sharing, factoring in of past experiences,
and savvy analysis, they identified the spatial and temporal variations of the
threat. Some situations called for heightened vigilance, such as festivities and
school holidays. These investigative activities involved participating in
exchange spaces within various interknowledge networks, but they also
exposed participants to the threat of rumor and armed violence. Similarly,
travel, relying ultimately on a person's familiarity with a place and its inhabitants, remained exposed to the possibility that conflict or increased repression
would call it into question. Uncertainty was also evident in the material
dimension, with budgeting by the families in the sierra always having to factor in the unpredictable nature of their incomes. Finally, adulthood for
young girls marked the beginning of a condition in which their interactions
with men raised the threat of rape. All of these events were decisive in the
social experience that I have tried to render here.

However, their similarity with other contexts of armed conflict and
uncertainty (the former Yugoslavia, Afghanistan, Iraq, Syria) ended with a
notable difference: none of my interlocutors made the connection between
the looming danger in their familiar spaces and a possible event that would
have marked a turning point, a break, an entry into the order of indeterminate situations. On the contrary, their analyses and the ways in which they
identified threats were intimately linked to a reading of their environment
rooted in past experiences. Thus, the uncertainty that hung over the slightest
interactions of daily life appeared to be closely linked to the conflicts around
the areas of poppy production, the modes of repression, fluid ways of affiliation with different groups, or involvement in neighborhood conflicts that
descended into armed violence. The uncertainty surrounding their lives
therefore did not stem from a shattering of relevant interpretive frameworks

that would make identifying the norms on which to base their behavior difficult. Instead, it was linked to a detailed knowledge of violent practices, the social and political logics which drove them, and their historicity.

This knowledge was informed by their past experiences and lodged in the objectivation operations they carried out. It did not preclude many formulations of a perceived stability in some social relationships. Recall the official, the son of a woman who had opened a restaurant-grocery store in the sierra, who told me: "I'm the one who harvests what my mother sowed." This statement was especially revelatory of this logic. That is to say, he expressed that it was possible to have an investment in sociability in a part of the sierra bear fruit outside it in another generation. Similarly, the importance of more or less strong contacts with the regional political elite was evident in the structuring of armed groups and in local political competition. More broadly, the figures of the marginalization entrepreneurs who had prospered from the 1940s to the 1960s revealed the continuity of ways and means for exercising domination. Of course, several notable reorientations and transformations did take place, including the gradual separation between participation in institutional politics and ostensible involvement in the poppy trade. Similarly, the hazards that punctuated the lives of the powerful (death, arrest) occasionally increased uncertainty. But the "great families of the past" and their descendants—whether they were engaged in a political career or in the drug trade—kept a lock on resources that invariably were decisive in the social game. The cornerstone of these relationships—a positioning that profited from the municipality's enclavement—was pervasive both in the organization of drug trafficking and in the strategies deployed by local politicians.

These dynamics reflected a tendency to reproduce the relationships of domination. The uncertainty that I have described, which was simultaneously situational, existential, and material, was not a manifestation of recent abrupt changes. On the contrary, the difficulty of anticipating a situation was part of a context in which the predictability of the social game was overwhelming. This articulation was particularly evident in some of the dynamics that appeared along the way. How the municipal government acted in the context of violence was paradigmatic. By producing solvable problems and an ironclad agenda, local elected officials sealed off the realm of institutional politics against the residents' concerns and related their treatment to violent social relationships. In this sense, maintaining the unwavering stability of the bureaucratic routine participated in the uncertainty regime imposed on the inhabitants. Where state and federal policies (repression, marginalization) contributed to the reproduction of local modes of domination, the daily administrative work of the town hall ensured its own reproduction by insulating itself from violent dynamics and therefore also contributed to their persistence.

The ephemeral nature of economic ascents through the drug trade showed the same relationship between domination and uncertainty. Going for a "ride"—smuggling a quantity of drugs across the US border—appeared to be one of the few ways of escaping this context of dependence. It required family and friendly networks along the migration route—a widespread resource— and thus could bypass the intermediaries installed in drug trafficking. But, as we have seen, it also exposed the "rider" to the threat of armed violence and contributed significantly to the difficulties of identifying those who were likely to kill and be killed. The possibility of a "ride" increased the uncertainty in neighbor and kinship relationships, as well as the threatening nature of gossip, fueling further conflicts that harked back to various old grievances. More specifically, the uncertainty of the "ride" referred to the fragility of the ascents that these opportunities allowed, exposing young men to death. Behind the accounts that emphasized the responsibility of those who "do not know how to administer" and were killed often hid the actions of those who *did* know how to administer, which is to say, those who benefited upstream from social, political, and violent resources in administering their affairs.

The same tension—this certainty of uncertainty—also raised its head in giving meaning to the violent acts. In this regard, the rare cases where armed violence was carried out by socially marginal persons were symptomatic of the logics lurking in the many formulations of self-protection. The differentiated treatment of violent acts committed by Martín's band highlighted two phenomena. On the one hand, the judgment on violence was included in the evaluations of the killers' social profile, which implied, conversely, that the use of violence and the profits from "rides" alone were not enough to make someone powerful; such a person also needed the means to "administer." On the other hand, blaming the victims of violence for their fate rested on the fact that the killing was done on behest of the powerful.

Thus, statements related to self-protection ("only those with unsettled accounts," "only those who stick their noses in others' business" were killed; "just behave well" or "he sure died for something") contradicted the practices of protection by asserting predictability in the very situations in which armed violence was especially a factor of uncertainty. These comments framed the violence of the powerful as the foundation of the social order, as punishment of deviant practices against norms known to all. Yet, the targets of these violent acts were in practice difficult to identify, which made it imperative to scrutinize and gather information among kin or neighbors, with the object of detecting, for example, a beginning economic ascent where none was expected.

As we saw in the case of the police chief "El Gallito," this paradoxical apprehending of violent acts did not depend on whether there was a legal basis for the violent act or not, but on the power attributed to the armed person, and then on its practical modalities. The incantatory formulas—such as the phrase "only those who . . ." for averting danger from the person speaking—was both a posture to make this experience acceptable ("here, everything is quiet") and a mechanism for assigning responsibility to the victims for their own death, in keeping with the Mexican national context. In Badiraguato, this imputation referred in particular to an economy of what could and could not be said. The unmentionable was twofold: it encompassed both the responsibility of the powerful in homicides and the uncertainty that their domination induced.

The context of Badiraguato therefore appeared as an assemblage of dynamics producing a configuration where the experience of uncertainty underpinned the reproduction of extremely unequal relationships. The case of land regulation was indicative of the uncoordinated but complementary interests that produced these tragic patterns: the application of agrarian legislation hand in glove with the military repression of the main livelihood made the legal "commons" susceptible to violent and individual land grabs and turned land security, the predictability of a person's rights to land, into a "theory" that put it out of reach of grower families. Uncertainty became a key element in the perpetuation of relationships of domination and dependence.

QUALIFICATION BY ARMS

Badiraguato's structuring around an extractive economy and the reproduction of the relations of domination through uncertainty both raise the question of how this context actualized itself at the situational, interactional level. Indeed, if this context induced a condition of precarity, it did not impose itself passively, the comments on a specific action being decisive in how the context affects a situation. Throughout this book I have emphasized the intense evaluation and qualification work that the people with whom I shared time performed on situations that confronted them and in which they were sometimes directly involved. In fact, there were many such situations in their daily lives which they had to interpret. These sensemaking operations sometimes resulted in their characterizing a situation as problematic—in the sense of unacceptable—and, on other occasions, qualifying it as in line with the order of things. In Badiraguato, the processes through which these definitions emerged highlighted the obstacles that hampered the emergence of a controversy in the sense of Luc Boltanski's pragmatic sociology: of generating conflicting interpretations, opening up the public space to unprecedented criticism, and ultimately raising the possibilities of an action transforming its context.[2]

In this regard, the periods of indeterminacy that violence opened were particularly revealing. Thus, the hours and days following Adriana's abduction by six armed men were occupied by attempts to define what had just transpired. Similarly, we saw that in the days following the dawn rising on a dead body, the residents conversed and deliberated. Although in the minor mode of implicitness, the operation had to do with whether he was "killed for a reason" or whether it was a problematic murder, one that needed more extensive commentary. These cases highlighted mechanisms that had wider ramifications: was the fencing of a parcel a matter of asserting a right, or an undue land grab?

As we have seen, these qualification processes invariably involved the search for imputations. Defining the situation, deciding what we were dealing with, required judgments about actors and actions: were we confronted with a dead man who was one of those responsible for their own death or, as in the case of Martín, this time was the killer a dangerous psychopath? Was it the chief of police or the three young men who were responsible for their deaths? So, was the killing of the chief of police a reprehensible act or a well-deserved punishment? Did Adriana provoke her rape or did her abductor go beyond what was acceptable? These judgments were very rarely expressed outright (except by Teófilo). In the kitchens, in front of the grocery stores, and in the streets of the town, it was the expression of their elaboration that manifested itself: the construction of a broader narrative, with a precise chronology and stress on this or that detail.

Thus, fragments of narrative emerged: Adriana was already "spending time with" her abductor; the third man was killed by "El Gallito" while he was unarmed, begging for his life; and the latter's death ensued after he had compounded his affront by offending the three victims' family. The narrative elements were reported in the exchanges as gossip—"they say that . . ."—but in fact indicated a staking-out of positions. Placing a given act in a narrative frame defined it, in the sense that the narrative lifted the veil on what the act achieved and, incidentally, attributed fault, imputed blame.

Judgments brought to bear by an individual appeared intrinsically linked to the assessment of whether or not this event would have a sequel. A consensus account of the deaths of the three young men spread in parallel with the tension of waiting for reprisals. Among the judgments passed by the neighbors on Adriana's abduction, we still saw the assessment of the possibility that her father would take revenge: one opined it as unlikely and suggested that Adriana was at fault; the other hoped for a reaction from the father and pointed to the unacceptable nature of the abductor's action; even more revealing, the requalification as a lover's quarrel took place after any possibility of retaliation was ruled out. The same process could be observed in the only slightly dissonant discourse following the death of Martín. While everyone urgently wanted to condemn the dead man and recall his offenses, in the grocery store they emphasized *both* betrayal as a modality of his murder and the possibility of reprisals.

Thus, judgments about action were caught up in self-preservation practices and were confounded by assessments geared to anticipating the possibility, or not, of retaliation. There was indeed a time of indeterminacy about the situation that had just occurred, a time for cautious qualifications—and possibly such an action might become the subject of conflicting interpretations and thereby acquire a capacity for transforming the context. However, the ordinary qualifications simultaneously constituted an anticipation of violence, which remained indeterminate, given the possibility that those involved would escalate. The exercise of violence thus became decisive in the very definition of the meaning of past actions. It was the people involved and, above all, their variable capacity to mobilize violent resources that affected this definition most substantively. In a way, they defined the situation by arms (the kidnapping was punished, therefore it was unacceptable), and this definition prevailed if necessary by a requalification after the fact. So, the distinguishing criterion between a "proper" stealing ("that's how we do it here"), "a lover's quarrel," and an unacceptable act of violence was inseparable from the assessment of the violent resources of the abductors, fathers, and other men involved. It was a matter of compelling necessity for living in this context of violence: not to see one's judgments contradicted or even sanctioned by those who wielded the weapons. The definition of problematic situations and their treatment thus carried over to the unequal social relations of predatory and violent capitalism.

The constraints on the evaluations of my interlocutors fit into a context where another qualifying operator entered into the picture—that is, the local level of the state. As we saw, one of the remarkable aspects of the public speeches by the town hall executives was precisely the fact that they refrained from commenting on these situations that occupied the rest of the town, which was constantly trying to define how problematic they were. Thus, the town hall did not participate in the process of qualifying the abduction and rape of Adriana or the many homicides that occurred in the municipality. The only case in which we saw these officials come up with a story about an act of violence—the death of the police chief in Culiacán—was because here the issues and expectations at the state and federal levels were what mattered. The local executives' main concern was how to distance themselves from the political fallout over the murder of the highest local security official.

On the other hand, these officials regularly performed generalization operations. In his office, the town hall secretary alluded to the "problem of stealing women," to the "problem of domestic violence," before concluding with a lapidary formula: "They kill you." Similarly, Gonzalo, the municipal executive, in explaining that the *cerco* and not the *ejido* determined access to land, could say: "If they kill each other over a simple look . . . you can imagine it for a *cerco*." The identification by state officials of "problems" immediately led to the reference to another form of regulation characterized by the use of violence. The impersonal "they" forms pertain both to an essentialization—a reprise of the alterity that underlies the collective criminalization in the national framework of "narco-trafficking"—and to the "sector," meaning "organized crime." This "sector," which required no further qualification, denoted the organization producing and trafficking drugs, one that would deal in practice with problems that were not solvable by institutional means: woman stealing, domestic violence, land disputes, dead bodies found on roadsides, depopulated hamlets, even sometimes the construction of roads, churches, or schools. Thus, the "criminal" characterization reduced all the conflicts and problems that posed themselves for the inhabitants to those concerning the organization of violence and the drug trade.

This recurring vision of a "dual government," of an opposition between a legal us and an illegal them, assumed that other institutions, with their own norms and hierarchies, would preside over the definition and treatment of these problematic situations. However, the experience of the inhabitants in these situations did not suggest regulation by an alleged "cartel." While some discourses referred to ad hoc interventions by a powerful someone, the vast majority of inhabitants did not benefit from the possible use of third parties to mediate, arbitrate disputes, and apply standards, thus proposing alternative definitions of what was or was not acceptable. Just as the legal concept of the *ejido* "commons" constituted a validation of the violent land-grabbing and a distancing from the agrarian courts that theoretically had jurisdiction over this kind of conflict, the transfer of the definition of problematic situations to "the sector" constituted a validation of how they were currently processed. In practice, this institutional treatment reinforced the preeminence of the exercise of violence by those involved in defining the problematic or non-problematic nature of situations.

The withdrawal of institutions from qualifying situations and their definition by arms is fundamentally a political problem. The detailed assessment of the ins and outs of each situation according to the violent resources of the people involved leads to a personalization and a singularization of conflicts. Conversely, for people to generalize their experience would require the possibility of seeing beyond the specificity of each situation and the people involved to detect common elements and denaturalize social relations. These obstacles to generalization are crucial for grasping the constraints that weighed on the emergence of a formalized discourse around a shared condition of the vulnerable inhabitants of Badiraguato—in short, their politicization. Thinking about modes of transformation would require a qualification of the context in which they lived, an explanation of their social position, and a sharing of individual experiences. However, in the context of Badiraguato, all the necessary precautions prescribed the singularization and personalization of evaluations. In a place where all inhabitants are tarred with being part of a criminal organization, this issue is crucial. It relates to the need to question the homogeneity of the framing generated by the municipality's reputation: a criminal society in which the distinctions between those who exploit and those who are exploited have no place.

. . .

One evening, at the beginning of my investigation, Teófilo and I were sitting outside our chambers' doors when I asked him why he was taking the risk of telling me all these stories. He said, "They're all dead anyway." This man, who said things in transgressive sallies, had seen many of the people with whom he had worked and lived disappear, and this condition was continuing. These people included not only those older than him, but also the younger ones. Antonio, in front of Yolanda's grocery store, kept repeating: "So many young men are getting killed." Tamara spoke of the hamlet of Chihuahua state where she grew up as a desolate place. Like Lamberto's family before her, she had left a place where "you couldn't live." When I temporarily shared their daily lives they were warm, but also worried and confronting uncertain horizons. Doña Irina, who insisted on her privileged circumstances, was constantly expressing her anguish about a "good match." One of her sons-in-law had already been killed and a good match would be above all one that would rescue one of her daughters from this limbo. By moving to the main town, Ismael and Adriana seemed to have managed to carve out a space for their aspirations—but only briefly. Teófilo, Gabriela and her husband, Rosa and her father, all exited, at one time or another, a place where "they killed too much."

To say "dawn rose on a dead body" every now and then is not to be the person killed or their killer. It is, however, to share the uncertainty of these women and men, to take your place with them among the ranks of the outcasts.

INTRODUCTION

1. Joaquin Guzman Loera, whose nickname "El Chapo" means "Shorty," hailed from La Tuna, a hamlet in the Badiraguato sierra, and was suspected by the DEA of running the "Sinaloa Cartel." From the early 2000s, following his first escape (he had been arrested in 1993), he became one of the DEA's most wanted; in 2009, 2010, and 2011 the magazine *Forbes* ranked him among the richest and most influential figures in the world. He was arrested in 2016 and extradited to the United States.

2. Rafael Caro Quintero was born in the hamlet of La Noria in the Badiraguato sierra. He was thought to have been one of the leaders of the "Guadalajara Cartel," the forerunner of the "Sinaloa Cartel." Accused of murdering DEA agent Enrique Camarena, he was arrested in 1985 and sentenced by the Mexican federal court to forty years in prison. He was accidentally released in 2013 due to a procedural defect, and was then hunted until his last arrest in 2022 in Choix, a municipality neighboring Badiraguato.

3. Between 2011 and 2018, the Mexican Human Rights Commission estimated that 8,726,375 people were forced to leave their homes either temporarily or permanently to escape fighting and violence in Mexico. See Brenda Gabriela Pérez Vázquez et al., *Episodios de desplazamiento interno forzado masivo en México. Informe 2018* (Mexico City: Comision Mexicana de Defensa y Promocion de los Derechos Humanos, 2019).

4. Several recent works highlight the place of armed violence in the formation of the Mexican state. See Gilbert Joseph and Daniel Nugent, eds., *Everyday Forms of the State. Revolution and the Negotiation of Rule in Modern Mexico* (Durham: Duke University Press, 1994); Benjamin Smith, *Pistoleros and Popular Movements: The Politics of State Formation in Postrevolutionary Oaxaca* (Lincoln: University of Nebraska Press, 2009); Wil Pansters, ed., *Violence, Coercion, and State-Making in Twentieth-Century Mexico: The Other Half of the Centaur* (Stanford: Stanford University Press, 2012); Alexander Aviña, *Specters of Revolution: Peasant Guerrillas in the Cold War Mexican Countryside* (Oxford: Oxford University Press, 2014); Luis

Astorga, *El siglo de las drogas: Del Porfiriato al nuevo milenio,* 2nd ed. (Mexico City: Penguin, 2016); Pablo Piccato, *A History of Infamy: Crime, Truth, and Justice in Mexico* (Oakland: University of California Press, 2017).

5. In April 2019, the United Nations High Commissioner for Human Rights estimated that more than 250,000 people had been killed and compared the situation to "a country at war." Based on official Mexican statistics, US academics tallied a death toll of 150,000 in connection with the so-called war on drugs, while admitting in a methodological appendix that it is impossible to distinguish these deaths from other homicides. More broadly, human rights groups suspect the existence of numerous mass graves, and the lack of investigation into most killings leads to chronic underestimation of the number of killings linked to drug trafficking and competition between armed organizations. For figures from the Office of the United Nations High Commissioner for Human Rights see https://www.ohchr.org/EN /NewsEvents/Pages/DisplayNews.aspx?NewsID=24467&LangID=E. For the study of the University of San Diego, see Laura Calderon et al., *Organized Crime and Violence in Mexico* (2019), https://justiceinmexico.org/wp-content/uploads /2021/10/OCVM-21.pdf.

6. My research takes its place among works that have highlighted the importance of not perceiving social groups through the legal categories imposed by states. See Sally Engle Merry, "The Criminalization of Everyday Life," in *Everyday Practices and Trouble Cases,* ed. Austin Sarat et al. (Evanston: Northwestern University Press, 1998), 14–40; Philippe Parnell and Stephanie Kane, eds., *Crime's Power: Anthropologists and the Ethnography of Crime* (New York: Palgrave Macmillan); Jean Comaroff and John Comaroff, eds., *Law and Disorder in the Postcolony* (Chicago: University of Chicago Press, 2006); Jane Schneider and Peter Schneider, "The Anthropology of Crime and Criminalization," *Annual Review of Anthropology* 37, no. 1 (2008): 35173.

7. Fernando Escalante Gonzalbo, *El crimen como realidad y representacion* (Mexico City: El Colegio de México, 2012). Therefore, I avoid the use of these terms as much as possible and their rare mentions are in quotation marks.

8. For an oral history of the massacre of Ayotzinapa see John Gibler, *I Couldn't Even Imagine That They Would Kill Us: An Oral History of the Attacks Against the Students of Ayotzinapa* (San Francisco: City Lights, 2017).

9. This perspective is particularly evident in the works that in taking a cultural anthropology approach bring together media designations ("narcofilm," "narcocorrido," "narcomanta," "narcojunior") in the concept of "narcoculture." See José Manuel Valenzuela Arce, *Jefe de Jefes: Corridos y narcocultura in México* (Mexico City: Plaza y Janés, 2001); Howard Campbell, *Drug War Zone: Frontline Dispatches from the Streets of El Paso and Juarez* (Austin: University of Texas Press, 2009). For a different perspective on these same cultural objects, see Luis Astorga, *Mitología del "narco-traficante" en Mexico* (Mexico City: Plaza y Valdes, 1995).

10. Revealingly, one of the important works on the violence of drug trafficking bears the title *El México Narco,* thus taking up the title of the classic work *México Profundo* by the anthropologist Guillermo Bonfil Batalla, in which he contrasted

the illusory modernity of metis Mexico with the authenticity of indigenous Mexico. See Guillermo Bonfil Batalla, *México profundo: una civilizacion negada* (Mexico City: Grijalbo, 1987); Rafael Rodriguez Castaneda, *El México Narco* (Mexico City: Booket, 2009).

11. William Roseberry, *Anthropologies and Histories: Essays in Culture, History and Political Economy* (New Brunswick: Rutgers University Press, 1989); Henry Bernstein, "'Changing Before Our Very Eyes': Agrarian Questions and the Politics of Land in Capitalism Today," *Journal of Agrarian Change* 4, no. 1-2 (2004): 190–225; Gavin Smith, "Selective Hegemony and Beyond-Populations with 'No Productive Function': A Framework for Enquiry," *Identities* 18, no. 1 (2011): 2–38; Tania Li, *Land's End: Capitalist Relations on an Indigenous Frontier* (Durham: Duke University Press, 2014); Susana Narotzky and Niko Besnier, "Crisis, Value, and Hope: Rethinking the Economy," *Current Anthropology* 55, no. 9 (2014): S4–S16.

12. For other examples of the linkages between politics and development of the agroindustry and structuring of the illegal economy in Mexico, see Victoria Malkin, "Narcotrafficking, Migration, and Modernity in Rural Mexico," *Latin American Perspectives* 28, no. 4 (2001): 101–28; James McDonald, "The Narcoeconomy and Small-Town, Rural Mexico," *Human Organization* 64, no. 2 (2005): 115–25; Salvador Maldonado Aranda, *Los márgenes del estado mexicano: Territorios ilegales, desarrollo y violencia en Michoacán* (Zamora: El Colegio de Michoacán, 2010).

13. In the same vein, see Christian Geffray, *Chroniques de la servitude en Amazonie brésilienne: Essai sur l'exploitation paternaliste* (Paris: Karthala, 1995). More broadly, on the centrality of flows in the predatory capitalism of drugs, see Philippe Bourgois, "Insecurity, the War on Drugs and Crimes of States," in *Violence at the Urban Margins,* ed. Javier Auyero, Philippe Bourgois, and Nancy Scheper-Hughes (London: Oxford University Press, 2015), 305–21.

14. Following David Harvey and Philippe Bourgois, I talk about predation to highlight the centrality of violent appropriations among forms of accumulation. See David Harvey, *A Brief History of Neoliberalism* (Oxford: Oxford University Press, 2005); Philippe Bourgois, "Decolonising Drug Studies in an Era of Predatory Accumulation," *Third World Quarterly* 39, no. 2 (2018): 385–98.

15. Carolyn Nordstrom, *A Different Kind of War Story* (Philadelphia: University of Pennsylvania Press, 1997); Linda Green, *Fear as a Way of Life: Mayan Widows in Rural Guatemala* (New York: Columbia University Press, 1999); Elisabeth Claverie, *Les guerres de la vierge: Une anthropologie des apparitions* (Paris: Gallimard, 2003); Henrik Vigh, *Navigating Terrains of War: Youth and Soldiering in Guinea-Bissau* (New York: Berghahn Books, 2006); Sverker Finnström, *Living with Bad Surroundings: War, History, and Everyday Moments in Northern Uganda* (Durham: Duke University Press, 2008); Ivana Macek, *Sarajevo Under Siege: Anthropology in Wartime* (Philadelphia: University of Pennsylvania Press, 2009); Stephen Lubkemann, *Culture in Chaos: An Anthropology of the Social Condition in War* (Chicago: University of Chicago Press, 2010).

16. Jeanne Favret-Saada, *Deadly Words: Witchcraft in the Bocage* (Cambridge: Cambridge University Press, 1980); Kimberly Theidon, *Intimate Enemies: Violence*

and Reconciliation in Peru (Philadelphia: University of Pennsylvania Press, 2013); Valérie Robin Azevedo, *Sur les sentiers de la violence: Politiques de la mémoire et conflit armé au Pérou* (Paris: Éditions de l'IHEAL, 2019).

17. Here we encounter the situations of extreme insecurity about which Judith Butler writes. See Judith Butler, *Precarious Life: The Powers of Mourning and Violence* (New York: Verso Books, 2006); Judith Butler, *Frames of War: When is Life Grievable?* (London: Verso Books, 2009).

18. Michel Naepels, *Dans la détresse: Une anthropologie de la vulnérabilité* (Paris: Éditions de l'EHESS, 2019).

19. Michel de Certeau, *The Practice of Everyday Life* (Berkeley: University of California Press, 1984); Bertrand Masquelier and Jean-Louis Siran, eds., *Pour une anthropologie de l'interlocution: Rhétoriques du quotidien* (Paris: L'Harmattan, 2000); Veena Das, *Life and Words: Violence and the Descent into the Ordinary* (Berkeley: University of California Press, 2007.

20. Here we find the impact of media and legal categories of violence on local social relationships in a context of violence. See Danny Hoffmann, "The Civilian Target in Sierra Leone and Liberia: Political Power, Military Strategy, and Humanitarian Intervention," *African Affairs* 103 (2004): 211–26; Elisabeth Claverie, "Mettre en cause la légitimité de la violence d'État," *Quaderni* 2 (2012): 67–83; Alice Goffman, *On the Run: Fugitive Life in an American City* (Chicago: University of Chicago Press, 2014).

21. On neoliberalism as a mode of individual responsibilization see Harvey, *A Brief History of Neoliberalism,* 76; Loïc Wacquant, "Crafting the Neoliberal State: Workfare, Prisonfare, and Social Insecurity," *Sociological Forum* 25, no. 2 (2010): 197–220.

22. Carolyn Nordstrom and Antonius Robben, eds., *Fieldwork Under Fire: Contemporary Studies of Violence and Culture* (Berkeley: University of California Press, 1995), 276–93; J. Christopher Kovats-Bernat, "Negotiating Dangerous Fields: Pragmatic Strategies for Fieldwork amid Violence and Terror," *American Anthropologist* 104, no. 1 (2002): 208–22.

23. As Noah Coburn's ethnography in a village of potters during the war in Afghanistan also shows, the choice of location and the angle of the inquiry at times makes it possible to avoid these difficulties to render *in situ* the daily experience of armed violence; see *Bazaar Politics: Power and Pottery in an Afghan Market Town* (Stanford: Stanford University Press, 2011).

24. I develop the conditions of my fieldwork in Adèle Blazquez, "Ethnographie d'un contexte violent: L'immanence de l'enquête (Sinaloa, Mexique)," *Monde commun* 1 (2018): 188–205.

25. Bronislaw Malinowski, *Argonauts of the Western Pacific: An Account of Native Enterprise and Adventure in the Archipelagoes of Melanesian New Guinea* (London: Routledge, 1922).

26. Jean Bazin, "Questions de sens," *Enquête* 6 (1998): 13–34; Jean Bazin, "Interpréter ou décrire: Notes critiques sur la connaissance anthropologique," in *Une école pour les sciences sociales: De la VIe section à l'EHESS,* ed. Jacques Revel and Nathan Wachtel (Paris: Le Cerf, 1996), 401–20.

27. Max Gluckman, "Analysis of a Social Situation in Modern Zululand," *Bantu Studies* 14 (1940): 1–30.

28. Alain Cottereau, "What's the Right Price for Babysitting? A Case Study in Ethno-Accounting," *Human Studies* 38, no. 1 (2015): 97–112. On this topic, also see Michel Naepels, *Histoires de terres kanakes: Conflicts fonciers et rapports sociaux dans la région de Houaïlou (Nouvelle-Calédonie)* (Paris: Belin, 1998), 16–19.

29. The "world" of given actions, as defined by Jean Bazin, is "a particular configuration, fleeting, more or less sustainable . . . of the space of the 'doable' for a given action (or for a series of relatively analogous actions). . . . The world the actions implied (what I need to know to describe them) is also the world they repeat day after day; it is the ordinary of social life as they contribute, by their fulfilment, to renewing it." See "Science des mœurs et description de l'action," *Le Genre humain* 35, no. 2 (1999): 43.

30. George Devereux, *From Anxiety to Method in the Behavioral Sciences* (Berlin: De Gruyter Mouton, 1967); Donna Haraway, "Situated Knowledges: The Science Question in Feminism and the Privilege of Partial Perspective," *Feminist Studies* 14, no. 3 (1988): 575–99; Michel Naepels, "L'épiement sans trêve et la curiosité de tout," *L'Homme* 203–4 (2012): 77–102.

31. Michel Naepels, "Une étrange étrangeté. Remarques sur la situation ethnographique," *L'Homme* 148 (1998: 185–99); Michel Naepels, "Note sur la justification dans la relation ethnographique," *Genèses* 64, no. 3 (2006), 110–26.

32. Drawing on the work of art historian George Didi-Huberman, Michel Naepels proposes a reflection on the production and recreation of ethnography as a montage, as a work of grouping discursivities and visibilities that takes into account their shortcomings, the path of the ethnographer, and the uniqueness of the experiences of those with whom he co-produces the material ("L'épiement sans trêve et la curiosité de tout.") See also Georges Didi-Huberman, *Images in Spite of All: Four Photographs from Auschwitz* (Chicago: University of Chicago Press, 2012).

33. René Char, *Retour amont* (Paris: Gallimard, 1966).

CHAPTER I

1. Deborah Poole speaks of the "visual economy" to account for visual images as part of a "comprehensive organization of people, ideas, and objects. . . . [T]his organization has as much to do with social relationships, inequality, and power as with shared meanings and community. In the more specific sense of a political economy, it also suggests that this organization bears some—not necessarily direct—relationship to the political and class structure of society as well as to the production and exchange of the material goods or commodities that form the life blood of modernity. See *Vision, Race, and Modernity: A Visual Economy of the Andean Image World* (Princeton: Princeton University Press, 1997), 8.

2. "En Badiraguato, Sinaloa, cuna de capos, el cultivo de drogas es una forma de ser y de pensar," *Proceso*, August 23, 1997.

3. Osorno's visit occurred before the welcoming arch was built.

4. Diego Osorno, *El Cártel de Sinaloa: una historia del uso político del narco* (Mexico: Penguin, 2011), 109–11.

5. Alis Krupskaia and Rafael Romo, "Code of Silence Reigns in El Chapo's Birthplace," *CNN*, January 19, 2016.

6. Nery Córdova, *La Narcocultura: Simbología de la transgresión, el poder y la muerte; Sinaloa y la "leyenda negra"* (Culiacán: Universidad Autónoma de Sinaloa, 2011).

7. https://www.youtube.com/watch?v = Pc-XmXvbv9U.

8. The use of the term is very common in the writings of Badiraguato intellectuals. It comes from a Spanish historian, Julián Juderías, who published *The Spanish Black Legend* (1914) in which he denounced as excessive the criticisms of the Kingdom of Spain of the colonial conquest, the extermination of the Amerindian populations, and the methods of the Inquisition. Its use refers to the wide dissemination of negative narratives of a place that are deemed exaggerated.

9. José Figueroa and Gilberto López Alanís, eds., *Encuentros con la Historia: Badiraguato* (Culiacán: Presagio, 2002), 6.

10. Linaloe Flores, "La 'cruzada' de EPN deja Badiraguato al narco," *Sin embargo*, August 23, 2013, https://www.sinembargo.mx/23-08-2013/728974.

11. Astorga, *El siglo de las drogas*, 84.

12. The military's Condor operation was launched in 1977 in the region with the official objective of eradicating plantings of poppies and marijuana. See chapter 2.

13. The places they came from is a classic element in stories about bandits; see Eric Hobsbawm, *Les bandits* (Paris: La Découverte, 2018).

14. Córdova, *La Narcocultura*, 145.

15. As Luis Astorga has shown, this dynamic dates back to the 1940s and 1950s, with the celebrity of people associated with drug trafficking stemming less from their place in the production and sale of drugs than from being identified and pursued by US authorities such as the FBI or DEA; see *El siglo de las drogas,* 158.

16. The treatment of the duel between Martín Elenes and Valente Quintero is indicative of what plays out in the reinterpretation of local history. The corrido "Valente Quintero" and the film of the same name suggest a political dispute between the two men as part of the revolutionary struggle, each belonging to a separate faction (https://www.youtube.com/watch?v = V6v9opfmrok). The "Corrido of Badiraguato," for its part, refers to the duel in these terms: "On this blessed ground walked Martín Elenes; the one who killed Valente in a dispute over women." In both cases, the attributes highlighted are those of violent masculinity, honor, and courage. In 1990, a local intellectual tried to put things right, writing that "Martín Elenes, originally from Santiago de los Caballeros, is much more than what the people of Mexico came to know through the also distorted version of Don Rosendo Monzón's *corrido*." But he apologizes for not being able to reveal the real story of the case, because "65 years later, there are still things that we cannot talk about carelessly, because we run the risk of unjustly hurting the self-esteem of people who do not deserve to be hurt. In any case, in the light of history, neither the mayor [Martín

Elenes], nor Valente, two figures of the revolution, deserved to die in this way, in this sad finale, that night of March 19, 1922, in Babunica." See Oscar Lara Salazar, *Sangre Caliente* (Culiacán: Talleres de Artes Gréficas Sinaloenses, 1990), 54. The power of framing it as drug trafficking is evident in the subsequent reinterpretation of the story: "Probably, says a Sinaloan writer [Herberto Sinagawa], the substance of the conflict to the death between the soldiers Valente Quintero and Martín Elenes was not only political differences as related by one of the most famous *corridos* but precisely drug issues and perhaps delimitation of certain territories" (Córdova, *La Narcocultura*, 142).

17. The region matches Karl Jacoby's definition of "borderlands" for territories close to the state border but also on the boundary between history and narrative. See *Des ombres à l'aube: Un massacre d'Apaches et la violence de l'histoire* (Toulouse: Anacharsis, 2015).

18. On the subject of the dam's construction, José de Jesús Caro Medina, mayor of Badiraguato in the late 1990s, remarked that the inhabitants in the vicinity only "saw the water go by . . . without receiving any benefit from it." Despite demands that supposedly were made for the nearby land to receive a certain allocation of water, nothing came of it. Thus, he stressed that this area today figures among the most marginalized in the municipality. José de Jesús Caro Medina, *Mi sueño . . . ver a Badiraguato convertido en un municipio de primera nivel en calidad de vida* (self-published, 1990).

19. This was the case in 1953; see Astorga, *El siglo de las drogas*, 114.

20. Osorno, *El Cártel de Sinaloa*, 114.

21. Using these airstrips amid the difficulties of landing on them due to their smallness and camouflaging was a classic status object. One of the grand personages of the 1980s, a native of the coastal plain, thus modestly called himself the "Lord of the skies"—evidently a reference to his *maestra* as a pilot.

22. Flores, "La 'cruzada' de EPN deja Badiraguato al narco."

23. This town hall in which I worked during the fieldwork was responsible for enrollments and follow-up of aid programs and delivering food aid to the hamlets.

24. One resident of a hamlet told me about the arrival of state policemen as one of the highlights of the last few months. He described the bewilderment of the residents, and then their relief at the sight of the police being accompanied by an important man from their hamlet—apparently about a stolen car.

25. The word *pesado* is in local use to describe the intermediaries of the drug trade. I explain their emergence and their specific traits in chapter 3.

26. "En la recta final de las campañas: Propaganda negra," *El Debate*, June 24, 2018. The place of PRI affiliation in travel and, more broadly, the party's long hegemony in the municipality waned in 2021 with the victory of the Morena National Regeneration Movement, the partisan formation of President Andrés Manuel López Obrador (2018–24).

27. Today called the "Badiraguato-Parral," it has become an important main road, both at the state and federal level, because it connects Sinaloa to the state of Chihuahua. Completing it was a campaign promise of President Lopéz Obrador.

28. The *sindicaturas* correspond to the municipality's internal administrative divisions. Until 2011, there were ten; four more were created in 2011, and one more in 2013. During my fieldwork, there were thus fifteen *sindicaturas*. At stake in them especially was the election of representatives for each; however, they were sometimes appointed by the town hall and paid 1,500 pesos (75 USD) bimonthly.

29. Praxedis Alarcón Valdez, *Radiografía política: Una visión retrospectiva* (Culiacán: Universidad Autónoma de Sinaloa, 2011), 65–66.

30. The group from N* notably stood out from the other armed groups in the municipality by the fact that they patrolled, wore military-style uniforms, were hired in other parts of the country, and practiced discipline.

31. *Checar* is an anglicism, derived from the verb "to check."

32. This may be because of the higher number of deaths in hamlet S*, but also because I stayed several times in S* and only once in N*.

33. *Compadre* or *comadre* is the person bound by *compadrazgo*, a term that refers to kinship ties constructed through the sponsorship of an important event in a person's life such as baptism, communion, marriage, or the birth of a child.

34. During this stay, I had no chance to go into the sierra, much less by bus to S*.

CHAPTER 2

1. Presence has been a classic dimension of anthropology since the seminal works of Bronislaw Malinowski. Following in the traces of the text by Clifford Geertz titled "Being There," several thinkers have stressed the constitutive dimension of presence in the knowledge produced by ethnography. See Clifford Geertz, "Being There: Anthropology and the Scene of Writing," in *Works and Lives: The Anthropologist as Author* (Stanford: Stanford University Press, 1988), 1–24; Conrad Watson, ed., *Being There: Fieldwork in Anthropology* (New York: Pluto Press, 1999); John Borneman and Abdellah Hammoudi, eds., *Being There: The Fieldwork Encounter and the Making of Truth* (Berkeley: University of California Press, 2009).

2. Alfred Schütz distinguishes between degrees of "relevance" of the attention that a person brings to their experience and the kind of knowledge that experience entails. His scale distinguishes "self-evident" actions and interactions, thus not requiring a deepening of their stakes and indeterminate interactions that induce operations of questioning and investigation. See "The Well-Informed Citizen: An Essay on the Social Distribution of Knowledge," *Social Research* 13, no. 4 (1946): 463–78.

3. In the case of the conflict in Colombia, Natalia Suárez Bonilla shows the information gathering operations undertaken by the inhabitants caught between the suspicions of the guerrillas and the military. See "Épreuves d'altérité dans les enclaves insurrectionnelles: Le cas de la Colombie," in *Sociétés en guerre,* ed. Rémy Bazenguissa-Ganga and Sami Makki (Paris: Éditions de la MSH, 2012), 129–44.

4. On information gathering as a social practice by individuals, see Bruno Karsenti and Louis Quéré, eds., *La croyance et l'enquête: aux sources du pragmatisme* (Paris: Éditions de l'EHESS, 2004).

5. In this regard, see the work of Alain Cottereau, inspired by Schütz's propositions ("What's the Right Price for Babysitting?").

6. For a consideration of the investigator's feelings as indicative of the experience of the people in question, see Green, *Fear as a Way of Life*; and Nicolas Duvoux, "La peur de l'ethnographe," *Geneses* 97, no. 4 (2014): 126–39. While I draw on the experience of the investigation to reproduce the conditions of description, the past experiences, horizons, and material conditions of my interlocutors differ greatly from mine. So I avoid attributing my fears and uncertainties to them. As Sverker Finnström (*Living with Bad Surroundings*) and Ivana Macek (*Sarajevo Under Siege*) point out, despite all the immersion efforts and the intensity of the investigative experience, I could buy a return ticket and leave Badiraguato, an option that my interlocutors did not have—and which was decisive for their experience of the context of violence.

7. I employ *don* and *doña* in the same way as I addressed some of my interlocutors during all or part of my investigation.

8. If, because of our relationship, Teófilo's information and interpretations took up a lot of space in my investigation in the main town, I often had to distance myself from them (again because of our relationship), and I was careful not to make his soundings the thread of my investigation. However, because of the extent of his networks, the way in which his words crosschecked with those of my other interlocutors often helped me to understand how information flowed.

9. As Alain Cottereau notes, these exchanges, which appear disjointed and incomprehensible to the outside observer, are characteristic of a form of intimacy tied to recurrent exchanges and shared concerns that unite the commenters ("What's the Right Price for Babysitting?").

10. Albert Piette, "Les détails de l'action. Écriture, images et pertinence ethnologique," *Enquête* 6 (1998): 109–28; Stanislas Deprez, "The Minor Mode: Albert Piette and the Reshaping of Anthropology," *Sociologus* 64, no. 1 (2014): 87–95.

11. This dimension of exchanges in the town is similar to the definition proposed by Tamotzu Shibutani for improvised news: "A recurring form of communication through which people sharing an ambiguous situation seek to construct a valuable interpretation by gathering their intellectual resources." See *Improvised News: A Sociological Study of Rumor* (Indianapolis: The Bobbs-Merrill Company, 1966), 17.

12. During a return visit to Badiraguato, a year after my investigation, I inquired of Teófilo who had killed a person during a series of past murders. He shot me a look but, since we were alone, he nevertheless agreed to tell me what was supposed to remain unsaid.

13. A metal plate over a wood fire.

14. I stayed in "the chambers" until January 2015, when I moved in with two sisters, Laura and Beatriz, whom I had met through Teófilo. Their mother, who was going through a separation from her husband, agreed to let me stay in a small stand-alone structure, which let me encounter another neighborhood network in the main town.

15. As much as I hope to avoid the pejorative connotation that attaches to "gossip," I take up Christiane Bougerol's distinction between rumor and gossip to keep

the first term for the circulation of a specific story. Even so, one of the determining features of information circulating in Badiraguato was the lack of "traceability." See Christiane Bougerol, "Commérages et adresses indirectes. L'exemple antillais," in *Pour une anthropologie de l'interlocution. Rhétorique du quotidien,* ed. Bertrand Masquelier and Jean-Louis Siran (Paris: L'Hamattan, 2000), 359–81; Christiane Bougerol, "Une rumeur à la Guadeloupe: De certaines pratiques supposées des Haïtiens," *Terrain* 54 (2010): 130–39.

16. On words as dangerous act per se, see Favret-Saada, *Deadly Words.* Framed in the war in Peru, the threats that gossip constituted were specifically raised, even leading to passage of a law against gossip (*ley contra chismes*). See Theidon, *Intimate Enemies,* 14–16; and Robin Azevedo, *Sur les sentiers de la violence,* 150.

17. Max Gluckman, "Gossip and Scandal," *Current Anthropology* 4, no. 3 (1963): 307–16.

18. The questions "What do you do for a living?" or "What kind of work do you do?" (*A qué se dedica?*) are paradigmatic direct questions that were totally off limits during my investigation.

19. Each of the destinations she ticked off featured in one or more stories as operational nodes in the trafficking network coming from Sinaloa. On Malaysia, see the investigative reporting of Víctor Hugo Michel on the threat of the death penalty hanging over the young men coming from a poor Culiacán neighborhood hired to do janitorial work in the chemical drug laboratories: *Morir en Malasia: Una crónica sobre los desechables del narco* (Mexico City: Océano, 2013).

20. My investigation took me to five different hamlets, three on the north road and two on the south road (see chapter 1). The stays in two of these hamlets were longer, and I was able to return several times. For reasons of anonymization, I simply present some members of the families of three of these hamlets, without specifying which one. This precaution holds true throughout the work and induces a limit on contextualization with the specificities of each hamlet. Therefore, although I myself registered the differences between each and the disparity between the areas, I am bound to talk about the sierra in general.

21. For an ethnography that shows the effects of a lack of meeting spaces in a village on the circulation of information see Léonore Le Caisne, *Un inceste ordinaire: Et pourtant tout le monde savait* (Paris: Belin, 2014).

22. Astorga, *El siglo de las drogas,* 141.

23. Francisco Ortiz Pinchetti, "La Operación Cóndor," *Proceso* (1981).

24. The most important subversive movement on the regional level was the "sick ones" (*enfermos*), based in the Autonomous University of Sinaloa.

25. Box 16, "Independiente Presidencia 1982," Badiraguato municipal archives.

26. The DEA's activities have a long history (notably peaking with the assassination in 1985 of one of its agents, Enrique Camarena, which was attributed to Rafael Caro Quintero and which led to stepped-up involvement by the US agency). As for the Mexican Navy, it went into action throughout the country as part of the "war against narcotrafficking" launched in 2006 by president Felipe Calderón.

27. The use of coded communication is not a hallmark of a centralized organization, but rather of managing the public nature of communication. In his book on Afghan migrants in the war, Alessandro Monsutti cites the example of coded communications concerning property, marital, and commercial issues difficult to keep from prying eyes that circulated between Afghanistan, Pakistan, and Iran. See *War and Migration: Social Networks and Economic Strategies of the Hazaras of Afghanistan* (New York: Routledge, 2005).

28. Elisabeth Claverie, "Techniques de la menace," *Terrain* 43 (2004): 15–30.

29. During another investigation in the state of Chihuahua, one of my interlocutors had very clearly formulated this identification. After a man involved in a conflict had gotten himself killed at a dance, this person exclaimed: "But why do they keep going to dances? You'd think they don't listen to the *narcocorridos*: they always catch them at the dances!"

30. Just one time (see chapter 6), this purported comparison was questioned: following the death of three of the town's young people in one night, Antonio asked me: "In your country do they kill like here?" But it must be said that Antonio showed an insatiable curiosity and systematically quizzed me about all manner of things (monetization, the need to convert national currencies, disappearance of mining, or military repression) if they took place "in [my] country."

31. Here we have a special form of "empty talk." See Claude Javeau, "Parler pour ne rien dire: 'Ça va ? Ça va!,'" *Ethnologie française* 26, no. 2 (1996): 255–63.

32. In the case of Guatemala and Peru, see respectively Green, *Fear as a Way of Life*, 68–69; Theidon, *Intimate Enemies*, 376. Ivana Macek, whose ethnography took place during the siege of Sarajevo, offers a variation on this argument. She stresses the contradictory nature of these discourses (employing the concept of "cognitive dissonance") and shows that they are linked to larger ensembles to rationalize their choices in confronting the imposition of ideologies by the nationalist parties; see *Sarajevo Under Siege*, 191.

33. Azevedo, *Sur les sentiers de la violence*.

34. Pablo Piccato, "Homicide as Politics in Modern Mexico: Homicide in Modern Mexico," *Bulletin of Latin American Research* 32, no. 1 (2013): 104–25; Piccato, *A History of Infamy*.

35. As noted by Pablo Piccato, this coverage fits into the continuity of the history of the press since the 1920s, an era when the crime columns "red note" (*nota roja*) appeared. See "Murders of Nota Roja: Truth and Justice in Mexican Crime News," *Past & Present* 223, no. 1 (2014): 195–231.

36. Akhil Gupta, "Blurred Boundaries: The Discourse of Corruption, the Culture of Politics, and the Imagined State," *American Ethnologist* 22, no. 2 (1995): 375–402.

37. Here we find the usual usage of humor in authoritarian settings to say the unsayable. See Macek, *Sarajevo Under Siege*, 51–61; Lisa Wedeen, "Ideology and Humor in Dark Times: Notes from Syria," *Critical Inquiry* 39, no. 4 (2013): 841–73.

38. Associated with poverty and misery, *guacho* has many different meanings depending on the Latin American country. In northern Mexico, it is a pejorative

term for soldiers, referencing the fact they are frequently recruited from the indigenous populations in the country's south.

CHAPTER 3

1. Juan Luis Sariego Rodriguez, *Enclaves y minerales en el norte de México: Social historia de los mineros de Cananea y Nueva Rosita, 1900–1970* (Mexico City: CIESAS, 1988).

2. Beginning in the 1960s, the decline in foreign investment in the mining sector prompted the government to push for the "Mexicanization" of the large mining companies. But, starting in the 1990s, as part of liberalization, Canadian companies in particular often operated alone or with a Mexican partner. See Juan Luis Sariego Rodriguez, "De minas, mineros, territorios y protestas social en México: Los nuevos retos de la globalizacion," *Cahiers des Amériques latines* 60–61 (2009): 173–92.

3. Sibely Cañedo, Marcos Vizcarra, and Sheila Arias, "Desplazados por el yugo narco-minero en Sinaloa," *Noroeste*, June 3, 2019. Natalia Mendoza Rockwell shows these intricacies in the neighboring state of Sonora in "La Privatizacion de la Ilegalidad," in *Si persisten las molestias,* ed. Fernando Escalante Gonzalbo (México: Cal y Arena, 2018), 28–51.

4. The presence of small companies grew out of the policy of boosting national mining activity launched by President Lázaro Cárdenas in 1934, including the establishment of cooperatives. Municipalities in the southern state of Sinaloa were much larger mining centers than Badiraguato, where the number of mines was still lower than the number listed. The activity of the *gambusinos,* on the other hand, was ignored by these censuses and, in the historical work on mining in the region, they appeared as the classic figures that always accompany monopolies in the making: thieves. See Rigoberto Arturo Romon Alarcon, "Auge y decadencia de la minería en Sinaloa 1910–1950," *Nueva Época* 4 (2004): 38; Francisco Javier Osuna Felix, "Crecimiento y crisis de la minería en Sinaloa (1907–1950)" (MA thesis, Universidad Autónoma de Sinaloa, Culiacán, 2014).

5. Juan Antonio Fernández Velázquez, "El narcotráfico en los Altos de Sinaloa (1940–1977)" (PhD diss., Universidad Veracruzana, 2016).

6. Osuna, *Crecimiento y crisis de la minería en Sinaloa*, 148.

7. Although technically called "don Melesio's crop," it is he in particular who distributed parcels for cultivation and bought back the gum.

8. Astorga, *El siglo de las drogas*. This rising production during the 1940s was the subject of a rumor about an official pact between the United States and Mexico for supplying the former with morphine, but Astorga notes that there is no archival evidence for the alleged agreement.

9. The revolution began in 1910, the constitution was adopted in 1917, and the end of the armed conflict between the various factions is generally dated to 1920. For a general history of the Mexican Revolution, see Alan Knight, *The Mexican Revolution* (Cambridge: Cambridge University Press, 1986).

10. Fernández Velázquez, "El narcotráfico en los Altos de Sinaloa (1940–1977)."

11. The *cacique* occupies a political intermediary's position with the state (on the administrative side) based on his economic resources and a strong social grounding, which lets him navigate between several regional social groups. See Guillermo de la Peña, "Poder local, poder regional: Perspectivas socioanthopológicas," in *Poder local, poder regional,* ed. Jorge Padua and Alain Vanneph (Mexico: Colegio de México, 1986), 27–56.

12. On the influence of Hector Cuén on the Autonomous University of Sinaloa, see Ana Luz Ruelas, *Crisis universitaria y ratio legis en Sinaloa* (Mexico City: Juan Pablos, 2010).

13. On the agrarian and political dynamics in the growth of Sinaloa's agroindustry, see Hubert Carton De Grammont, *Empresarios agrícolas y el estado: Sinaloa, 1893–1984* (Mexico City: Universidad Nacional Autónoma de México, 1990).

14. Jorge Durand, "El programa bracero (1942–1964): Un balance crítico," *Migración y Desarrollo* 9 (2007): 27–43. The demise of the program did not put an end to immigration; it just made it illegal. As Juan Vicente Palerm shows in the case of California, while the mechanization of agriculture might have ended the need for some kinds of labor, the shift to more profitable crops (berries, grapes) from the mid-1970s on actually increased the use of manual labor. As a result, the number of Mexican agricultural day laborers swelled despite a growing anti-immigration stance by US institutions. See "The Expansion of California Agriculture and the Rise of Peasant-Workers Communities," in *Immigration: A Civil Rights Issue for the Americas,* ed. Susanne Jonas and Suzanne Dod Thomas (Wilmington: Scholarly Resources Inc., 1998), 45–68. See also Yerko Castro Neira, *En la orilla de la justicia. Migración y justicia en los màrgenes del Estado* (Mexico: Universidad Autónoma Metropolitana, 2009).

15. Jorge Durand and Douglas Massey, *Clandestinos: Migración México-Estados Unidos en los albores del siglo XXI* (Zacatecas: Universidad Autónoma de Zacatecas, 2003); Guillermo Ibarra Escobar, *Migrantes en mercados de trabajo globales: Mexicanos y sinaloenses en Los Ángeles* (Culiacán: Universidad Autónoma de Sinaloa, 2005).

16. In the towns of Sinaloa, as in other parts of the country, the means deployed for Operation Condor and the media veneer offered by the criminalization of drugs were harnessed to the political repression of the social movements of the 1970s. For an analysis of this instrumentalization in the state of Guerrero, see Aviña, *Specters of Revolution.*

17. The defoliant used the most was paraquat (Gramoxone). Despite the initial official declarations that the agents used were not ecocides, it quickly became obvious that these pesticides had devastating effects. The United States used paraquat in the Vietnam war and the stockpiles were distributed to the Mexican and Venezuelan governments for the war against marijuana and opium cultivation. See Ortiz Pinchetti, "La Operación Cóndor"; Astorga, *El siglo de las drogas,* 150.

18. Anna L. Tsing, *The Mushroom at the End of the World: On the Possibility of Life in Capitalist Ruins* (Princeton: Princeton University Press, 2015).

19. Natalia Mendoza Rockwell, *Conversaciones de desierto* (Mexico: CIDE, 2007); Jorge Alan Sánchez Godoy, "Procesos de institucionalización de la narcocultura en Sinaloa," *Frontera Norte* 21, no. 41 (2009): 77–103; Fernández Velázquez, "El narcotráfico en los Altos de Sinaloa (1940–1977)."

20. Sabine Guez takes up the free-spending 1980s and the money that even trickled into activities only indirectly linked to trafficking. However, the financial benefits she describes appeared to be limited to urban centers, places of consumption and spending for people enriched by the transportation and sale of drugs. In the production regions, opportunities remained limited to activities directly exposed to repression and violence and did not translate into an influx of money into the sierra. See "Les années 1980 ou le temps de l'innocence: Un tournant sociétal dans l'histoire du trafic de drogue au Mexique," *Outros Tempos* 14, no. 24 (2017): 161–183.

21. Here we have a dynamic similar to that described in Michoacán by Salvador Maldonado Aranda: money from drugs making up for the collapse of rural economies linked to the development of agroindustrial enterprises. See "Drogas, violencia y militarización en el México rural: el caso de Michoacán," *Revista mexicana de sociología* 74, no. 1 (2012): 15–16.

22. Anna Tsing, *Friction: An Ethnography of Global Connection* (Princeton: Princeton University Press, 2005).

23. During my fieldwork, marijuana, which had been an important crop in the area, turned marginal because of the drop in prices caused by legalization in parts of the United States.

24. Ronaldo González Valdés, et al., *La cultura en Sinaloa: narrativas de lo social y la violencia* (Culiacán: Honorable Ayuntamiento de Culiacán/Instituto Municipal de Cultura Culiacán, 2013); Córdova, *La Narcocultura.*

25. Astorga, *El siglo de las drogas.*

26. Unlike marijuana seeds that are the subject of research into higher quality seeds, usually sold by the buyer of the crop, poppy seeds are collected from the same flowers after the gum is collected.

27. Since harvesting required more hands, on large plots under special agreements, people were brought up from the plain to incise and harvest.

28. In addition to the proximity of his hamlet to the hamlet of a powerful man, I had observed in this area one of these very large fields, whose stability contrasted with the situation of small growers. Facilities had been built for the armed men who watched it day and night during harvest periods and, for several years, a large quantity of gum (40 kilograms) was harvested in this field.

29. Anton Blok, *The Mafia of a Sicilian Village, 1860–1960: A Study of Violent Peasant Entrepreneurs* (New York: Harper and Row, 1975).

30. In this respect, the poppy growers were no different from other farmers who no longer could make a living from agricultural work. In practice, their subsistence depended routinely on other forms of income: work, remittances from relatives abroad, subsidies or social welfare. See Michael Kearney, *Reconceptualizing the Peasantry: Anthropology in Global Perspective* (New York: Avalon Publishing, 1996).

31. This system is reminiscent of the classic techniques of indebtedness and sale of products at prohibitive prices on the plantations. Called *tiendas de raya* (literally "stores of the dash") after the marks used to record the debts, they were generally associated with the social organization of the Porfirio Díaz era and demands by the 1910 revolutionaries. For other cases of using indebtedness to keep laborers in peonage, see Christian Geffray, "La dette imaginaire des collecteurs de caoutchouc," *Cahiers des Sciences Humaines* 28, no. 4 (1992): 705–25; Tania Li, *Land's End: Capitalist Relations on an Indigenous Frontier* (Durham: Duke University Press, 2014).

32. Contrary to the forecast by this young grower, fentanyl arriving on the illegal market has caused a drastic drop in the price of poppy gum since 2017, with some newspaper articles reporting price declines of 90 percent. See Kirk Semple, "Mexican Opium Prices Plummet, Driving Poppy Farmers to Migrate," *The New York Times*, July 7, 2019.

33. María Celia Toro, *Mexico's "War" on Drugs: Causes and Consequences* (Boulder: Lynne Rienner, 1995).

34. Birgit Müller, "La loi du marché comme idéologie: Les agriculteurs du Saskatchewan face au système économique néo-libéral," *Cahiers du GEMDEV* 31 (2007): 52–65.

35. François-Xavier Dudouet shows in this regard that the drug is not subject to a general prohibition, but to the construction of a legal market for drugs supplying hospitals, doctors, and pharmacies. Thus, the prohibition of part of the production of opium (and coca) is part of a much larger flow whose main profits are not captured by the major figures in the sale of heroin and cocaine, but by the few pharmaceutical companies that share the market. As Dudouet explains, prohibition, and the resulting illegality, protects the margins of this oligopoly. See *Le Grand deal de l'opium: Histoire du marché légal des drogues* (Paris: Syllepse, 2009).

36. Operations for dismantling laboratories, heavily covered by the media, occurred frequently during my fieldwork and accelerated after El Chapo's arrest in 2016.

37. Christian Geffray, *Chroniques de la servitude en Amazonie brésilienne: Essai sur l'exploitation paternaliste* (Paris: Karthala, 1995).

38. Marshall Sahlins, *Stone Age Economics* (Chicago: Aldine-Athertone, 1972).

39. Claudio Lomnitz, "Sobre reciprocidad negativa," *Revista de Antropología Social* 14 (2005): 311–34.

40. Laurent Bazin thus analyzes the use of the vocabulary of kinship in hierarchical relationships in business as they relate to dependence and subjection. See "La parenté: miroir and enlisement des hiérarchies en Côte-d'Ivoire," *Journal des anthropologues* 77–78 (1999): 193–215.

CHAPTER 4

1. This phrase constitutes one of the fundamental principles of the *ejido* regime, which goes back to how important this demand was during the 1910 Revolution. The goal was to give everyone access to land so they could see to their needs. This land was meant to be inalienable, and its fruits were to go to those who worked it.

2. Sara Berry, *No Condition Is Permanent: The Social Dynamics of Agrarian Change in Sub-Saharan Africa* (Madison: University of Wisconsin Press, 1993;) Monique Nuijten, *Power, Community and the State: The Political Anthropology of Organisation in Mexico* (New York: Pluto Press, 2003); Jesse Ribot and Nancy Peluso, "A Theory of Access," *Rural Sociology* 68, no. 2 (2009): 153–81; Thomas Sikor and Christian Lund, "Access and Property: A Question of Power and Authority," *Development and Change* 40, no. 1 (2009): 1–22.

3. On ejidal status in Mexico as a form of citizenship to which people aspire because of the rights that come with it, see Helga Baitenmann, "Reforma agraria y ciudadanía en el México del siglo XX," in *Paisajes mexicanos de la reforma agraria: Homenaje a William Roseberry*, ed. William Goméz (Zamora: El Colegio de Michoacán, 2007), 71–97; Éric Léonard and Emilia Velázquez, "Citoyenneté locale et réappropriation du changement légal au Mexique: Une analyse des conflits autour des transferts fonciers à Soteapan, Veracruz," in *Politique de la terre et de l'appartenance: Droits fonciers et citoyenneté locale dans les sociétés du sud*, ed. Jean-Pierre Jacob et Pierre-Yves Le Meur (Paris: Karthala, 2010), 61–94.

4. Elected president in 1934, Lázaro Cárdenas systematized the land reform that until then had been applied sporadically in response to recurrent peasant mobilizations. His land redistribution policy relied on massive expropriations that led to a reorganization of land structures in many of the country's regions.

5. The eight owners probably enjoyed other support, but only the mayor wrote to the commission and, while he did not claim to support the "owners," he denounced the behavior of the "*ejidatarios*," saying that they "misrepresented the agrarian cause," and that it was their fault that the other inhabitants regarded this cause "with horror, envy and contempt." Moreover, the eight owners affected by the possible endowment did not claim property rights but questioned the petitioners' status as "landless peasants." See letter from the Mayor of Badiraguato dated February 20, 1940, in the file "ejido de Badiraguato," National Agrarian Register.

6. The administrative process of setting up the *ejidos* involved a series of steps. Once the petitioners' request reached the governor, it was published in the official gazette. The Joint Agrarian Commission then went to work on the technical details, including topographical measurements and surveys of people meeting the criteria for benefiting from the endowment, owners whose land was subject to being seized, possible common boundaries with other *ejidos*, and available agrarian and livestock resources. If, on the basis of these measures, the Commission issued a favorable opinion, the governor was bound to establish a provisional endowment. This in turn allowed the Ministry of Land Reform to make its seizures; it could also issue further notices and possibly modify the endowment. The final step was the signature by the President of the Republic of the act of endowment. Here, between 1938 and 1941, despite the Joint Agrarian Commission's recommendation, the governor's provisional endowment never arrived, until in 1962 it was finally accorded on the basis of the previously completed technical work.

7. For the *ejidos* involving issues linked to poppy production, I anonymized those I mention by giving each a number from 1 to 4. Other *ejidos* were the subject

of later presidential resolutions (the last in 1984). Furthermore, the ensuing stages could take a long time, and some *ejidos* that I discuss here were not finally "executed" until the late 1970s.

8. Frans Schryer, "Peasants and the Law: A History of Land Tenure and Conflict in the Huasteca," *Journal of Latin American Studies* 18, no. 2 (1986): 283–311; Maldonado Aranda, *Los márgenes del Estado mexicano.*

9. The initial petitions often dated from the 1930–40s, but they were not necessarily the sign of a local mobilization: during distribution campaigns, people systematically submitted petitions for endowment of as many places as possible. See Éric Léonard, "Réforme agraire et reconfiguration du régime de gouvernementalité dans Les Tuxtlas, Mexique, 1920–1945," *Critique internationale* 75, no. 2 (2017): 53–69.

10. *Querencia,* literally the act of loving or desiring (from the verb *querer*), designates both a profound attachment to a place and the pasture where an animal grazes regularly. In some areas higher up *querencias* still exist and many open lands remain.

11. In some areas, *querencias* (and "free" lands) still existed during my fieldwork. I distinguish between the two kinds of *cerco* for the sake of analytical clarity, but it goes without saying that the two coexist and that the two uses are intertwined, especially as often one justifies the other.

12. Jean-Philippe Colin, Pierre-Yves Le Meur, and Éric Léonard, "Identifier les droits et dicter le droit: la politique des programmes de formalisation des droits fonciers," in *Les politiques d'enregistrement des droits fonciers: du cadre légal aux pratiques locales,* ed. Jean-Pierre Colin, Pierre-Yves Le Meur and Éric Léonard (Paris: Karthala, 2009), 10–16.

13. Pierre Bourdieu, "Droit et passe-droit," *Actes de la Recherche en Sciences Sociales* 81, no. 1 (1990): 86–96.

14. Badiraguato's breeders' association historically performed the role of middleman in cattle sales. While it did little more than register the cattle and issue permits for their transport, it was also a political sphere by virtue of its affiliation with the breeder's association for the whole state of Sinaloa, a powerful regional interest group.

15. For the concept of "legibility" as a process of standardization as well as organization and mapping for the purpose of applying the state's categories to its rural peripheries, see James C. Scott, *Seeing like a State: How Certain Schemes to Improve the Human Condition Have Failed* (New Haven: Yale University Press, 1999).

16. On the legal framework of the reform and its application on a national scale, see Emmanuelle Bouquet and Jean-Philippe Colin, "L'Etat, l'ejido et les droits fonciers: Ruptures et continuités du cadre institutionnel formel au Mexique," in Colin, Le Meur, and Léonard, *Les politiques d'enregistrement des droits fonciers,* 299–332.

17. Hector Robles Berlanga shows that moving to private land ownership was a limited phenomenon; see "Tendencias del campo mexicano a la luz del Programa de

Certificación de los Derechos Ejidales (Procede)," in *Políticas y regulaciones agrarias: dinámicas de poder y juegos de actores en torno a la tenencia de la tierra,* ed. Eric Léonard, André Quesnel, and Emilia Velázquez (Mexico: CIESAS/IRD, 2003), 131–56.

18. Odile Hoffmann, "L'ejido: laboratoire des pratiques sociales et fondement de la ruralité contemporaine au Mexique," in *La ruralité dans les pays du Sud à la fin du vingtième siècle,* ed. Jean-Marc Gastellu (Paris: Orstom, 1997), 401–16.

19. I did not have access to the Procede archives, but several of my interlocutors became *ejidatarios* during the reform.

20. On translation as a practice that produces public policies, see Alejandro Agudo Sanchíz, *Una etnografía de la administracion de la pobreza: La produccion social de los programas de desarrollo* (Mexico: Universidad Iberoamericana, 2015).

21. Éric Leonard, "Titularización agraria y apropiación de nuevos espacios económicos por los actores rurales: El Procede en los Tuxtlas, estado de Veracruz," in Leonard, Queznel, and Velázquez, *Políticas y regulaciones agrarias,* 297–328.

22. For other dynamics that preside over the choice of a common regime during the Procede reform in Mayan communities, see Gabriela Torres Mazuera, "Formas cotidianas de participación política rural: el Procede en Yucatán," *Estudios sociológicos* 32, no. 95 (2014): 295–322.

23. Boaventura De Sousa Santos, *Toward a New Legal Common Sense: Law, Globalization, and Emancipation* (Cambridge: Cambridge University Press, 2002), 91.

24. On the concept of "forum shopping," see Keebet von Benda-Beckmann, "Forum Shopping and Shopping Forums: Dispute Processing in a Minangkabau Village in West Sumatra," *The Journal of Legal Pluralism and Unofficial Law* 13, no. 19 (1981): 117–59.

CHAPTER 5

1. On the notion of a continuum between the modes of domination and physical violence perpetrated by men on women, see, see Liz Kelly, "The Continuum of Sexual Violence," in *Women, Violence and Social Control,* ed. Jalna Hanmer and Mary Maynard (London: Palgrave Macmillan, 1987), 46–60.

2. Elizabeth Schneider, "The Violence of Privacy," *Connecticut Law Review* 23 (1991): 973–99; Christine Delphy, "L'état d'exception: La dérogation au droit commun comme fondement de la sphère privée," *Nouvelles Questions Féministes* 16, no. 4 (1995): 73–114.

3. Following Joan Scott and Christine Delphy, by gender relations I mean a system of unequal division from which male and female terms flow. See Joan Scott, "Gender: A Useful Category of Historical Analysis," *American Historical Review* 91, no. 5 (1986), 1053–75; Christine Delphy, *L'ennemi principal: Penser le genre* (Paris: Syllepse, 2001).

4. During the 1970s Claude Meillassoux underlined this linkage between the production system and household economies; see *Femmes, greniers et capitaux* (Paris: Maspéro, 1975).

5. Nicole-Claude Mathieu, "When Yielding Is Not Consenting: Material and Psychic Determinants of Women's Dominated Consciousness and Some of Their Interpretations in Ethnology," *Feminist Issues* 9 (1989): 3–49.

6. On forgetting as constitutive of relationships initiated by coercion and predation, see C. Lomnitz, "Sobre reciprocidad negativa," 323.

7. The same blaming of victims is found in the case of the Ciudad Juarez femicides, with the same term "spending time with" (*tratarse*), but, probably because of the urban context, more of an insistence on being out at night and going to entertainment venues. See Chiara Calzolaio, "Les féminicides de Ciudad Juárez: Reconnaissance institutionnelle, enjeux politiques and moraux de la prise en charge des victims," *Problèmes d'Amérique latine* 84, no. 2 (2012): 61–76. This logic of social control by putting the onus on victims can be found in other contexts of armed violence, for example in Colombia; see Natalia Suarez Bonilla, "Viol, Blâme de la victime et contrôle social: Le cas des enclaves paramilitaires en Colombie," in *Viols en temps de guerre*, ed. Raphaëlle Branche and Fabrice Virgili (Paris: Payot, 2011): 83–93.

8. *Quinceañera* is a celebration of a girl's fifteenth birthday. Depending on the family's means, it includes a party, a religious ceremony, a dance, many photos, and, for the richest, going on a trip.

9. Maintaining this fiction did not come without challenges. For example, the mayor's wife gave me away to her husband and other men. Having met her before I had grasped that I ought to be saying I was married, I had told her I was not married. When, several months later, her husband importuned me for the umpteenth time that he was going to marry me, I told him that it was up to me alone and that I was already married, on which she contradicted me publicly.

10. On the difficulty of grasping certain dimensions of gender relations by the discourses and on the advantages of experimenting with them in a situated manner, see Haraway, "Situated Knowledge." That said, I want to stress the distance that remained between my interlocutors and me. See Mathieu, "When Yielding Is Not Consenting"; and Odile Journet-Diallo, "Catégories de genre et relation ethnographique," in *Femmes plurielles: Les représentations des femmes: discours, normes et conduites*, ed. Danielle Jonckers and Marie-Claude Dupré (Paris: Éditions de la MSH, 1999), 21–22.

11. Literally, a "quick lunch." A *comida corrida* is a small, cheap restaurant, sometimes set up in the cook's kitchen, where set menus are served at midday.

12. "The plane of death," celebrated in particular in a song by the band Los Tigres del Norte, refers to the story of Manuel Atilano, a pilot who was a victim of repression during Operation Condor in the late 1970s. Captured by the military and taken to the Badiraguato military base, he was tortured until he agreed to take the soldiers to the clandestine airstrips from which marijuana and poppy gum were airlifted. Once on the plane, Atilano managed to take the controls and dove the plane into a Badiraguato hill. His words were recorded by the plane's radio and an article of the time recounted the episode: "A piloto estrella su avion para matar a sus torturadores [A pilot crashed his plane to kill his torturers]," *Proceso*, April 14, 1979.

13. I thought for a time that Teófilo persisted in refusing to understand my work, but it finally dawned on me that he presented me in the town in the terms that worked best to keep me out of trouble.

14. Some ethnographers have reported various stratagems for playing on gender relations in pursuing their investigations. See Marie Goyon, "La relation ethnographique: une affaire de genres," *Socio-anthropologie* 16 (2005); and Ghislaine Gallenga, "Ethnologue à marier: La neutralisation des attributs sexués en entreprise," *Ethnologies* 29, no. 1-2 (2007): 303–14.

15. The different forms of women's participation in stealing practices and the moral condemnation of the person abducted refer to a problem well-identified by researchers studying violence carried out by women and children. It emphasizes in particular the need to think concertedly about their conditions as victims and perpetrators of violence, and thus to recognize both the constraints that weigh on them and their autonomy of action under these constraints. See Erin Baines, "Complex Political Perpetrators: Reflections on Dominic Ongwen," *The Journal of Modern African Studies* 47, no. 2 (2009): 163–91; and Coline Cardi and Geneviève Pruvost, eds., *Penser la violence des femmes* (Paris: La Découverte, 2012).

16. Christine Delphy, *L'ennemi principal: L'économie politique du Patriarcat* (Paris: Syllepse, 2001).

17. The program was restricted to mothers to avoid delivering the aid to men likely to spend it in their leisure time, including alcohol and gambling. See Alejandro Agudo Sanchíz's ethnography around this program and, more broadly, around public policies to combat poverty (*Una etnografía de la administración de la pobreza*).

18. The express divorce is a process that lets a spouse demand·divorce unilaterally, without requiring the consent of the other spouse.

19. Dessert prepared with buns drizzled with water flavored with cloves, cinnamon, and cane sugar, with bananas, grapes, apples, and nuts. It is traditionally eaten at Easter.

20. A cold soup of pasta, ham, pineapple, cream, and mayonnaise.

21. I was given the same line about the "new anti-corruption laws" ("See, for example, if I have a problem that I have to deal with here in my office and I call my wife from that phone to pick up the children from school . . . Bang! It's corruption!") Similarly, the "transparency law" was routinely cited in response to any of my requests: asserting my "inalienable right" to consult "all documents" was generally a way to avoid giving me access to them right then and there. The absurdity of the argument appears here as a tool that reinforces the arbitrary way in which certain policies are applied, as emphasized by Akhil Gupta, *Red Tape: Bureaucracy, Structural Violence, and Poverty in India* (Durham: Duke University Press, 2012).

22. I relate this story in chapter 1.

CHAPTER 6

1. For an interactional definition of violence, see Randall Collins, *Violence: A Micro-sociological Theory* (Princeton: Princeton University Press, 2008). On the

necessity of linking this definition so that it registers in its context, see Michel Naepels, "The Complexity of a Murder: Situational Dynamics, Social Relations, and Historical Context," *International Journal of Conflict and Violence* 11, no. 1 (2017).

2. In this respect, it should be noted that my interlocutors rarely made sense of violent acts in spiritual terms or intangible phenomena. It may be that this specificity had to do with the relative proximity and interknowledge between my interlocutors and the perpetrators of the violence. For a reverse case, see Finnström, *Living with Bad Surroundings*.

3. Contrary to the usual praise lavished on presence in anthropology, Anna Tsing emphasizes the paradoxically beneficial absence of the ethnographer for capturing narrative settings because it alleviates the impulse of confronting ethnographic subjects with her own version of the facts (*Friction*, 248–49).

4. In this respect, the difficulties linked to the impossibility of mourning the dead and going to the funeral brings to mind the loss expressed by the relatives of the disappeared, as well-evoked in several ethnographies. See Federico Mastrogiovanni, *Ni vivos ni muertos: La desaparición forzada en México como estrategia de terror* (Mexico: Penguin, 2014); Carolina Robledo Silvestre, *Drama social y política de duelo: Las desapariciones de la guerra contra las drogas en Tijuana* (Mexico: El Colegio de México, 2017); and Sergio Salazar Araya, *Violencia y valor en el tránsito migratorio centro-americano: La masacre de Cadereyta (2012) y la lucha por el retorno de los cuerpos,* forthcoming.

5. Lara Salazar, *Sangre Caliente*.

6. Paris Martinez, "98% de los homicidios cometidos en 2012 están impunes," *Animal Político,* July 17, 2013.

7. Concerning the media treatment of organized crime, see Pablo Piccato, *The Tyranny of Opinion: Honor in the Construction of the Mexican Public Sphere* (Durham: Duke University Press, 2010); Pablo Piccato, "Murders of Nota Roja: Truth and Justice in Mexican Crime News," *Past & Present* 223, no. 1 (2014): 195–231; and Patricia Figueroa Sauceda, *Ética en tiempos de guerra y narcotráfico* (Culiacán: Moby Dick, 2017).

8. Badiraguato and, more broadly, Mexico illustrate the logic of social invisibilization of the lives and the deaths that accompany blaming the victims of violence. See Butler, *Precarious Life*.

9. John Gibler, *To Die in Mexico: Dispatches from Inside the Drug War* (San Francisco: City Lights, 2011).

10. Gibler, *To Die in Mexico*.

11. Transferring the responsibility for deaths in Mexico's public arena has a long history. See Piccato, "Homicide as Politics in Modern Mexico." In Badiraguato, the deaths of twelve people in 1971 during a raid by the army on a baptism ceremony gave rise to condemnations on the regional level, with the inhabitants of Badiraguato all being tarred as criminals; see Astorga, *El siglo de las drogas,* 141.

12. These evaluations fit the Sinaloa context. It seems that in certain of the country's other regions, these dynamics are at least somewhat distinct (for example, in Ciudad Juarez). Moreover, the murder of the journalist Javier Valdez in 2017 may

have transformed these evaluations: despite his fame, his family received no word of any inquiry, but the killing was said to be linked to an interview during the succession conflict after El Chapo's extradition.

13. Figueroa Sauceda, *Ética en tiempos de guerra y narcotráfico.*

14. The interpretation of the shooting is one of the forms of intelligence gathering and is the subject of many discussions. Thus, the sound of a truck unloading rubble can initially be interpreted as machine-gun fire and talked about as such between people in the vicinity. In the scene recounted by Teófilo, the reason the audience did not react much was probably due to the hypothesis that this was celebratory gunfire related to the party.

15. Ismael told me about the same murder a few months later, following his sister's abduction (chapter 5). That Armando might return to the chambers worried us, which we tried to alleviate with jokes. One had Armando breaking down a door, but—as they were all identical—only to find the fat Teófilo in place of the beautiful Adriana. The imagined scene reminded Ismael of the murder that had taken place right there and that he told me about in much the same terms: "I said to him, ayyy, don Teódoro [his nickname for Teófilo], let me stay with you!!"

16. This was the case with Creel, for example. See Adèle Blazquez, "Lecture d'un ordinaire en situation de violence dans le Nord du Mexique: Déguisements du quotidien et contournement de la tension" (MA thesis, EHESS, 2013).

17. Martín Gastelum, "El Gallito paseaba a sus hijos cuando fue asesinado," *El Debate,* March 24, 2015.

CHAPTER 7

1. The free municipality was a demand of the Mexican revolutionaries of 1910 and makes up one of the key principles structuring the postrevolutionary Mexican state (Knight, *The Mexican Revolution,* 32).

2. During 2000–14, money transfers to states and counties rose to 335 billion USD, triple the amount of the Marshall Plan. See Héctor Aguilar Camín, "La parranda local," *Milenio,* February 19, 2015.

3. My argument here joins that of Akhil Gupta when he shows the structuring and partly arbitrary effects of war-on-poverty policies in India and underlines the defining character of the incoherence of different levels of government (*Red Tape*).

4. The practices I describe recall those studied by Ferguson, Li, and Müller, with one other notable difference: the development mechanisms here function without the intervention of international organizations. See James Ferguson, *The Anti-Politics Machine: "Development," Depoliticization, and Bureaucratic Power in Lesotho* (Minneapolis: University of Minnesota Press, 1994); Tania Li, *The Will to Improve: Governmentality, Development, and the Practice of Politics* (Durham: Duke University Press, 2007); and Birgit Müller, "Lifting the Veil of Harmony: Anthropologists Approach International Organisations," in *The Gloss of Harmony: The*

Politics of Policy-Making in Multilateral Organisations, ed. Birgit Müller (London: Pluto Press, 2013), 1–20.

5. In the 2021 elections, Morena ended that hegemony by winning the mayoralty of Badiraguato. Consequently, the political scenario described here has just been reconfigured.

6. Larissa Adler Lomnitz, Claudio Lomnitz-Adler, and Ilya Adler analyze this process for the 1988 presidential campaign, when the PRI's nomination was still tantamount to an appointment. Following the nomination of the candidate, while there was no uncertainty about the election, the campaign was the time for building presidential stature by having the candidate embody, via his biography, ties with all regions of the country and social sectors. See *El fondo de la forma: actos publicos de la campaña presidencial del Partido Revolucionario Institucional* (Mexico City: 1988; Notre Dame, IN: The Kellogg Institute, 1990.

7. In the months that followed, Gabriela and her husband were no longer able to cover living expenses for their son, who was staying free of charge with a relative while studying in Culiacán. He was forced to return to Badiraguato and, while his parents pressed him more by the day to find a job, he failed to find one. He kept reminding them that "without influence (*palanca*), you find nothing." Gabriela's husband looked for odd jobs and for a time struck a deal with Joaquín to repair his *cercos* for a fee. But, after he had already started, Gabriela told him to quit, because apparently Joaquín actually wanted to pay her husband in kind with goods from his grocery store. Gabriela compared prices and, as groceries were always much more expensive than the supermarket next door, she reckoned that this deal was tilted in Joaquín's favor. The situation worsened when their adult daughter returned with her own daughter: her husband was locked up in Islas Marias prison where they, the mother and daughter, had also been living. Having had enough of the difficult prison conditions, she decided to leave, but had no other place to stay and no livelihood.

8. "Opacidad y falta de regulación. Sueldos de los 18 alcaldes de Sinaloa," Culiacán, Iniciativa Sinaloa, 2013.

9. "Alcaldes de Sinaloa justifican elevados sueldos," *El Debate,* February 4, 2016.

10. *Zócalo* being the Mexican name for the main plazas of the big cities, the mayor's use of the term was grandiloquent.

11. Mexico's independence day, September 16, is celebrated by recreating the parish priest Hidalgo's yell (*grito*) from on high in a church that is thought to have been the starting gun for the armed uprising for independence.

12. "Se inaugura el zócalo municipal y la reubicación de la fuente," *El Debate,* March 3, 2014.

13. "Inician remodelación de plazuela municipal de Badiraguato," *Linea Directa,* June 27, 2019.

14. Marco Antonio Lizárraga, *Ayuntamiento de Badiraguato acondiciona el Parque Alameda para Semana Santa,* March 2015, http://www.entreveredas.com .mx/2015/03/ayuntamiento-de-badiraguato-acondiciona.html.

15. In Jalisco, Shinji Hirai thus speaks of a "political economy of nostalgia" in the migration framework. He notably highlights the use of nostalgic sentiments in

municipal politics and urban renewal projects that seek to turn migrants into a source of revenue. As such, the local authorities, like Badiraguato's, try to attract migrants living in the United States to come back as tourists to their native municipality. See *Economía política de la nostalgia: un estudio sobre la transformación del paisaje urbano en la migración transnacional entre México y Estados Unidos* (Mexico City: Universidad Autónoma Metropolitana, 2009).

16. "Se inaugura el zócalo municipal y la reubicación de la fuente," *El Debate,* March 3, 2014.

17. "'Saldo Blanco' en el festejo del 411 aniversario de Badiraguato," October 22, 2016, http://www.adiscusion.com/Noticia.aspx?q=%22Saldo-blanco%22-en-feste-jos-del-411-aniversario-de-Badiraguato-, accessed August 10, 2019.

18. Monique Nuijten underlines the depoliticizing character of the citizen participation discourse and local organization in Mexico. She thus sizes up the Mexican state as a "hope generating machine," while in practice its government, enrolled in patronage networks, replicates above all the inequalities and forms of subordination (*Power, Community and the State,* 152–93).

19. Carlos Rosas, "'¡Chingada madre! No me van a decir que fue un pleito de chicles': El asesinato de 'El Gallito': Alcalde de Badiraguato," March 24, 2015, https://cafenegroportal.com/2015/03/24/chingada-madre-no-me-van-a-decir-que-fue-un-pleito-de-chicles-el-asesinato-de-el-gallito-alcalde-de-badiraguato, accessed on July 14, 2017.

20. We find in Badiraguato the same elements regularly described in the contexts of armed conflicts: the staging of a program to legitimize the state and local institutions, instrumentalizing the program for recovering some material advantages by exchanging obsolete weaponry, and in general conserving arms. Among an abundant literature, see the stories by Danny Hoffman on the demobilization programs in Liberia in *The War Machines: Young Men and Violence in Sierra Leone and Liberia* (Durham: Duke University Press, 2011).

21. Müller, "Lifting the Veil of Harmony"; Alessandro Monsutti, "Fuzzy Sovereignty: Rural Reconstruction in Afghanistan, between Democracy Promotion and Power Games," *Comparative Studies in Society and History* 54, no. 3 (2012): 563–91; and Agudo Sanchíz, *Una etnografía de la administración de la pobreza.*

22. This practice refers to what they call in Mexico *el acarreo* (literally transport, the convoy), the act of bringing the public to political events. See Adler Lomnitz, Lomnitz-Adler, and Adler, *El fondo de la forma*; and Claudio Lomnitz, *Las salidas del laberinto: Cultura e ideología en el espacio nacional mexicano* (Mexico City: Joaquín Moritz, 1995), 393.

23. She was elected to the state parliament in 2016, in part thanks to the policy of parity that inspired her husband to one of his most memorable public interventions. In a speech on the fact that democracy was not a question of gender but of "electoral profitability," he challenged the PRI leadership by stating in the press that, to prove the absurdity of this policy, he should have "had surgery and changed sex to make him eligible to campaign" for the position to which his wife was appointed. The technique of provocation by way of the press appeared to be one of his impor-

tant modes of distinction within political circles. His appointment as leader of the Revolutionary Juvenile Front stemmed from his orotund statements. In 2011, according to Praxedis Alarcón in the local press, the fact that he was the only one to react forcefully to the announcement of the nomination of Ángel Robles Bañuelos for the municipal election earned him the "consolation prize": the appointment as candidate for the state parliament that let him step up to the post of mayor in the next term.

24. This time, I talk about vulnerability not as a condition but as the construction of an administrative category. For an analysis of how the category of vulnerables is produced, see Michel Agier, "Le camp des vulnérables," *Les Temps Modernes* 627, no. 2 (2004): 120–37.

25. Pierre Bourdieu emphasized how the mastery of the calendar and time constitutes a definitive element in the autonomization of state institutions; see *On the State: Lectures at the Collège de France, 1989–1992* (Cambridge: Polity, 2014).

26. "¿Badiraguato, alegre por fuga de 'El Chapo'?," *El Debate,* July 19, 2015; "Badiraguato 'llora' por la captura del 'Chapo' Guzmán," *Expansión*, January 11, 2016; Daniel Flores, "Entre llanto y tristeza, Badiraguato sufre por El Chapo, pero rezan por su tercer escape," *Publimetro México,* March 3, 2019.

27. Also going by "El Lic." *Licenciado* is the form of address for someone with a diploma or license.

28. Irene González, "Presidenta del PRI molesta por declaraciones del alcalde de Badiraguato al diario El País," February 23, 2015, https://cafenegroportal.com/2015/02/23/presidenta-del-pri-molesta-por-declaraciones-del-alcalde-de-badiraguato-al-diario-el-pais, accessed August 10, 2019.

CONCLUSION

1. For the article and a transcript of the interview, see "El Chapo Speaks," *Rolling Stone,* January 10, 2016.

2. Luc Boltanski and Laurent Thevenot, *De la justification. Les économies de la grandeur* (Paris: Gallimard, 1991).

BIBLIOGRAPHY

Adler Lomnitz, Larissa, Claudio Lomnitz-Adler, and Ilya Adler. *El fondo de la forma: Actos públicos de la campaña presidencial del Partido Revolucionario Institucional.* Mexico City: 1988; Notre Dame, IN: The Kellogg Institute, 1990.

Agier, Michel. "Le camp des vulnérables." *Les Temps Modernes* 627, no. 2 (2004): 120–37.

Agudo Sanchíz, Alejandro. *Una etnografía de la administración de la pobreza: La producción social de los programas de desarrollo.* Mexico City: Universidad Iberoamericana, 2015.

Alarcón Valdez, Praxedis. *Radiografía política: Una visión retrospectiva.* Culiacán: Universidad Autónoma de Sinaloa, 2011.

Astorga, Luis. *Mitología del "narcotraficante" en México.* Mexico City: Plaza y Valdes, 1995.

———. *El siglo de las drogas: Del Porfiriato al nuevo milenio.* 2nd ed. Mexico: Penguin, 2016.

Aviña, Alexander. *Specters of Revolution: Peasant Guerrillas in the Cold War Mexican Countryside.* Oxford: Oxford University Press, 2014.

Baines, Erin. "Complex Political Perpetrators: Reflections on Dominic Ongwen." *The Journal of Modern African Studies* 47, no. 2 (2009): 163–91.

Baitenmann, Helga. "The Article 27 Reforms and the Promise of Local Democratization in Central Veracruz." In *The Transformation of Rural Mexico: Reforming the Ejido Sector,* edited by Wayne Cornelius and David Myhre, 105–23. San Diego: UCSD, 1998.

———. "Reforma agraria y ciudadanía en el México del siglo XX." In *Paisajes mexicanos de la reforma agraria: homenaje a William Roseberry,* edited by William Goméz, 71–97. Zamora: El Colegio de Michoacán, 2007.

Bazin, Jean. "Interpréter ou décrire : notes critiques sur la connaissance anthropologique." In *Une école pour les sciences sociales: De la VIe section à l'EHESS,* edited by Jacques Revel and Nathan Wachtel, 401–20. Paris: Le Cerf, 1996.

———. "Questions de sens." *Enquête* 6 (1998): 13–34.

————. "Science des moeurs and description de l'action." *Le Genre humain* 35, no. 2 (1999): 33–58.

Bazin, Laurent. "La parenté : miroir and enlisement des hiérarchies en Côte-d'Ivoire." *Journal des anthropologues* 77–78 (1999): 193–215.

Benda-Beckmann, Keebet von. "Forum Shopping and Shopping Forums: Dispute Processing in a Minangkabau Village in West Sumatra." *The Journal of Legal Pluralism and Unofficial Law* 13, no. 19 (1981): 117–59.

Bernstein, Henry. "'Changing Before Our Very Eyes': Agrarian Questions and the Politics of Land in Capitalism Today." *Journal of Agrarian Change* 4, no. 1-2 (2014): 190225.

Berry, Sara. *No Condition is Permanent: The Social Dynamics of Agrarian Change in Sub-Saharan Africa*. Madison: University of Wisconsin Press, 1993.

Blazquez, Adèle. "Lecture d'un ordinaire en situation de violence dans le Nord du Mexique. Déguisements du quotidien and contournement de la tension." MA thesis, EHESS, Paris: 2013.

————. "Ethnographie d'un contexte violent: L'immanence de l'enquête (Sinaloa, Mexique)." *Monde commun* 1 (2018): 188–205.

Blok, Anton. *The Mafia of a Sicilian Village, 1860–1960: A Study of Violent Peasant Entrepreneurs*. New York: Harper & Row, 1975.

Boltanski, Luc, and Laurent Thevenot. *De la justification. Les économies de la grandeur*. Paris: Gallimard, 1991.

Bonfil Batalla, Guillermo. *México profundo: Una civilizacion negada*. Mexico: Grijalbo, 1987.

Borneman, John, and Hammoudi Abdellah, eds. *Being There: The Fieldwork Encounter and the Making of Truth*. Berkeley: University of California Press, 2009.

Bougerol, Christiane. "Commérages and adresses indirectes: L'exemple antillais." In *Pour une anthropologie de l'interlocution. Rhétorique du quotidien,* edited by Bertrand Masquelier and Jean-Louis Siran, 359–81. Paris: L'Harmattan, 2000.

————. "Une rumeur à la Guadeloupe: De certaines pratiques supposées des Haïtiens." *Terrain* 54 (2010): 130–39.

Bouquet, Emmanuelle, and Jean-Philippe Colin. "L'État, l'ejido and les droits fonciers: Ruptures and continuités du cadre institutionnel formel au Mexique." In *Les politiques d'enregistrement des droits fonciers: du cadre légal aux pratiques locales,* edited by Jean-Philippe Colin, Pierre-Yves Le Meur and Éric Léonard, 299–32. Paris: Karthala, 2009.

Bourdieu, Pierre. "Droit and passe-droit." *Actes de la Recherche en Sciences Sociales* 81, no. 1 (1990): 86–96.

————. *On the State: Lectures at the Collège de France, 1989–1992*. Cambridge: Polity, 2014.

Bourgois, Philippe. "Insecurity, the War on Drugs, and Crimes of States." In *Violence at the Urban Margins,* edited by Javier Auyero, Philippe Bourgois, and Nancy Scheper-Hughes, 305–21. London: Oxford University Press, 2015.

————. "Decolonising Drug Studies in an Era of Predatory Accumulation." *Third World Quarterly* 39, no. 2 (2018): 385–98.

Butler, Judith. *Precarious Life: The Powers of Mourning and Violence*. New York: Verso Books, 2006.

———. *Frames of War: When is Life Grievable?* London: Verso Books, 2009.

Calzolaio, Chiara. "Les féminicides de Ciudad Juárez : Reconnaissance institutionnelle, enjeux politiques and moraux de la prise en charge des victims." *Problèmes d'Amérique latine* 84, no. 2 (2012): 61–76.

———. "Contre la violence: Fabriquer des 'bons citoyens' à Ciudad Juárez (Mexique, XXIst siècle)." *Clio* 43 (2016): 117–38.

Campbell, Howard. *Drug War Zone: Frontline Dispatches from the Streets of El Paso and Juárez*. Austin: University of Texas Press, 2009.

Cardi, Coline, and Geneviève Pruvost. *Penser la violence des femmes*. Paris: La Découverte, 2012.

Carton de Grammont, Hubert. *Empresarios agrícolas y el estado: Sinaloa, 1893–1984*. Mexico City: Universidad Nacional Autónoma de México, 1990.

Castro Neira, Yerko. *En la orilla de la justicia: Migración y justicia en los márgenes del Estado*. Mexico City: Universidad Autónoma Metropolitana, 2009.

Char, René. *Retour amont,* Paris: Gallimard, 1966.

Claverie, Elisabeth. *Les guerres de la vierge: Une anthropologie des apparitions*. Paris: Gallimard, 2003.

———. "Techniques de la menace." *Terrain* 43 (2004): 15–30.

———. "Mettre en cause la légitimité de la violence d'État." *Quaderni* 2 (2012): 67–83.

Coburn, Noah. *Bazaar Politics: Power and Pottery in an Afghan Market Town*. Stanford: Stanford University Press, 2011.

Colin, Jean-Philippe, Pierre-Yves Le Meur, and Éric Léonard. "Identifier les droits and dicter le droit : la politique des programmes de formalisation des droits fonciers." In *Les politiques d'enregistrement des droits fonciers: du cadre légal aux pratiques locales,* edited by Jean-Pierre Colin, Pierre-Yves Le Meur, and Éric Léonard, 5–68. Paris: Karthala, 2009.

Collins, Randall. *Violence: A Micro-Sociological Theory*. Princeton: Princeton University Press, 2008.

Comaroff, Jean, and John Comaroff, eds. *Law and Disorder in the Postcolony*. Chicago, University of Chicago Press, 2006.

Córdova, Nery. *La Narcocultura: Simbología de la transgresión, el poder y la muerte; Sinaloa y la "leyenda negra."* Culiacán: Universidad Autónoma de Sinaloa, 2011.

Cottereau, Alain. "Contextualiser dans un monde auto-interprétant. 'Quel prix pour la garde d'un bébé?' Un exemple d'anthropologie de l'évaluation ou 'ethno-comptabilité.'" In *Des contextes en histoire,* edited by Florent Brayard, 123–50. Paris: CRH, 2011.

Das, Veena. *Life and Words: Violence and the Descent Into the Ordinary*: Berkeley, University of California Press, 2007.

De Certeau, Michel. *The Practice of Everyday Life*. Berkeley: University of California Press, 1984.

Delphy, Christine. "L'état d'exception : la dérogation au droit commun comme fondement de la sphère privée." *Nouvelles Questions Féministes* 16, no. 4 (1995): 73–114.

———. *L'ennemi principal: L'économie politique du Patriarcat.* Paris: Syllepse, 2001.

———. *L'ennemi principal: Penser le genre.* Paris: Syllepse, 2001.

Deprez, Stanislas. "The Minor Mode: Albert Piette and the Reshaping of Anthropology." *Sociologus* 64, no. 1 (2014): 87–95.

Devereux, Georges. *De l'angoisse à la méthode dans les sciences du comportement.* Paris: Aubier, 1980.

Didi-Huberman, Georges. *Images in Spite of All: Four Photographs from Auschwitz.* Chicago: University of Chicago Press, 2012.

Dudouet, François-Xavier. *Le Grand deal de l'opium: Histoire du marché légal des drogues.* Paris: Syllepse, 2009.

Durand, Jorge. "El programa bracero (1942–1964): Un balance crítico." *Migración y Desarrollo* 9 (2007): 27–43.

Durand, Jorge, and Douglas Massey. *Clandestinos: Migración México-Estados Unidos en los albores del siglo XXI.* Zacatecas: Universidad Autónoma de Zacatecas, 2003.

Duvoux, Nicolas. "La peur de l'ethnographe." *Genèses* 97, no. 4 (2014): 126–39.

Engle Merry, Sally. "The Criminalization of Everyday Life." In *Everyday Practices and Trouble Cases,* edited by Austin Sarat, Marianne Constable, David Engle, Valerie Hans, and Susanne Lawrence, 14–40. Evanston: Northwestern University Press, 1998.

Escalante Gonzalbo, Fernando. *El crimen como realidad y representación.* Mexico: El Colegio de México, 2012.

Favret-Saada, Jeanne. *Deadly Words: Witchcraft in the Bocage.* Cambridge: Cambridge University Press, 1980.

Ferguson, James. *The Anti-Politics Machine: "Development," Depoliticization, and Bureaucratic Power in Lesotho.* Minneapolis: University of Minnesota Press, 1994.

Ferme, Mariane, and Daniel Hoffman. "Combattants irréguliers et discours international des droits de l'homme dans les guerres civiles africaines." *Politique africaine* 88, no. 4 (2002): 27–48.

Fernández Velázquez, Juan Antonio. "El narcotráfico en los Altos de Sinaloa (1940–1977)." PhD diss., Universidad Veracruzana, 2016.

Figueroa, José, and Alanís Gilberto López, eds. *Encuentros con la Historia: Badiraguato.* Culiacán: Presagio, 2002.

Figueroa Sauceda, Patricia. *Ética en tiempos de guerra y narcotráfico.* Culiacán: Moby Dick, 2017.

Finnström, Sverker. *Living with Bad Surroundings: War, History, and Everyday Moments in Northern Uganda.* Durham: Duke University Press, 2008.

Gallenga, Ghislaine. "Ethnologue à marier: La neutralisation des attributs sexués en entreprise." *Ethnologies* 29, no. 1–2 (2007): 303–14.

Geertz, Clifford. "Being There: Anthropology and the Scene of Writing." In *Works and Lives: The Anthropologist as Author,* 1–24. Stanford: Stanford University Press, 1988.

Geffray, Christian. "La dette imaginaire des collecteurs de caoutchouc." *Cahiers des Sciences Humaines* 28, no. 4 (1992): 705–25.

———. *Chroniques de la servitude en Amazonie brésilienne: Essai sur l'exploitation paternaliste.* Paris: Karthala, 1995.

Gibler, John. *To Die in Mexico: Dispatches from Inside the Drug War.* San Francisco: City Lights, 2011.

———. *I Couldn't Even Imagine That They Would Kill Us: An Oral History of the Attacks Against the Students of Ayotzinapa.* San Francisco: City Lights, 2017.

Gluckman, Max. "Analysis of a Social Situation in Modern Zululand." *Bantu Studies* 14 (1940): 1–30.

———. "Gossip and Scandal." *Current Anthropology* 4, no. 3 (1963): 307–16.

Goffman, Alice. *On the Run: Fugitive Life in an American City.* Chicago: University of Chicago Press, 2014.

González Valdés, Ronaldo, Jorge Gastélum Escalante, Adrián López Ortiz, and Ruth Franco Zazueta. *La cultura en Sinaloa: narrativas de lo social y la violencia.* Culiacán: Honorable Ayuntamiento de Culiacán/Instituto Municipal de Cultura Culiacán, 2013.

Goyon, Marie. "La relation ethnographique: Une affaire de genres." *Socio-anthropologie* 16 (2005).

Green, Linda. *Fear as a Way of Life: Mayan Widows in Rural Guatemala.* New York: Columbia University Press, 1999.

Guez, Sabine. "Les années 1980 ou le temps de l'innocence: Un tournant sociétal dans l'histoire du trafic de drogue au Mexique." *Outros Tempos* 14, no. 24 (2017): 161–83.

Gupta, Akhil. "Blurred Boundaries: The Discourse of Corruption, the Culture of Politics, and the Imagined State." *American Ethnologist* 22, no. 2 (1995): 375–402.

———. *Red Tape: Bureaucracy, Structural Violence, and Poverty in India.* Durham: Duke University Press, 2012.

Haraway, Donna. "Situated Knowledges: The Science Question in Feminism and the Privilege of Partial Perspective." *Feminist Studies* 14, no. 3 (1988): 575–99.

Harvey, David. *A Brief History of Neoliberalism.* Oxford: Oxford University Press, 2007.

Hirai, Shinji. *Economía política de la nostalgia: un estudio sobre la transformación del paisaje urbano en la migración transnacional entre México y Estados Unidos.* Mexico City: Universidad Autónoma Metropolitana, 2009.

Hobsbawm, Eric. *Les bandits.* Paris: La Découverte, 2018.

Hoffman, Danny. "The Civilian Target in Sierra Leone and Liberia: Political Power, Military Strategy, and Humanitarian Intervention." *African Affairs* 103 (2004): 211–26.

———. *The War Machines: Young Men and Violence in Sierra Leone and Liberia.* Durham: Duke University Press, 2011.

Hoffmann, Odile. "L'ejido: Laboratoire des pratiques sociales and fondement de la ruralité contemporaine au Mexique." In *La ruralité dans les pays du Sud à la fin du vingtième siècle,* edited by Jean-Marc Gastellu, 401–16. Paris: Orstom, 1997.

Ibarra Escobar, Guillermo. *Migrantes en mercados de trabajo globales: Mexicanos y sinaloenses en Los Ángeles.* Culiacán: Universidad Autónoma de Sinaloa, 2005.

Jacoby, Karl. *Des ombres à l'aube: Un massacre d'Apaches and la violence de l'histoire.* Toulouse: Anacharsis, 2015.

Javeau, Claude. "Parler pour ne rien dire: 'Ça va? Ça va!'" *Ethnologie française* 26, no. 2 (1996): 255–63.

Joseph, Gilbert, and Daniel Nugent, eds. *Everydays Forms of the State: Revolution and the Negotiation of Rule in Modern Mexico* (Durham: Duke University Press, 1994).

Journet-Diallo, Odile. "Catégories de genre and relation ethnographique." In *Femmes plurielles. Les représentations des femmes: Discours, normes and conduites,* edited by Danielle Jonckers and Marie-Claude Dupré, 21–36. Paris: Éditions de la MSH, 1999.

Karsenti, Bruno, and Louis Quéré Louis. *La croyance and l'enquête: Aux sources du pragmatisme.* Paris: Éditions de l'EHESS, 2004.

Kearney, Michael. *Reconceptualizing the Peasantry: Anthropology in Global Perspective.* New York: Avalon Publishing, 1996.

Kelly, Liz. "The Continuum of Sexual Violence." In *Women, Violence and Social Control,* edited by Jalna Hanmer and Mary Maynard, 46–60. London: Palgrave Macmillan, 1987.

Knight, Alan. *The Mexican Revolution.* Cambridge: Cambridge University Press, 1986.

Kovats-Bernat, J. Christopher. "Negotiating Dangerous Fields: Pragmatic Strategies for Fieldwork amid Violence and Terror." *American Anthropologist* 104, no. 1 (2002): 208–22.

Lara Salazar, Oscar. *Sangre Caliente.* Culiacán: Talleres de Artes Gráficas Sinaloenses, 1990.

Le Caisne, Léonore. *Un inceste ordinaire: Et pourtant tout le monde savait.* Paris: Belin, 2014.

Léonard, Éric. "Titularización agraria y apropiación de nuevos espacios económicos por los actores rurales: El Procede en los Tuxtlas, estado de Veracruz." In *Políticas y regulaciones agrarias: dinámicas de poder y juegos de actores en torno a la tenencia de la tierra,* edited by Eric Léonard, André Quesnel, and Emilia Velázquez, 297–328. Mexico City: CIESAS/IRD, 2003.

———. "Réforme agraire and reconfiguration du régime de gouvernementalité dans Les Tuxtlas, Mexique, 1920–1945." *Critique internationale* 75, no. 2 (2017): 53–69.

Léonard, Éric, and Emilia Velázquez. "Citoyenneté locale and réappropriation du changement légal au Mexique: Une analyse des conflits autour des transferts fonciers à Soteapan, Veracruz." In *Politique de la terre and de l'appartenance: Droits fonciers and citoyenneté locale dans les sociétés du sud,* edited by Jean-Pierre Jacob and Pierre-Yves Le Meur, 61–94. Paris: Karthala, 2010.

Li, Tania. *The Will to Improve: Governmentality, Development, and the Practice of Politics.* Durham: Duke University Press, 2007.

————. *Land's End: Capitalist Relations on an Indigenous Frontier.* Durham: Duke University Press, 2014.

Lomnitz, Claudio. *Las salidas del laberinto: Cultura e ideología en el espacio nacional mexicano.* Mexico City: Joaquín Moritz, 1995.

————. "Sobre reciprocidad negative." *Revista de Antropología Social* 14 (2005): 311–34.

Lubkemann, Stephen. *Culture in Chaos: An Anthropology of the Social Condition in War.* Chicago: University of Chicago Press, 2010.

Macek, Ivana. *Sarajevo Under Siege: Anthropology in Wartime.* Philadelphia: University of Pennsylvania Press, 2009.

Maldonado Aranda, Salvador. *Los márgenes del estado mexicano: Territorios ilegales, desarrollo y violencia en Michoacán.* Zamora: El Colegio de Michoacán, 2010.

————. "Drogas, violencia y militarización en el México rural: el caso de Michoacán." *Revista mexicana de sociología* 74, no. 1 (2012): 5–39.

Malinowski, Bronislaw. *Argonauts of the Western Pacific: An Account of Native Enterprise and Adventure in the Archipelagoes of Melanesian New Guinea.* London: Routledge, 1922.

Malkin, Victoria. "Narcotrafficking, Migration, and Modernity in Rural Mexico." *Latin American Perspectives* 28, no. 4 (2001): 101–28.

Masquelier, Bertrand, and Jean-Louis Siran. *Pour une anthropologie de l'interlocution: Rhétoriques du quotidien.* Paris: L'Harmattan, 2000.

Mastrogiovanni, Federico. *Ni vivos ni muertos: La desaparición forzada en México como estrategia de terror.* Mexico City: Penguin, 2014.

Mathieu, Nicole-Claude. "When Yielding Is Not Consenting: Material and Psychic Determinants of Women's Dominated Consciousness and Some of Their Interpretations in Ethnology." *Feminist Issues* 9 (1989): 3–49.

McDonald, James. "The Narcoeconomy and Small-Town, Rural Mexico." *Human Organization* 64, no. 2 (2005): 115–25.

Meillassoux, Claude. *Femmes, greniers and capitaux.* Paris: Maspéro, 1975.

Mendoza Rockwell, Natalia. *Conversaciones de desierto.* Mexico City: CIDE, 2007.

————. "La Privatizacion de la Ilegalidad." In *Si persisten las molestias,* edited by Fernando Escalante Gonzalbo, 28–51. Mexico City: Cal y Arena, 2018.

Michel, Víctor Hugo. *Morir en Malasia: Una crónica sobre los desechables del narco.* Mexico City: Océano, 2013.

Monsutti, Alessandro. *War and Migration: Social Networks and Economic Strategies of the Hazaras of Afghanistan.* New York: Routledge, 2005.

————. "Fuzzy Sovereignty: Rural Reconstruction in Afghanistan, between Democracy Promotion and Power Games." *Comparative Studies in Society and History* 54, no. 3 (2012): 563–91.

Müller, Birgit. "La loi du marché comme idéologie: Les agriculteurs du Saskatchewan face au système économique néo-libéral." *Cahiers du GEMDEV* 31 (2007): 52–65.

———. "Lifting the Veil of Harmony: Anthropologists Approach International Organisations." In *The Gloss of Harmony: The Politics of Policy-Making in Multilateral Organisations*, edited by Birgit Müller, 1–20. London: Pluto Press, 2013.

Naepels, Michel. *Histoires de terres kanakes: Conflicts fonciers and rapports sociaux dans la région de Houaïlou (Nouvelle-Calédonie).* Paris: Belin, 1998.

———. "Une étrange étrangeté: Remarques sur la situation ethnographique." *L'Homme* 148 (1998): 185–99.

———. "Note sur la justification dans la relation ethnographique." *Genèses* 64, no. 3 (2006): 110–26.

———. "L'épiement sans trêve and la curiosité de tout." *L'Homme* 203–4 (2012): 77–102.

———. "The Complexity of a Murder: Situational Dynamics, Social Relations, and Historical Context." *International Journal of Conflict and Violence* 11, no. 1 (2017).

———. *Dans la détresse: une anthropologie de la vulnérabilité.* Paris: Éditions de l'EHESS, 2019.

Narotzky, Susana, and Niko Besnier. "Crisis, Value, and Hope: Rethinking the Economy: An Introduction to Supplement 9." *Current Anthropology* 55, no. S9 (2014): S4–S16.

Nordstrom, Carolyn. *A Different Kind of War Story.* Philadelphia: University of Pennsylvania Press, 1997.

Nordstrom, Carolyn, and Antonius C. G. M. Robben, eds. *Fieldwork Under Fire: Contemporary Studies of Violence and Culture.* Berkeley: University of California Press, 1995.

Nuijten, Monique. "Family Property and the Limits of Intervention: The Article 27 Reforms and the PROCEDE Programme in Mexico." *Development and Change* 34, no. 3 (2003): 475–97.

———. *Power, Community and the State: The Political Anthropology of Organisation in Mexico.* New York: Pluto Press, 2003.

Ortiz Pinchetti, Francisco. "La Operación Cóndor." *Proceso* (1981).

Osorno, Diego. *El Cártel de Sinaloa: Una historia del uso político del narco.* Mexico City: Penguin, 2011.

Osuna, Felix Francisco Javier. "Crecimiento y crisis de la minería en Sinaloa (1907–1950)." MA thesis, Universidad Autónoma de Sinaloa, Culiacán, 2014.

Palerm, Juan-Vincent. "The Expansion of California Agriculture and the Rise of Peasant-Workers Communities." In *Immigration: A Civil Rights Issue for the Americas,* edited by Susanne Jonas and Suzanne Dod Thomas, 45–68. Wilmington: Scholarly Resources Inc., 1998.

Pansters, Wil, ed. *Violence, Coercion, and State-Making in Twentieth-Century Mexico: The Other Half of the Centaur.* Stanford: Stanford University Press, 2012.

Parnell, Philip C., and Stephanie C. Kane, eds. *Crime's Power: Anthropologists and the Ethnography of Crime.* New York: Palgrave Macmillan, 2003.

Peña, Guillermo de la. "Poder local, poder regional: Perspectivas socioanthopológicas." In *Poder local, poder regional,* edited by Jorge Padua and Alain Vanneph, 27–56. Mexico City: Colegio de México, 1986.

Pérez Vázquez, Brenda Gabriela, Daniela Bachi Morales, Barbosa Magalhães Lígia de Aquino, and Castillo Portillo Montserrat. *Episodios de desplazamiento interno forzado masivo en México. Informe 2018.* Mexico: Comisión Mexicana de Defensa y Promoción de los Derechos Humanos, 2019.

Piccato, Pablo. *The Tyranny of Opinion: Honor in the Construction of the Mexican Public Sphere.* Durham: Duke University Press, 2010.

———. "Homicide as Politics in Modern Mexico: Homicide in Modern Mexico." *Bulletin of Latin American Research* 32, no. 1 (2013): 104–25.

———. "Murders of Nota Roja: Truth and Justice in Mexican Crime News." *Past & Present* 223, no. 1 (2014): 195–231.

———. *A History of Infamy: Crime, Truth, and Justice in Mexico.* Oakland: University of California Press, 2017.

Piette, Albert. "Les détails de l'action: Écriture, images and pertinence ethnologique." *Enquête* 6 (1998): 109–28.

Poole, Deborah. *Vision, Race, and Modernity: A Visual Economy of the Andean Image World.* Princeton: Princeton University Press, 1997.

Ribot, Jesse, and Nancy Peluso. "A Theory of Access." *Rural Sociology* 68, no. 2 (2009): 153–81.

Robin Azevedo, Valérie. *Sur les sentiers de la violence: Politiques de la mémoire and conflit armé au Pérou.* Paris: Éditions de l'IHEAL, 2019.

Robledo Silvestre, Carolina. *Drama social y política de duelo: las desapariciones de la guerra contra las drogas en Tijuana.* Mexico City: El Colegio de México, 2017.

Robles Berlanga, Hector. "Tendencias del campo mexicano a la luz del Programa de Certificación de los Derechos Ejidales (Procede)." In *Políticas y regulaciones agrarias: dinámicas de poder y juegos de actores en torno a la tenencia de la tierra,* edited by Eric Léonard, André Quesnel, and Emilia Velázquez, 131–56. Mexico City: CIESAS/IRD, 2003.

Rodriguez Castaneda, Rafael. *El México Narco.* Mexico: Booket, 2009.

Román Alarcón, Rigoberto Arturo. "Auge y decadencia de la minería en Sinaloa 1910–1950." *Nueva Época* 4 (2004): 38.

Roseberry, William. *Anthropologies and Histories: Essays in Culture, History, and Political Economy.* New Brunswick: Rutgers University Press, 1989.

Ruelas, Ana Luz. *Crisis universitaria y ratio legis en Sinaloa.* Mexico City: Juan Pablos, 2010.

Sahlins, Marshall. *Stone Age Economics.* Chicago: Aldine-Athertone, 1972.

Salazar Araya, Sergio. *Violencia y valor en el tránsito migratorio centro-americano: La masacre de Cadereyta (2012) y la lucha por el retorno de los cuerpos.* Forthcoming.

Sánchez Godoy, Jorge Alan. "Procesos de institucionalización de la narcocultura en Sinaloa." *Frontera Norte* 21, no. 41 (2009): 77–103.

Sariego Rodríguez, Juan Luis. *Enclaves y minerales en el norte de México: Historia social de los mineros de Cananea y Nueva Rosita, 1900–1970.* Mexico City: CIESAS, 1988.

————. "De minas, mineros, territorios y protestas sociales en México: Los nuevos retos de la globalización." *Cahiers des Amériques latines* 60–61 (2009): 173–92.

Schneider, Elizabeth. "The Violence of Privacy." *Connecticut Law Review* 23 (1991): 973–99.

Schneider, Jane, and Peter Schneider. "The Anthropology of Crime and Criminalization." *Annual Review of Anthropology* 37, no. 1 (2008): 351–73.

Schryer, Frans. "Peasants and the Law: A History of Land Tenure and Conflict in the Huasteca." *Journal of Latin American Studies* 18, no. 2 (1986): 283–311.

Schütz, Alfred. "The Well-Informed Citizen: An Essay on the Social Distribution of Knowledge." *Social Research* 13, no. 4 (1946): 463–78.

Scott, James. *Seeing like a State: How Certain Schemes to Improve the Human Condition Have Failed.* New Haven: Yale University Press, 1999.

Scott, Joan. "Gender: A Useful Category of Historical Analysis." *American Historical Review* 91, no. 5 (1986): 1053–75.

Shibutani, Tamotsu. *Improvised News: A Sociological Study of Rumor.* Indianapolis: The Bobbs-Merrill Company, 1966.

Sikor, Thomas, and Christian Lund. "Access and Property: A Question of Power and Authority." *Development and Change* 40, no. 1 (2009): 1–22.

Smith, Benjamin. *Pistoleros and Popular Movements: The Politics of State Formation in Postrevolutionary Oaxaca.* Lincoln: University of Nebraska Press, 2009.

Smith, Gavin. "Selective Hegemony and Beyond-Populations with 'No Productive Function': A Framework for Enquiry." *Identities* 18, no. 1 (2011): 2–38.

Sousa Santos, Boaventura de. *Toward a New Legal Common Sense: Law, Globalization, and Emancipation.* Cambridge: Cambridge University Press, 2002.

Suárez Bonilla, Natalia. "Viol, blâme de la victime and contrôle social: Le cas des enclaves paramilitaires en Colombie." In *Viols en temps de guerre,* edited by Raphaëlle Branche and Fabrice Virgili, 83–93. Paris: Payot, 2011.

————. "Épreuves d'altérité dans les enclaves insurrectionnelles: Le cas de la Colombie." In *Sociétés en guerre,* edited by Rémy Bazenguissa-Ganga and Sami Makki, 129–44. Paris: Éditions de la MSH, 2012.

Theidon, Kimberly. *Intimate Enemies: Violence and Reconciliation in Peru.* Philadelphia: University of Pennsylvania Press, 2012.

Toro, María Celia. *Mexico's "War" on Drugs: Causes and Consequences.* Boulder: Lynne Rienner, 1995.

Torres Mazuera, Gabriela. "Formas cotidianas de participación política rural: El Procede en Yucatán." *Estudios sociológicos* 32, no. 95 (2014): 295–322.

Tsing, Anna. *Friction: An Ethnography of Global Connection.* Princeton: Princeton University Press, 2005.

————. *The Mushroom at the End of the World: On the Possibility of Life in Capitalist Ruins.* Princeton: Princeton University Press, 2015.

Valenzuela Arce, José Manuel. *Jefe de Jefes: Corridos y narcocultura en México.* Mexico: Plaza y Janés, 2001.

Vigh, Henrik. *Navigating Terrains of War: Youth and Soldiering in Guinea-Bissau.* New York: Berghahn Books, 2006.

Wacquant, Loïc. "Crafting the Neoliberal State: Workfare, Prisonfare, and Social Insecurity." *Sociological Forum* 25, no. 2 (2010): 197–220.

Watson, Conrad, ed. *Being There: Fieldwork in Anthropology.* New York: Pluto Press, 1999.

Wedeen, Lisa. "Ideology and Humor in Dark Times: Notes from Syria." *Critical Inquiry* 39, no. 4 (2013): 841–73.

INDEX

abandonment: of hamlets, 1–2, 24, 71, 98, 99, 120, 194, 209–10; of insoluble problems by municipal administration, 229; of mines, 93

abduction: in the continuum of gender violence, 157–60; and domestic violence, 178–80; and marriage, 172–78; as motive for killing, 204–5; of single women, 169–71; by soldiers, 66; victim blaming for, 155–56, 160–71, 180–81, 252–53, 285n7. *See also* predation, gendered

accessibility/inaccessibility of Badiraguato, 16–18, 25–30, 40, 44–45, 97–98, 117, 241–45, 254

accumulation strategies, 5, 44–45, 94–97, 101–2, 256, 257–58

action, fundamental logics of, 8–9

"administering" violence, 210–11, 260

administration, municipal: daily movements of municipal employees, 22, 25–31; federal policies in political economy of, 211–12; in isolating Badiraguato, 16–18; political games in, 212–19; production of solvable problems by, 224–31, 259–60; public programs and events by, 220–24, 231–41; in public works, 220–24; as qualifying operator, 264; rhythm of office activities, 235–37; siloing by, 241–50. *See also* mayors of Badiraguato

Adolfo López Mateos Dam, 17–18, 98

agrarian administration and courts, 97, 124, 127–30, 145, 146–51. *See also* land regime and structures

agriculture: agribusinesses, 17–18, 97–98, 101–2, 122; and the *ejidos,* 129, 130–31, 132–33, 141–42, 145; growing cycle, in travel, 44; in the imposition of poppy monoculture, 97–98, 101–2, 122; mechanization of, in emigration, 279n14; military in constraints on, 104; in the Procede reform, 148

Alarcón Valdez, Praxedis: *Political Radiography,* 215–17

alcohol consumption, 76–77, 184–85, 186–87, 201–2

ambiguity: in municipal presentation of anti-gun programs, 230–31; of the power of *pesados,* 87, 109; in predatory gender relations, 158, 163, 168–69, 175–76; of relationships between residents and the military, 82, 106–7, 109; between state and non-state violence, 203–4

anticipation of violence: in daily movements, 10; in the "El Gallito" murders, 204–5, 210; information-gathering in, 52, 72, 88; in municipal event planning, 223–24; in qualification by arms, 263–64; in uncertainty, 259–60

anticorruption policies, 211–12, 286n21

ascents, economic, 60–61, 99, 101, 196–97, 260–61

assassinations, 43, 120–21, 191, 203–7, 211, 243–44. *See also* killings

Atilano, Manuel, 285n12

"El Gallito" murders, 198–209. *See also*
Guerrero Reyes, José Guadalupe ("El
Gallito")
emigrants/emigration. *See* migration/
migrants
employment/unemployment: domination
and reciprocity in, 119, 120–21, 122; in
grower-buyer relationships, 120–21; in
household economies, 114; and the
imposition of poppy monoculture,
91–93, 99–102; in municipal administration, 212–15, 221; in Sinaloa state, 1–2
enclavement, 5, 10–21, 24, 122, 253–57, 259
enclosure. *See* *cercos* ("fenced-in" parcel and
land)
entrepreneurs: in extraction and enclavement, 254–57; in fencing in, 124–25,
129, 145, 146–49, 150–51; in the imposition of poppy monoculture, 93–98, 122;
of marginalization, 93–98, 117, 122,
150–51, 254–57, 259 (See also *pesados*
(armed strongmen)); in uncertainty, 117,
259
enunciation regimes, 47–48, 88–89, 231
euphemisms: in the context of violence,
85–87; for gender predation, 162–63; in
making sense of repression, 106–7; for
protection, 110; for violence, 59–60,
80–81, 120–21, 183, 229
exceptionalism of Badiraguato, 1–2, 4–5,
14, 255
executives, municipal: community events
in visibility of, 235, 236–37; in constraints on contesting violence, 264;
elections in visibility of, 30; in extraction and enclavement, 254–55; in gender
predation, 166–67; in the manufacture
of solvable problems, 225–26, 228–29; in
the Procede reform, 149–50; in siloing,
245–50. *See also* administration, municipal; mayors of Badiraguato
experiences: of past repression, and sociability in the hamlets, 65–69; relevance
of, 274n2; in social practices, 46; in
threat identification, 71, 73–74, 75–76,
258–59
exploitation, 5, 8–9, 91–92, 115–18, 121–23,
152, 172–78, 253–57

extortion, 110–13, 114–18, 122–23, 197–98,
252, 255
extraction/extractive economy, 17, 101–2,
103, 253–57, 261–62. *See also* mining

familiarity, 6–8, 20–21, 29, 30, 31–45,
248–49, 258–59
Family Affairs, State Department of. *See*
DIF (Desarollo Integral de la Familia)
federal government and federal programs:
ejidos as interlocutor for, 143–45, 149–
50; escort of federal officials in siloing,
245; in the imposition of poppy monoculture, 95; in isolating Badiraguato, 17;
in moving around, 22–23, 29–30; and
municipal administration, 211–12, 231,
253
fentanyl, 256–57
food crops, 97–98, 99–100, 122
food distribution/aid, 28, 62
framings: of Badiraguato, in daily narratives, 6; in characterizing context,
81–82; of drug trafficking as organized
crime, 3–4; in enclavement, 265; institutional, for killings, 209; of killers as
deviant, 193–94, 197; of *pesados* in the
media, 119–20; in siloing, 250
friendship: domination and reciprocity in,
120–22; and the hazards of the hamlets,
70; in moving around, 36; political,
94–95, 96, 217–18; and proximity, 49,
57, 60–61; threat identification in,
74–75
funerals/funeral vigils, 76, 185–86, 192, 198

gambling, 184–85, 186–87
gambusinos (independent prospectors),
90–94, 95, 278n4
gavillas (armed gangs): constraints on
characterizing, 86; in daily movements
in the sierra, 24–25, 28–29, 39–41,
42–43, 44; in desertion of hamlets, 1–2;
El Rancho band, 188–98, 209–10,
288n14; in local vigilance, 60, 258; and
the profits of the *ejido*, 143–44; in
rhetoric against organized crime, 3–4;
silence of municipal administration
on, 231

gender relations, 8, 27, 63–65, 156, 163–64, 179–80. *See also* predation, gendered

generalizations: in calls to mistrust, 58–59; context in, 84, 85–86; on daily gun violence, 152; in discourse on killings, 186–87; on domestic violence, 178–79; and experience, in threat identification, 71, 73–74, 75–76; of violence, by municipal administration, 264, 265

gold mining, 90–93

gossip, 57–58, 60, 61, 88, 160–61, 164–65, 191, 262–63. *See also* rumors

graves, 15–16, 188, 242–43, 268n5

grower-buyer relationships: domination and reciprocity in, 118–22; exploitation in, 115–18; in extraction and enclavement, 255–57; hierarchies in, 120–21

"guacho," meaning of, 85–86, 277–78n38

guardedness, 5–6, 21, 58–59, 72, 159, 166–67. *See also* trust/mistrust

Guerrero Reyes, José Guadalupe ("El Gallito"), 198–209, 226–27, 228–29

gun buyback program, 229–31

Guzman Loera, Joaquín ("El Chapo"), 1–2, 12, 42–43, 244, 246–49, 255, 267n1

harvests, 44–45, 103–4, 106–9, 110–16, 117–18, 122–23, 134, 255–56

heroin production, 116–18

hierarchies, 120–21, 207, 231, 249, 250

holidays, in heightened threat of violence, 75–77, 258

homicides. *See* killings

inclusion/exclusion, 4–6, 136, 137, 151–53, 224

incursions: daily movement as, 16–17, 27–28, 42–43; military, 64, 66–67, 69, 85, 108–22, 252; in siloing, 244–45

information gathering: in daily life and self-protection, 47–61, 66–69, 72, 88–89, 260–61; in the organization of production, 103–5; in threat identification, 73–74, 77, 258

infrastructure: in enclavement and extraction, 247, 248–49, 254; in moving around, 16, 17–20, 22–23, 37–40, 251–

52; in uncertain profits, 122. *See also* public works

interknowing, networks of, 36–37, 57–60, 191, 202, 258

intermediaries, local: in dominance and uncertainty, 260; in extraction and enclavement, 254–56; in land use and access, 137–38, 147–50; and marginalized independent armed groups, 196–97; in moving around, 36–37; in siloing by escort, 241–42, 244–45; in the structure of poppy production, 93–98, 101–2, 115–18, 119–22, 255–56. *See also* caciques (local political bosses); pesados (armed strongmen)

investigation/investigative activity. *See* information gathering

isolation: academic literature in, 12–13; in extraction and enclavement, 17–18, 254, 257; in moving around, 17–18, 39–40, 44–45; in the structure of poppy cultivation, 93, 95, 101–2, 103, 117, 122, 254–55. *See also* enclavement

Joint Agrarian Commission, 128–29, 282n6

journalists, 3–4, 11–12, 16–17, 187–88, 200, 241–50, 254–55. *See also* media

kidnapping. *See* abduction

killings: causes of, 183–88, 209–10; in daily life, 53, 71, 80–81, 184; El Gallito killings, 198–209, 210; El Rancho killings, 188–98; in enclavement, 12–13; and gender predation, 171; irrationality of, 188–98, 209–10; motives for, 183–98, 202–3, 204–5; "organized crime" in discourse on, 3–4; and politically induced vulnerability, 253; in Potemkin village politics, 241, 243–44; power in, 198–210, 260; as risk in moving around, 33, 41; in the social fabric, 9; underestimation of, 268n5; as unsolvable problem, 228, 229

kinship, 42, 53–54, 63–64, 95–97, 99, 260

Landell, "Nachillo," 219
Landell, Nacho, 93–98, 129, 131, 135

land regime and structures: *cercos* in, 125–
27, 130, 132–40, 142, 146–49, 150, 151–
53, 264; certainty and uncertainty in,
135–36, 147–48, 151–52, 211, 261; confusion around, 124–27, 252, 253; in
enclavement and extraction, 254–55;
land grabbing, 134–40, 146–51, 152–53,
252, 261; in poppy production, 94–95,
97, 102–3, 104, 106–7, 109–10, 115–16;
Procede reform in, 146–51; uncertainty
in, 135–36, 147–48, 151–52, 211, 261. See
also *ejidos* (communal land tenure
system)
League of Agrarian Communities, 128
liberalization, economic, 3–4, 146
linguistics: of Badiraguato media discourse,
248; linguistic uncertainty, 126–27, 138
livestock, 93–95, 106–7, 134–35, 138–39
Loera, Mara Consuelo (mother of "El
Chapo"), 246–47, 267n1
López, Mario Valenzuela, 214–15, 220–24,
242–51
López Obrador, Andrés Manuel, 3

marginalization: drug laws in, 254; entrepreneurs of, 94–98, 117, 122, 129, 150–51,
254, 257, 259; fragmentation of the sierra
in, 37; in killings, 194–98, 210, 253, 260;
in poppy monoculture, 94–98, 122; and
relationships, in the threat of violence,
55–57; socioeconomic, 4–5, 16–18,
196–97, 210, 256, 260; in the structure
of poppy production, 103
marijuana, 11–12, 22–23, 65–66, 97–98,
115–16, 256–57
markets/market forces, 115–16, 118, 146,
256–57, 281n32, 281n35
marriage, 158–59, 165–66, 169–71, 172–80
mayors of Badiraguato: in local political
games, 212–19; in the manufacture of
solvable problems, 224–25, 226–27,
229–31; as mayors of the "cradle of drug
trafficking," 241–46; in municipal
development, 220–21, 222–24; and the
Procede reform, 148–50; in public events,
233–34, 235–36; and public safety issues,
211, 226–27; response to the "El Gallito"
killings by, 201–2, 205; in siloing, 241–50.

See also administration, municipal;
executives, municipal; *name of mayor*
media: causal explanations for killings in,
209; characterization of daily life in,
80–82; in enclavement, 11–13, 16, 256;
escorts for, in siloing, 241–50; framings
of Badiraguato by, 6; on killings, 187–
88, 200, 205, 209; solidarity and reciprocity in framings by, 119–20. *See also*
journalists
methamphetamine labs, 247
Mexican Farm Labor Agreement, Mexico-
US, 98
middle men. *See* intermediaries, local;
pesados (armed strongmen)
migration/migrants: in the imposition of
poppy monoculture, 97–99, 101–2,
279n14; municipal employment of, 214;
and the political economy of nostalgia,
289–90n15; and the Procede reform,
147–48; return of, in heightened threat,
75–76, 79; stigmatization in, 24; and
the threat of reprisal murders, 194–95;
in tourism revenue, 222, 289–90n15
military: in daily life, 58, 63–64, 65–69,
71–72, 86–87, 88, 252; in daily movements, 11–12, 16, 31–34; in displacement
of Badiraguato's inhabitants, 1–2; "El
Gallito's" assassination in threat of
reinforcement by, 205–6; in extraction
and enclavement, 254, 255; as *gavillas*,
195–96; physical abuse of trafficker
family members by, 247, 249–50; positive recharacterizations of, in self-protection, 82–85; in the structure of poppy
cultivation, 101–8, 109–23, 252, 254–55,
256; in the war on drug trafficking, 3.
See also repression
mining, 90–97, 122, 278n4
monitoring. *See* surveillance
monopolies, 241–42, 244–45, 250, 252, 256,
257–58
mule paths, 36–42, 93
multiparty competition, 216–17

"negative reciprocity," 121
negotiations: domestic, 174–76; with the
ejido assembly, 144–45, 148–49, 150–51,

153; for employment in municipal administration, 214–15, 216–17; with military and politicians, in success in the drug trade, 101; in moving around, 25–26, 29, 30, 44–45, 251; in protection from gender predation, 161–62, 169–70

neoliberalism/neoliberal logics, 6, 228–29, 255

officials: municipal, 22, 25–31, 178–80, 205–8, 245 (*See also* administration, municipal; executives, municipal); state and federal, 16–17, 149–50, 231, 245, 250, 253

Olivas Alarcón, Fidel, 218

Operation Condor (1977), 65–66, 99, 106–7, 285n12

Operation Intercept (1969), 99

"organized crime," 3–4, 205, 211, 243, 245–46, 264. *See also* "the sector"

otherizing, 4, 7, 81–82, 188

patronage, 40, 139, 215, 219, 250

Peasant Trade Unions of Sinaloa, 128

Peña Nieto, Enrique, 3

Pérez Olivas, Lorena, 214–15, 220–21

Pericos, Sinaloa and Perricos-Badiraguato road, 14–15, 17–18, 19–21, 37

Permanent Campaign for the Donation and Voluntary Registration of Firearms, 229–31

pesados (armed strongmen): activities of, in information gathering, 252; control of roads by, 28; in daily life, 69–72, 86–87; in the El Rancho killings, 193, 196–98; in extraction and enclavement, 255; gender predation by, 170, 177, 179–80; and land use regimes, 129–31, 134, 138–40, 150–51; in the structure of poppy cultivation, 109–10, 114–15, 116–23, 252. *See also* intermediaries, local

pistoleros (armed professionals), 196

police, 27, 187–88, 189, 198–209, 210, 226–27

policies, state and federal, 102–3, 211–12, 259–60

politicians: in enclavement, 13; in local political games, 212–19; manufacture of

solvable problems by, 224–31; media exposure in the sierra in campaigns of, 245; and the power of the *ejido,* 142–43; in public projects and events, 220–24; in sidelining woman stealing, 180; in siloing, 241–50. See also under *name of politician*

politics: challenge of violence in, 250; dependence on state and federal authorities in, 250; and the *ejidos,* 142–44, 148–50; folksiness in, 237; in the imposition of poppy monoculture, 94–97, 101–2; in infrastructure investments, 40; in judging public works, 221; in material security, 215; mayoral media strategies, 241–50; in municipal administration, 212–19

poppy cultivation: in enclavement and extraction, 253–55; in the hazards of being in the hamlets, 62–64; as monoculture, 90–102, 122, 253–55; operations of, 102–9; soldiers and *pesados* in uncertain profits from, 109–22

poppy gum, 103, 114–18, 196–97, 256, 260

post-revolutionary narratives, 125–26, 127, 151

power/power relationships: to "administer," 260; in daily life, 71–72, 82, 86–87, 88; in extraction and enclavement, 254, 255, 256; in gender predation, 162–63, 169, 178–79, 180; in killings, 194, 195–210, 260–61; in land rights and use, 130, 132–40, 142–43, 151–52, 264–65; of local administration, 227–29, 250; in moving around, 42; in the structure of poppy cultivation, 96, 110, 116, 119–20, 121–22, 254, 255

precarity: in everyday life, 2–3, 69–70; in exploitation, 256; in moving around, 31–43; in poppy cultivation, 109–10; potential of armed violence in, 261–62; and uncertain profits, 115, 119, 121

precautions: killings in, 183–84; in moving around, 29, 35; in the structure of poppy production, 107–8; threat identification in, 76, 88–89; against woman stealing, 162–63

roads: armed roadblocks, 28–29, 41; construction and maintenance of, 143–44, 151; in moving around, 22–23, 28–29, 32–34, 37–43

Robles, Ángel Bañuelos, 13, 216–17, 220–21, 243–44

rumors, 5–6, 54–55, 155, 198, 206–7, 258, 275–76n15. *See also* gossip

search-and-destroy operations, 108, 111–13, 117–18, 122–23

"the sector," 24–25, 178–80, 229, 264–65. *See also* "organized crime"

see also administration, municipal

sense-making: characterizing context in, 80, 88–89; in the context of armed violence, 261–62; and gender predation, 155–56; information gathering in, 60–61, 73–74; and killings, 183, 184–86, 188–98, 200, 204–5, 209–10

sexual violence, 26, 156–60, 178–81, 264. *See also* predation, gendered; rape

siloing by escort, 241–50

Sinaloa Cartel, 2–3, 68–69, 241–42, 243–44, 255

sindicaturas, 274n28

SNTE (National Union of Education Employees), 2219

sociability/social relations: and access to land, 150–53; daily, and self-protection, 8–9, 55–61; in daily life, 46–47, 48–61, 62–72, 85, 88; and killings, 182–83, 201–2, 208–9, 210; in moving around, 20–21, 30–31, 34–35, 36, 37–40, 44; in the structure of poppy cultivation, 99, 104–5, 114–15, 119; uncertainty in, 257–58, 259; visual economy of, 271n1; in vulnerability to abduction, 160–64; in women's work, 177–78. *See also* relationships, personal

Social Development, State Ministry of (SEDESOL), 142–43, 235–36

social order, 210, 224–31, 250, 260–61

soldiers. *See* military

solidarity, 44, 58–59, 67–68, 119–20

spaces: communal, 55–57, 60–61, 63–64, 126, 127, 134, 231–37, 241; domestic, 63–65, 172–80; social, 76–77, 172

state government of Sinaloa: *ejiditarios* as interlocutors for, 143–44; in formation of the *ejidos,* 130; in the imposition of poppy monoculture, 96–97; in local policies, 225–26; manipulation of Badiraguato politics by, 215–17; as qualifying operator, 264

state violence, 188, 203–4

status, social: in the "El Gallito" murders, 210; municipal events in bridging gaps in, 237; in protection of wives, 176–77; in the violence of the powerful, 198–209

stereotyping, 24–25, 172–73

stigmatization, 4, 6, 12–13, 24–25, 199–200, 243–44, 256

street-watching, 48–50, 52–55, 60–61

structures, economic and political: of dependence and domination, 118–22; in enclavement and extraction, 253–57; of exploitation by subcontracting, 115–18; in gender predation, 168–71, 176–77; global economy, 4–5; inclusion and exclusion in, 4–5; in killings, 196, 209–10; of land use regimes, 127–32, 137, 140, 142–44, 148–50, 251–52; in moving around, 20–21, 36–41, 42–43; and nostalgia, 289–90n15; of poppy cultivation, 90–102; of poppy monoculture, 97–103; of the Procede reform, 146, 150–51

subcontracting, 115–18, 255–57

surveillance, 14–16, 21, 66–69, 100–101, 103–5

suspicion, 6, 54–55, 63, 188, 191, 244–45. *See also* trust/mistrust

threats of violence: anticipation of, in public celebrations, 223–24; of armed violence in handling domestic violence, 179–80; identification of, in daily life, 60–61, 71, 72–77, 252, 258; past experiences in identifying, 76, 258–59; to the poppy crop, 106–9; of reprisals for killings, in migration from the sierra, 191; to single women and girls, 161–64

tolls, 28–29, 110–11, 113

torture, 65–66, 83–84, 285n12

tourism, 22–24, 220–21, 222, 241, 289–90n15